Cleveland

DOUGLAS TRATTNER

Contents

Discover Cleveland.......**20**
Planning Your Trip.............22
The Three-Day Best of Cleveland..25
Rain or Shine Family Fun........26
Extreme Sports...............28

Sights....................**29**

Restaurants..............**58**

Nightlife **103**

Arts and Culture........**125**

Sports and Activities **151**

Shops **180**

Hotels...................**212**

**Excursions
  from Cleveland**........**229**

Background **269**

Essentials................**291**

Resources...............**302**

Index.....................**310**

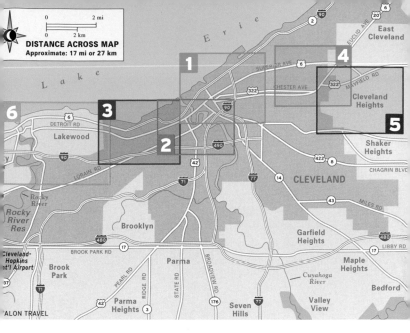

Maps

MAP 1: **Downtown** 4-5

MAP 2: **Ohio City and Tremont** 6-7

MAP 3: **Detroit Shoreway and Edgewater** 8-9

MAP 4: **University Circle and Little Italy** 10-11

MAP 5: **Cleveland Heights and Shaker Heights** 12-13

MAP 6: **Lakewood** 14-15

MAP 7: **Greater Cleveland** 16-17

MAP 8: **Rapid Transit System and Downtown Trolleys** 18-19

SIGHTS

2	U.S.S. *COD* SUBMARINE
3	ROCK AND ROLL HALL OF FAME AND MUSEUM
4	GREAT LAKES SCIENCE CENTER
19	*FREE STAMP*
21	CUYAHOGA COUNTY COURTHOUSE
31	OLD STONE CHURCH
33	WAR MEMORIAL FOUNTAIN
34	FEDERAL RESERVE BANK
36	CLEVELAND PUBLIC LIBRARY, MAIN BRANCH
38	OLD FEDERAL BUILDING
39	THE ARCADE
44	SOLDIERS AND SAILORS MONUMENT
46	TERMINAL TOWER
89	TROLLEY TOURS OF CLEVELAND
95	HOPE MEMORIAL BRIDGE

RESTAURANTS

7	SLYMAN'S DELI
11	SUPERIOR PHO
12	LI WAH
13	WONTON GOURMET BBQ
14	SZECHUAN GOURMET
16	KOKO BAKERY
25	BLUE POINT GRILLE
29	JOHNNY'S LITTLE BAR
30	NAUTI MERMAID
42	MARKET CAFÉ
51	PURA VIDA
52	NOODLECAT
59	GREENHOUSE TAVERN
60	LOLA
61	ERIE ISLAND COFFEE
63	RED, THE STEAKHOUSE
64	CLEVELAND PICKLE
74	COWELL & HUBBARD
77	DISTRICT

NIGHTLIFE

24	VELVET DOG
26	D'VINE WINE BAR
27	ANATOMY
50	HORSESHOE CLEVELAND
57	KEVIN'S MARTINI BAR
62	SOCIETY LOUNGE
65	WILBERT'S FOOD & MUSIC
81	PEABODY'S CONCERT CLUB
87	SHOOTER'S

© AVALON TRAVEL

⑥ ARTS AND CULTURE

5	OMNIMAX THEATER
8	CONVIVIUM33 GALLERY
9	FRONT ROOM GALLERY
10	ZYGOTE PRESS
18	WOOLTEX GALLERY
22	CLEVELAND POLICE HISTORICAL SOCIETY AND MUSEUM
35	MONEY MUSEUM AT FEDERAL RESERVE BANK
47	TOWER CITY CINEMAS
53	HOUSE OF BLUES
58	HILARITIES 4TH STREET THEATER
68	QUICKEN LOANS ARENA
72	PLAYHOUSESQUARE
72	DANCECLEVELAND
73	CLEVELAND PLAY HOUSE
75	ART GALLERY AT CLEVELAND STATE UNIVERSITY
78	GREAT LAKES THEATER FESTIVAL
79	BONFOEY GALLERY
82	WOLSTEIN CENTER
86	CLEVELAND AGORA
88	THE IMPROV
90	GREATER CLEVELAND AQUARIUM
92	JACOBS PAVILION AT NAUTICA
93	SPACES GALLERY
96	ROCK AND ROLL HALL OF FAME LIBRARY AND ARCHIVES

Ⓐ SPORTS AND ACTIVITIES

1	*GOODTIME III*
6	CLEVELAND BROWNS
37	CLEVELAND PUBLIC LIBRARY EASTMAN READING GARDEN
55	THE CORNER ALLEY
66	CLEVELAND BIKE RACK
67	CLEVELAND TOURS
69	CLEVELAND CAVALIERS
69	CLEVELAND GLADIATORS
69	LAKE ERIE MONSTERS
70	PROGRESSIVE FIELD
83	CLEVELAND STATE UNIVERSITY VIKINGS
84	YMCA OF GREATER CLEVELAND
91	TROLLEY TOURS OF CLEVELAND
94	WESTERN RESERVE ROWING ASSOCIATION

Ⓢ SHOPS

15	TINK HOLL
17	CLEVELAND METROBARK
28	SURROUNDINGS HOME DECOR
40	MARENGO LUXURY SPA
48	THE ONLY CLEVELAND STORE
48	TOWER CITY CENTER
54	CLE CLOTHING CO.
56	5TH STREET ARCADES

Ⓗ HOTELS

20	WESTIN CLEVELAND DOWNTOWN
23	ALOFT CLEVELAND DOWNTOWN
32	MARRIOTT DOWNTOWN AT KEY CENTER
41	HYATT REGENCY AT THE ARCADE
43	HOLIDAY INN EXPRESS HOTEL AND SUITES
45	RENAISSANCE CLEVELAND HOTEL
49	THE RITZ-CARLTON
71	HILTON GARDEN INN
76	WYNDHAM CLEVELAND AT PLAYHOUSE SQUARE
80	COMFORT INN DOWNTOWN
85	BROWNSTONE INN

DISTANCE ACROSS MAP
Approximate: 3.2 mi or 5.1 km

0   300 yds

0   300 m

SEE MAP 1

To A1 Wendy Park at Whiskey Island

VETERANS MEMORIAL BRIDGE

Cuyahoga River

To Hope Memorial Bridge

2 A

St. John's Episcopal Church
3 N   4

5

R 6
7 C

R 8

SEE DETAIL

Franklin Castle 10 H
9

A 11

Fairview Park

12 N

RTA
West 25th–Ohio City

13
14
St. Patrick's Church
17 C   16
18
15   John Heisman's Birthplace

N 21

St. Ignatius High School
19   20

Carnegie West Library

OHIO CITY

22

23
Jay Avenue Homes
24   31
25   28   N   32
26   A S
27   R   33
30   34

35 S   37
36 N   38
39
40

41
43   R N   42
44   45   50   48   West Side Market
49   R   51   46   47   A 10
52

53

54 S
55 S
56 H

SEE MAP 3

0   100 yds
0   100 m

0   300 yds
0   300 m

DISTANCE ACROSS MAP
Approximate: 2.6 mi or 4.2 km

© AVALON TRAVEL

A 88

Ohio City and Tremont

SIGHTS

4 ST. JOHN'S EPISCOPAL CHURCH
9 FRANKLIN CASTLE
15 JOHN HEISMAN'S BIRTHPLACE
16 ST. PATRICK'S CHURCH
19 CARNEGIE WEST LIBRARY
20 ST. IGNATIUS HIGH SCHOOL
23 JAY AVENUE HOMES
48 WEST SIDE MARKET
77 LINCOLN PARK
84 ST. THEODOSIUS RUSSIAN ORTHODOX CATHEDRAL
89 A CHRISTMAS STORY HOUSE

SPORTS AND ACTIVITIES

1 WENDY PARK AT WHISKEY ISLAND
2 VETERANS MEMORIAL BRIDGE TOUR
5 OHIO CITY BICYCLE CO-OP
11 FAIRVIEW PARK/ KENTUCKY GARDENS
27 JOY MACHINES BIKE SHOP
33 VISION YOGA & WELLNESS
88 DICKEY'S LANES

RESTAURANTS

6 RISING STAR COFFEE ROASTERS
8 THE HARP
13 MOMOCHO MOD MEX
14 JOHNNY MANGO
18 LE PETIT TRIANGLE CAFÉ
26 ORALE!
30 OLD ANGLE
30 BOGTROTTERS DOORSTEP
34 BLACK PIG
37 SOHO KITCHEN & BAR
39 NATE'S DELI
41 BAR CENTRO
44 FLYING FIG
47 WEST SIDE MARKET CAFÉ
49 SOUPER MARKET
51 BONBON PASTRY & CAFÉ
52 CROP BISTRO
57 SOKOLOWSKI'S UNIVERSITY INN
58 FAT CATS
59 LOOP CAFÉ
60 PARALLAX
61 SOUTH SIDE
62 A COOKIE AND A CUPCAKE
63 BARRIO
64 LOLITA
65 DANTE
65 GINKO
67 CIVILIZATION
70 TREMONT SCOOPS
73 FAHRENHEIT
74 TY FUN THAI BISTRO
78 TREMONT TAPHOUSE
80 DERVISH TURKISH CUISINE
82 LUCKY'S CAFÉ
85 BAC

NIGHTLIFE

3 UNION STATION/BOUNCE
21 VELVET TANGO ROOM
31 NANO BREW
36 ABC THE TAVERN
40 MARKET GARDEN BREWERY
42 MCNULTY'S BIER MARKT
43 GREAT LAKES BREWING CO.
46 MARKET AVENUE WINE BAR
71 SPOTTED OWL
75 FLYING MONKEY PUB
79 PROSPERITY SOCIAL CLUB
86 LAVA LOUNGE

ARTS AND CULTURE

7 TRANSFORMER STATION
17 NEAR WEST THEATRE
69 PAUL DUDA GALLERY
76 CONVERGENCE-CONTINUUM

SHOPS

22 UNIQUE THRIFT
24 ELEGANSIA
25 JOHNNYVILLE SLUGGER
28 DEERING VINTAGE
32 GLASS BUBBLE PROJECT
35 ZEN METRO SPA
38 SOMETHING DIFFERENT
45 MARKET AT THE FIG
50 OPEN AIR IN MARKET SQUARE
53 HANSA IMPORT HAUS
54 ROOM SERVICE
55 CAMPBELL'S SWEETS FACTORY
66 BANYAN TREE
68 VISIBLE VOICE BOOKS
72 PINKY'S DAILY PLANNER
81 EVIE LOU
83 LILLY HANDMADE CHOCOLATES
87 CLEVELAND BREW SHOP

HOTELS

10 STONE GABLES BED AND BREAKFAST
12 CLIFFORD HOUSE BED AND BREAKFAST
29 J. PALEN HOUSE
56 CLEVELAND HOSTEL

TREMONT

Lincoln Park

St. Theodosius Russian Orthodox Cathedral

Tremont Valley Field

A Christmas Story House 89

DISTANCE ACROSS MAP
Approximate: 2.6 mi or 4.1 km

EDGEWATER

CUDELL

WEST BOULEVARD

SEE MAP 6

West Blvd-Cudell

Cudell Commons Park

⊙ SIGHTS
1   LAKEFRONT RESERVATION
22 GORDON SQUARE ARTS DISTRICT
31 ST. STEPHEN CATHOLIC CHURCH

Ⓡ RESTAURANTS
3   DINER ON CLIFTON
13 PARKVIEW NITE CLUB
19 SWEET MOSES SODA FOUNTAIN
20 LUXE KITCHEN & LOUNGE
23 GYPSY BEANS & BAKERY
24 XYZ THE TAVERN
28 SPICE KITCHEN & BAR
29 MINH-ANH VIETNAMESE RESTAURANT

Ⓝ NIGHTLIFE
4   TWIST
6   BROTHERS LOUNGE
14 STONE MAD IRISH PUB
27 HAPPY DOG

Ⓖ ARTS AND CULTURE
11 STUDIOS AT WEST 78TH STREET
12 BLANK CANVAS THEATRE
17 CAPITOL THEATRE
25 1POINT618 GALLERY
26 CLEVELAND PUBLIC THEATRE

Ⓐ SPORTS AND ACTIVITIES
2   LAKEFRONT RESERVATION
30 THERE'S NO PLACE LIKE OM

Ⓢ SHOPS
5   FLOWER CHILD
7   HECK'S REVIVAL
8   PET-TIQUE
9   CHRISTOPHIER CUSTOM CLOTHIER
10 BENT CRAYON RECORDS
15 HAUSFRAU RECORDS
16 GUIDE TO KULCHUR
18 YELLOWCAKE SHOP
21 THE CLEVELAND SHOP
32 REINCARNATION VINTAGE DESIGN
33 LORAIN AVENUE ANTIQUES DISTRICT
34 SUITE LORAIN

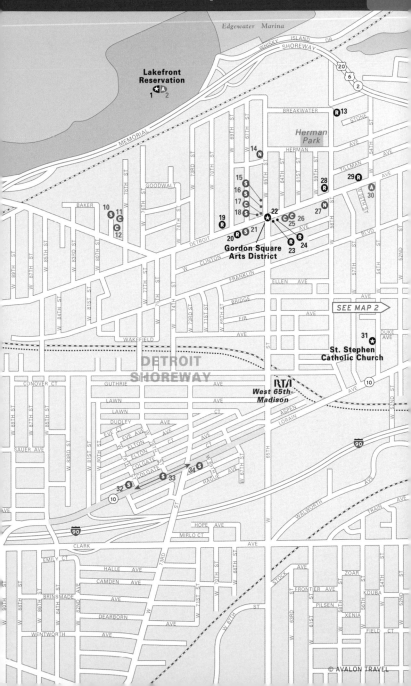

Edgewater Marina

WHISKY ISLAND DR.

SHOREWAY

Lakefront Reservation

1 ★ A 2

BREAKWATER

R 13

STONE

Herman Park

14 N

HERMAN

15 S

16 S

17 S

28 R

29 R

A 30

18 S

22 ★

C C

25 26

27 N

19 R

20 R 21

S

23 R 24

Gordon Square Arts District

10

11 S

C 12

BAKER

GOODWALT

DETROIT

CLINTON

FRANKLIN

ELLEN AVE

SEE MAP 2

BRIDGE

FIR

WAKEFIELD

AVE

31 ★

St. Stephen Catholic Church

DETROIT
SHOREWAY

CONOVER CT

GUTHRIE AVE

LAWN

LAWN

DUDLEY AVE

EVE CT

ELTON

COLGATE

32 S

33 S

34 S

RTA
West 65th-Madison

LORAIN

ASPEN

10

I-90

10

HOPE AVE

MIRLO CT

CLARK

EMILY CT

HALLE AVE

CAMDEN AVE

BRINSMADE

DEARBORN AVE

WENTWORTH AVE

WALWORTH

TRAIN AVE

ZOAR

FRONTIER AVE

KOUBA

PILSEN

XENIA

STOCK

FIELD CT

© AVALON TRAVEL

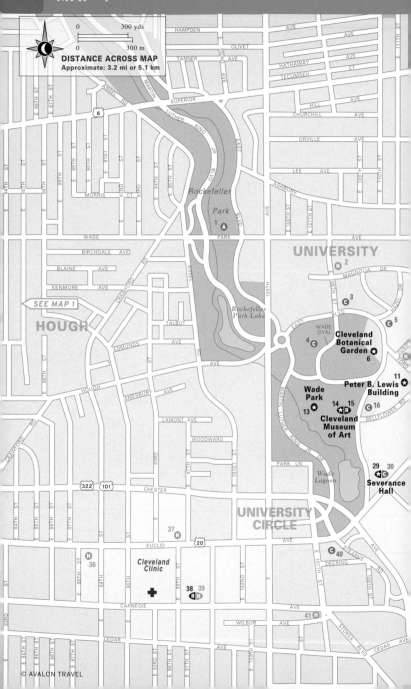

SIGHTS

6	CLEVELAND BOTANICAL GARDEN	13	WADE PARK
11	PETER B. LEWIS BUILDING	14	CLEVELAND MUSEUM OF ART
12	HESSLER ROAD AND HESSLER COURT	29	SEVERANCE HALL

RESTAURANTS

9	ARABICA CAFÉ	25	LA DOLCE VITA
10	L'ALBATROS	26	CORBO'S BAKERY
15	PROVENANCE AND CAFÉ	31	CLUB ISABELLA
17	COQUETTE PATISSERIE	32	ALGEBRA TEA HOUSE
18	MI PUEBLO	33	WASHINGTON PLACE BISTRO
20	MITCHELL'S HOMEMADE ICE CREAM	34	MICHAELANGELO'S
24	PRESTI'S BAKERY & CAFÉ	35	VALENTINO'S PIZZA
		38	TABLE 45

NIGHTLIFE

8	BARKING SPIDER TAVERN	23	THE BEER MARKET

ARTS AND CULTURE

3	WESTERN RESERVE HISTORICAL SOCIETY	22	MUSEUM OF CONTEMPORARY ART
4	CLEVELAND MUSEUM OF NATURAL HISTORY	27	MURRAY HILL SCHOOL HOUSE GALLERIES
5	CLEVELAND INSTITUTE OF MUSIC	30	CLEVELAND ORCHESTRA
16	CLEVELAND INSTITUTE OF ART CINEMATHEQUE	40	CHILDREN'S MUSEUM OF CLEVELAND
16	REINBERGER GALLERIES		

SPORTS AND ACTIVITIES

1	ROCKEFELLER PARK	19	CLEVELAND YOGA

SHOPS

21	ANNE VAN H. BOUTIQUE

HOTELS

2	UNIVERSITY CIRCLE BED AND BREAKFAST	37	CLEVELAND CLINIC GUESTHOUSE
7	GLIDDEN HOUSE	39	INTERCONTINENTAL HOTEL AND CONFERENCE CENTER
28	COURTYARD BY MARRIOTT	41	DOUBLETREE BY HILTON
36	INTERCONTINENTAL SUITES HOTEL		

SEE MAP 4

Finnigan Fields

Euclid-E 120th RTA

DISTANCE ACROSS MAP
Approximate: 3.2 mi or 5.2 km

0   300 yds
0   300 m

Lake View Cemetery

SEE MAP 4

LITTLE ITALY

Case Western Reserve University

Fairmount Boulevard District

RESTAURANTS

2	PACIFIC EAST	31	ANATOLIA CAFÉ
8	TOMMY'S	32	STONE OVEN
12	INN ON COVENTRY	33	SWEETIE FRY
15	VERO BISTRO	36	FELICE URBAN CAFÉ
17	ALADDIN'S EATERY	37	BIG AL'S DINER
18	LUNA BAKERY AND CAFE	43	SASA MATSU
22	KATZ CLUB DINER	45	FIRE FOOD & DRINK
29	DEWEY'S PIZZA	49	ON THE RISE

NIGHTLIFE

11	WINKING LIZARD TAVERN	23	KATZ CLUB
13	GROG SHOP	24	BOTTLEHOUSE BREWERY
13	LA CAVE DU VIN	27	PARNELL'S PUB
14	NIGHTTOWN		

ARTS AND CULTURE

21	EVANS AMPHITHEATER	35	DOBAMA THEATRE
26	CEDAR LEE THEATRE	42	SHAKER SQUARE CINEMAS
28	HEIGHTS ARTS GALLERY		

Shaker Lakes

Park

Lower Shaker Lak

SHAKER HEIGHTS

Shaker Square RTA

Shaker Square

Coventry RTA

Shaker Square Shopping Center

COVENTRY VILLAGE

Cumberland Park

CLEVELAND HEIGHTS

Cain Park

The Commercial Districts of Cleveland Heights

Nature Center at Shaker Lakes

Horseshoe Lake

Southern Park

Severence Town Center

SIGHTS
1 LAKE VIEW CEMETERY
19 FAIRMOUNT BOULEVARD DISTRICT
20 CAIN PARK
25 THE COMMERCIAL DISTRICTS OF CLEVELAND HEIGHTS
44 SHAKER SQUARE
47 NATURE CENTER AT SHAKER LAKES

SPORTS AND ACTIVITIES
34 ATMA CENTER

SHOPS
3 UTRECHT ART SUPPLIES
4 PASSPORT TO PERU
5 COVENTRY CATS
6 BIG FUN
7 MAC'S BACKS BOOKS
9 CITY BUDDHA
10 RECORD REVOLUTION
30 QUINTANA'S BARBER SHOP

HOTELS
16 THE ALCAZAR

50 HORSESHOE LAKE PARK
38 FINE POINTS
39 HEIDE RIVCHUN CONSERVATION STUDIOS
40 GENTLEMAN'S QUARTERS/FROG'S LEGS
41 LOGANBERRY BOOKS
46 PLAYMATTERS TOYS
48 DUOHOME

© AVALON TRAVEL

✪ SIGHTS
1 OLDEST STONE HOUSE
2 LAKEWOOD PARK
9 THE BECK CENTER FOR THE ARTS

℞ RESTAURANTS
3 PIER W
5 TARTINE BISTRO AND WINE BAR
6 BLACKBIRD BAKING COMPANY
8 WEST END TAVERN
10 THE SWEET SPOT
14 EL CARNICERO
18 ROOT CAFÉ
19 DEAGAN'S KITCHEN & BAR
20 MELT BAR AND GRILLED
27 BUCKEYE BEER ENGINE
28 MALLEY'S CHOCOLATES
29 PLAYERS ON MADISON
32 BARROCO GRILL

N NIGHTLIFE
7 AROUND THE CORNER SALOON
17 HUMBLE WINE BAR
23 FIVE O'CLOCK LOUNGE
33 WINCHESTER TAVERN AND CONCERT CLUB

✪ ARTS AND CULTURE
11 BECK CENTER FOR THE ARTS
12 SOMETHING DADA
34 SCREW FACTORY ARTISTS

Ⓐ SPORTS AND ACTIVITIES
16 PUMA YOGA
25 41° NORTH KAYAK ADVENTURES
26 LAKEWOOD OFF-LEASH DOG PARK
31 MAHALL'S TWENTY LANES
35 SERPENTINI ARENA
38 HALLORAN ICE SKATING RINK

Ⓢ SHOPS
13 REAGLE BEAGLE
15 MY MIND'S EYE RECORDS
21 GEIGER'S CLOTHING & SPORTS
22 PAISLEY MONKEY
24 INN THE DOGHOUSE
30 PLAY IT AGAIN, SAM
37 CAROL & JOHN'S COMIC BOOK SHOP

Ⓗ HOTELS
4 DAYS INN
36 EMERALD NECKLACE INN

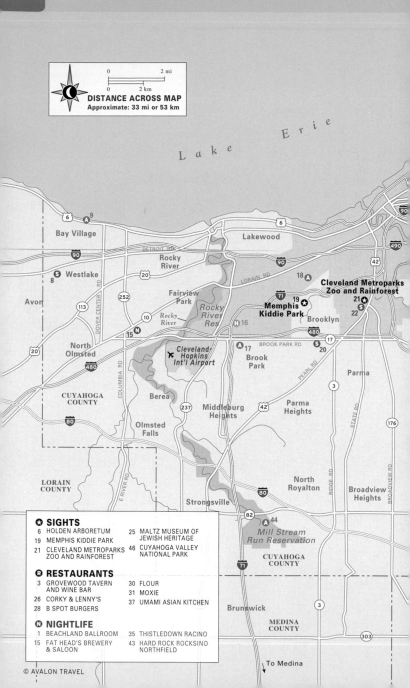

DISTANCE ACROSS MAP
Approximate: 33 mi or 53 km

SIGHTS
6 HOLDEN ARBORETUM
19 MEMPHIS KIDDIE PARK
21 CLEVELAND METROPARKS ZOO AND RAINFOREST
25 MALTZ MUSEUM OF JEWISH HERITAGE
46 CUYAHOGA VALLEY NATIONAL PARK

RESTAURANTS
3 GROVEWOOD TAVERN AND WINE BAR
26 CORKY & LENNY'S
28 B SPOT BURGERS
30 FLOUR
31 MOXIE
37 UMAMI ASIAN KITCHEN

NIGHTLIFE
1 BEACHLAND BALLROOM
15 FAT HEAD'S BREWERY & SALOON
35 THISTLEDOWN RACINO
43 HARD ROCK ROCKSINO NORTHFIELD

© AVALON TRAVEL

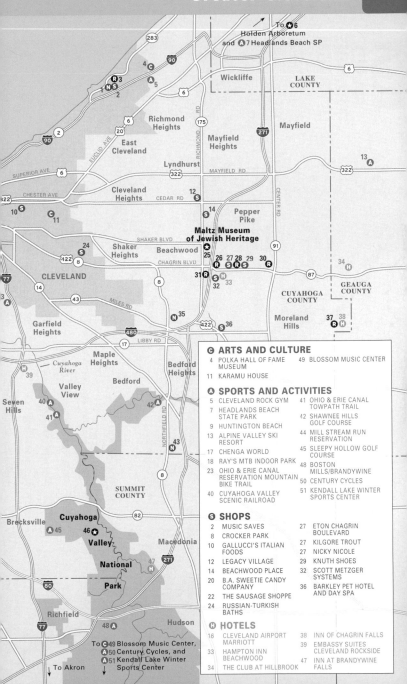

To **49** 6
Holden Arboretum
and **47** Headlands Beach SP

Wickliffe

LAKE COUNTY

4 C
R 3
1 N S
2
5

Richmond Heights

Mayfield

Mayfield Heights

East Cleveland

Lyndhurst

MAYFIELD RD

13 A

SUPERIOR AVE

CHESTER AVE

Cleveland Heights

CEDAR RD

Pepper Pike

12 S

14 S

10 S

C **11**

Maltz Museum of Jewish Heritage

24 S
8

Shaker Heights

Beachwood

CHAGRIN BLVD

25 **26** **27** **28** **29** **30**
R **S** **S** **S** **R**
31 **R**
32 S **33**

34 H

CLEVELAND

14

43

MILES RD

8

87

CUYAHOGA COUNTY

GEAUGA COUNTY

Garfield Heights

N **35**

Moreland Hills

37 **38**
R **H**

480

17

LIBBY RD

422 S **36**

Maple Heights

Bedford Heights

Valley View

Bedford

Cuyahoga River
39

Sewen Hills

40 A
41 A

42 A

43
N

8

SUMMIT COUNTY

Cuyahoga

46

Valley

Macedonia

National

47 H
271

Park

Brecksville

45 A

48 A

Hudson

Richfield

To C **49** Blossom Music Center,
A **50** Century Cycles, and
A **51** Kendall Lake Winter
Sports Center

To Akron

C ARTS AND CULTURE

4 POLKA HALL OF FAME MUSEUM
11 KARAMU HOUSE
49 BLOSSOM MUSIC CENTER

A SPORTS AND ACTIVITIES

5 CLEVELAND ROCK GYM
7 HEADLANDS BEACH STATE PARK
9 HUNTINGTON BEACH
13 ALPINE VALLEY SKI RESORT
17 CHENGA WORLD
18 RAY'S MTB INDOOR PARK
23 OHIO & ERIE CANAL RESERVATION MOUNTAIN BIKE TRAIL
40 CUYAHOGA VALLEY SCENIC RAILROAD
41 OHIO & ERIE CANAL TOWPATH TRAIL
42 SHAWNEE HILLS GOLF COURSE
44 MILL STREAM RUN RESERVATION
45 SLEEPY HOLLOW GOLF COURSE
48 BOSTON MILLS/BRANDYWINE
50 CENTURY CYCLES
51 KENDALL LAKE WINTER SPORTS CENTER

S SHOPS

2 MUSIC SAVES
8 CROCKER PARK
10 GALLUCCI'S ITALIAN FOODS
12 LEGACY VILLAGE
14 BEACHWOOD PLACE
20 B.A. SWEETIE CANDY COMPANY
22 THE SAUSAGE SHOPPE
24 RUSSIAN-TURKISH BATHS
27 ETON CHAGRIN BOULEVARD
27 KILGORE TROUT
27 NICKY NICOLE
29 KNUTH SHOES
32 SCOTT METZGER SYSTEMS
36 BARKLEY PET HOTEL AND DAY SPA

H HOTELS

16 CLEVELAND AIRPORT MARRIOTT
33 HAMPTON INN BEACHWOOD
34 THE CLUB AT HILLBROOK
38 INN OF CHAGRIN FALLS
39 EMBASSY SUITES CLEVELAND ROCKSIDE
47 INN AT BRANDYWINE FALLS

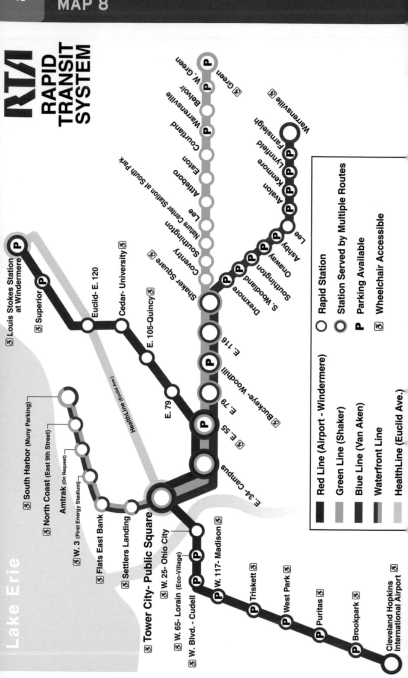

RTA RAPID TRANSIT SYSTEM

Lake Erie

Louis Stokes Station at Windermere ♿
Superior ♿ P
Superior ♿ P
Euclid- E. 120
Cedar- University ♿
E. 105-Quincy ♿
E. 116
HealthLine (Euclid Ave.)
E. 79
Buckeye- Woodhill ♿
E. 55 ♿
E. 79 ♿
E. 34- Campus

W. Green ♿
Green P
Belvoir P
Warrensville P
Courtland
Eaton
Lee
Attleboro
Nature Center Station at South Park ♿
Southington
Coventry
Shaker Square ♿
Drexmore
S. Woodland
Southington
Onaway
Ashby
Lee
Avalon
Kenmore
Lynnfield
Farnsleigh
Warrensville ♿

South Harbor (Muny Parking)
North Coast (East 9th Street)
Amtrak (On Request)
W. 3 (First Energy Stadium) ♿
Flats East Bank ♿
Settlers Landing
Tower City- Public Square ♿
W. 25- Ohio City ♿
W. 65- Lorain (Eco-Village) ♿
W. Blvd.- Cudell ♿
W. 117- Madison ♿
Triskett ♿
West Park ♿
Puritas ♿
Brookpark ♿
Cleveland Hopkins International Airport

Legend

━━━	Red Line (Airport - Windermere)
━━━	Green Line (Shaker)
━━━	Blue Line (Van Aken)
━━━	Waterfront Line
━━━	HealthLine (Euclid Ave.)

○ Rapid Station
◉ Station Served by Multiple Routes
P Parking Available
♿ Wheelchair Accessible

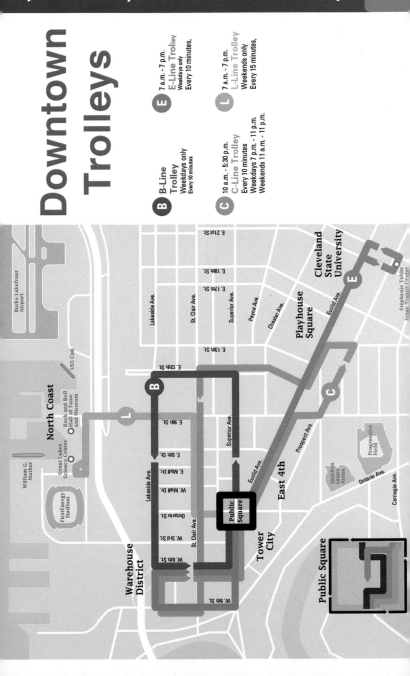

Downtown Trolleys

B B-Line Trolley
Weekdays only
Every 10 minutes

C 10 a.m. - 5:30 p.m.
C-Line Trolley
Every 10 minutes
Weekdays 7 p.m. - 11 p.m.
Weekends 11 a.m. - 11 p.m.

E 7 a.m. - 7 p.m.
E-Line Trolley
Weekdays only
Every 10 minutes,

L 7 a.m. - 7 p.m.
L-Line Trolley
Weekends only
Every 15 minutes,

Cleveland

There's a level of enthusiasm and optimism in Cleveland, the likes of which hasn't been felt in decades. Population in the city center has more than doubled in the past 10 years, introducing an abundance of fresh energy to downtown streets. Many of those new residents are young professionals, who bring with them all the positive trappings of a modern generation. Look around today and you'll see more bikes, breweries, food trucks, urban gardens, creative start-ups, and a slower pace to the day.

Those outside the region are taking notice, too. Major film studios have recently discovered that Cleveland's grand 20th-century architecture makes a fine backdrop to just about any story. The dining scene continues to attract more than its fair share of attention, creating a boom in food-related tourism. And more than $2 billion worth of recent development has doubled the number of annual visitors, who beat a path to Cleveland's world-class museums and stages.

But more than anything, there is a genuine sense of civic pride. After decades of serving as the nation's favorite punch line, Cleveland finally seems to have shaken off the rust, put its house in order, and emerged as a contemporary city with solid Midwestern roots. Rather than wait for others to label and define their town, locals simply are appreciating the affordability, accessibility, and beauty of this city on a Great Lake.

These days, it seems you can't pick up a magazine or newspaper without reading another story about Cleveland's "Rust Belt Revival." Around here, folks just call that Tuesday.

Planning Your Trip

Where to Go

Downtown

From nine to five, downtown serves as the financial, legal, and governmental nucleus of the entire county. After dark, though, the vibrant Warehouse District and East 4th Street teem with restaurants, nightclubs, and live-music venues like the House of Blues. Downtown also is the place to enjoy live theater, cheer on professional sports teams, and explore the ephemera at the Rock and Roll Hall of Fame and Museum. Clean, compact, and walkable, downtown rewards urban hikers with an abundance of glorious classical architecture, and the largest stock of hotels can be found here as well.

Ohio City and Tremont

The 19th-century homes in Ohio City make strolling its leafy lanes feel like a trip back in time, but the neighborhood's not stuck in the past. The celebrated West Side Market and fine eateries like Flying Fig and Momocho make the area ground zero for adventurous foodies, while new breweries attract craft beer fans from far afield. Nearby Tremont has an equally high concentration of chef-owned bistros, like Lolita, Fahrenheit, and Parallax, but is better known for its creative energy, on display in the monthly ArtWalks; architecture fans enjoy the historic churches in this former university neighborhood, and shoppers come for the upscale boutiques.

Cleveland Museum of Art in University Circle

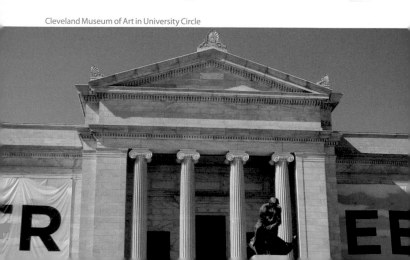

Detroit Shoreway and Edgewater

Some of Cleveland's most exciting changes are taking place in these near-west neighborhoods. Ecoconscious residents are moving here to live in green-built homes, raise backyard chickens, and frequent new farm-to-table eateries like Toast and Spice Kitchen. Building on the 20-year history of the Cleveland Public Theatre, the animated Gordon Square Arts District is home to art galleries, design studios, and thriving neighborhood theater. Antiques hunters prowl the secondhand shops of Lorain Avenue in hopes of scoring a treasure.

University Circle and Little Italy

Often referred to as "One Perfect Mile," University Circle is home to an unmatched concentration of educational, medical, and cultural institutions, including the Cleveland Museum of Art and Museum of Contemporary Art, both of which are better than ever. The Old World is alive and well in neighboring Little Italy, a lively borough featuring redbrick lanes, authentic Italian eateries, and eclectic art galleries.

Cleveland Heights and Shaker Heights

Incorporated in the early 1900s, the neighboring communities of Cleveland Heights and Shaker Heights developed as leafy streetcar suburbs on the fringes of town. Today, these popular inner-ring cities boast all the amenities of a self-sufficient town. The Main Street-like districts of Shaker Square, Cedar-Lee, and Coventry keep residents and visitors alike entertained with restaurants, jazz clubs, and movie theaters, and sightseeing drives allow one to explore the impressive mansions built by Cleveland's wealthy industrialists.

Lakewood

The bulk of the commercial activity in this West Side neighborhood is found on the thoroughfares of Detroit, Madison, and Clifton, which are dotted with funky shops, restaurants, and bars. But one of the biggest draws here is the Rocky River Reservation, part of the Cleveland Metroparks system. Boasting a dog park, a web of trails, and a scenic strip of rushing river, this picturesque retreat attracts joggers, bicyclists, anglers, and picnickers. Lakewood is also home to the Beck Center for the Arts, a long-standing community arts beacon.

Greater Cleveland

The Greater Cleveland area stretches for miles in every direction save for north, where it is bounded by Lake Erie. Much of that real estate is consumed by bedroom-community suburbs, but that doesn't mean you should just hole up downtown. The majestic Cuyahoga Valley National Park is just south of town, while the equally verdant Holden Arboretum can be found out east. In the wintertime, mountain bike enthusiasts travel from throughout the Midwest to hit Ray's MTB Indoor Park. Meanwhile, shoppers flock to upscale boutiques in Beachwood, Rocky River, and Chagrin Falls, and live music fans venture to the Beachland Ballroom and Blossom Music Center.

When to Go

Fall is the best time to visit Cleveland, to savor the vibrant fall foliage and crisp, dry air by hitting hike-and-bike trails, apple orchards, and football games. Autumn also signals the start of the abundant performing-arts calendar, filled with dance, theater, and musical productions.

If you really can't stand cold weather, it's best to avoid Cleveland December through March—but you will be missing out on quite a bit. The winter holidays here can be Dickensian, with downy-white snow blanketing the region as residents make the rounds at museums, theaters, and restaurants.

Spring can be frustratingly wet, even snowy, but it also can offer glimpses of the warm days to come. Folks here take advantage of these rare days atop bikes, in gardens, and on restaurant patios.

Summer is filled with Indians baseball games, rounds of golf, neighborhood festivals, visits to farmers markets, and fishing trips on Lake Erie. Nearly every restaurant takes advantage of the season by offering alfresco seating.

Lake View Cemetery

The Three-Day Best of Cleveland

Day 1

▶ Visit the bustling West Side Market, a public market that is a treat not just for cooks, but also people-watchers and architecture buffs. Grab a cup of coffee from City Roast and peruse the 80 or so stalls that sell everything from goat to goat cheese. For brunch, eat like a local by ordering a sausage sandwich from Frank's Bratwurst. Get it with kraut, horseradish, and brown mustard on a hard roll. Don't leave without checking out the detached vegetable annex.

▶ If it's between Memorial Day and Labor Day, set aside some time to prowl the knickknacks at Open Air in Market Square, an outdoor flea market and block party that takes place across the street from the West Side Market. Stroll north on W. 25th Street and check out the various shops that dot the eclectic urban strip. Hit Deering Vintage for glam vintage threads, Glass Bubble Project for original blown-glass art objects, and Johnnyville Slugger for your very own custom baseball bat.

▶ Before dinner, walk down Jay Avenue to see what Cleveland looked like 150 years ago and admire blocks of restored 19th-century homes.

▶ When hunger sets in, hit Bar Cento for Neapolitan-style pizza or SOHO Kitchen for new takes on Southern classics, or stop by Crop Bistro for contemporary American fare dished up in the city's most attractive dining room.

▶ For a post-meal nightcap, go directly to Velvet Tango Room, a polished speakeasy that mixes up the most divine classic cocktails in the region.

Day 2

▶ Start your day with a little Parisian flair by grabbing breakfast at Le Petit Triangle Café, a quaint and quiet café that serves savory crepes, fluffy omelets, and ethereal café au laits.

▶ Make your way over to Nautica entertainment complex on the west bank of the Flats and hop aboard Lolly the Trolley, which offers a number of fun and informative sightseeing tours.

▶ When the trolley ride is over, make your way to the North Coast Harbor and into the Rock and Roll Hall of Fame. Though the museum looks small from the outside, it can devour entire afternoons in a single visit.

Rain or Shine Family Fun

Progressive Field, home to the Cleveland Indians

Top Choices for Sun-Soaked Cleveland Family Fun

- Take in an **Indians** baseball game at **Progressive Field.** To snag player **autographs,** arrive up to 45 minutes before the first pitch and head to sections 125-134 or 169-175.

- Hop aboard the *Goodtime III* for a **narrated cruise** on Lake Erie and the Cuyahoga River. Bring a camera to capture the amazing skyline.

- What child doesn't love primates? Go bananas at the **Cleveland Metroparks Zoo,** with its gorillas, chimps, lemurs, and baboons.

Rainy Day in Cleveland? No Problem.

- Manageable in size, completely undercover, and loaded with 42 tanks filled with one million gallons of water and thousands of fish, the **Greater Cleveland Aquarium** is a great place to kill an hour or so in inclement weather.

- **The Museum of Natural History** is loaded with cool stuff: a Foucault pendulum, tyrannosaur and stegosaur skeletons, and a **planetarium,** to name a few.

- Take the **Cuyahoga Valley Scenic Railroad** through the scenic forests, wetlands, and prairies of the lush Cuyahoga Valley National Park.

If the kids are in tow, swap the Rock Hall for a visit to the adjacent Great Lakes Science Center.

► If the Indians are in town, check the box office at Progressive Field for last-minute bleacher seats, where you'll enjoy cold beer, hot dogs, and great baseball. Otherwise, go gallery hopping in eclectic Tremont, where artsy shops like Paul Duda Gallery and Banyan Tree sit side-by-side with architecturally impressive churches.

- Grab a glass of wine at Press Wine Bar before hitting any of the amazing chef-driven bistros in the area.

- For upscale pasta and pizza in a lively setting visit Fahrenheit. Or, go to Michael Symon's charming neighborhood bistro Lolita for Mediterranean fare.

- After dinner peruse the wonderful collection of art, film, and music books at Visible Voice Books, or grab a chocolate-covered banana at Tremont Scoops.

Day 3

- If it's Sunday, join the locals for a long, leisurely dim sum brunch at Li Wah. If you prefer upscale breakfast fare served in an elegantly restored diner car, head to Katz Club Diner in Cleveland Heights.

- For proof that there's more to do in Cleveland than eat and drink, head to University Circle for a day filled with art, architecture, and history. The Cleveland Museum of Art just wrapped up a seven-year, $350 million overhaul and has never looked better. Science and history nerds would do well to spend some time exploring the Cleveland Museum of Natural History, while the horticulturally minded might prefer the Cleveland Botanical Garden. Contemporary art fans and architecture buffs both will appreciate the Museum of Contemporary Art.

- For lunch, try Coquette Patisserie, a petite bakery café across the street from the Museum of Contemporary Art that offers authentic French pastries, savory small plates, and champagne by the glass.

- Thrift, salvage, and antiques buffs should stroll the Lorain Avenue Antiques District, a collection of thrift, consignment, antiques, and restoration shops.

- For a full farm-to-table feast not far from the antiques, head to Spice Kitchen, a handsome American bistro that buys local, cooks seasonal, and always hits the mark.

- On warm or chilly nights, the outdoor courtyard at Stone Mad Irish Pub is the place to be thanks to a towering four-sided fireplace. Inside, a meticulously crafted Irish bar complete with sunken bocce court offers a unique form of after-dinner fun.

Ray's MTB Indoor Park

Thanks to an incredible diversity of geography, Greater Cleveland has no shortage of extreme sports opportunities.

Take a sunset kayak tour along Lake Erie's shore, right by the Rock and Roll Hall of Fame, with **41° North Kayak Adventures.** Paddlers of all skill levels are welcome.

Learn the basic fundamentals of competitive rowing from some of the best scullers around. **Western Reserve Rowing Association** offers social summer and fall rowing leagues that take place on the Cuyahoga River.

Bundle up and zip down the twin refrigerated tobogganing chutes at the **Mill Stream Run Reservation** of the Cleveland Metroparks. Hike 110 steps up then zip 70 feet down and 1,000 feet out on this exhilarating thrill ride.

The indoor climbing gym at **Cleveland Rock Gym** is comprised of 30-foot top-rope walls and numerous bouldering areas, some featuring near-horizontal overhangs. Introductory classes are available for newbies.

Encompassing more than 100,000 square feet of indoor mountain bike paradise, **Ray's MTB Indoor Park** is the only attraction of its kind in the country. Race down paths, around steeped embankments, over uneven bridges, and into the air off vertical jumps.

The Olympic-style bicycle racing track at the **Cleveland Velodrome** is the only one of its kind in the region. The outdoor steel and wood track features banked turns and smooth straightaways.

Ride (or walk, or jog) along the 80 miles or so of crushed-limestone path that is the **Ohio & Erie Canal Towpath Trail.** For the best scenery, enjoy the portions that pass through the Cuyahoga Valley National Park.

Well-stocked rivers and streams provide some of the best **steelhead trout fly-fishing** in the country. Professional guides are available to show you the way to the best spots around.

Dense forests, lush wetlands, and grassy prairies provide the ideal **hunting** grounds for white-tailed deer, wild turkey, grouse, and pheasant. A hunting license is required for most pursuits.

Alpine Valley Ski Resort gets around 120 inches of snowfall a year, making it the best place nearby to downhill ski, snowboard, or snow tube. There are 11 trails covering 72 skiable acres.

Sights

Downtown 32

Ohio City and Tremont 42

Detroit Shoreway and Edgewater. .46

University Circle and Little Italy 48

Cleveland Heights
    and Shaker Heights 51

Lakewood 54

Greater Cleveland 55

Look for ★ to find
recommended sights.

HIGHLIGHTS

★ **Most Amazing Old Mall:** Built in 1890, **The Arcade** is an absolutely breathtaking Victorian-style atrium that flaunts a 300-foot-long, 100-foot-high skylight comprised of 1,800 panes of glass (page 32).

★ **Most Controversial Pop Art:** Love it or loathe it, the **Free Stamp** never fails to incite an opinion. Sure, artist Claes Oldenburg's 30-foot-tall faux rubber stamp is silly—bordering on ridiculous. But the fact that we're still discussing it after all these years has to account for something (page 33).

★ **Most Iconic Bridge Art:** The art deco statues carved into the 43-foot sandstone pylons of the **Hope Memorial Bridge** are fondly referred to as the "guardians of traffic." Eight separate figures stand sentry at either end of the mile-long bridge, making even the worst commute a little easier to stomach (page 35).

★ **Best-Sounding History Lesson:** If all school was as entertaining as this "school of rock," there would be no more truancy. The **Rock and Roll Hall of Fame and Museum** boasts a dizzying kaleidoscope of rock memorabilia, both familiar and obscure (page 37).

★ **Most Famous Church:** Featured in the Academy Award-winning film *The Deer Hunter,* the 13 onion-shaped domes atop **St. Theodosius Russian Orthodox Cathedral** hover like a battalion of faded copper weather balloons (page 45).

★ **Best Old-World Grocery Store:** Other cities have grand old public markets; too bad most of them have replaced the actual food stalls with shops selling T-shirts and candles. At Ohio City's beloved **West Side Market,** people actually shop—for pork, halibut, sausage, pierogies, tomatoes, and everything in between. Look up at the barrel-vaulted ceiling and you'll forget everything on your shopping list (page 45).

★ **Most Extreme Makeover:** Art fans endured an eight-year, $350 million renovation and expansion, but in 2013, the **Cleveland Museum of Art** officially said goodbye to the scaffolding. Now, the breathtaking spaces somehow manage to make the impressive art collection look even better (page 49).

★ **Best Show of Homes:** In the early 1900s, Cleveland's rich and famous employed the architect hotshots of the day to build stately homes in the **Fairmount Boulevard District** in Cleveland Heights. Park your ride and take a stroll past Georgian mansions, terra-cotta-clad Italian villas, and wildly asymmetrical Tudor Revivals (page 52).

★ **Finest Final Resting Place: Lake View Cemetery,** a 290-acre oasis on the border of Cleveland Heights, is equal parts botanical garden, history lesson, and alfresco art gallery. Approximately 400,000 people visit the grounds each year, many to gander at Wade Chapel's Tiffany interior (page 53).

To rip off Dickens: Cleveland is a tale of two cities. By 1920, the city on a lake, a river, and a grand canal had grown to become the fifth most populous city in the United States. Cleveland's early successes in steel, rail, and automotive production, not to mention oil, banking, and chemical manufac-turing, led to very prosperous times. As the city expanded, so too did its need for new local, county, and federal buildings. Fortu-itously, that need happened to coincide with the City Beautiful movement, a progressive philosophy that a well-planned, visually appealing downtown could go a long way toward boosting the spirit of its inhabitants. Those heady times left a lasting legacy of monumental classical architectural, world-class cultural institu-tions, and idyllic residential suburbs on the fringes of town.

It would take Cleveland another 75 years to match its building boom of the early 20th century. But in the mid-1990s, shaking off the chains of its Rust Belt reputation, the rebounding city pulled off a slew of public projects that included sporty new baseball, bas-ketball, and football venues, a state-of-the-art science and technol-ogy museum, and a glass-and-steel temple to rock and roll. More recently, the city added a new medical mart and convention center, downtown aquarium, and urban casino. After an eight-year, $350 million renovation and expansion, the Cleveland Museum of Art has never looked better.

In revitalized old neighborhoods like Ohio City, Tremont, and Detroit Shoreway, the Gothic steeples of 100-year-old churches cast slender shadows across sleek new townhomes. Brick-paved lanes are dotted with decades-old ethnic restaurants, but also trendy chef-owned bistros. If you keep your eyes open at the West Side Market, you'll spot Polish pierogies and Hungarian sausage along with wild Alaskan salmon and squid-ink pasta. And if you keep your ears open, you'll pick out a dozen different native tongues along the way.

That happy juxtaposition between newfangled and old-fashioned, contemporary and classical, punk and polka seems to permeate the whole of Cleveland. With one foot pleasantly planted in the present, the other stubbornly stuck in the past, this city has a knack for surprising visitors of all stripes.

Downtown

Map 1

★ The Arcade

Easily one of the most glorious Cleveland interiors, this Victorian-style atrium flaunts a 300-foot-long, 100-foot-high skylight comprised of 1,800 panes of glass. Fabricated in 1890 and modeled after a similar structure in Milan, Italy, the building holds the dubious distinction of being this country's first indoor shopping mall. The staggering-for-its-time price tag of $875,000 was covered by John D. Rockefeller and other wealthy Cleveland industrialists. Five years after it was built, the grand space hosted the National Republican Convention. While lost on many of the commuters who routinely navigate its corridors, the Arcade's intricate brass-and-iron detail can stop a visitor dead in his or her tracks. Especially appealing is the cadre of cast-iron griffons and gargoyles that rings the skylight. A well-executed $60 million renovation of the historic structure in 1999 repurposed much of the upper floors into hotel rooms for the **Hyatt Regency at The Arcade.** Shops, services, and restaurants occupy the lower levels of this five-story gem.

MAP 1: 420 Superior Ave., 216/696-1408, www.thearcade-cleveland.com; free

Cleveland Public Library, Main Branch

The main branch of the Cleveland Public Library, one of the nation's most respected urban library systems, is comprised of two buildings linked by a subterranean passageway. Built in 1925 by the noted architecture firm Walker & Weeks, the talent behind Severance Hall, the main library is a neoclassical citadel. This building sits in stark contrast to the Louis Stokes Wing, a striking postmodern tower added in the mid-1990s as part of a $90 million expansion. Look closely, however, and a nexus can be found. With a nod to the original structure, the annex features a facade of the same height and stone. Rising from that six-story marble frame, the 10-story glass tower matches the height of the neighboring Federal

Reserve Bank. Inside the glorious old frame, a magnificent globe-shaped chandelier greets visitors, and grand marble stairs lead to upper floors. Vaulted ceilings, some 44 feet high, contain vivid geometric patterns and paintings of historical figures. Leaded-glass windows flood the reading rooms with light. Decorative friezes, original paintings and sculpture, and New Deal-commissioned murals are sprinkled throughout.

MAP 1: 325 Superior Ave. NE, 216/623-2800, www.cpl.org; Mon.-Sat. 9am-6pm, Sept.-May Sun. 1pm-5 pm

Cuyahoga County Courthouse

A county courthouse must possess a certain amount of charm for it to become popular with brides as a wedding site. Photographers love this historic building because the beaux arts interior serves as the most dramatic backdrop a shutterbug could hope for: sweeping marble staircases, soaring three-story vaulted ceilings, jaw-dropping stained glass, and art deco light fixtures. Along with city hall, the building serves as the northern terminus of the 1903 Group Plan, which arranged local and federal buildings around a public mall.

MAP 1: 1 Lakeside Ave., 216/443-8800

Federal Reserve Bank

Headquarters of the Fourth Federal Reserve District, the Federal Reserve Bank of Cleveland is an opulent palace of prosperity, security, and wealth. Designed by the noted Cleveland firm of Walker & Weeks, the 12-story granite and marble fortress resembles a Medici-style palazzo. The gilded interior features hand-painted vaulted ceilings, polished marble walls and pillars, and intricately detailed ironwork. Surprisingly, visitors are free to enter the bank's lobby, Learning Center, and **Money Museum.** Tours, offered Tuesday at 2pm and Thursday at 10am, fill up fast, so it is wise to reserve a spot well in advance.

MAP 1: 1455 E. 6th St., 216/579-2000, www.clevelandfed.org; Mon.-Thurs. 10am-2pm, closed holidays; free

★ Free Stamp

The *Free Stamp* has placed Cleveland squarely on the pop art map. Located on an expanse of green just east of city hall, the comically large aluminum-and-steel sculpture of a rubber office stamp was created by artist Claes Oldenburg for Standard Oil (SOHIO). When Standard Oil was purchased by BP, new management wanted nothing to do with the modern sculpture, so it was relegated to storage out of state. Tired of paying storage fees for years, BP ultimately offered the work to the City of Cleveland—for free. A new site was selected, the artist modified the design to better suit the locale, and

City Beautiful

In the late 1800s, as city populations continued to rise, so too did the levels of crime, poverty, and disease. Fresh on the heels of the 1893 Chicago World's Fair, the City Beautiful movement began to creep across the land. Advocates behind this civic-minded movement believed that a beautiful city could go a long way toward improving the moral spirit and caliber of its inhabitants. In cities like Chicago, Washington DC, and Cleveland, the initiative took the form of architectural "group plans"—cohesive arrangements of similar structures positioned around a great public mall.

The movement reached the shores of Lake Erie at an opportune time as federal, county, and municipal governments all were planning to erect sizable new structures. Cleveland's Group Plan of 1903, supported by Ohio governor George Nash and executed by New York and Chicago architects Daniel Burnham, John Carrere, and Arnold Brunner, advocated a monumental grouping of civic buildings around a mall. Built in the beaux arts style, which emphasizes symmetry, uniformity, and harmony, the structures all share similar scale and design. Six of the classically designed buildings were completed: the **Old Federal Building, Cleveland Public Library, City Hall, Cuyahoga County Courthouse, Public Auditorium,** and **Board of Education building.** A rail station, proposed for the northern boundary of the plan, was abandoned in favor of the **Terminal Tower.**

Sitting like near-identical twins to the south are the Old Federal Building and Cleveland Public Library. To the north, the Cuyahoga County Courthouse and City Hall are similar in height and mass, but not identical. Classic design, comparable scale, and the use of noble material like granite and marble in the whole of the buildings created a unified sense of dignity and order. But these reserved exteriors belie the grandeur of the interiors within, most featuring soaring vaulted ceilings, polished marble staircases, intricate ironwork, and original commissioned artwork. Linking all the buildings is an expanse of green space known as the Mall, which forms a corridor from Public Square to Lake Erie. Eventually, height limitations and "grand plans" gave way to modern skyscrapers. But the Group Plan, an ambitious schematic hatched more than a century ago, still serves as the backbone of this city.

the *Free Stamp* was officially dedicated in 1991. To this day many abhor its design—but just count the number of folks scrambling for a picture.

MAP 1: Williard Park, E. 9th St. and Lakeside Ave.

Great Lakes Science Center

Along with the Rock Hall and Cleveland Browns Stadium, the Great Lakes Science Center commands a prominent spot along the lakefront in North Coast Harbor. With the stated goal of making science, technology, and the local environment fun and accessible, this modern steel-and-glass structure boasts some 400 hands-on activities on three floors of exhibits. One of the largest science centers in the country, the 165,000-square-foot museum lures schoolchildren and adults with an edifying roster of permanent, temporary, and traveling exhibits. Favorites include the indoor twister, static generator, and photoluminescence shadow wall. The "Great Lakes Story" explores the physical characteristics, geography, and geology that make the Great Lakes region unique. The complex is also home to a 320-seat OMNIMAX theater and the Science Store, a great source for science-related books, games, and kits. A brand-new NASA Glenn Visitor Center opened at the Great Lakes Science Center in 2013. The hands-on exhibit lets visitors explore the actual 1973 Skylab 3 Apollo Command Module, see a real moon rock from the *Apollo 15* mission, and check out actual space suits worn by astronauts, including Buzz Aldrin. The exhibit also answers burning questions you might be afraid to ask, like how do astronauts go to the bathroom in space? The discovery gallery highlights the science and engineering behind space travel and even lets visitors experiment with a pressurized bottle rocket.

Out front, a single 150-foot wind turbine generates enough juice to satisfy 7 percent of the center's electrical needs. Open May through October, the adjacent Steamship *William G. Mather* is a retired Great Lakes freighter that offers a glimpse of life aboard a commercial vessel.

MAP 1: 601 Erieside Ave., 216/694-2000, www.glsc.org; daily 10am-5pm, closed Thanksgiving and Christmas; $9.50 adult, $7.50 child, $8.50 senior

★ Hope Memorial Bridge

Bridges typically are utilitarian affairs, elevated roadways designed to move commuters from here to there. But the Hope Memorial Bridge, also known as the Lorain-Carnegie, is beautiful to behold. Built in 1932, the gently arched span over the Cuyahoga River connects the East and West Sides of town. For most commuters, the highlight of each crossing is not safe arrival on the other side, but the epic sculptures that sit sentry on either end. Carved into the bridge's 43-foot sandstone pylons, the art deco figures are known fondly as the "guardians of traffic." Like bookends, the monuments stand back-to-back, for a total of eight unique designs. Cradled in the hands of each is a mode of transportation, from covered wagon and stagecoach to automobile and truck. The mile-long bridge features generous walkways on either side, offering easy passage from downtown to Ohio City, as well as fantastic vantage points for skyline photos.

MAP 1: Connects Carnegie Ave. and Lorain Ave. where they cross the Cuyahoga River; free

Old Federal Building

Originally constructed as a U.S. post office, customs house, and courthouse, the so-called Old Federal Building was the first structure built under the 1903 Group Plan, setting the tone for

clockwise from top left: Great Lakes Science Center, downtown; tulips in bloom at the Cleveland Botanical Garden; Rock and Roll Hall of Fame and Museum, downtown

the five buildings that followed. Today, the building is known as
the Howard M. Metzenbaum U.S. Courthouse, housing district
and bankruptcy courts, as well as Departments of Homeland
Security and Agriculture. The inspiration for this classical beaux
arts beauty is said to be the Place de la Concorde in Paris. Clad
in gray granite, and mirroring in size and scope the nearby public library, the majestic landmark occupies a full city block. Artist
Daniel Chester French created two monumental sculptures for the
exterior, *Jurisprudence* and *Commerce,* which flank the Superior
Avenue entrance. Climb the stone steps and enter the magnificent
marble lobby, taking in its grand vaulted ceiling, turn-of-the-20th-
century chandeliers, and original postal windows.

MAP 1: 201 Superior Ave. NE, 216/615-1235; Mon.-Fri. 7am-5pm; free

SIGHTS
DOWNTOWN

Old Stone Church

This church is formally called First Presbyterian Society, but because it is the oldest surviving structure on Public Square, and
because it was constructed of hand-hammered native sandstone,
the church has become known simply as the Old Stone Church.
Twice ravaged by fire, the Romanesque Revival structure was
thrice built—in 1855, 1858, and 1884. The awe-inspiring interior
boasts a barrel-vaulted ceiling, handsome oak pews, and a 3,000-
pipe Cleveland-built Holtkamp organ. Perhaps more impressive
are the four Louis Comfort Tiffany stained-glass windows, all of
which have undergone complete restoration. But this building is not
relegated to forgotten-museum status; it is a contemporary place of
worship for its congregants, and families gather for weekly prayer,
attend free organ concerts (row 77 center is the sweet spot), or practice yoga. Dwarfed by modern skyscrapers, this elegant old church
also serves as a gentle reminder that sanctuary is never too far away.

MAP 1: 91 Public Sq., 216/241-6145, www.oldstonechurch.org

★ Rock and Roll Hall of Fame and Museum

They say you can't cage an animal like rock and roll, but this iconic
shrine does a laudable job of telling the story of rock's gritty past,
present, and future. Some 150,000 square feet of space is crammed
with permanent and temporary exhibits, interactive displays, and
live-performance spaces. An incredible array of memorable costumes, instruments, personal effects, and ephemera provide visitors with a unique perspective on rock's roots and culture. Sure,
the entry fee is a bit steep. And, yes, it stinks that you can't take
photographs inside the building. But where else are you going to
see a Janis Joplin blotter acid sheet drawn by comic book artist
Robert Crumb and the hand-written lyrics of "Lucy in the Sky with
Diamonds" in one afternoon? To take a little bit of rock home with
you, stop by the well-stocked museum store, which is loaded with

How Cleveland Landed the Rock Hall

Since opening its doors in 1995, the Rock and Roll Hall of Fame has become such a symbol of Cleveland that the notion of it being located anywhere else seems absurd. Yet, despite the fact that "Cleveland Rocks"—thank you very much, Ian Hunter—this city had to pull off nothing short of a miracle to land the big prize.

When the Rock and Roll Hall of Fame Foundation was established in New York in 1985, with the aim of creating a museum to honor the legends of rock and roll, Cleveland wasn't even considered as a potential site. It took heroic efforts by Cleveland-based rock historian Norm N. Nite to convince the board to humor a contingent of city boosters. Those in attendance, including Ahmet Ertegun of Atlantic Records and Jann Wenner of Rolling Stone, were impressed enough by the presentation to schedule a fact-finding mission to C-Town.

Cleveland certainly had the rock chops to warrant that trip. This is where celebrated DJ Alan Freed and Record Rendezvous owner Leo Mintz first popularized the phrase "rock and roll." The Moondog Coronation Ball, considered the world's first rock concert (and subsequent rock concert fracas), took place in the Cleveland Arena in 1952. Groundbreaking DJs like Bill Randle, Pete "Mad Daddy" Myers, Casey Kasem, and Kid Leo all worked the turntable and microphone here. The region has a proven track record for delivering stars, from Joe Walsh and Chrissie Hynde to Eric Carmen and Nine Inch Nails. All the biggest names in rock made certain to stop and say "Hello, Cleveland" when touring, including Elvis, the Beatles, the Rolling Stones, David Bowie, Led Zeppelin, and the Who. Those big names performed, and their successors continue to do so, in some of the best live-music venues in the land, like Public Music Hall, Cleveland Agora, Peabody's, Beachland Ballroom, Grog Shop, and House of Blues. Ahead of its time, the album-oriented WMMS—Home of the Buzzard—was one of the most important rock-and-roll radio stations in the country. Jane Scott, one of the greatest, and most unlikely, rock reporters of anybody's generation made her living at the Cleveland Plain Dealer.

But ultimately it was the good people of Cleveland who tipped the scales in their own favor. When a USA Today telephone poll asked its readers to cast a vote for their choice of home for the Rock Hall, Cleveland trounced the competition, garnering 15 times the votes of second-place Memphis. When the foundation did eventually make that fact-finding tour to Cleveland, it was an impromptu pit stop at the original (now gone) Record Rendezvous that sealed the deal for some decision makers.

Cleveland officially won the Hall in 1986, but it would take an additional nine years and $90 million to see it through to completion. Today, the iconic I. M. Pei-designed glass-and-steel pyramid is a globally recognized affirmation of this city's rock-and-roll clout. And the museum has been a smash hit: Drawing more than six million guests since its opening, the Rock Hall is the most-visited hall of fame in the world.

Despite all the success, Cleveland was far from content. The Rock and Roll Hall of Fame Foundation's most prominent event, the annual induction ceremony, maintained a permanent residence at New York's Waldorf-Astoria hotel. Lobbying once again paid off: Starting in 2009, Cleveland began hosting the Hall of Fame induction gala every three years, a fitting tribute to a city that has proven that the Rock Hall belongs on the shores of Lake Erie.

music-themed books, CDs, and genuine memorabilia. This pyramidal building on Lake Erie's shore may look modest from the outside, but like a Grateful Dead concert, it will devour entire portions of one's day.

MAP 1: 1100 Rock and Roll Blvd., 216/781-7625, www.rockhall.com; Thurs.-Tues. 10am-5:30pm, Wed. 10am-9pm, closed Thanksgiving and Christmas; $22 adult, $13 child, $17 senior, free 8 and under

Soldiers and Sailors Monument

Since 1894, this stately bronze-and-granite statue has served to commemorate the men and women of Cuyahoga County who served their country during the Civil War. Situated in the heart of Cleveland's Public Square, the monument features a 125-foot spire, four exterior sculptural groupings, and an interior Memorial Hall. A walk around the base reveals arresting scenes of the four principal branches of service—infantry, artillery, cavalry, and navy—in the throes of battle. Wander inside to see the carved names of 9,000 Civil War veterans, some stained-glass windows, and the base of the spire, which bears bronze panels of Abraham Lincoln proclaiming emancipation.

MAP 1: 3 Public Sq., 216/621-3710, www.soldiersandsailors.com; Mon.-Sat. 9am-4pm, closed Thanksgiving, Christmas, and New Year's Day; free

Terminal Tower

When it was completed in 1930, this graceful skyscraper was the second-tallest building in the world. Rising 710 feet above Public Square, the building was the crown jewel of the Terminal Tower Complex, an ahead-of-its-time mixed-use development that included Cleveland Union Terminal rail station, hotels, department stores, and a post office. While it no longer competes for height records, Terminal Tower still serves as a beautiful reminder of this city's once-lofty status as the nation's fifth-largest city. Belying its neoclassical exterior, the building's interior spaces ooze with beaux arts and art deco details. Today, the complex houses hotels, office towers, a modern mall with restaurants, shops, and movie theaters, and a terminal for Cleveland's light-rail system, RTA. Tunnels and pathways connect to Progressive Field and Quicken Loans Arena. A five-year, $40 million restoration, that wrapped up in 2012, has repaired damaged exterior portions, restored the cupola to its original golden hue, modernized the tower's 21 elevators, replaced 2,000 windows, and added splashy new exterior lighting. The 42nd-floor observation deck, which had been closed since September 11, 2001, is now open to visitors on select weekends. Tickets ($5) are required. *Life* magazine photographer Margaret Bourke-White's famous black-and-white shot of Terminal Tower is said to have launched her noteworthy career. Bird-watchers should keep an eye out for

Downtown Development Boom

Not since the mid 1990s, when Cleveland unveiled the Rock Hall, Great Lakes Science Center, Gund Arena (now Quicken Loans), Browns Stadium (now FirstEnergy) and Jacob's Field (now Progressive) to great fanfare, has the city experienced such an explosive downtown development boom. In just a few short years, the city experienced a multibillion dollar face-lift that shows little sign of abating.

Completed in summer of 2013, the $465 million Global Center for Health Innovation and Cleveland Convention Center enjoys a commanding presence just off Public Square. As the world's only facility targeted specifically to the medical and health-care industries, the complex boasts 120,000 square feet of showroom space for major medical manufacturers and service providers. The attached state-of-the-art Convention Center features 300,000 square feet of exhibit space and 100,000 square feet of high-tech meeting rooms.

A few short blocks away is the new **Horseshoe Casino Cleveland,** a $350 million Las Vegas-style casino in the heart of downtown. Built within the walls of the historic Higbee department store building, the casino is one of the most attractive to hit any strip. Inside, 2,100 slot machines, 63 table games, a World Series of Poker room, and tons of amenities service millions of visitors per year.

Down in the Flats, a long-dormant entertainment district along the banks of the Cuyahoga, a $275 million multiuse development has come to life. The centerpiece of Flats East Bank, as it's known, is the 18-story, 500,000-square-foot Ernst & Young office tower. A 150-room **Aloft Hotel** joins new restaurants, clubs, and a riverfront boardwalk. A $120 million second phase will include 200 apartments and even more entertainment amenities.

Just across the river, on the west bank of the Flats, the $35 million **Greater Cleveland Aquarium** saw more than 400,000 visitors during its first year. Designed by New Zealand-based Marinescape, the one-million-gallon aquarium features a walk-through SeaTube, multiple exhibits and offers a "diving with sharks" program that allows certified SCUBA divers to take a very special plunge.

A new eight-story, 220,000-square-foot Cuyahoga County headquarters is going up at a cost of roughly $75 million at E. Ninth Street and Prospect Avenue in downtown Cleveland. It should be completed in mid-2014.

PlayhouseSquare, the second-largest performing arts center in the nation, underwent a $16 million beatification endeavor that added new lighting and seating and park space. In the Warehouse District, $1 million bought wider sidewalks and patios, flower planters, and improved pedestrian traffic.

peregrine falcons, which nest high on the tower and occasionally swoop down for a meal of fresh pigeon.

MAP 1: 50 Public Sq., 216/623-4750, www.towercitycenter.com; daily 24 hours; $5

Trolley Tours of Cleveland

The clang, clang, clang of Lolly the Trolley is a familiar sound for locals, who for years have observed these bright-red open-air carriages shuttling the curious about town. Despite the hokeyness factor, these trolleys provide a wonderful perspective on a city that often obscures its assets, with seasoned guides weaving historical, architectural, cultural, and political tidbits into a memorable excursion. General one- and two-hour tours hit the major sights of North Coast Harbor, the Warehouse District, Ohio City, PlayhouseSquare, Millionaire's Row, and University Circle, while numerous specialty tours focus on Little Italy and Lake View Cemetery, ethnic markets of Cleveland, unique churches about town, and the trail of Eliot Ness. Tours, which leave from the **Powerhouse at Nautica Entertainment Complex** in the Flats, run year-round, but leave more frequently from Memorial Day to Labor Day. All customers are required to call to reserve a spot in advance. Children under five are not permitted on the two-hour tour.

SIGHTS
DOWNTOWN

MAP 1: 2000 Sycamore St., 216/771-4484, www.lollytrolley.com; one-hour tour $11 adult, $8 child, $10 senior; two-hour tour $17 adult, $12 child, $16 senior

U.S.S. *COD* Submarine

Launched in 1943, this 312-foot fleet submarine made seven war patrols in the South Pacific during World War II. She is credited with sinking a Japanese destroyer, minesweeper, several cargo ships, and troop transports with her steam-powered torpedoes. The *COD* also performed the only international sub-to-sub rescue in history, saving 56 Dutch sailors before destroying their grounded ship. A popular tourist attraction since 1976, the *COD* is unique among restored display submarines in that visitors use the very same ladders and hatches employed by the crew (making it challenging for elderly and handicapped). On shore is a Mark 14 steam-driven torpedo, a five-bladed 2,080-pound bronze sub propeller, and a plaque honoring submariners who have lost their lives throughout the history of the United States. Military in uniform and wives and family of active-duty submariners are admitted free.

MAP 1: E. 9th St. and N. Marginal Rd., 216/566-8770, www.usscod.org; May-Sept. daily 10am-5pm; $6 adult, $3 student, $5 senior, free for military in uniform

War Memorial Fountain

Alternatively known as the Fountain of Eternal Life, Peace Arising from the Flames of War, or simply, the Green Guy, this regal statue enjoys prominent placement in a large open space called the Mall. The 35-foot granite-and-bronze sculpture depicts a stately male figure rising from the flames of war, his outstretched arm reaching toward the heavens. Illuminated fountains ring the base. Designed by a Cleveland Institute of Art graduate, the monument serves as a memorial to those who perished during World War II and the Korean War. During the planning stages, in the mid-1960s, conservative city officials insisted that the artist "cover up" his too-naked male form, which he did with strategically placed flames.

MAP 1: Veterans' Memorial Plaza, St. Clair Ave. NE and W. Mall Dr.

Ohio City and Tremont Map 2

Carnegie West Library

Outside of philanthropist Andrew Carnegie's hometown of Pittsburgh, more Carnegie libraries were constructed in Cleveland than anywhere else. Of the 15 built here, all but three are still used as libraries. One of them is this graceful Renaissance Revival structure, a triangular-shaped edifice designed by Edward Tilton and completed in 1910. The interior of this Ohio City branch of the Cleveland Public Library boasts Corinthian columns, expansive windows, and room-illuminating skylights. Original Arts and Crafts touches can be found throughout the warm space, like the charming green-glazed Alice in Wonderland tiles, crafted by noted potter William Grueby, that frame the fireplace in the children's room. Set on a roomy and open green space, the library forms a graceful backdrop for impromptu strolls, neighborhood gatherings, and lazy Sunday mornings with coffee and the paper.

MAP 2: 1900 Fulton Rd., 216/623-6927, http://cpl.org; Mon., Tues., and Thurs. 9:30am-8pm, Wed., Fri., and Sat. 9:30am-6pm

A Christmas Story House

People thought Brian Jones, a West Coaster who had never stepped foot in Cleveland, was out of his mind when he purchased the house that served as the visual backdrop for the classic film *A Christmas Story*. A lifelong fan of the flick, Jones bought the 1895 Tremont structure sight unseen, with plans of restoring the "Parker house" to its original movie splendor. Every effort was made to recapture the authentic look and feel of the times, including exchanging vinyl siding with real wood, ditching the replacement windows, and converting the building from a duplex back to a single-family home. Jones took pains to match the interior layout of the movie home, scouting out identical furnishings. Fans of the movie will recognize the familiar yellow-and-green of the building's exterior. Directly across the street from the house is a gift shop and museum, where film buffs can view original props, costumes, and memorabilia. Feel deserving of a "major award?" Pick up a full-size replica of the notorious leg lamp to take home and proudly display in the front window.

MAP 2: 3159 W. 11th St., 216/298-4919, www.achristmasstoryhouse.com; Wed.-Sat. 10am-5pm, Sun. noon-5pm, closed Thanksgiving and Christmas; $7 adult, $5 child, $6 senior

Cleveland neighborhoods are graced with scores of architecturally stunning churches, their steeples and bell towers visible from area highways. And thanks to a generous donation by a retired dentist, many are visible day or night.

Before he died, **Reinhold W. Erickson** saw to it that his life savings of $370,000 would be used to improve his city's image to outsiders. His plan was specific: By illuminating church steeples along Cleveland interstates,

he could give folks arriving via Cleveland Hopkins International Airport something beautiful to look at during their ride into the city. His goal was to light 20 churches along the oft-traveled I-90 and I-71 corridors.

Today, the Reinhold W. Erickson Fund is managed by the Cleveland Foundation and the Cleveland Restoration Society. So far, a dozen churches have participated in the ambitious **Steeple Lighting Program.** See how many you can spot along the way.

Franklin Castle

This 9,000-square-foot, carved-sandstone Gothic mansion is presently unoccupied—and some say that is a good thing. Host to many unspeakable acts, the house is long rumored to be haunted by unhappy spirits. Built in the late 1800s by a wealthy banker, the mansion boasts 26 rooms, five marble fireplaces, and some 80 windows. It is also, according to lore, the sight of a few grisly slayings, including that of a housekeeper who was murdered on her wedding day. Passersby regularly claim to see a ghost in the upstairs window, while others hear blood-curdling cries. Stroll by at night—if you dare.

MAP 2: 4308 Franklin Blvd.; not open to the public

Jay Avenue Homes

Jay Avenue can be viewed as a microcosm of the whole of Ohio City. Not long ago, this leafy tree-lined block in Cleveland's oldest neighborhood was a picture of despair, with once majestic Victorians inching ever closer to collapse and oblivion. Today, nearly every one of those homes has been thoughtfully restored, transforming each from eyesore to attraction. Stroll south on Jay from West 25th to its terminus at West 30th and explore the Archibald Willard House (2601 Jay), built in 1860 and once home to the famous painter of *The Spirit of '76,* and the Marquard Mansion (2920 Jay), built in 1903 by Philip Marquard, owner of the Marquard Sash and Door Co.

MAP 2: Jay Ave. btwn. W. 25th and W. 30th Sts.

John Heisman's Birthplace

Sports fans know that the Heisman (officially the Heisman Memorial Trophy) is awarded annually to the best athlete in college football. Most, however, do not know that John W. Heisman was born in Ohio City and, according to many, in this very house. A commemorative plaque marks the site, but the house is not open to the public. Heisman was a wildly successful coach at Oberlin College, University of Akron, Auburn, Clemson, and Georgia Tech, where he guided his team to a mind-boggling 222-0 victory over the Cumberland College Bulldogs.

MAP 2: 2825 Bridge Ave.

Lincoln Park

Once part of Cleveland University, a short-lived mid-1800s college, this leafy green expanse is Tremont's version of Public Square. Ringed by bars, restaurants, and lovingly restored century-old homes, this park sees activity all day long. It is the site of numerous neighborhood festivals, alfresco summer concerts, and even Civil War encampments. Throughout the summer, free dance and music concerts attract large picnicking crowds at night, while the park's municipal swimming pool attracts overheated locals during the day. A stroll around the park's perimeter will unearth such haunts as Sanctuary (coffeehouse), Dish (deli), and Prosperity Social Club (neighborhood pub). Over on Starkweather Avenue, sharp modern townhomes occupy the Lincoln Park Bath building, which was constructed in 1921 as a public bathhouse for the many residents who still lacked modern plumbing.

MAP 2: Starkweather Ave. and W. 14th St.

St. Ignatius High School

With 13 majestic buildings spread across a lush 16-acre campus, St. Ignatius High School looks more like a tony liberal arts college than a Catholic prep school for boys. Founded in the late 1800s by a group of German Jesuits, the school is both a neighborhood icon and a Cleveland educational institution. Along with the West Side Market's clock tower, St. Ig's 160-foot redbrick spire is one of the most recognizable skyline landmarks in the area. Respected equally for its athletics and academic excellence, this school has graduated both Olympic gold medalists and Ohio Supreme Court justices. Ohio City is often filled with the youthfully exuberant sounds of lacrosse, football, and track-and-field athletes as they compete on the pro-style turf field.

MAP 2: 2825 Bridge Ave., 216/651-6313, www.ignatius.edu

St. John's Episcopal Church

Cleveland's oldest church, this Ohio City landmark was built by a Connecticut settler in 1836. Beloved for its Gothic Revival style and its facade of local sandstone, the building has survived both a devastating fire and a violent tornado. In the mid-1800s, Ohio offered safe passage for tens of thousands of slaves; St. John's was the last stop on the so-called Underground Railroad before arriving in Canada. The newest acquisition for this storied church is a fully restored 500-pipe organ, originally crafted in 1926, which has made its way through at least three separate places of worship.

MAP 2: 2600 Church Ave., 216/781-5546

St. Patrick's Church

The story of this church's construction in 1873 truly is an inspiring tale of commitment and allegiance. When parishioners outgrew their original place of worship, land at the present site was purchased, an architect was hired, and plans for a Gothic Revival structure were drawn up. And that was the easy part. Offered all the free blue limestone they could cut and carry, parishioners made weekly trips to a quarry 65 miles away, where they would cut stone for days on end before returning by wagon to Cleveland. The parishioners who remained on-site had the task of sizing and positioning the stone. This process continued for a full two years. These days, neighbors often gather and cheer as newlyweds make their way down the church steps.

MAP 2: 3602 Bridge Ave., 216/631-6872, www.stpatrickbridge.org

★ St. Theodosius Russian Orthodox Cathedral

Fans of *The Deer Hunter* will surely recognize the characteristic onion-shaped domes that dot the top of this magnificent cathedral, which served as the backdrop for that film's wedding scenes. The 13 copper-clad domes that rise above the structure represent Christ and the 12 apostles. At 112 years old, St. Theodosius is the oldest Russian Orthodox cathedral in Ohio, and it is considered one of the finest examples of traditional orthodox architecture in the country. Nearly every inch of the interior is adorned with vivid religious murals, icons, and holy pictures, the highlight of which is a screen bearing images of Christ, the Virgin Mary, the 12 apostles, and St. Theodosius. A 2001 renovation has breathed fresh life into the historic church.

MAP 2: 733 Starkweather Ave., 216/741-1310, www.sttheodosius.org

★ West Side Market

Though it looks like a grand railway station, the building that houses this historic public market was constructed expressly to sell food. Built in 1912, and added to the National Register of Historic Places in the mid-1970s, the West Side Market attracts food fans, architecture buffs, and campaigning politicians. But mostly it functions as the city's most fantastic supermarket, where residents buy their weekly eggs, meat, produce, and bread. Unlike prominent public markets elsewhere that stock everything from incense to T-shirts, this market is almost exclusively focused on food. Some 80 individually operated stalls hawk everything from Polish pierogies and Hungarian sausage to fresh pasta and exotic herbs and grains. There are multiple butchers for poultry, pork, beef, lamb, and goat, three separate fishmongers, and a handful of artisan bakers. Notice the conspicuous absence of fresh produce? That's because it's all next door in the fruit and vegetable annex, situated on the north and east sides of the complex.

MAP 2: 1979 W. 25th St., 216/664-3387, www.westsidemarket.com; Mon. and Wed. 7am-4pm, Fri.-Sat. 7am-6pm

Detroit Shoreway and Edgewater

Map 3

Gordon Square Arts District

Thanks to a multi-year, multi-million dollar revitalization project, this arts-focused district has become the nucleus not only of the Detroit Shoreway neighborhood, but likely the entire near-West Side of Cleveland. Two miles west of downtown, with easy access to Lake Erie, the district is the site of ambitious new residential, commercial, and cultural development. Anchored by the 20-year-old Cleveland Public Theatre, the walkable area boasts a restored 1921 art-house movie theater, a pedestrian-friendly streetscape, and soon the new home of 275-seat Near West Theatre. Already, the vibrant area is picking up steam. Shoppers are beginning to discover funky new boutiques, design studios and art galleries, and book and record shops. Sharp new cafés, restaurants, and bars keep the diverse streets peopled day and night.

MAP 3: Centered around Detroit Ave. and W. 65th St., www.gordonsquare.org; hours vary

Lakefront Reservation

Lakefront Reservation may not have the blushing pink sands of a Bahamas beach, or the jet-set crowds of the French Riviera, but it does have something only a handful of beaches in the world can claim: remarkable Cleveland skyline views. Amateur and professional shutterbugs flock to this urban sanctuary for breathtaking city, lake, and sunset views. This sprawling lakefront park is comprised of two main areas: an elevated bluff and a lake-level beach. On sweltering summer days, largely working-class families seek relief in the cool lake waters (despite the lake's less-than-stellar water quality). But most visitors don't come here to swim. Kite-flyers enjoy steady breezes nearly 12 months out of the year. Walkers, joggers, and bicyclists crisscross the park on paved pathways. Anglers

Lolly the Trolley

Lolly the Trolley on Public Square

For more than 20 years, Sherrill Paul Witt has been leading narrated sightseeing tours through Cleveland on bright red vehicles called Lolly the Trolley. In that time, the company has grown from one trolley and one guide to eight trolleys and 10 guides. The clientele has shifted from mostly locals to mostly out-of-towners, including visitors from every U.S. state and most countries. We asked Witt some questions about the city she loves to show off.

How did the trolley tours start?

I began giving tours of Playhouse-Square theaters and loved it. Soon, I was leading walking and bus tours of Cleveland. When I went to Boston for a wedding and saw a trolley tour, I decided Cleveland needed one.

What opinions do first-time visitors often have of Cleveland?

Some think we are provincial and have a rust-belt-city mentality. They don't know that Cleveland is a sophisticated multicultural city with all the big-city pluses and few of the minuses. There is a tremendous amount of quiet wealth in the area, and people are generous to a fault.

What are some of your favorite places to take visitors?

I love the Arcade. It is a Victorian de-light that opened in 1890, and its huge glass ceiling and fabulous wrought-iron railings just stun people. Also, Lake View Cemetery has the Garfield Memorial, John D. Rockefeller's gravesite, and Wade Chapel, the only Tiffany-designed interior in the United States.

What do kids get a kick out of?

They love the lake, U.S.S. *COD* Submarine, and the jets on display at Burke Lakefront Airport. They also love all of our professional sports venues and bridges.

What impression of Cleveland do your customers leave with?

People always say what a beautiful city we have. They love the classical downtown architecture and how clean our streets and Lake Erie are. Also, they like how affordable Cleveland is both for visitors and residents. You can go to Broadway shows for a fraction of the cost of the East Coast.

What's the best excursion from town?

Pedaling along the Ohio & Erie Canal Towpath in Cuyahoga Valley National Park.

drop lines off a nearby fishing pier. Boaters launch their watercraft from various ramps. And winter at the park is just as spectacular thanks to the dramatic ice sculptures that form along the rocks. Wise Clevelanders know to exit this park before dark.

MAP 3: 6500 Memorial Shoreway, 216/881-8141, www.ohiodnr.com/parks; daily 6am-11pm

St. Stephen Catholic Church

This stunning Gothic-style church was built in 1881 to serve the West Side's large contingent of German-speaking Catholics—by 1900 there were nearly 40,000. Many of the original parishioners agreed to mortgage their homes to insure that construction was completed. What distinguishes a German Catholic church from, say, a Roman Catholic one? For starters, the interior features a blond Virgin Mary, the hand-carved altars and statuary were imported from Munich, and the image of the Lord is a bearded one. Mass is still held in German on the first Sunday of each month. The freestanding hand-carved oak pulpit, a 25-foot tower of ornamental figurines, was initially exhibited at the Chicago World's Fair. Basket-weave marble tiles cover the sanctuary floor. St. Stephen's imported stained-glass windows were shattered by a tornado in 1999 and have since been replaced.

MAP 3: 1930 W. 54th St., 216/631-5634, www.saintstephenchurch.org

University Circle and Little Italy

Map 4

Cleveland Botanical Garden

With origins in a converted boathouse on nearby Wade Park Lagoon, the botanical garden moved to its current site in 1966. The facility's most conspicuous asset is the 18,000-square-foot Glasshouse, which contains faithful re-creations of two fragile ecosystems, a Costa Rican cloud forest and the desert of Madagascar. Inside, visitors glide from biome to biome, immersed in environments rich with magical fauna and flora. Some 400 varieties of plants and animals take up residence in the conservatory, including 20 species of butterfly, the world's most diminutive orchids, and an army of hungry leaf-cutter ants. Perhaps even more spectacular are the 10 acres of award-winning outdoor gardens. Among them are a traditional Japanese dry garden, a show-stopping rose garden, perennial and woodland gardens, and an herb garden with 4,000 distinct plants. The Hershey Children's Garden caters specifically to the littlest green thumbs in the bunch with mini forests, caves, worm bins, and a wheelchair-accessible tree house. An on-site library houses one of the largest repositories of gardening information in the country, with more than 17,000 garden-related books and periodicals. All gardens are open year-round except the Children's Garden, which closes during winter.

MAP 4: 11030 East Blvd., 216/721-1600, www.cbgarden.org; Mon.-Sat. 10am-5pm, Sun. noon-5pm, open late Wed.; $7.50 adult, $3 child

★ Cleveland Museum of Art

The Cleveland Museum of Art has always been regarded as one of the nation's finest repositories of art and antiquities. Thanks to an ambitious, and some might say long overdue, expansion and renovation, visitors now enjoy a much improved art-viewing experience. The first phase of the $350 million project saw the reopening of the original 1916 building following three years of construction; the entire project, which was completed in 2013, replaced outmoded additions with two new wings, uniting all with a massive central atrium. Restored to its original glory, the classical marble-clad main building now gives the art a wider berth and visitors an easier path to navigate. Restored skylights create optimal lighting conditions for viewing the work, while state-of-the-art mechanicals provide a more comfortable environment. Thanks to 40,000 square feet of new gallery space, there's more room now than ever to exhibit the museum's vast permanent collection of 43,000 works of art. Among the permanent exhibits on display are 17th century to early 19th century European art; 18th century and 19th century American art; 19th century European sculpture, paining, and decorative arts; and Islamic, Medieval, and Renaissance art, textiles, and manuscripts. Long a favorite of young and old, the Armor Court contains one of the largest and finest compilations of medieval and Renaissance arms and armor. Set on a picturesque bluff in University Circle, the museum presides over a sweeping landscape designed by Frederick Law Olmsted Jr., whose father created New York's Central Park. Photography without a flash is permitted.

MAP 4: 11150 East Blvd., 216/421-7340, www.clevelandart.org; Tues., Thurs., and Sat.-Sun. 10am-5pm, Wed. and Fri. 10am-9pm; free

Hessler Road and Hessler Court

It may not look like much at first blush, but these two tiny lanes in University Circle have been the site of many battles, protests, and celebrations. The buildings here date back to the early 1900s, so it's understandable that folks didn't take too kindly to the notion of their neighborhood being demolished to make room for parking lots. A vigilant street association formed in 1969 and managed to fight off the proposed development. Before long, the neighborhood was declared a historic district and was placed on the National

Register of Historic Places. Hessler Court is just 300 feet long and is the only street in Cleveland that is paved with wood blocks. Held each May, the Hessler Street Fair is a spirited block party that unites friends and neighbors through art, music, food, and dance.

MAP 4: Ford Dr. and Hessler Rd.

Peter B. Lewis Building

Set amid the tranquil tree-lined streets that make up the campus of Case Western Reserve University, the Peter B. Lewis Building doesn't just stand out, it explodes onto the landscape. Home to the Weatherhead School of Management, the Frank Gehry-designed building is precisely what one would expect from the acclaimed avant-garde architect. Seemingly lacking even a single right angle, the twisting brick structure corkscrews out of the ground. There is no roof, per se, but rather a riot of stainless steel ribbons that festoon the top, reflecting whatever the sky happens to be doing at any given moment. Like the coiling tail of a rambunctious fish, the scaly steel tiles provide a flurry of movement and whimsy. Visible for blocks and blocks, the architectural landmark has become an attraction all to itself. Group tours can be arranged by calling ahead two weeks in advance.

MAP 4: Bellflower Rd. and Ford Dr., 216/368-4771, www.weatherhead.case.edu; free

Severance Hall

The saga of Severance Hall is a love story. One month after tycoon and Cleveland Orchestra president John Long Severance committed to building the concert hall, his wife, Elisabeth, died suddenly of a stroke. Vowing to dedicate the venue to the memory of his beloved partner, Severance went on to build a performance hall that rivals in beauty and sound of any found in Vienna, Boston, or New York. Severance Hall was designed by Walker & Weeks, Cleveland's leading architecture firm throughout the 1920s and 1930s, and it mimics a Greek temple. The majestic building's neoclassical facade, with its Ionic column-supported pediment, harmonizes with the nearby Cleveland Museum of Art. Tributes to Mrs. Severance can be found throughout the hall. Silvery shapes high above the main concert floor are reported to be modeled after the lace from her bridal veil. Lotus blossoms, Elisabeth's favorite flower, appear in the grand foyer's terrazzo floor and elsewhere. Entering the Grand Foyer, visitors are immersed in an opulent environment of two-story red marble columns, art deco chandeliers, decorative metalwork, and dazzling floors. A $40 million renovation and restoration has updated the facility while remaining faithful to the original design. Severance Hall is, and always has been, a fitting home for the "Best Band in the Land." Concerts and tours are held year-round except during the summer months, when the orchestra performs at Blossom Music Center.

MAP 4: 11001 Euclid Ave., 216/231-1111, www.clevelandorchestra.com; cost varies by performance

Wade Park

Not just any ordinary park, Wade is the epicenter of arts, culture, and education in Cleveland, surrounded by the city's finest museums, performing-arts venues, and universities. It is also the site of Wade Oval and Wade Lagoon. Whether one is off to a museum, concert, or lunch date—or none of the above—time should be set aside for a leisurely stroll through this urban oasis. The grounds are dotted with alluring public art, architecturally stunning buildings, and meticulously tended gardens. On sunny spring, summer, and fall days, it isn't uncommon to see numerous newlywed couples roaming the green space with photographer in tow. During a random stroll, a visitor might encounter Rodin's *The Thinker,* a garden designed by Frederick Law Olmsted Jr., or a colorful neighborhood parade. Wade Oval is the site of WOW!, weekly free outdoor concerts held on Wednesday June through August.

MAP 4: Bordered by East Blvd. and Martin Luther King Jr. Blvd.

Cleveland Heights and Shaker Heights

Map 5

Cain Park

The crown jewel of this 22-acre urban park is the Evans Amphitheater, a 1,200-seat covered venue with accompanying open-air lawn for outdoor seating. Despite its meager size, the stage attracts top-talent touring acts who appreciate the intimacy of the setting. Pick a show, pack a picnic, and spend a glorious summer night under the stars. Varied performances on either of the two stages include dance, cabaret, singer-songwriters, and Broadway musicals. In addition to some modest biking and hiking trails, the wooded parkland contains basketball and tennis courts, a toboggan hill, and a skate park. Every July, Cain Park hosts one of the most impressive arts festivals in the region. For three full days, thousands gather to shop the wares of some 150 artists, covering a broad swath of disciplines.

MAP 5: Superior Ave. at Lee Rd., 216/371-3000, www.cainpark.com

Cleveland Heights is a progressive and diverse inner-ring suburb of about 45,000 residents. The area's unique physical layout and history as a "streetcar city" caused the creation of various commercial districts within its environs, each boasting its own look, feel, and flair. **Cedar-Lee,** so named for the major intersection in its midst, acts as "Main Street" for Cleveland Heights. This walkable mile-long strip of shops, services, restaurants, and bars serves the students, young professionals, and families who call the neighborhood home. Running south from Cain Park to the public library, the street includes the Cedar Lee Theatre, a local hardware store, a yoga studio, numerous galleries and boutiques, and countless bars and restaurants. There is rarely a time of day or night that finds the street totally deserted. **Coventry Village** is perhaps best known for its counterculture past, a time when underground cartoonists R. Crumb and Harvey Pekar made the street their living room. Sadly, the strip has succumbed to more than a few national chains, causing a slow and steady erosion of its infamous indie spirit. But all is not lost; Coventry still deserves attention thanks to a quirky amalgam of shops, restaurants, bars, and clubs. This is the only place in the world you'll find Big Fun, the Grog Shop, and Tommy's restaurant. We'll forgive Cedar-Fairmount its Starbucks, mainly because this picturesque gathering of Tudor-style buildings looks today much as it did in 1920. Known as the "Gateway to the Heights," the district sits at the pinnacle of Cedar Hill. That aforementioned coffeehouse teems with activity all day long, while world-renowned jazz club Nighttown bops all night. A spirited mix of independent shops includes a bookstore, wine shop, Pilates studio, gelato parlor, pool hall, and martini bar. The nearby professional buildings are filled with architects, lawyers, psychiatrists, and doctors.

MAP 5: Cedar-Lee: Lee Rd. btwn. Superior and Dellwood; Coventry Village: Coventry Rd. btwn. Mayfield Rd. and Euclid Heights Blvd.

★ Fairmount Boulevard District

In the early 1900s, industry tycoons began migrating from the city core to the eastern suburbs. At the time, Cleveland Heights still was considered far out in the country despite being a mere nine miles from Public Square. Serviced by the Cleveland Electric Railway, which traveled from downtown up Cedar Hill, the area quickly became home to the city's wealthiest residents. Employing the architect hotshots of the day, those business moguls built some of the finest homes of the 1910s and 1920s. Today, Fairmount Boulevard in Cleveland Heights is dotted with stately Georgian mansions, terra-cotta-clad Italian villas, and wildly asymmetrical Tudor Revivals. Park your car on any of the side streets and make the trek on foot in order to enjoy architectural details like original copper gutters, leaded-glass windows, steeply pitched slate roofs, and wrought-iron balconies. The annual Heights Heritage Home Tour, held in September, offers participants intimate access to some of these homes and their magnificent gardens.

MAP 5: Fairmount Blvd. from Cedar Rd. to Wellington Rd.

★ Lake View Cemetery

This 290-acre plot of land is much more than just a final resting place for loved ones; it is an outdoor museum visited by approximately 400,000 people each year. Botanical garden, history lesson, and art gallery all in one, Lake View is a tranquil oasis in the middle of a congested urban environment. Best known as the burial site for many of this city's movers and shakers, the cemetery is "home" to John D. Rockefeller, Eliot Ness, and 22 Cleveland mayors. The most notable resident, perhaps, is President James A. Garfield, whose stately memorial provides views clear to Lake Erie. Hidden behind the simple, classical lines of the Jeptha Wade Memorial Chapel is a fairy-tale interior designed by Louis Comfort Tiffany. Four-ton bronze doors protect a deliriously beautiful stained-glass window, worthy of a crosstown visit itself. A few hours spent wandering the grounds and viewing the architecturally appealing markers and headstones is time well spent. Numerous walking tours are offered during spring and summer. Both the Garfield Memorial and Wade Chapel are open April 1-November 19, 9am-4pm.

MAP 5: 12316 Euclid Ave., 216/421-2665, www.lakeviewcemetery.com; daily 7:30am-5:30pm; free

Nature Center at Shaker Lakes

Armed with the slogan "Better ducks than trucks," a vigilant ladies garden club managed to save this bucolic 200-acre preserve from becoming another four-lane superhighway. That was in the late 1960s. Today the Shaker Lakes, and the single-minded Nature Center that serves as their environmental steward, attract thousands of ecoconscious visitors each year thanks to an absolute embarrassment of wildlife riches. The parklands encompass lakes, streams, marshes, fields, and dense forest, providing natural habitats for a host of native flora and fauna. Two trails—one wheelchair-accessible, the other more rugged—wind through this incredible landscape, providing the day-tripper an up close and immersive experience. Die-hard bird-watchers flock here for regularly scheduled walks, ticking off warblers, thrushes, catbirds, juncos, red-tailed hawks, and barred owls on their checklists. Innovative programs held throughout the year inspire visitors to live greener lives.

MAP 5: 2600 South Park Blvd., 216/321-5935, www.shakerlakes.org; Mon.-Sat. 10am-5pm, Sun. 1pm-5pm, trails open dawn to dusk; free

Shaker Square

More an octagon than a square, Shaker Square is the heart of a spirited and diverse neighborhood six miles east of downtown. Built in the late 1920s, and connected to downtown via the Rapid Transit line, the square is considered the second-oldest outdoor shopping district in the nation. But more than just a collection of shops, the square is a public space, where neighbors meet over coffee, take in a summer concert, or simply wander the circumference with a baby stroller. On warm nights, the roomy front patios of the numerous restaurants fill with diners. A movie theater shows both the latest releases as well as more offbeat indie flicks. Coffee, ice cream, and popcorn, all available on the square, provide the perfect post-movie nosh. A smattering of galleries, boutiques, and shops make for entertaining window-shopping. Held every Saturday morning mid-April through fall, the North Union Farmers Market attracts a massive sampling of small growers and producers, making it the largest fresh-food bazaar in the region.

MAP 5: Shaker Blvd. and N. and S. Moreland, www.shakersquare.net

Lakewood

Map 6

The Beck Center for the Arts

The Beck is the largest nonprofit performing-arts and arts-education organization on the West Side of Cleveland. In addition to professional theatrical productions, which take place on two stages, the center offers comprehensive arts-education programming in dance, music, theater, and visual arts. Lead by artistic director Scott Spence, Beck's productions of musicals, dramas, and comedies consistently draw rave reviews from area critics and fans. The center's ambitious schedule of offerings attracts 100,000 people per year. Folks looking to try something new scramble for spots in classes that range from hip-hop to life drawing from the nude. Two on-site art galleries regularly feature the works of local, regional, and nationally recognized artists.

MAP 6: 17801 Detroit Ave., 216/521-2540, www.beckcenter.org

Lakewood Park

One of 15 city parks in neighboring Lakewood, Lakewood Park is a 31-acre lakefront recreational area with eight tennis courts, three sand volleyball courts, two softball fields, an outdoor swimming pool, picnic pavilions, a skateboard park, and a kid-friendly playground. The park's band shell offers free Friday night movies and Sunday night concerts throughout the summer. On or around the Fourth of July, thousands gather here for a celebration of games,

food, music, and fireworks. The Oldest Stone House is also located
within the confines of this park.

MAP 6: Belle and Lake Aves., 216/529-4081, www.ci.lakewood.oh.us

Oldest Stone House

In the 1830s, Lakewood was a densely forested hamlet populated by a handful of rugged pioneer types. Back then, now-busy
Detroit Road was a dusty trail dotted with log-cabin homes. In
1838, John Honam built this small stone house out of locally
quarried sandstone, pretty much signaling the end for log-cabin
construction. The building, which served at various times as
a residence, post office, and barbershop, remained at its original location for 117 years. In the mid-1950s, at a cost of around
$10,000, the solidly built stone house was moved to its current
location and established as the home of the Lakewood Historical
Society and Museum. Though tiny, the museum boasts a rich
tapestry of pioneer relics, including a preserved pioneer kitchen,
four-harness loom, furnished parlor with horsehair sofa, and
bedrooms with roped beds and homespun sheets. The museum
also displays samplers, quilts, and folk art. An on-site herb garden is representative of those pioneer families would maintain
as a source of scents, dyes, and food seasonings. Tours of the
museum are conducted by costumed hostesses on Wednesday
and Sunday 2pm-5pm

MAP 6: 14710 Lake Ave., 216/221-7343, www.lakewoodhistory.org; Feb.-Nov. Wed.
1pm-4pm, Sun. 2pm-5pm, closed major holidays; free

Greater Cleveland   Map 7

Cleveland Metroparks Zoo and RainForest

With more than a million visitors each year, the zoo continues to
be one of the region's top draws. Spread across 170 acres, the park
contains 3,000 animals representing 600 different species. The
most popular attraction is the RainForest, a two-acre, two-story
steam bath jammed with a cornucopia of plants and animals, including birds, monkeys, and odd-smelling beasts. A simulated
tropical rainstorm washes over the room every few minutes. 'Roo
fans will hop over to Australian Adventure, home to parrots, koa-
las, and kangaroos. Like an African safari in Ohio, the Savannah
teems with lions, rhinos, giraffes, zebras, and gazelles. Black bears
and grizzlies take up residence in the Northern Trek, while tortoises and cheetahs race behind the Primate Building. In 2008,
the zoo broke ground on a $25 million elephant habitat due to
be completed in 2011. There are numerous fast and casual food

options at the park, but guests are free to bring in a packed lunch to save money.

MAP 7: 3900 Wildlife Way, Cleveland, 216/661-6500, www.clemetzoo.com; daily 10am-5pm, Memorial Day through Labor Day until 7pm Sat., Sun., and holidays; Apr.-Oct. $10 adult, $6 child, Nov-Apr. $7 adult, $5 child

Cuyahoga Valley National Park

This 33,000-acre national park follows the twists and turns of the Cuyahoga River for 22 miles. Thanks to a wide range of habitats, from deep ravines and wetlands to open prairie and grasslands, the park is home to a great diversity of wildlife. Bird-watchers routinely spot great blue herons, short-eared owls, bobolinks, even bald eagles. Anglers pluck from the rushing waters steelhead trout, bullhead, bluegill, and bass. White-tailed deer seem to be everywhere, coyotes prowl the hillsides, and spring peepers provide the evening soundtrack. Bicycling is likely the most popular activity in the park, taking place along four major trails, including the perennially popular Towpath Trail, which follows the path of the historic Ohio & Erie Canal for 20 miles. Over 125 miles of hiking trails wend and weave their way through the park, offering treks of varying degrees of difficulty. In wintertime, folks don snowshoes, cross-country skis, and ice skates for some blustery fun. The Cuyahoga Valley Scenic Railroad provides a decidedly more passive park experience, giving riders an eagle's-eye view of the landscape from the comfort of a vintage railcar. Cyclists hop the train with bicycle in tow to get to or from favorite paths.

MAP 7: 7104 Canal Rd., Valley View, 216/524-1497, www.nps.gov/cuva

Holden Arboretum

This nature preserve east of Cleveland began as a modest 100-acre parcel of land. Today it encompasses 3,500 acres and includes more than 120,000 diverse plants, making it one of the largest arboretums and botanical gardens in the country. The lush and rambling landscape features a vast array of natural habitats, including bogs, gulches, ponds, lakes, rivers, meadows, and forests, combining to create a wildlife lover's paradise. Various display and specimen gardens specialize in trees, shrubs, and herbaceous perennials, colorful butterfly-attracting plants, even nut-bearing trees. Classes are offered in a range of disciplines, from utilizing native plants at home to propagating deciduous woody perennials. Winter is no time to shun the arboretum; it evolves into an absolute wonderland punctuated by bounding deer, frozen-in-time waterfalls, and a downy blanket of snow. Numerous guided tours (held largely from spring through fall) focus on various regions of the park, while 20 miles of pathways offer visitors a host of self-guided treks through easy, moderate, and rugged terrain.

MAP 7: 9500 Sperry Rd., Kirtland, 440/946-4400, www.holdenarb.org; daily 9am-5pm, closed Thanksgiving and Christmas; $6 adult, $3 child, $5 senior

Jewish or not, visitors to this East Side museum typically leave moved beyond words: This museum tells the story of 200 years of Jewish-American history, but it could just as easily be recounting the experience of every American immigrant. Opened in 2005, the Maltz Museum is modern, well-planned, and thoughtfully executed. It was created by the folks behind the International Spy Museum in Washington DC, and like that highly immersive facility, it relies on cutting-edge interactive exhibits to tell its tales. Through oral histories, artifacts, and films, visitors experience what it might be like to leave everything behind to start life anew in a foreign place. Yes, there is reference to the dark days of the Holocaust, but there are also humorous examinations into the contribution of Jews to the world of entertainment. The museum's Temple-Tifereth Israel Gallery is a treasure trove of significant Judaica, including scrolls and documents of antiquity, European silverwork, and 18th-century tapestries.

MAP 7: 2929 Richmond Rd., Beachwood, 216/593-0575, www. maltzjewishmuseum.org; Tues.-Sun. 11am-5pm, until 9pm Wed., closed Rosh Hashanah, Yom Kippur, and Thanksgiving; $7 adult, $5 senior and student, free under 12

Memphis Kiddie Park

This is the amusement park where little ones get revenge on all those other parks—you know, the ones that say you have to be "this tall" to ride the rides. At Memphis, children must be *under* 50 inches tall to enjoy most rides. Not far from the zoo, this cherished Cleveland landmark has been putting smiles on kids' faces for more than 50 years. Pint-size thrill seekers scramble for seats on trains, in boats, aboard spaceships, and high (well, not so high) atop the Ferris wheel. For something both young and old can get behind, consider an 18-hole round of championship minigolf. Good clean fun abounds at this tidy family-friendly park. Memphis runs on tickets, with each ride a pay-as-you-go affair.

MAP 7: 10340 Memphis Ave., Cleveland, 216/941-5995, www.memphiskiddiepark. com; Apr.-Sept. daily 10am-9pm; no admission fee, but a book of 25 ride tickets costs $21.50

Restaurants

Downtown........................61

Ohio City and Tremont 68

Detroit Shoreway and Edgewater. .82

University Circle and Little Italy 85

Cleveland Heights
   and Shaker Heights 90

Lakewood.........................95

Greater Cleveland 100

PRICE KEY

$ Entrées less than $15

$$ Entrées $15–25

$$$ Entrées more than $25

Top of the Cleveland dining scene has received loads of positive national attention lately. Glossy magazines such as *Food & Wine, Esquire,* and *Bon Appétit* all have singled out local chefs and restaurants for inclusion in articles. A number of high-profile food and travel shows have made pit stops here to film episodes. And the local visitors and convention bureau is seeing a steep rise in food-focused visits by out-of-towners. Certainly, celebrity chef Michael Symon gets and deserves much of that interest, but there are dozens of other talented chefs who are making waves and drawing praise.

For a city its size, Cleveland boasts a disproportionately high number of independent chef-owned restaurants. Sure, the suburbs are littered with the identical national chains that exist in most metro areas, but alongside those repetitive eateries are scores of ambitious bakeries, bistros, gastropubs, and trattorias. Nestled in the fertile Cuyahoga Valley, Cleveland is well ahead of the national curve when it comes to its sophisticated system of farmers markets. In turn, chefs here are able to offer their customers farm-to-table cuisine crafted from local, seasonal, and sustainable ingredients. In fact, that progressive stance is quickly undoing Cleveland's reputation as a stodgy meat-and-potatoes burg.

Not that there is anything wrong with meat and potatoes. Cleveland's charm lies in the very juxtaposition of new and old, classic and cutting-edge. It is a place where ambitious bistros rub shoulders with old-school cafeterias and mom-and-pop ethnic eateries. Folks here are just as zealous about whole roasted heritage pig

HIGHLIGHTS

★ **Best Bowl of Pho Bar None:** Long before pho became a fixture on the Cleveland culinary landscape there was **Superior Pho.** Find the odd little Golden Plaza, park in back, and take a seat in this plain-jane eatery to enjoy the city's best bowl of soup (page 61).

★ **Dig Into a Roasted Pig Face:** Admittedly, a roasted pig face does not sound all that appetizing. But people travel near and far to visit **Greenhouse Tavern** to enjoy chef Jonathon Sawyer's interactive, shareable and, yes, delicious half a pig face (page 64).

★ **World's Best Corned-Beef Sandwich:** We know the term "best" gets bandied about when discussing corned beef, but **Slyman's Deli** really is the best around. Don't take our word for it—visit this always-popular diner to see what mile-high perfection tastes like (page 66).

★ **Finest Raw Fish:** At **Ginko,** a grotto-style bistro, Japanese sushi chefs craft pristine fish into edible art (page 68).

★ **Tastiest Hangover Cure:** Head to **Lucky's Café** for a brunchtime Shipwreck, bound to cure any ailment—including those self-induced. This mad jumble of scrambled eggs, bacon, cheddar, and fried potatoes seems to have magical healing powers. Either that, or the dish leaves diners too stuffed to notice (page 70).

★ **Best Cup of Joe:** Cleveland is fortunate to have no shortage of good, locally roasted coffee. But the best can be found at **Rising Star Coffee Roasters,** a former firehouse turned roastery that attracts the most serious bean heads (page 73).

★ **Best Cafeteria Meal:** Clevelanders of all stripes can't seem to get enough of **Sokolowski's University Inn.** This institution dishes up old-school Eastern European classics like stuffed cabbage, potato pierogies, and chicken paprikash in a tchotchke-filled cafeteria setting (page 78).

★ **Best Late-Night Chow:** Bar Cento serves food until 2am every single day of the year, including Christmas, New Year's, and Arbor Day. The hardworking chefs here turn out approachable Mediterranean fare like charcuterie, warm herbed olives, Neapolitan-style pizza, and grilled Ohio meats (page 78).

★ **Best Hope for a Vegetarian: Tommy's** began in the 1970s as a hippie-run soda fountain. Today, it is the most popular eatery on Coventry Road. While not solely a vegetarian restaurant, Tommy's has a wildly eclectic menu with loads of delicious meat-free options (page 91).

★ **Best New Use of an Old Diner:** For a decade, this pair of old diner cars suffered through a litany of failed eateries. But then chef Doug Katz took them over and opened **Katz Club Diner** and everything changed. This stunningly renovated diner serves upscale comfort food morning, noon, and night (page 92).

cheeks as they are mile-high corned beef sandwiches. The region's diverse immigrant population bestows culinary gifts in the form of Lebanese falafel, Slovenian pierogies, Polish kielbasa, and Jewish matzo-ball soup. Cleveland has an entire neighborhood of Chinese, Korean, and Vietnamese markets and restaurants.

So take a bite of what some national writers are calling the Rust Belt Revival.

Downtown Map 1

ASIAN
Li Wah $

Dim sum is a popular weekend brunch activity in Cleveland, and not just for Asian Americans. Hit Li Wah on a Saturday or Sunday morning to join entire families feasting on steamed dumplings, crispy duck, turnip cakes, and scores of other exotic dishes. Get here early for a table; the cavernous hall fills up fast. Once seated, you simply point to the items that interest you as they roll past on countless steam carts. Items are ridiculously inexpensive, so be adventurous. When the teapot runs dry, prop open the lid so your server knows to refill it.

MAP 1: 2999 Payne Ave., Asia Plaza, 216/696-6556, www.liwahcleveland.com; Mon.-Thurs. 10am-midnight, Fri.-Sun. 10am-1:30am

Noodlecat $$

Chef Jonathon Sawyer is such a fan of Japanese noodle bars that he flew to Tokyo and returned with Noodlecat. Okay, not exactly, but he did soon open this freewheeling downtown noodle shop. Both traditional and modern versions of ramen-, udon-, and soba-based soups are on the menu, as are Asian-inspired starters, salads, steam buns, and sides. Cold soba and dashi, pork miso ramen, and spicy tofu udon all are big bowls full of lovin.' Beer, wine, sake, and cocktails are available.

MAP 1: 234 Euclid Ave., 216/589-0007, www.noodlecat.com; Mon.-Sun. 11am-11pm

★ Superior Pho $

Long before pho became a fixture on the Cleveland culinary land-scape, there was Superior Pho. This low-profile restaurant is tucked away in Golden Plaza, a small collection of shops and services. Park in back and take a seat in this clean but spare eatery to enjoy the city's best bowl of pho, bar none. To round out the meal order one of their amazing banh mi, a Vietnamese sandwich stuffed with sliced roast pork, grated radish, jalapeño, fresh cilantro, chicken-liver pâté, and mayo.

MAP 1: 3030 Superior Ave., 216/781-7462, www.superiorpho.com; Tues.-Sat. 10am-8pm, Sun. 11am-7pm

Szechuan Gourmet ⊖

Located inside Tink Holl, a wonderful Asian foods market, this eatery quickly rose to the top of the list thanks to its brilliant and authentic Szechuan cuisine. Fire engine red dishes look more dangerous than they are thanks to a shrewd balance of flavors. Comforting ma po tofu features soft, silky cubes of tofu set off by finely ground and sautéed pork. Fried fish dry pot is a wok-size bowl filled with tender fish and tongue-tingling peppers. Bright sautéed greens with garlic are sweet and savory.

MAP 1: 1735 E. 36th St., in Tink Holl, 216/881-9688; Mon.-Sat. 11:30am-11:30pm, Sun. noon-10pm

Wonton Gourmet BBQ ⊖

Ever get the feeling that others are eating better than you? That is often the case at Chinese restaurants, where native-tongued diners order off super-secret menus reserved for those who speak Mandarin. Not so at this popular AsiaTown eatery, where the walls are shellacked with color photos of every dish, making ordering an easy point-and-pick affair. Consider "pointing" to plump chive and pork-filled pot stickers, panfried turnip cakes, beef chow fun, golden roast duck, and garlicky sautéed greens. At lunch, head straight for the shrimp dumpling noodle soup, a winter warmer if ever there was one.

MAP 1: 3211 Payne Ave., 216/875-7000; Wed.-Mon. 11am-11pm

CAFÉS

Erie Island Coffee ⊖

Modeled after a Pacific Northwest coffeehouse, Erie blends a rustic chic aesthetic with top-notch java. Since opening in early 2009, the shop has brewed up a devoted fan base thanks to its stellar coffee, espresso, and cappuccino. From bean to barista, every step is taken to assure a consistently delicious cup. While caffeine is the company's stock in trade, customers also can fuel up from the light menu of salads, breakfast and lunch sandwiches, and real-fruit smoothies.

MAP 1: 2057 E. Fourth St., 216/394-0093, www.erieislandcoffee.com; Mon.-Thurs. 6:30am-8pm, Fri. 6:30am-10pm, Sat. 9am-10pm, Sun. 9am-4pm

Koko Bakery ⊖

Pretty as a picture, this contemporary Asian bakery sports coolers filled with vibrantly hued fruit tarts, cakes, and pastries. On-the-go eaters have at their disposal a large self-serve display of freshly steamed and baked buns filled with barbecued pork, curried beef, and ham and eggs. At lunch Koko offers bowls brimming with steamed rice, vegetables, and panko-crusted pork. Koko is also the best source for bubble tea, fruit smoothies, and Taiwanese shaved ice, made with fruit and condensed milk.

MAP 1: 3710 Payne Ave., 216/881-7600; Wed.-Mon. 9am-7pm

Market Café $

Within the diverse family of food establishments, cafeterias rarely earn props. And why should they, with their reputation of steam tables, gray vegetables, and hairnets? But this cafeteria is different. For starters, it's beautiful, thanks to Amish-built communal tables, chandeliers made from recycled milk jugs, and honey-jar accent walls. Various food stations offer seasonal soups, custom salads, fresh-baked calzones, grilled-to-order burgers, kebabs and fish, and hot pressed sandwiches. Better still, much of the product is locally sourced, and the kitchen uses only sustainable seafood, cage-free eggs, BGH-free dairy products, antibiotic-free beef and poultry, and trans fat-free cooking oils. Great prepackaged food items are on display for convenient carryout.

MAP 1: 1801 E. 9th St., 216/394-0124, www.themarketcafeandwinebar.com; Mon.-Fri. 7am-8pm

CONTEMPORARY

Cowell & Hubbard $$$

Zack Bruell's fifth Cleveland restaurant, C & H brings high-caliber service, drop-dead aesthetics, and modern French-American cuisine to the heart of PlayhouseSquare. Pop in before or after a show—or any other meal of the week—and tuck into beet and beef cheek salads, roasted bone marrow, succulent lamb breast, or pristine redfish. Bruell's restaurants have a knack for making diners feel special, and this gem in no different.

MAP 1: 1305 Euclid Ave., 216/479-0555, www.cowellhubbard.com; Mon.-Wed. 11am-10pm, Thurs.-Fri. 11am-11pm, Sat. 4pm-11pm, Sun. 4pm-8pm

District $$$

This attractive bistro owns the sweet spot between casual and upmarket, dishing up food that's refined yet approachable. A 90-seat dining room ensures that the kitchen can handle both time-sensitive theatergoers and leisurely diners. An Israeli-born chef with Mediterranean leanings turns out hearty but right-sized plates like chickpea and lentil salad, chicken liver pâté, goat cheese-stuffed calamari, goose confit and pappardelle marinara. Lunch and dinner service.

MAP 1: 1350 Euclid Ave., 216/858-1000, www.districtcleveland.com; Mon. 11am-9pm, Tues.-Fri. 11am-11pm, Sat. 4pm-11pm, Sun. 4pm-9pm

RESTAURANTS
DOWNTOWN

Dim Sum and Then Some: A Guide to AsiaTown

golden roast ducks in AsiaTown

The Chinese are Cleveland's oldest Asian immigrant group, dating all the way back to the 1860s, but the area that used to be called Chinatown is now referred to as AsiaTown to better reflect the residents who call the area home. Recent decades have welcomed arrivals from Korea, Vietnam, and Thailand, and immigrants from each of these countries have established restaurants and markets in this area.

Some 33,000 Cuyahoga County residents identify themselves as Asian American, making them one of the larger ethnic populations. Many reside or do business in **AsiaTown** (www. asiatowncleveland.com), an area just east of downtown that is loosely bordered by East 30th and 40th Streets, and St. Clair and Payne Avenues. This vibrant, diverse neighborhood is teeming with Asian-owned shops, restaurants, and markets. A visit here is a must for ethnic food fans, adventurous home cooks, and lovers of all things exotic.

Pho has become an absolute food craze in Cleveland, with at least a dozen shops devoted to the tasty brew. This Vietnamese meal in a bowl features noodles, beef, broth, and veggies in a plentiful, affordable, and delicious package. Cleveland's best bowl bar none can be found at **Superior Pho,** a hard-to-find but worth-the-effort gem. This place also happens to sell Cleveland's best banh mi sandwich.

Dim sum is a popular weekend brunch in Cleveland—the practice of selecting food as it rolls by on carts is pretty much a universal delight. Some Chinese restaurants

★ Greenhouse Tavern $$$

Popular chef Jonathon Sawyer proves that being green is not only attractive, but delicious. Ohio's first "certified green restaurant" reinterprets French-inspired fare through a heavy reliance on local, seasonal, and sustainable ingredients. That translates to steak frites with Ohio beef, roast chicken featuring local poultry, and a salad goosed with Ohio goat confit. Here, everyday items are elevated to extraordinary, like grilled bread with wide array of spreads, hand-ground beef tartare, chicken wings fried in duck fat, and clams simmered in a foie gras-enriched broth. If it's nice, check out the rooftop bar.

MAP 1: 2038 E. Fourth St., 216/393-4302, www.thegreenhousetavern.com; Mon.-Thurs. 11am-11pm, Fri. 11am-1am, Sat. 5pm-1am, Sun. 4pm-10pm

are designed specifically with dim sum in mind, with cavernous dining rooms capable of handling hundreds of guests at once. Two local dim sum institutions are **Bo Loong** (3922 St. Clair Ave., 216/391-3113) and **Li Wah** (2999 Payne Ave., Asia Plaza, 216/696-6556, www.liwahcleveland.com). Both have wonderful selections, efficient service, and reasonable prices. Try the barbecue pork buns, turnip cakes, shrimp dumplings, crisp-skinned duck, and, if you're brave, chicken feet. A notable newcomer on the dim sum circuit is **Emperor's Palace** (2136 Rockwell Ave., 216/861-9999) on the edge of AsiaTown. While they skip the carts in favor of menus, the range and quality of the food makes the experience every bit as enjoyable.

There are few greater culinary joys than a platter of fresh-grilled and garlicky beef *bulgogi*, served alongside a wide array of *banchan*, those pungent condiments like kimchi that accompany every Korean meal. That's precisely why in-the-know folks flock to **Miega Korean BBQ** (3820 Superior Ave., 216/432-9200, www.miegabbq.com), an upstairs eatery in Asian Town Center mall.

AsiaTown is blessed with great ethnic markets that transform an everyday grocery trip into a culinary expedition. These bustling groceries stock exotic live seafood items like frogs and eels, hard-to-find herbs and spices, and even dirt-cheap cookware. One of Cleveland's oldest and best is **Tink Holl** (1735 E. 36th St., 216/881-6996), a large, bright space crammed with everything from baby bok choy to shrimp chips. For a treat, purchase half a roasted duck. Hacked into pieces, this bird blows away the Colonel's. There is also an excellent restaurant, **Szechuan Gourmet,** located within the complex. Try the ma po tofu or the fried fish dry pot. Also worthy of a visit is **Koko Bakery** (3710 Payne Ave., 216/881-7600), a contemporary shop that sells an amazing selection of Asian baked goods. Come here for sweet and savory buns, Chinese cakes, egg custards, and bubble tea.

Lola $$$

This uber-cosmopolitan restaurant is the nucleus of food celeb Michael Symon's ever-growing empire. Along with Lolita in Tremont and Roast in Detroit, Lola is where Symon spends his time satisfying fans one forkful at a time. In addition to having a winning personality, the dude can cook. Come here to sample creative Midwestern fare constructed from local, seasonal, and artisanal ingredients. Pierogies are stuffed with slow-braised beef cheeks; crisp pork belly is gilded with warm poached egg; a well-marbled rib eye gets an over-the-top push from buttery bone marrow. Sweets fans will doubtless swoon over this restaurant's dessert selections. Even if you can't score a dinner reservation (check www.opentable.com), grab a stool at the glowing alabaster bar for a cocktail and an appetizer. Wherever you sit, you might hear Symon's trademark laugh.

MAP 1: 2058 E. 4th St., 216/621-5652, www.lolabistro.com; Mon.-Thurs.

11:30am-2:30pm and 5pm-10pm, Fri. 11:30am-2:30pm and 5pm-11pm, Sat. 5pm-11pm

Pura Vida $$$

Successful chef Brandt Evans has brightened up Public Square, long a restaurant no-man's-land, with this gleaming white bistro. Fresh, seasonal, global, and almost always flawlessly prepared, Pura Vida's food is at once rustic and refined. A stickler for flavor, technique, and presentation, Evans pays equal attention to every element of a dish. Spotless salads, balanced soups and chowders, brilliant sandwiches, and heavenly meat, fish, and vegetarian-friendly entrées all are dished up daily.

MAP 1: 170 Euclid Ave., 216/987-0100, www.puravidabybrandt.com; Mon.-Sat. 11:30am-2pm, 4pm-close

DELIS

Cleveland Pickle $

Chef-owner Josh Kabat has single-handedly upped the downtown sandwich scene with his "nu-skool" creations. A dozen or so Cleveland-themed hoagies are well balanced, with a good meat-to-fixings ratio, and include the Payne Avenue ($9), a twist on the Vietnamese banh mi, the Terminal with Black Forest ham and brie, and the Classic Pickle, loaded with Italian meats and cheeses. Breakfast sandwiches, soup, salads, and deviled eggs round out the menu. There are a handful of seats in the small dining room.

MAP 1: 850 Euclid Ave., 216/575-1111, www.clevelandpickle.com; Mon.-Fri. 11am-4pm, Sat. noon-4pm

★ Slyman's Deli $

According to such definitive sources as *Esquire* magazine and the Barenaked Ladies, Slyman's really does have the best corned-beef sandwich in America. (*Esquire*'s Scott Raab wrote, "I've noshed deli across the globe, and no corned-beef sandwich anywhere knuckles up to this.") Just before noon on weekdays, a line begins forming at the deli counter. Soon, that line is snaking down the sidewalk. But don't worry, it moves quickly, and waiting at the other end is a fat, buttery, gut-busting beauty about which you too might pen songs. Order your sammy "natural" if you like it plain, "original" for mustard only, and "all the way" for swiss, mustard, and horseradish.

MAP 1: 3106 St. Clair Ave., 216/621-3760, www.slymans.com; Mon.-Fri. 6:30am-2:30pm

Restaurant Weeks

Two different organizations host separate events that each offer diners great deals when eating out. Held in late February, **Downtown Cleveland Restaurant Week** (www.downtowncleveland.com) encourages guests to dine downtown with specially priced multicourse lunches and dinners. Special parking deals also help budgets. Held the first two weeks in March, **Cleveland Independents Restaurant Week** (www.clevelandindependents.com) is broader in both geography and participation, with upward of 90 independent restaurants getting in on the action. Those restaurants typically offer special three-course menus for around $30 per guest. Many offer lunch deals as well.

PUBS

Johnny's Little Bar $

The Little Bar is indeed little, tucked away as it is in an alley off the main drag. But what this popular watering hole lacks in stature it makes up for in attitude. During the day, downtown suits duck in here for iceberg wedge salads, matchless burgers, and hearty home-style entrées. After work, the genial bar takes on a more neighborly vibe as downtown residents pop in for happy hour beers and upscale pub grub. If the Browns are on the small screen, Little Bar becomes game central.

MAP 1: 614 Frankfort Ave., 216/861-2166, www.johnnyscleveland.com; Mon.-Fri. 11am-2:30am, Sat. 5pm-2:30am, Sun. 7pm-2:30am, opens at 10am for Browns Sunday home games

STEAK AND SEAFOOD

Blue Point Grille $$$

Ask a random Clevelander where to go for upscale seafood and you'll invariably be directed here. In the business of fish since 1998, this Warehouse District mainstay serves up some of the most consistently delicious seafood in the city. The drop-dead gorgeous warehouse space boasts soaring ceilings, castle-thick brick walls, and modest nautical accents. Blue Point is famous for its crab cakes, chowders, surf and turf, and grouper with lobster mashed potatoes. Meat lovers are in good hands here too, since this small restaurant group also operates a wonderful steak house. For a more affordable way to savor the atmosphere, grab seats at the bar and enjoy the best oyster selection around. Reservations are recommended for weekends.

MAP 1: 700 W. St. Clair Ave., 216/875-7827, www.bluepointgrille.com; Mon.-Fri. 11:30am-3pm and 5pm-10pm, Sat. 5pm-11pm, Sun. 4pm-10pm

Nauti Mermaid ⑤⑤

Often the best places to enjoy seafood are the most laid-back, and this casual fish-shack tavern is proof of that. Equal parts bar and restaurant, this unpretentious Warehouse District eatery serves raw-bar items, fried fish, and whole Maine lobsters. Favorites here include crab cakes, lobster nachos, fried lake-perch platters, and whole steamed lobsters. If you're looking for a fun, reasonably priced, and atypical place to grab a quick bite, consider a visit to the Mermaid. This is also a great spot to enjoy a craft beer and watch the Cavs, Indians, or Brownies on the telly.

MAP 1: 1378 W. 6th St., 216/771-6175, www.thenautimermaid.com; daily 11am-10pm

Red, the Steakhouse ⑤⑤⑤

Restaurateur Brad Friedlander has opened a glitzy downtown version of his uber-popular Beachwood steak house. The Brat Pack-style decor offers a touch of Old Vegas, with red, white, and black splashes throughout. Here, high rollers win big with the city's best steaks, freshest seafood, and chef-driven specials. There's a reason why *Playboy, USA Today* and *Esquire,* have all proclaimed their love for Red.

MAP 1: 417 Prospect Ave., 216/664-0941, www.redthesteakhouse.com; Mon.-Wed. 11:30am-10pm, Thurs.-Fri. 11:30am-11pm, Sat. 4pm-11pm

Ohio City and Tremont   Map 2

ASIAN

Bac ⑤⑤

"Bac" means "north" in Vietnamese, and while the menu is a melting pot of classic Asian and Asian American cuisine, the restaurant's name more accurately is a tribute to the chef's birthplace in northern Vietnam. Unlike your typical mom-and-pop ethnic shop, this trendy neighborhood bistro is modern, casual, and easygoing. Classics like summer rolls and gyoza join updated takes on basil fried rice and pad Thai. The lunchtime bento box lets diners combine three items for just $10. A full bar with specialty cocktails and a roomy patio add to the appeal of this popular spot.

MAP 2: 2661 W. 14th St., 216/938-8960, www.bactremont.com; Mon.-Thurs. 11am-10pm, Fri.-Sat. 11am-11pm

★ Ginko ⑤⑤⑤

Ginko is a paean to fish, most of it raw, some of it rolled, all of it exceptional. Most of the seats in this grotto-style den are at a large horseshoe-shaped sushi bar, where diners can watch Japanese sushi chefs craft edible art. Brilliant sashimi, sushi, and rolls are the main order of the day here, as are fish-focused starters and salads. Diners seated at one of the two booths can also enjoy shabu-shabu.

MAP 2: 2247 Professor Ave., 216/274-1202, www.restaurantdante.us; Tues.-Thurs. 4:30pm-11pm, Fri. 11:30am-2:30pm and 4:30pm-1am, Sat. 4:30pm-1am

Ty Fun Thai Bistro ⑤⑤

We wouldn't go so far as to say Ty Fun is the most authentic Thai restaurant in town, but it may be the sharpest. This petite urban bistro is tastefully decorated, with long banquettes dotted with vivid fabric and silky cushions. Food is presented on dramatic tableware, with intricately carved vegetable garnishes adorning each dish. The kitchen does wonders with soups and starters, like the perfectly balanced coconut chicken soup, moist chicken *satay,* and spicy fried fish cakes. Ty Fun also serves wonderful curries and a more than respectable pad Thai.

MAP 2: 815 Jefferson Ave., 216/664-1000, www.tyfunthaibistro.com; Mon.-Thurs. 5pm-10pm, Fri.-Sat. 5pm-11pm, Sun. 5pm-9pm

BREAKFAST AND BRUNCH

Bonbon Pastry & Café ⑤

Award-winning pastry chef Courtney Bonning covers both sweet and savory at this cute-as-a-cupcake café. Like a big-city patisserie, the café is intimate, elegant, and attractive enough to warrant a visit every day. In addition to the delectable sweets—fruit-laced linzer tortes, sugar-dusted lemon squares, chocolate éclairs—the café dishes up breakfast, lunch, and weekend brunch. The quiche of the day, meat-filled Cornish pasties, and a killer Ohio beef burger are just a few of the offerings.

MAP 2: 2549 Lorain Ave., 216/458-9225, www.bonboncleveland.com; Mon. 6:30am-3pm, Tues.-Fri. 6:30am-8pm, Sat. 7am-8pm, Sun. 9am-3pm

Le Petit Triangle Café ⑤

As the name suggests, this café is a wee wedge of a place, with scarcely two dozen seats in all. On balmy days, that capacity jumps considerably thanks to a grouping of bright-red bistro furniture that tumbles out onto the sidewalk. Inside or out, this charming neighborhood spot captures the carefree insouciance of a Parisian café, complete with sweet and savory crepes, fluffy omelets, and ethereal café au laits. On wintery nights, this tiny spot is like a warm embrace, made all the balmier thanks to French onion soup, piping-hot cassoulet, and red wine. Get here early on weekend mornings to enjoy an authentic slice of Ohio City life along with your fluffy smoked-salmon omelet.

MAP 2: 1881 Fulton Rd., 216/281-1881, www.lepetittrianglecafe.com; Tues.-Thurs. 11am-10pm, Fri.-Sat. 11am-11pm, Sun. 10am-3pm

Food Trucks

weekly food truck round-up known as Walnut Wednesday

In 2011, the City of Cleveland eased long-standing restrictions that made owning and operating a food truck within city limits nearly impossible. The positive effects of those changes were felt almost immediately. And in the short while since, Cleveland's food truck scene jumped from being one of the worst around to one of the best.

It's only natural that a thriving food truck scene would arise given Cleveland's progressive and robust dining scene. Having a bumper crop of excellent restaurants not only cranks out culinary rock stars, many of whom go on to launch food trucks, but also fuels an ever-growing base of adventurous diners.

Much of the food truck momentum can be credited to chef Chris Hodgson, who burst onto the scene at the outset with his rolling kitchen Dim and Den Sum. His adventurous cuisine and infectious personality not only ignited a trend, it landed him a spot on Food Network's *The Great Food Truck Race*, where he almost won.

These days, some two dozen food trucks call Cleveland home, dishing up everything from freshly fried doughnuts and pulled pork sandwiches to crawfish jambalaya and

★ **Lucky's Café** $

In addition to being the de facto java stop for many Tremont residents, Lucky's features one of the most popular weekend brunches in town. Chef-owner Heather Haviland scours the countryside in search of local eggs, sustainable produce, and ecofriendly meats. Hearty breakfast here means big plates of Ohio sweet-corn waffles with strawberry-rhubarb compote, fresh-baked cheddar-scallion scones topped with scrambled eggs and sausage gravy, and a delicious disaster dubbed the Shipwreck featuring scrambled eggs, bacon, white cheddar, and fried potatoes. Haviland is also a prominent pastry chef, so you can count on phenomenal sweets, tortes, brownies, and cakes.

MAP 2: 777 Starkweather Ave., 216/622-7773, www.luckyscafe.com; Mon.-Sat. 7am-5pm, Sun. 8am-5pm

small-batch ice cream. While rigs are always coming and going, some of the most consistent operators (and their Twitter handles) include: Umami Moto (@UmamiMoto), StrEat Mobile Bistro (@streatmobile), The Nosh Box (@theNoshBox), JiBaro Gourmet (@JibaroWorldEats), and Hodgson's new rig, Hodge Podge (@HodgePodgeTruck).

One of the easiest ways to track down food trucks is to attend **Walnut Wednesdays,** a weekly food truck roundup that runs May through September in downtown Cleveland (E. 12th and Chester Ave.). At least 10 food trucks sell food 11:30am to 1:30pm, attracting upward of 2,000 diners on a nice day. A nearby park provides live music and plenty of seating.

Pop Up Party at the Plaza, an alfresco happy hour featuring food trucks and beer lands at Perk Plaza (E. 12th and Chester Ave.) third Thursdays 5 to 8pm during the summer. Even the City of Cleveland gets in on the action with **Food Truck Friday,** which takes place downtown 11am to 2pm on Fridays June to October at Willard Park (601 Lakeside Ave.).

Here are some tips that will help you navigate the food truck scene:

- **Check Facebook and Twitter.** These are the best sources of information when it comes to seeing which trucks will be where.

- **Do your homework.** Most trucks post what they're serving online ahead of time so you can decide long before you walk up to the rig.

- **Get there early.** Food trucks run out of food all the time.

- **Make the rounds before ordering.** Lots of trucks mean lots of options.

- **Know what you want.** Don't waste everybody's time by being unprepared.

- **Expect to wait.** Large crowds mean that diners wait in lines to order, then wait for their food.

- **Don't stray too far.** You should be within earshot of the truck while waiting for your food.

- **Preorder via email.** Most trucks will have your food ready if you email ahead.

- **Bring cash.** Because cash is king.

West Side Market Café $

On Saturday, the busiest shopping day at the West Side Market, this café is absolutely buzzing with activity as folks fuel up on eggs Benedict, corned-beef hash, and righteous blueberry pancakes. Weekday mornings, lunches, and dinners are decidedly calmer affairs, but still worth a visit thanks to quality ingredients and consistent attention to detail. Fans of stick-to-your-ribs diner fare will dig this café not only for its food but also its decor, which features original fixtures and historic photos of the market's earliest days.

MAP 2: 1995 W. 25th St., 216/579-6800, www.westsidemarketcafe.com; Mon.-Thurs. 7am-4pm, Fri.-Sat. 7am-9pm, Sun. 9am-3pm

Foodie Heaven: Best of the West Side Market

The West Side Market is a big, bustling bazaar, with more than 100 food stands and dozens more next door in the produce annex. Here's a taste of what's inside.

- Many shoppers begin or end their visit with a quick and tasty meal. The best options include **Maha's Falafel** for fresh-fried falafel sandwiches, **Kim Se** for prepared Thai and Cambodian dishes, **Crepes DeLuxe** for amazing savory crepes filled with fresh ingredients, or **Frank's Bratwurst** for, you guessed it, bratwurst sandwiches. (Ask for horseradish.)

- Diet-shattering baked goods are around every turn. For artisan-style European bread, hit **Mediterra Bakehouse.** If your tooth leans more sweet than savory, wander over to **Cake Royale,** where the luscious pastries are made from scratch. Over at **Campbell's Popcorn,** the sugary offerings include cotton candy, chocolate-covered pretzels, and amazing cheesy popcorn.

- **Ohio City Pasta** supplies dozens of upscale restaurants with fresh pasta, ravioli, and gnocchi. At the ever-popular **Pierogi Palace,** dozens of varieties of stuffed Polish dumplings are sold frozen to go. Hit **Orale Mexican Cuisine** for empanadas, corn husk-wrapped tamales, fresh-fried chips, and the best salsas in town.

- Adventurous home cooks shop at **Urban Herbs** and **Narrin's Spice** to track down hard-to-find herbs, spices, grains, and chiles. Narrin's also stocks a wide assortment of hot sauces. And if **Mediterranean Imported Foods** doesn't carry the ingredient you're looking for, it probably doesn't exist. Tucked into the corner of the market, this jam-packed Italian grocery offers a dizzying array high-quality cheeses, olives, salamis, dried fruit, and nuts.

- To purchase old-world Hungarian-style meats, like double-smoked bacon, rice sausage, and cottage ham, stroll over to **Dohar Meats. Old Country Sausage** sells authentic German favorites like liverwurst and Black Forest salamis.

CAFÉS

Civilization $

This European-style coffeehouse is right on Lincoln Park and features a generous sidewalk patio for enjoying a post-dinner espresso. The beans are locally roasted by the owner, who also runs the City Roast Coffee stand at the West Side Market. The rustic 100-plus-year-old storefront feels like a general store from days gone by. The fare here is light and simple, such as pastries, soups, and sandwiches.

MAP 2: 2366 W. 11th St., 216/621-3838, www.cafecivilization.com; Mon.-Thurs. 7am-7pm, Fri.-Sat. 7am-8:30pm, Sun. 7:30am-6pm

Johnny Mango $

Ohio City's other pie-shaped café, the Mango is as lovably quirky as its setting. With its rattan ceiling fans and vividly hued walls, the interior looks as if it had been plucked from a Mexican beer commercial. That seems to suit the locals just fine, as many of them are sporting flip-flops and tattoos as bright as the surroundings. Borrowing elements from Caribbean, Mexican, and Asian kitchens, the menu melds widely disparate foodstuffs into a seamless global cuisine. Vegetarians dig the juice bar and fried tofu, while carnivores tuck into Jamaican jerk chicken and gaucho steak. Toss in pad Thai, shrimp-fried rice, and a robust weekend brunch, and you end up with an eclectic neighborhood hangout.

MAP 2: 3120 Bridge Ave., 216/575-1919, www.jmango.com; Mon.-Thurs. 11am-10pm, Fri. 11am-11pm, Sat.-Sun. 9am-10pm

Loop Café ⑤

If you're in the market for both a delicious cappuccino and the latest release from the Black Keys, Loop is the place for you. This sharp café inside a converted Tremont home has an upstairs record shop that carries a good selection of vinyl and CD indie releases. The main floor is largely devoted to the business of brewing high-quality coffee and tea. Loop is a great place to start the day or to kill an hour or two doing absolutely nothing important.

MAP 2: 2180 W. 11th St., 216/298-5096; Mon.-Thurs. 7am-9pm, Fri. 7am-10pm, Sat. 8am-10pm, Sun. 10am-6pm

★ Rising Star Coffee Roasters ⑤

Since setting up shop in 2012 in a former Ohio City firehouse, Rising Star Coffee has quickly become the bean of choice at numerous coffee shops, restaurants, and bakeries. It's also stop number one for coffee geeks thanks to quality beans, obsessive technique, and proper equipment. Pour-over, aeropress, and vacuum pot brewers turn out the city's best espressos, cappuccinos, lattes, and macchiatos. House-roasted beans are sold by the pound.

MAP 2: 1455 W. 29th St., 216/273-3573, www.risingstarcoffee.com; Mon. 6:30am-2pm, Tues.-Fri. 6:30am-6pm, Sat. 8am-6pm, Sun. 9am-2pm

CONTEMPORARY AMERICAN
Black Pig ⑤⑤⑤

The phrase "black pig" is shorthand for any number of heritage breeds of pig. Chef-owner Mike Nowak sources his high-quality pork from a local farmer to craft some of this city's most agreeable pork-centric fare. The farm-to-table menu features French-inspired dishes braised pork belly, pork schnitzel, pasta and smoked trotters, butter-poached pork loin, and roasted duck breast with confit crepinette and hominy. An elevated chef's table in front of the open kitchen provides a few lucky diners with great views of the piggy action.

MAP 2: 1865 W. 25th St., 216/862-7551, www.theblackpigcleveland.com; Tues.-Fri. 4pm-close, Sat. noon-close, Sun. 11am-close

Crop Bistro $$$

Since the day Crop burst onto the Cleveland dining scene, there has been near-unanimous consent that the restaurant is among the best in town. Now that it has moved to its new home in Ohio City, it has managed to get even better. Certainly the jaw-dropping bank lobby setting has something to do with it, but chef-owner Steve Schimoler's contemporary American food will always be the main draw. Lighthearted starters like balsamic popcorn, deviled eggs, and cherry bombs—deep-fried sausage and cheese-stuffed tomatoes—join others starring pork belly and foie gras. Mains built around scallops, pork chops, tuna, and beef keep the flavor train rolling merrily along at this beloved boisterous bistro.

MAP 2: 2537 Lorain Ave., 216/696-CROP, www.cropbistro.com; lunch Mon.-Fri. 11:30am-2pm, dinner Mon.-Thurs. 5pm-9:30pm, Fri.-Sat. 5pm-11pm

Fahrenheit $$$

Chef Rocco Whalen picked up his pizza-making skills directly from Wolfgang Puck, so you can assume the gourmet pies here are super-lative. But this hopping Tremont bistro goes well beyond pizza, venturing into Asian-inspired starters, seasonal pastas, hearty chops, and, perhaps, the city's finest short ribs. Seafood fans will have no difficulty enjoying a meal here; the menu usually features oysters, scallops, and walleye. Or, enjoy a cocktail in Fahrenheit's sharp lounge before or after having dinner elsewhere. Reservations are highly recommended for weekends.

MAP 2: 2417 Professor Ave., 216/781-8858, www.fahrenheittremont.com; Mon.-Thurs. 5pm-11pm, Fri.-Sat. 5pm-1am

Flying Fig $$$

Located on a charming brick-paved lane in Ohio City, this bistro is among the city's very best places to dine. Frequented by fawn-ing locals and well-heeled travelers alike, the Fig's crowd is an eclectic blend of young and old, tattooed and suited, liberal and conservative. Chef-owner Karen Small works closely with local farmers, farmers markets, and artisanal producers to craft a menu that changes nearly as frequently as the calendar. Savory starters include crispy sweetbreads and chorizo-stuffed dates. Entrées run the gamut from braised and grilled short ribs to pristine halibut. Hit this restaurant's famous happy hour for heavily discounted drinks, nibbles, and house-made chips. Reservations are recommended for weekends.

MAP 2: 2523 Market Ave., 216/241-4243, www.theflyingfig.com; Mon.-Thurs. 5pm-11pm, Fri.-Sat. 5pm-11:30pm, Sun. 5pm-10pm

Parallax ⑤⑤⑤

While not technically an Asian restaurant, Parallax is beloved for its sparkling sushi. The selection of raw fish is not as extensive as one might find at a Japanese restaurant, but what is prepared here is beyond reproach. Operated by noted chef and restaurateur Zach Bruell, Parallax is an elegant and stylish bistro that specializes in impeccable fish and seafood, whether served raw, poached, fried, grilled, or roasted. The Alaskan black cod with miso glaze is an absolute winner of a dish, but the menu might also include monkfish, salmon, tuna, and lobster. Meat eaters can choose from grilled hanger steak, braised short ribs, and Bruell's famous chicken *pommes frites* with beurre blanc. Reservations are a necessity on weekends.

MAP 2: 2179 W. 11th St., 216/583-9999, www.parallaxtremont.com; Mon.-Thurs. 5pm-11pm, Fri.-Sat. 5pm-midnight

SOHO Kitchen & Bar ⑤⑤

Rising star chef Nolan Konkoski seems to have formulated the near-perfect alignment of location, concept, execution, and timing with his "New Southern" bistro. Short for Southern hospitality, SOHO serves fresh takes on Dixie-inspired fare like shrimp and grits, catfish po'boys, and chicken and waffles, all dressed up for a more demanding modern audience. Jars of pimento cheese, plates of oysters Rockefeller, and bowls of sausage stew will transport diners straight to the Low Country. Even the cocktails scream Deep South, with bourbon, rye, and moonshine-fueled bevies going down like sweet tea on a sticky summer day.

MAP 2: 1889 W. 25th St., 216/298-9090, www.sohocleveland.com; Tues.-Thurs. 5pm-10pm, Fri.-Sat. 11:30am-2:30pm, 5pm-11pm, Sun. 11am-2pm

DELIS

Bogtrotters Doorstep ⑤

Colossal, dripping with juice, and unwieldy as a Vaseline-coated baby, these hoagies require a diner's complete attention. All the meats are marinated, brined, and roasted in-house, and the drippings from each are used as gravy. The Philly is loaded with roast beef, grilled onions, and cheese sauce; the Porkopolis is crammed with sliced pork loin, bitter greens, and provolone. Others are built around roast turkey, Italian sausage, or roasted veggies. Order your sammie "wet with crunch" and it will be doused with gravy and topped with chips. Bogtrotters essentially is a carryout-only operation.

MAP 2: 1848 W. 25th St., 216/861-5515; Tues.-Thurs. 11:30am-10pm, Fri.-Sat. 11am-3am

Nate's Deli $

A local institution, Nate's is reflective of Cleveland's rich ethnic diversity and the city's love for all things delicious. Possessing a sort of edible split personality, this austere café serves traditional deli-style breakfast and lunch alongside Middle Eastern specialties. This means that while diners at one table are enjoying pastrami on rye and char-grilled burgers, their neighbors are cooing over a platter of hummus, tabbouleh, and stuffed grape leaves. On Saturdays this deli buzzes with shoppers fueling up for their trip to the nearby West Side Market.

MAP 2: 1923 W. 25th St., 216/696-7529; Mon.-Fri. 10am-5pm, Sat. 10am-4pm

Souper Market $

Around the corner from Ohio City's main drag, this tiny soup house is worth finding. The attraction here, of course, is the handcrafted soup, made daily with house-brewed stocks, wholesome ingredients, and ladlefuls of patience. An ever-rotating roster keeps fans coming back time and again for beautiful bisques, broths, and bouillabaisses. There are always veggie options like chunky mushroom and tomato-ginger, hearty stews like jambalaya and mulligatawny, and, in the summer, refreshing chilled soups such as gazpacho and strawberry bisque. Most diners get their soup to go, as there's only enough room for a few people to stand at a window-facing counter.

MAP 2: 2528 Lorain Ave., 216/737-7687, www.thesoupermarket.com; Mon.-Fri. 11am-7pm, Sat. 11am-6pm

DESSERT

A Cookie and a Cupcake $

Wendy Thompson, long an executive pastry chef, opened up this boutique bakeshop in 2008, next to Eye Candy Gallery. Wander in for handcrafted cookies, brownies, macaroons, cupcakes, and vintage-style cakes. The signature cupcakes come in a dozen flavors that mirror those of the cakes: red velvet, German chocolate, carrot cake, and grasshopper, to name a few. Thompson also creates one-of-a-kind cakes for weddings and other special occasions; you can watch her decorate them in the shop's open kitchen.

MAP 2: 2173 Professor Ave., 216/344-9433, www.acookieandacupcake.com; Mon.-Sat. 11am-7pm

Tremont Scoops $

This great neighborhood ice-cream shop serves hand-dipped cups, cones, and sundaes in a wide variety of flavors. Delicious creations like milk shakes and floats are served up alongside novelties like ice cream sandwiches and chocolate-covered cheesecake on a stick.

New ownership in 2013 has updated every aspect of this long-running business.

MAP 2: 2362 Professor Ave., 216/781-0352, www.tremontscoops.com; Mon.-Fri. 4pm-10pm, Sat.-Sun. noon-10pm

EASTERN EUROPEAN AND MEDITERRANEAN

Dervish Turkish Cuisine $$

This urban outpost of the suburban original dishes up the same high-quality and healthful Turkish cuisine in a cozy storefront setting. There are vegetarian spreads, flavorful grilled meat kebabs, and simply prepared seafood items. Comfort foods like stuffed peppers and Turkish pizza transcend cultural borders.

MAP 2: 2505 Professor Ave., 216/298-4450, www.dervishgrill.com; Mon.-Sat. 11am-10pm, Sun. 11am-9pm

Fat Cats $$

Along with Michael Symon's original Lola locale, Fat Cats was one of the first restaurants to set up shop in Tremont. Today, thanks to pioneering eateries such as these, Tremont has blossomed into a gourmand's playground. Fat Cats is tucked into an old house on the far end of a residential block, and this cozy bistro never fails to delight first-time visitors. Guests might come for the charm, but they invariably return for the delicious, eclectic comfort food. The seasonal Mediterranean offerings might include steamed mussels, roasted monkfish, grilled skirt steak, or braised veal shank. Copious portions, hospitable service, and modest prices make this restaurant a popular destination for both lunch and dinner.

MAP 2: 2061 W. 10th St., 216/579-0200, www.coolplacestoeat.com; Mon.-Thurs. 11am-3pm and 4pm-10pm, Fri. 11am-3pm and 4pm-midnight, Sat. 4pm-midnight

Lolita $$

Michael Symon's downtown restaurant Lola may garner most of the national accolades, but many local Symon fans actually prefer this more inviting neighborhood bistro. Dimly lit and tragically hip, this place feels more like a wine bar than a restaurant. But the food, a well-executed blend of Mediterranean small, medium, and large plates, is far beyond what you'd ever find in an enoteca. Start with platters of house-cured charcuterie before moving on to wood-fired pizzas topped with roast suckling pig, duck prosciutto, or plump white anchovies. Amazing pastas, fresh fish, and wood-fired meats are good enough to leave even a politician speechless. Hit Lolita for happy hour 5pm-6:30pm or 10pm to close, when a half-pound Kobe burger topped with cheddar, bacon, and a fried egg costs just $5.

MAP 2: 900 Literary Rd., 216/771-5652, www.lolitarestaurant.com; Tues.-Thurs. 5pm-10pm, Fri.-Sat. 5pm-midnight, Sun. 4pm-9pm

★ **Sokolowski's University Inn** $$

There may be no more uniquely Cleveland restaurant than Sokolowski's, which opened in 1923 on the edge of Tremont. What makes this restaurant unique is the cafeteria-style dining. What makes it "Cleveland" is the smorgasbord of Eastern European delicacies. All manner of folks work their way down the chow line, loading up trays with heaping portions of stuffed cabbage, potato pancakes, pierogies, chicken paprikash, and rice pudding. This is comfort food in its purest form. The homey lodge-like dining room features a fireplace, live piano music, and the curious collection of ephemera that 90 years in business inevitably generates. Fans of the Travel Channel's *No Reservations* will undoubtedly recall the Cleveland episode where Tony Bourdain swooned over this place.

MAP 2: 1201 University Rd., 216/771-9236, www.sokolowskis.com; Mon.-Thurs. 11am-3pm, Fri. 11am-3pm and 5pm-9pm, Sat. 4pm-9pm

ITALIAN
★ Bar Cento $$

The lively, mostly youthful staff at this bustling wine bar keep the mood buoyant. But that playfulness belies the serious culinary talent in the kitchen. Meals here can be as delightfully uncomplicated as bottles of wine and plates of thin-sliced charcuterie, or as substantial as grilled Ohio meats with seasonal treatments. Picture-perfect Neapolitan-style pizzas fly out of the brick ovens topped with clams, pancetta, or locally foraged ramps. Open every day of the year until 2am, Bar Cento is the favored late-night hangout for chefs and night owls.

MAP 2: 1948 W. 25th St., 216/274-1010, www.barcento.com; Sun.-Fri. 4:30pm-2am, Sat. noon-2am

Dante $$$

Native Clevelander and Michelin-starred chef Dante Boccuzzi has worked his way around the globe, with stints in London, Milan, Hong Kong, San Francisco, and New York. At this contemporary Tremont bistro, the chef showcases his knack for Italian, American, and Asian cuisines. Here, a diner can glide from grilled octopus to porcini risotto to grilled skirt steak and not get gastronomic whiplash. No meal is complete without a sample of the chef's killer pasta, polenta or risotto, all available by the taste.

MAP 2: 2247 Professor Ave., 216/274-1200, www.restaurantdante.us; Mon.-Thurs. 4:30pm-11pm, Fri.-Sat. 4:30pm-1am

MEXICAN
Barrio $

This Tremont taqueria puts the power of the pen in the diner's hand. Guests design their own tacos from a list of some 30

clockwise from top left: West Side Market Café, Ohio City; Rising Star Coffee Roasters, Ohio City; Tremont Taphouse, Tremont

Weihenstephaner HEFE WEISSBIER 17%

Triple White 8.0% $8.0
10oz

Duvel Single 6.8% .25L $7.5

PALM Belgian Pale Ale 5.4% $5.5
16oz

3 Fonteinen Zwet be Porter SOUR 7.0% $8.5
10oz

Founders Old Curmudgeon Ale 9.8% $6.5
12oz

BELL'S AMBER 6.0% $4.5
14oz

ROCK MILL CASK AGED Tripel 10.5% $9.5
10oz

components—from shell to filling to salsa to toppings. The best part: They are all just a few bucks each. This blissfully informal approach is a great fit for the unpretentious food. In addition to the tacos, the menu features a few starters and sides, not to mention a landslide of tequilas and margaritas.

MAP 2: 806 Literary Rd., 216/999-7714; Mon.-Sun. 4pm-2:30am

Momocho Mod Mex ⑤⑤

Not your typical chips-and-salsa Mexican joint, this dark, clubby eatery elevates south-of-the-border cuisine to a delicious art form. Set in a two-story colonial, Momocho features a lively 1st-floor lounge and a more serene upstairs dining room. Locals stop in for a festive meal of appetizers and margaritas, starring smoked-trout guacamole and the rightly famous duck tamales. The smart ones stick around for the adobo braised pork or the *pepita*-crusted trout. When the weather is cooperating, this restaurant's lush and leafy patio comes alive with drinkers, diners, and daters.

MAP 2: 1835 Fulton Rd., 216/694-2122, www.momocho.com; Tues.-Sat. 5pm-2am, Sun. 4pm-9:30pm

Orale! ⑤⑤

For years, chef Roberto Rodriguez has run a popular Mexican foods stand at the West Side Market. Now he operates a restaurant of the same name in a funky double storefront down the block. The 50-seat eatery serves contemporary Mexican cuisine like chicken mole tamales, jalapeño-dough empanadas, fish tacos, and tequila-friendly snacks to go with the killer margaritas. A display cooler stocks many of the prepared foods sold at the market.

MAP 2: 1834 W. 25th St., 216/862-3117, www.oralecmc.com; Tues.-Thurs. 11am-10pm, Fri.-Sat. 11am-11pm

PUBS

The Harp ⑤⑤

Clevelanders have been coming to The Harp for years to enjoy hearty Irish fare, wonderful drink, and a great patio with Lake Erie views. Best sellers, apart from the Guinness and Jameson, include the corned beef and sauerkraut rolls, shepherd's pie, and the salmon boxty, a large potato pancake folded around salmon, veggies, and pesto cream sauce. Most of the items are made from the owner's traditional family recipes. There is festive live Irish music on Wednesday, Friday, and Saturday.

MAP 2: 4408 Detroit Ave., 216/939-0200, www.the-harp.com; Mon.-Thurs. 11am-10pm, Fri.-Sat. 11am-11pm, Sun. 11am-9pm

Old Angle $

Set in a former hardware store, this is not your typical shot-and-a-beer Irish pub. An ambitious renovation of the 100-year-old building resulted in a sleek, contemporary space boasting tin ceilings, tile flooring, and a lengthy mahogany bar. The food, too, rises above standard pub fare with an eclectic mix of appetizers, sandwiches, and entrées. Best among them are the fried ravioli, lamb stew, falafel, and hot ham sandwich. With plenty of hard surfaces, this joint can get rather loud when there is a band playing or a can't-miss sporting event on the large screen.

MAP 2: 1848 W. 25th St., 216/861-5643, www.oldangletavern.com; Mon.-Thurs. 4pm-2:30am, Fri.-Sun. 11:30am-2:30am

South Side $$

Besides having the absolute largest patio in Tremont, South Side has a great bar scene. Upscale comfort food, a rambunctious atmosphere, and friendly bartenders keep this joint jumping most hours of the day. For something different, try the chicken and waffles, a Tremont take on the Harlem classic. The menu also features fresh salads, tasty burgers, and quality pastas. The South Side can get extremely loud and crowded, especially during important televised sporting events or when there is live music. But if you snag a seat at the bar early enough, you should be in for a great night. The genial neighborhood vibe makes this pub a popular meet-and-greet spot.

MAP 2: 2207 W. 11th St., 216/937-2288, www.southsidecleveland.com; Mon.-Sat. 11am-2am, Sun. 10am-2am

Tremont Taphouse $$

As Cleveland's first true gastropub, the Taphouse has been dispensing high-caliber grub and high-test craft beer for a handful of years. Though others have followed suit, this off-the-beaten-path pub still shows how it's done thanks to flavorful small plates, killer burgers, great pizza, and chef-driven entrées. But it's the city's best beer list that keeps beer geeks and neighborhood folks beating a path to its door. Check out the great patio on warm days.

MAP 2: 2572 Scranton Rd., 216/298-4451, www.tremonttaphouse.com; daily 4pm-2am

RESTAURANTS

OHIO CITY AND TREMONT

Detroit Shoreway and Edgewater

Map 3

CAFÉS AND DINERS

Diner on Clifton $

Since it opened in 1998, the Diner on Clifton has quietly become a Cleveland landmark. In the beginning it seemed the place had the feel of one of those flashy urban diners that focused more on beauty than bacon. Fortunately, that could not have been further from the truth. On top of a full slate of genuinely crafted and generously portioned diner classics (Greek salad, hot roast turkey, patty melt), Clifton offers wonderful breakfast items, some served all day long. Try the great stuffed omelets, corned-beef hash, pancakes, and French toast.

MAP 3: 11637 Clifton Blvd., 216/521-5003, www.dineronclifton.com; Mon.-Fri. 7am-11pm, Sat. 9am-11pm, Sun. 8am-11pm

Gypsy Beans & Bakery $

Situated at the epicenter of the burgeoning Detroit Shoreway neighborhood, and serving as its unofficial community center, Gypsy Beans is an independently owned and operated café. Open from early morning until late in the evening, the attractive double storefront serves coffee drinks, fresh-baked muffins and croissants, pasta salads, thick-crust pizza by the slice, and overstuffed sandwiches. This is a great place to meet up before or after a show at Cleveland Public Theatre.

MAP 3: 6425 Detroit Ave., 216/939-9009, www.gypsybeans.com; Mon.-Sat. 7am-9pm, Sun. 9am-9pm

CONTEMPORARY AMERICAN

Spice Kitchen & Bar $$$

Chef-owner Ben Bebenroth is widely regarded as one of the leading farm-to-table chefs in the region, and as such his restaurant is a locavore's dream. Approachable, elegant, and expertly crafted, the food evolves with the seasons but always manages to hit the right spot. Polenta fries combine the crunch of a fry with the creaminess of soft polenta; flatbread is layered with house-smoked trout; soups swing from potato and sunchoke to chilled beet and pickled squash. While dishes frequently change, diners can count on options built around sustainable fish and local pork, chicken, and beef.

MAP 3: 5800 Detroit Ave., 216/961-9637, www.spicekitchenandbar.com; Tues.-Sat. 5pm-11pm

DESSERT

Sweet Moses Soda Fountain $

Grab a stool at the antique soda fountain and watch soda jerks skillfully create classic sundaes, floats, and malts using the shop's own homemade ice cream. Savor the aroma as the kitchen churns out batches of hot fudge, caramel sauce, baked goods, chocolates, and caramel corn. Then step over to the candy counter, and take home more sweet memories with a box of handmade confections and treats. If this throwback sounds like candy-covered dream, that's because it is.

MAP 3: 6800 Detroit Ave., 216/651-2202, www.sweetmosestreats.com; Sun.-Thurs. noon-11pm, Fri.-Sat. noon-midnight

MEDITERRANEAN

Luxe Kitchen & Lounge $$

With a wide range of small plates, shared plates, pizzas, and prix fixe dinners, this super-cool Mediterranean restaurant satisfies just about every taste, mood, and budget. A couple can sit in the lounge and nibble on a charcuterie plate and cheese board and split a bottle of wine for about $25. Small plates include pork and chicken kebabs, bacon-wrapped shrimp, and veal-stuffed peppers. For the main event there are thin-crust pizzas, pastas, and fun-spirited family-style meals. The stylish space features a salvaged art deco bar, shabby-chic chandeliers, and a wine cellar built into an old bank vault. A DJ plays an amazing mix of retro and contemporary tunes. All bottles on the wine list are sold at $10 over retail. You can also grab wine to go at retail prices.

MAP 3: 6605 Detroit Ave., 216/916-8732, www.luxecleveland.com; Mon.-Sat. 5pm-midnight, Sun. 10am-9pm

PUBS

Parkview Nite Club $

You won't find a cooler old-school Cleveland watering hole than the Parkview. Hidden away at the end of a block, this rowdy club pretty much has its own neighborhood. The crowd is as agreeably disparate as one can find, with rough-and-tumble blue collars, musicians, reporters, and politicians all seeking shelter from more conspicuous spots. This tavern's age and history are evident in the photos, memorabilia, and detritus that plaster the weathered walls. Come here for great burgers, fried walleye sandwiches, house-smoked pulled pork, and the ever-popular Sunday brunch featuring eggs Benedict and Bloody Marys. On Wednesday night, the Parkview hosts a rousing live blues jam.

MAP 3: 1261 W. 58th St., 216/961-1341, www.parkviewniteclub.com; Mon.-Sat. 11am-11pm, Sun. 11am-10pm

clockwise from top left: Provenance Restaurant and Café, Cleveland Museum of Art; Melt Bar & Grilled, Lakewood; Neapolitan-style pizza at Vero Bistro, Cleveland Heights

XYZ the Tavern $$

Eclectic and affordable pub-style comfort food is the name of the game at this popular neighborhood saloon. Great burgers, corned beef and chicken sandwiches, and daily special flush out the home-style menu. Don't miss the house-made chips and the killer chicken and waffles. More than 70 varieties of whiskey, scotch, bourbon, and rye and a killer craft beer list make this lively American pub a winner.

MAP 3: 6419 Detroit Ave., 216/706-1104, www.xyzthetavern.com; daily 4pm-2am

VIETNAMESE
Minh-Anh Vietnamese Restaurant $

What you won't find at Minh-Anh are swanky table settings and gregarious servers. What you will find is authentic home-style Vietnamese cuisine. This simple restaurant serves lacy crepes loaded with shrimp, vegetables, and fresh herbs. There are nearly a dozen soups, best of which is the cinnamon beef soup with rice noodles. Numerous vermicelli noodle dishes come topped with egg rolls, shrimp on sugarcane, or grilled pork. After dinner, walk next door to the Asian market to load up on ingredients like Sriracha hot sauce, fresh lemongrass, and fermented shrimp paste.

MAP 3: 5428 Detroit Ave., 216/961-9671, www.minh-anh.com; Mon.-Thurs. 11am-9:45pm, Fri. 11am-10:45pm, Sat. noon-10:45pm, Sun. noon-8:45pm

University Circle and Little Italy

Map 4

AMERICAN
Washington Place Bistro $$$

This well-appointed American bistro stands out in Little Italy, a neighborhood chock-full of Italian restaurants. Formerly the Baricelli Inn, the stately mansion has received a top-to-bottom makeover, adding a bar and lounge while freshening up the dining rooms. The menu is full of unique and captivating items, much of it comfort foods updated by choice seasonal ingredients and chef-driven technique. Oxtail pierogies and shrimp and grits make fine starters, while chicken confit, fork-tender pot roast, and veal meat loaf round out the business end of the meal. On Wednesday, couples can eat well for just $40.

MAP 4: 2203 Cornell Rd., 216/791-6500, www.washingtonplacelittleitaly.com; Mon.-Fri. 11:30am-10pm, Sat. 10am-10pm, Sun. 10am-8pm

BAKERIES

Corbo's Bakery $

Not to name-drop, but super-chef Mario Batali said, "Corbo's Bakery has the best *cassata* (cake) I have tried in the U.S.A." This long-standing Little Italy bakery is known far and wide as the source for delectable Italian sweets, treats, and classic desserts. If there is an Italian wedding happening within 100 miles of the shop, chances are good the bride and groom will be slicing into a Corbo's *cassata*. A move down the block has sacrificed a bit of the old-school charm in favor of space, comfort, and modernity, but there has been no loss in quality.

MAP 4: 12210 Mayfield Rd., 216/421-8181, www.corbos.com; Tues.-Thurs. and Sun. 8am-6pm, Fri.-Sat. 8am-10pm

Presti's Bakery & Café $

In Little Italy, Presti is a name that carries some clout. To foodies, it is synonymous with killer cannoli. This airy corner café is busy morning, noon, and night thanks to a full range of necessities, delicacies, and delights. Espresso and cappuccino attract the early-morning set, who on nice days take their cups outside to enjoy along with the newspaper. At lunch, students from nearby Case Western Reserve University pop in for slices of pizza, sandwiches, and soda. After work, folks drop by to pick up tidy white boxes laden with buttery cookies, flaky pastries, and those amazing cannoli.

MAP 4: 12101 Mayfield Rd., 216/421-3060, www.prestisbakery.com; Mon.-Thurs. 6am-9pm, Fri.-Sat. 6am-10pm, Sun. 6am-6pm

CAFÉS

Algebra Tea House $

As much a funky living collage as it is a teahouse, Algebra is the de facto bohemian hangout in Little Italy. The inside of this quirky gypsy den is filled with original furniture, wall hangings, and paintings. The floor is a one-of-a-kind mosaic; the ceiling is hand-painted; the cups and saucers are the handiwork of artist-owner Ayman. Tea fans will find dozens of superior-quality flavors, including house blends. Light eats run mainly to salads, Lebanese dishes, and desserts. Try the hummus and pita platter or the toasted pita sandwich with cheese and veggies.

MAP 4: 2136 Murray Hill Rd., 216/421-9007, www.algebrateahouse.net; daily 10am-11pm

Arabica Café $

The Arabica name has been a symbol of quality coffee in Cleveland for decades, with numerous outposts scattered about town. This café can be considered the headquarters if for no other reasons than size and location. Built into an old mansion on University Circle, the rambling coffeehouse features rooms of various shapes and sizes, plus a lovely patio. Popular with students from nearby Case Western Reserve University, who sip in the constant company of their laptops, Arabica serves salads, sandwiches, and desserts along with hot and cold caffeinated beverages.

MAP 4: 11300 Juniper Rd., 216/791-0300, www.arabica-cafe.com; Mon.-Fri. 7am-10pm, Sat.-Sun. 7:30am-8pm

DESSERTS
Coquette Patisserie $

As Cleveland's first truly authentic French pastry producer, Coquette Patisserie introduced a whole host of locals to the supreme pleasures of rainbow-colored macarons, airy German-style cheesecakes, and magnificent chocolate *triomphes.* A move to a charming retail location now expands on those beautifully composed pastries by adding artisanal cheeses, small plates, and other savory fare to the mix. Fine coffees, craft beers, boutique wines, and handcrafted cocktails make Coquette a wonderful pre- or post-event stop.

MAP 4: 11607 Euclid Ave., 216/570-7193, www.coquettepatisserie.com; Tues.-Sun. 10am-midnight

Mitchell's Homemade Ice Cream $

Cleveland's favorite homegrown brand crafts top-notch ice creams using the freshest ingredients. The small-batch products are made with local milk from grass-fed cows and flavored with fresh, seasonal fruits. While most of the scoop shops are scattered in the suburbs, this location in University Circle brings candy-coated smiles to urban-minded students and culture seekers.

MAP 4: 11444 Uptown Ave., 216/229.9402, www.mitchellshomemade.com; Sun.-Thurs. 11am-10pm, Fri.-Sat. 11am-11pm

GLOBAL
Table 45 $$$

In addition to Tremont's popular Parallax and nearby L'Albatros, chef Zack Bruell also operates this ultracontemporary restaurant inside the InterContinental Hotel. Relying on influences as varied as Moroccan, Indian, Asian, and Latin American, Table 45's eclectic menu might feature green-tomato gazpacho, naan pizza, five-spice short ribs, and tandoor-roasted chicken. Despite the range, these dishes have amazing focus, and the flavors come across like a bolt of genius. Architecture and design fans will undoubtedly get a kick out of the minimal digs, which embrace white like no other.

MAP 4: 9801 Carnegie Ave., 216/707-4045, www.tbl45.com; Sun.-Fri. 11am-11pm, Sat. 3pm-11pm

MEDITERRANEAN

Club Isabella $$$

This reborn rendition of a long-standing classic sparkles, from the gorgeous old-meets-new setting to the original and progressive cuisine. Chef-owner Fabio Mota manages to twist high-quality but familiar ingredients into surprising and delicious new tastes. Start with a meat and fish tartare tasting with fried soft-cooked egg. If the buttery frogs' legs are on the menu, get them, along with monkfish in smoky bacon-studded cream sauce or scallops with braised pork belly. On nice days, the front of the restaurant opens up to the spacious front patio.

MAP 4: 2175 Cornell Rd., 216/229-1111, www.clubisabella.com; lunch Mon.-Fri. 11:30am-3pm, dinner Mon.-Sat. 5pm-10pm

La Dolce Vita $$

On pleasant days and nights, the prime sidewalk space surrounding this popular Little Italy restaurant is flooded with diners. The attitude is festive and lighthearted; the food is flavorful and unfussy. Consistently satisfying salads, pizzas, pastas, and Italian classics are dished up in large portions. Try the clams Tarantino, a pasta dish with clams and fresh zucchini, or the veal Pavarotti, made with portobello mushrooms and marsala wine. Visit on a Monday night and you'll enjoy live opera with your pizza.

MAP 4: 12112 Mayfield Rd., 216/721-8156; Mon.-Thurs. 5pm-10pm, Fri.-Sat. noon-11pm, Sun. noon-10pm

L'Albatros $$

Situated inside a completely modernized 19th-century carriage house, L'Albatros is a contemporary French brasserie with loads of style. Set against this ultra-sleek backdrop is a menu overflowing with bistro classics, like onion soup gratinée, escargot, pork terrine, and cassoulet. For those who prefer less far-flung tastes, there are pasta, fish, and poultry dishes that satisfy just as heartily. Popular with the pretheater and orchestra set, the lively restaurant features items specifically selected for rapid enjoyment. In warm weather, in-the-know folks flock to this restaurant's idyllic tree-shaded patio for fine food and drink.

MAP 4: 11401 Bellflower Rd., 216/791-7880, www.albatrosbrasserie.com; Mon.-Wed. 11:30am-11pm, Thurs.-Sat. 11:30am-midnight

Michaelangelo's $$$

In a neighborhood that often dumbs down Italian food to match tourists' expectations, Michaelangelo's is a magnificent exception. Authentic and ambitious northern Italian cuisine is the order of the day at this elegant, well-appointed trattoria. Run by a Piedmont-trained chef, the restaurant serves cold and hot antipasti, handmade pastas in luxurious cream sauces, wine-braised meats, including boar, rabbit, and lamb, and fresh fish specials. If the veal cannelloni is on the menu, get it. Ethereal crepes are filled with ground veal and ricotta cheese and topped with a mascarpone cream sauce.

MAP 4: 2198 Murray Hill Rd., 216/721-0300, www.mangelos.com; Mon.-Thurs. 5:30pm-10pm, Fri.-Sat. 5:30pm-11pm, Sun. 5pm-9pm

Provenance Restaurant and Café ⑤⑤⑤

As part of the Cleveland Museum of Art's massive renovation and expansion, art and food lovers both won big thanks to these two new on-site eateries. Provenance is a 75-seat fine-dining restaurant, while Provenance Café is a sporty quick-service yet high-quality cafeteria. Located shoulder-by-shoulder at the far end of the cavernous atrium, the twin eateries are pretty as a picture, bringing both form and function to museum dining. Both are overseen by chef Doug Katz.

MAP 4: 11150 E. Blvd., in Cleveland Museum of Art, 216/421-7350, www. clevelandart.org; Tues., Thurs., Sat., and Sun. 10am-5pm, Wed. and Fri. 10am-9pm

Valentino's Pizza ⑤

You might expect a neighborhood called Little Italy to be crawling with amazing pizza joints, but in Cleveland you'd be wrong. Fortunately, there's Valentino's, the closest thing to a New York pie this side of Manhattan's West Side Highway. Thin-crusted yet floppy enough to fold, the pepperoni pizza is the real deal. But unlike in New York, you can enjoy your slice on a leafy outdoor patio. This small takeout-only shop also sells salads, meatball sandwiches, and above-average pasta dishes.

MAP 4: 2197 Murray Hill Rd., 216/795-0463, www.valentinospizzacleveland.com; Mon.-Fri. 11am-11pm, Sat. 3pm-11pm

MEXICAN

Mi Pueblo ⑤

This laid-back Mexican restaurant serves some of the best chips and salsa, authentic soft tacos, and boozy margaritas in town. If you can steer yourself away from the chorizo tacos, try an order of the amazing enchiladas *suizas* (chicken-stuffed tortillas topped with creamy tomatillo sauce). Mole fans will want to try Mi Pueblo's version, which is dark, stormy, and sufficiently complex. On weekends, specials like *menudo* (tripe soup) and goat stew are available, and a strolling mariachi band adds a festive note.

MAP 4: 11611 Euclid Ave., 216/791-8226, www.mipueblocleveland.com; Mon.-Wed. 11:30am-10pm, Thurs.-Sat. 11:30am-11pm, Sun. noon-9pm

Cleveland Heights and Shaker Heights

Map 5

BAKERIES

Luna Bakery and Cafe ⓢ

This small and tidy space in the Cedar-Fairmount District is as crisp and cosmopolitan as a bespoke suit. More bakery than café, the shop specializes in sweets of every size, color, and seductiveness. Cupcakes, scones, sugar cookies, cakes, brownies, croissants, and pastel-hued macarons are just some of the offerings. Rounding out the menu are breakfast sandwiches, panini, and French crepes, both sweet and savory. Seating is available inside and out.

MAP 5: 2482 Fairmount Blvd., 216/231-8585, www.lunabakerycafe.com; Mon.-Fri. 7am-7pm, Sat.-Sun. 8am-7pm

On the Rise ⓢ

Cleveland Heights is blessed to have a trio of fantastic bakeries, and this charming little shop is one of them. Artisan baker Adam Gidlow and his team craft everything by hand the old-fashioned European way, and eager fans arrive every morning to grab their daily bread and coffee. Come here for buttery scones and cookies, flaky croissants, dense and chewy focaccia and sourdough, and the best French baguette in Cleveland, if not Ohio. At lunch, a line forms out the door for incredible sandwiches like grass-fed roast beef, smoked brisket, and Vietnamese banh mi. There is very limited seating inside, but on nice days you can sit outside.

MAP 5: 3471 Fairmount Blvd., 216/320-9923, www.ontheriseartisanbreads.com; Tues.-Fri. 7am-6pm, Sat. 8am-5pm, Sun. 8am-2pm

CAFÉS

Aladdin's Eatery ⓢⓢ

This local chain is popular for its reliably fresh, healthy, and tasty Lebanese cuisine. Bountiful salads like fattoush join hearty soups like lentil and veggie as great places to start. Falafel, shawarma, and shish tawook are packed into pitas with tahini and rolled up tight. Thanks to countless veggie and vegan items, Aladdin's has become hugely popular with those who avoid meats. Fruit and veggie juices and fruit smoothies are made to order.

MAP 5: 12447 Cedar Rd., 216/932-4333, www.aladdinseatery.com; Mon.-Thurs. 10:30am-10:30pm, Fri.-Sat. 11am-11:30pm, Sun. 11am-10pm

This other fine Cleveland Heights bakeshop is one of the most popular spots on Lee Road for a quick, casual lunch or dinner. This bright, airy contemporary café specializes in soups made daily, fresh salads, and gourmet sandwiches. Built atop wonderful house-baked bread, the sandwiches include egg salad and chive, chicken curry salad, and roast beef and swiss with horseradish mayo. There is also a wonderful selection of pastries, cookies, and cakes. Outdoor dining is available behind the restaurant.

MAP 5: 2267 Lee Rd., 216/932-3003, www.stone-oven.com; Mon.-Thurs. 7am-9pm, Fri. 7am-10pm, Sat. 8am-10pm, Sun. 8:30am-8pm

★ Tommy's $

What started out in the 1970s as a hippie-run soda fountain has become the anchor not only of Coventry Road, but of Coventry Village. Multiple locations and incarnations later, this bustling family-friendly café now commands a large and lovely space in the middle of the action. A lengthy menu features an amazing range of vegan, vegetarian, and meaty options, many of which are named after the owner's friends and customers. Soups are made daily from scratch, an entire page is devoted to fresh and inventive salads and meat and spinach pies, falafel sandwiches come with fillings too numerous to list, and the hand-dipped milk shakes are the best in the city.

MAP 5: 1824 Coventry Rd., 216/321-7757, www.tommyscoventry.com; Sun.-Thurs. 9am-9pm, Fri. 9am-10pm, Sat. 7:30am-10pm

CONTEMPORARY

Felice Urban Café $$

When it comes to curb appeal, Felice pretty much has a lock on the competition. Set in a restored Craftsman-style home, this intimate eatery is as cozy as they come. Arriving here for dinner feels more like dropping in on a friend than entering a public restaurant. Inside, diners discover the original leaded-glass windows, warm wooden fixtures, and historic hearth. The eclectic menu features Mediterranean-inspired treats like grilled baby octopus, chorizo-spiked mussels, lamb sliders, and skirt steak with *chimichurri*. Out back there is a beautiful flagstone courtyard set beneath a towering oak.

MAP 5: 12502 Larchmere Blvd., 216/791-0918, www.coolplacestoeat.com; Tues.-Thurs. 4pm-10pm, Fri.-Sat. 4pm-midnight

Fire Food & Drink $$$

Relying almost exclusively on local, seasonal, and sustainable ingredients, widely praised chef Doug Katz is well ahead of the national curve when it comes to "slow food." Located at Shaker Square, just steps from the largest farmers market in the region, this snazzy bistro serves simply prepared and robustly flavored American fare. Sit at the poured-concrete bar and enjoy a glass of wine and a clay-oven pizza. Or sit in the industrial-chic dining room and tuck into crispy chicken livers, tandoor-roasted pork chops, or diver scallops with Ohio sweet corn. Fire has an incredible Sunday brunch and boasts an expansive sidewalk patio overlooking the square.

MAP 5: 13220 Shaker Sq., 216/921-3473, www.firefoodanddrink.com; Tues.-Thurs. 5pm-10pm, Fri.-Sat. 5pm-11pm, Sun. 10am-2pm and 5pm-10pm

DESSERT
Sweetie Fry ❺

"What a strange concept," said neighborhood residents when they learned of Keith Logan's idea to combine ice cream and french fries in a single shop. But a handful of years into his kooky project, Logan has made belly-rubbing believers of us all. His homemade ice cream is appropriately creamy and delicious, but it's the "impossibly good fries" that pleasantly shock newcomers. Topped with everything from bacon and cheddar to and parmesan and truffle oil, the regular and sweet potato fries are out of this world.

MAP 5: 2307 Lee Rd., 216/932-2300, www.sweetiefry.com; Tues.-Thurs. 3pm-11pm, Fri.-Sat. 3pm-12:30am, Sun. 2pm-10pm

DINERS
Big Al's Diner ❺

Greasy spoon? Neighborhood diner? Working-class lunch spot? Whatever you call it, Al's is a cherished East Side institution. Get here before church lets out on weekends and you'll score one of the coveted booths, which offer room enough for both a newspaper and a plate of corned-beef hash. On the border of Cleveland and Shaker Heights, this popular diner is as diverse as they come, with progressive politicians rubbing shoulders with hungover hipsters and oil-stained auto mechanics. The draws here are monster portions of hearty home-style grub, like biscuits and gravy, blueberry pancakes, three-egg omelets, and the aforementioned corned-beef hash. Pay at the counter when you're done.

MAP 5: 12600 Larchmere Blvd., 216/791-8550; Mon.-Sat. 6:30am-2:30pm,Sun. 8am-2:30pm

★ Katz Club Diner ❺❺

Set inside a stunningly renovated historic diner, this neighborhood gem is jumping breakfast, lunch, and dinner. Operated by popular chef Doug Katz, the 45-seat restaurant serves comfort foods like eggs Benedict, corned-beef hash, chicken salad sandwich, and meat loaf with mashed potatoes. Everything is made from scratch in-house or bought from a quality local vendor. In the morning, a

well-tended coffee bar dispatches cups of locally roasted espresso,
cappuccino, and French press coffee.

MAP 5: 1975 Lee Rd., 216/932-3333, www.thekatzclubdiner.com; Tues.-Thurs. and
Sun. 7am-10pm, Fri.-Sat. 7am-midnight

Inn on Coventry ⑤

This homey café is *the* place to go on Coventry Road for hearty
home-cooked breakfast fare. Ricotta pancakes, overstuffed omelets, and delish French toast are just a few of the reasons this place
gets slammed most weekend mornings. The intimate place fills up
fast and there is often a wait for a table, so once served and sated, a
diner might feel rushed to move on. But take your time and enjoy
creative wholesome and fresh breakfast fare before exploring the
shops of Coventry.

MAP 5: 2785 Euclid Heights Blvd., 216/371-1811, www.innoncoventry.com;
Mon.-Thurs. 7am-2:45pm, Fri. 7am-8:30pm, Sat.-Sun. 8am-2:45pm

JAPANESE
Pacific East ⑤⑤

When it comes to sushi, diners have two choices in this area for
wonderful quality and construction. Pacific East lacks the polished
decor of Sasa Matsu, and the sushi bar is small by comparison, but
the à la carte sushi selection here is much more diverse. Sample
crunchy freshwater crabs, monkish liver, tuna belly, and broiled
yellowtail collar along with standards like salmon, sea urchin, and
eel. The Japanese menu also offers the usual host of Asian salads,
tempuras, yakitori, noodle bowls, and creative rolls. Unique to this
locale is the region's only Malaysian menu.

MAP 5: 1763 Coventry Rd., 216/320-2302, www.pacificeastcoventry.com;
Mon.-Fri. 11am-10pm, Sat. noon-11pm, Sun. 3pm-10pm

Sasa Matsu ⑤⑤

Cleveland's first and only *izakaya,* or Japanese-style tapas bar, Sasa
is a treat for adventurous diners. In addition to wonderful sushi,
sashimi, and specialty rolls, this contemporary lounge at Shaker
Square boasts pages of out-of-the-ordinary small and medium-size
plates. Dishes can be as simple as fresh-steamed edamame with sea
salt or as elaborate as marinated sliced beef cooked tabletop on a
heated river rock. Try the Kobe beef gyoza, addictive Sasa fries, or
the best grilled mackerel around. For dessert, try the house-made
chai ice cream. Sasa also has the largest sake selection in town, with
approximately 40 imported and domestic varieties that range from
crisp and cold to unfiltered and sweet.

MAP 5: 13120 Shaker Sq., 216/767-1111, www.sasamatsu.com; Mon.-Sat.
5pm-midnight, Sun. 5pm-10pm

PIZZA
Dewey's Pizza ⑤⑤

Kids love visiting Dewey's because they can watch through the glass as the pizza chefs toss, twirl, and stretch the dough. Parents love Dewey's because it is attractive, contemporary, and serves good beer and wine. The menu here is delightfully uncomplicated, featuring just fresh salads, hand-tossed pizzas and calzones, and a few desserts. Diners can design their own pies from a list of sauces, cheeses, and toppings, or simply select from a dozen gourmet pizzas.

MAP 5: 2194 Lee Rd., 216/321-7355, www.deweyspizza.com; Mon.-Thurs. 11am-10pm, Fri.-Sat. 11am-11pm, Sun. 4pm-10pm

Vero Bistro ⑤⑤

Boasting one of the very few wood-burning ovens in this part of town, Vero turns out some of the most authentic Neapolitan-style pizza around. Owner Marc-Aurele Buholzer inherited the oven with the space, but has seriously elevated the product and the experience. An airy, chewy outer crust blistered with char gives way to a thin, crisp inner crust supporting a few choice ingredients. These pies are meant to be enjoyed fresh from the oven. Vero also serves beer and wine.

MAP 5: 12421 Cedar Rd., 216/229-8383, www.verocleveland.com; Tues.-Thurs. 4pm-10pm, Fri.-Sun. noon-10pm

TURKISH
Anatolia Café ⑤⑤

This roomy upscale Turkish restaurant does a brisk business in refreshing dips, flavorful spit-roasted meats, and aromatic stews. Start with fresh-baked pita and platters of hummus and smoky baba ghanoush, a wonderfully aromatic lentil soup, lemony sautéed calf's liver, or fried phyllo fingers stuffed with feta and parsley. For dinner, choose from numerous grilled meat and fish kebabs. Better yet, order anything made with Anatolia's delicious *doner,* thin-shaved spit-roasted meat. In the *iskender,* the *doner* is stacked on pita chips, topped with tomato sauce, and served with creamy yogurt.

MAP 5: 2270 Lee Rd., 216/321-4400, www.anatoliacafe.com; Mon.-Fri. 11am-11pm, Sat. noon-11pm,Sun. noon-10pm

Lakewood Map 6

BREAKFAST
West End Tavern ⑤

This comfortable neighborhood tavern has been a fixture in the
western 'burbs for over two decades. You know the type: repurposed old storefront, creaky wood floors, tin ceilings, uncomfortable booths, gregarious bartenders, amazing wings. In addition to
the great vibe, cold beer, and decent jukebox, the West End dishes
up some mighty fine pub grub. Come on weekends for the beloved
brunch starring the infamous Bloody Mary bar, where diners get to
doctor up their hair of the dog any way they choose. There's food,
too, like great eggs Benedict, stuffed French toast, roast-beef hash,
and big-as-a-dinner-plate omelets.

MAP 6: 18514 Detroit Ave., 216/521-7684, www.westendtav.com; daily 11am-2am

CASUAL AMERICAN
Buckeye Beer Engine ⑤

Artificially carbonated kegs, which essentially dispense themselves, rendered old-fashioned beer engines obsolete. But because
this West Side tavern serves unfiltered, unpasteurized, and naturally carbonated cask-conditioned ale, that antiquated beer pump
isn't so obsolete after all. Co-owned by the brewmaster of a local
craft brewery, the Beer Engine takes suds seriously. Hopheads will
find dozens of spectacular and hard-to-find drafts here, all served
in style-appropriate glassware. And to go with those brews is a
menu crammed with some 20 different half-pound burgers, with
toppings that include pulled pork, smoked bacon, and fried eggs.
The kitchen also offers hearty platters of pot roast, Wiener schnitzel, and fish-and-chips.

MAP 6: 15315 Madison Ave., 216/226-2337, www.buckeyebeerengine.com;
Mon.-Sat. 11am-midnight, Sun. 10am-midnight

Deagan's Kitchen & Bar ⑤⑤

This lively establishment is a food lover's gastropub, where the chef-
driven bistro fare rivals the matchless craft beer list for attention.
Small plates like deviled eggs, fried oysters, and sausage samplers
join soul-enriching entrées like fish-and-chips and bacon-studded
mac and cheese. Popular weekly events include Taco Tuesday and
Vegetarian Wednesday. Regardless the day, the setting, service, and
satisfying fare are worth checking out.

MAP 6: 14810 Detroit Ave., 216/767-5775, www.deagans.com; Mon.-Sat.
11am-2am, Sun. 10am-2am

Cleveland's Ethnic Smorgasbord

Cleveland's melting pot past and present mean that fans of ethnic food have their pick of delicious, adventurous options. For those who prefer to stay at home, the region is blessed with extraordinary markets and groceries that cater to individual ethnicities and tastes.

To say that the Greater Cleveland area is home to a lot of ethnic eateries is a major understatement. For every bland national chain there are a dozen mom-and-pop shops dishing up authentic foods from the homeland. Scattered like mustard seeds across the landscape, these gems are just waiting to be discovered by adventurous eaters.

For an appetizer, consider the fact that Cleveland has restaurants devoted to Italian, Greek, German, Irish, Lebanese, Turkish, Hungarian, Slovenian, Ethiopian, Indian, Mexican, Central American, and Jewish foods, to name a few. Some neighborhoods, like Little Italy and AsiaTown, are densely populated with restaurants serving a specific cuisine. And for some reason, the West Side is disproportionately endowed with Latin eateries.

So, how do you choose? Consider beginning with something you've never tried before, like Ethiopian food at **Empress Taytu** (6125 St. Clair Ave., 216/391-9400). Meals here are served family-style at traditional basket tables, and silverware is replaced with spongy flatbread called *injera*. Ever tried Turkish food? It's a lot like Lebanese, only tastier. Visit **Anatolia Café** (2270 Lee Rd., 216/321-4400, www.anatoliacafe.com) to see how good shish kebab can be. For amazing Middle Eastern food pencil in a trip to **Nate's Deli** (1923 W. 25th St., 216/696-7529) in Ohio City.

There may be no finer comfort food than Polish stuffed cabbage, and there may be no finer version than the one served at **Sokolowski's University Inn** (1201 University Rd., 216/771-9236, www.sokolowskis.com). Folks come here for not just the rib-sticking food but also the quirky cafeteria arrangement and the cozy lodge-like setting. As much a part of the Cleveland landscape as the

Melt Bar & Grilled $$

In the relatively brief period since this restaurant opened in 2006, it has received props from *Esquire, USA Today,* and numerous food-themed TV shows. What's all the fuss about? Grilled cheese—nearly three dozen wild and wonderful versions are currently on the menu. At this cool rock-fueled tavern, everybody's favorite childhood comfort food is contorted into tasty variations on the bread-and-cheese theme. Fillings range from crab cakes to peanut butter and banana. The Wake & Bacon is loaded with bacon, egg, and cheese; the Parmageddon is an intimidating stack of potato pierogies, kraut, onions, and cheese; and the Lake Erie Monster nets a diner deep-fried walleye, jalapeño tartar sauce, and—wait for it—*cheese!* Melt also has a superb beer selection.

MAP 6: 14718 Detroit Ave., 216/226-3699, www.meltbarandgrilled.com; Mon.-Thurs. 11am-11pm, Fri.-Sat. 11am-midnight, Sun. 10am-10pm

Cuyahoga River, **Sterle's Country House** (1401 E. 55th St., 216/881-4181, www.sterlescountryhouse. com) attracts folks by the busload with made-from-scratch Eastern European delicacies like liver and onions, roast pork with gravy, and heavenly strudel. The Hungarian food at **Balaton Restaurant** (13133 Shaker Sq., 216/921-9691) includes paprikash, goulash, and roast duck, but one out of four diners orders the Wiener schnitzel. These platter-size cutlets are pounded thin, breaded, and fried, and served with spaetzle and applesauce.

If you've never tried a Colombian *arepa* or a Salvadorian *pupusa* head straight to **Barroco Grill** (12906 Madison Ave., 216/221-8127, www. barrocogrill.com) and **Pupuseria La Bendicion** (3685 W. 105th St., 216/688-0338), respectively. At the first, super-thick corn tortillas are griddled, split, and filled with ingredients like spicy Mexican-style chorizo or steak, mushrooms and cheese. At the latter, corn dough is filled with cheese and pork and griddle-fried till crisp and corny.

Not far from Barroco is **Mi Pueblo Taqueria** (12207 Lorain Ave., 216/671-6661), a casual-style taqueria that serves the best and most authentic tacos around. Warm corn tortillas are stuffed with carne asada, chorizo, beef tongue, and chicken. Also on the near-west side of town is a fantastic Latin grocery called **La Plaza Supermarket** (13609 Lakewood Hts. Blvd., 216/476-8000), where you can score fresh-fried pork rinds, amazing salsas, and hard-to-find Latin ingredients. If the taco cart is out front, order some.

Indian-food lovers come in one of two categories: vegetarian or omnivore. **Udupi Café** (6339 Olde York Rd., 440/743-7154) caters to the first group with vegetarian-only fare from southern India. Meat lovers might want to bypass Udupi in favor of **Café Tandoor** (2096 S. Taylor Rd., 216/371-8500, www.cafetandoorcleveland. com), a comfortable East Side restaurant serving mildly spiced northern Indian food.

CAFÉS

Root Café ⑤

This roomy and woodsy corner storefront is where a good many Lakewood residents stop on their way to work or simply stop and work. Like any great neighborhood café, this is a true "third place," where locals spend a good deal of time. The Root offers vegetarian items built of local, sustainable, and organic ingredients. Fresh salads, house-made soups, straightforward veggie sandwiches, pizzas, and calzones fill the concise menu. Superbly brewed locally roasted coffee pairs beautifully with Root's house-baked vegan and vegetarian pastries.

MAP 6: 15118 Detroit Ave., 216/226-4401, www.theroot-cafe.com; Mon.-Fri. 6:30am-10pm, Sat. 7am-10pm, Sun. 8am-8pm

Blackbird Baking Company $

Nothing lifts a neighborhood like a great bakery. And for many residents in west Lakewood, Blackbird Baking Company does just that. Months were spent remodeling the structure from a shabby building into a sleek metropolitan bakery. The open design gives customers views of the kitchen, including its flour-dusted work tables and massive ovens. Everything is made from scratch daily and displayed on counters and baker's racks. Bread fans will crow about Blackbird's baguettes, batards, focaccia, and ciabatta. Sweets fans will head straight for the pecan sticky buns, cherry scones, apricot croissants, and dreamy chocolate chip cookies.

MAP 6: 1391 Sloane Ave., 216/712-6599, www.blackbirdbaking.com; Tues.-Fri. 6am-6pm, Sat.-Sun. 7am-5pm

DESSERT

Malley's Chocolates $

The Malley family has been making and selling fine chocolates in and around Cleveland since 1935. At this old-fashioned ice-cream parlor, guests can sit at a real soda fountain and pig out on amazing cones, shakes, and sundaes. This being a chocolate company, anything with hot fudge pretty much rules the night. Kids just love the decor, a pink-hued playground reminiscent of Grandma's kitchen. The candy counter is stocked with unique bars, holiday sweets, chocolate-covered cookies, dark chocolate-covered marshmallow, pecan-and-caramel clusters called Billy Bobs, and many others. Malley's is so popular in Cleveland that the store's characteristic "CHOC" stickers can be spotted on car bumpers throughout the city.

MAP 6: 14822 Madison Ave., 216/529-6262, www.malleys.com; Mon.-Thurs. 10am-10pm, Fri.-Sat. 10am-11pm, Sun. noon-10pm

The Sweet Spot $

The Sweet Spot features homemade, all-natural gelato made with the best local, seasonal organic ingredients. Popular flavors range from classics like cookies and cream and pistachio to some that are bit more out there like fig hazelnut and porter beer. Vegan, sugar-free, and sorbet options are available as well.

MAP 6: 17806 Detroit Ave., 216/221-8870, www.thesweetspotcleveland.com; Sun.-Thurs. noon-10pm, Fri.-Sat. noon-11pm

FRENCH

Tartine Bistro and Wine Bar $$

This welcoming bistro and wine bar feels like an authentic slice of Paris in sleepy Rocky River, Ohio. Exposed-brick walls, a blood-red tin ceiling, and a sturdy old bar give this place its charm. A tightly constructed menu of French-inspired small plates and entrées is designed to pair well with the appealing old-world wine list.

A tiny kitchen offers charcuterie plates, *tartines* (open-faced sand-wiches), hearty mains, and really good pizza. A facade of French doors opens on warm evenings, uniting the outside and inside.

MAP 6: 19110 Old Detroit Rd., Rocky River, 440/331-0800, www.tartinebistro.com; Tues.-Thurs. 4:30pm-10pm, Fri.-Sat. 11:30am-2:30pm and 4:30pm-11pm, Sun. 5pm-9pm

LATIN
Barroco Grill ⑤

This small, upbeat café is run by a Colombian family, who for years operated a street cart in that country. Lucky for us they've imported wonderful foods like Cubanos and arepas, puffy corn tortillas filled with chorizo, grilled steak, pork, or chicken. In one wildly addictive dish, arepas are cut into fingers, deep-fried, and served with cheese fondue for dipping. Best late-night grub ever. BYOB.

MAP 6: 12906 Madison Ave., 216/221-8127, www.barrocogrill.com; Mon.-Thurs. 11am-10pm, Fri.-Sat. 11am-11pm, Sun. 11am-9pm

El Carnicero ⑤⑤

Chef-owner Eric Williams, also of Momocho, opened this big, brash bar of a place, decorated it with Mexican professional wres-tling paraphernalia, and began dishing out flavorful platters of Latin-themed small plates and entrées. Freshly made tamales are topped with ancho-braised brisket, adobo-braised pork, and beer-braised lamb. Small, warm corn tortillas are filled with shrimp Veracruz, chile-glazed salmon, and grilled steak. Start with amaz-ing chips, salsa, and guacamole. There's a lengthy tequila list, a concise beer list, and margaritas are available by the sampler.

MAP 6: 16918 Detroit Ave., 216/226-3415, www.elcarnicerolakewood.com; Tues.-Thurs. 4pm-10:30pm, Fri.-Sat. 11am-11pm, Sun. 11am-9:30pm

MEDITERRANEAN
Pier W ⑤⑤⑤

Despite being situated on the shores of a Great Lake, Cleveland is woefully underserved when it comes to lakeside restaurants. But hav-ing this sparkling West Side gem seems to make up for that deficiency. In a ritzy high-rise west of town, the restaurant offers stunning views of the lake and Cleveland skyline. A tiered dining room means that none are left out on the fun. Unlike most "view" restaurants, this one actually serves great food. Diners can expect contemporary seafood dishes, like updated versions of crab Louis, bouillabaisse, and surf and turf. A great lounge offers a small-plate menu with mini-hali-but tacos, Kobe sliders, and shrimp tempura. Come for the Sunday brunch; it's a bit pricey, but you won't be disappointed.

MAP 6: 12700 Lake Ave., 216/228-2250, www.selectrestaurants.com; Mon.-Fri. 11:30am-2:30pm and 5pm-10pm, Sat. 5pm-11pm, Sun. 9:30am-2:30pm and 4:30pm-9pm

Players on Madison $$

Housed in a light-filled double storefront, this bistro has a decidedly California feel to it. Blond hardwood flooring, a copper-top bar, and lemony walls give this popular date-night restaurant a cheery vibe. Diners can create their own pizza, calzone, or pasta dish by mixing and matching from a lengthy list of noodles, sauces, and gourmet toppings. There are also a number of creative appetizers, salads, and entrées, such as chipotle braised short ribs, pear-and-walnut-stuffed pork chops, and pumpkin ravioli. Players has a charming enclosed garden patio for outdoor dining, weather permitting.

MAP 6: 14523 Madison Ave., 216/226-5200, www.playersonmadison.com; Mon.-Thurs. 5pm-10pm, Fri.-Sat. 5pm-11pm,Sun. 5pm-9pm

Greater Cleveland

Map 7

ASIAN
Umami Asian Kitchen $$$

What this petite, jewel box of a bistro lacks in size, it more than makes up for in style. At this 30-seat, chef-driven restaurant there are nods to Chinese, Thai, and Japanese cuisine, with stellar ingredients buoyed by complementary flavors and spices. Sushi and seafood shine, as do heartier meats like pork belly and duck. Vegetarians can even dine well on crispy tofu and pad Thai. Seasonal cooking means diners can always look forward to something new, delicious, and fresh.

MAP 7: 42 N. Main St., Chagrin Falls, 440/247-8600, www.umamiasiankitchen.com; lunch Tues.-Sat. 11:30am-2pm, dinner Tues.-Sun. 5pm-9pm

CASUAL AMERICAN
B Spot Burgers $

When Iron Chef Michael Symon set out to craft Cleveland's best burger, he didn't take the task lightly. Built with beef supplied by legendary New York purveyor Pat LaFrieda, the burgers explode with beefy goodness. A dozen versions range from Plain Jane to the ever-popular Fat Doug, topped with coleslaw, pastrami, and swiss. Other "Bs" include brats, bologna, and "Bad Ass" milk shakes, which are spiked with booze. Tack on orders of rosemary-scented Lola fries, golden brown onion rings, and blazing-hot Sriracha wings.

MAP 7: 28699 Chagrin Blvd., Woodmere, 216/292-5567, www.bspotburgers.com; Sun.-Thurs. 11:30am-9:30pm, Fri.-Sat. 11:30am-10:30pm

Flour $$$

Paul Minnillo, one of Cleveland's founding fathers of haute cuisine, has ditched the white tablecloths and starched linens of fine dining and opened this breezy suburban bistro. As one of the city's best restaurants, it's more than worth the drive. Italian classics are reworked into dishes that look familiar but taste entirely new. A wood-fired kiln turns out craftsman-quality Neapolitan-style pies. Also here are some of the best pastas, risottos, and Italian entrées around. The Sunday brunch menu is crammed with creative takes on breakfast-friendly items like eggs Benedict, French toast, and biscuits and gravy. Sit in the bar for the most upbeat atmosphere.

MAP 7: 34205 Chagrin Blvd., Moreland Hills, 216/464-3700, www. flourrestaurant.com; Mon.-Thurs. 11:30am-9:30pm, Fri.-Sat. 11:30am-10:30pm, Sun. 11am-8pm

Grovewood Tavern and Wine Bar $$

This unassuming tavern, slipped into a blue-collar neighborhood east of town, has consistently exceeded the expectations of diners who travel here for a delicious change of pace. The unpretentious saloon looks like any other buffalo wing-flinging bar, except this one serves upscale grub like barbecue fried crawfish, prosciutto-wrapped scallops, and honey-and-lavender-glazed chicken. And unlike any corner tavern we've experienced, this one offers more than 100 wines by the bottle, with most of those also available by the glass. Pair a visit here for dinner with a show at nearby Beachland Ballroom.

MAP 7: 17105 Grovewood Ave., Cleveland, 216/531-4900, www.grovewoodtavern. com; Sun.-Thurs. 5pm-10pm, Fri.-Sat. 5pm-11pm

Moxie $$$

Despite its suburban digs, this progressive American bistro has the contemporary feel of a downtown hot spot. And when the editors of *Gourmet* magazine pieced together their 2004 list of the best places to eat in America, Moxie made the cut. Praising chef Jonathan Bennett's dedication to quality ingredients and practiced technique, the magazine announced to the nation what Clevelanders have known for years: Bennett has a knack for assembling inventive, forward-thinking dishes that remain exceedingly approachable. Think artisanal cheese plates, roasted chicken livers with squash puree, house-smoked duck breast, and butter-roasted lobster knuckle with parsnip risotto. An in-house pastry chef crafts some of the finest desserts on the East Side.

MAP 7: 3355 Richmond Rd., Beachwood, 216/831-5599, www. moxietherestaurant.com; Mon.-Thurs. 11:30am-10pm, Fri. 11:30am-11pm, Sat. 5:30pm-11pm

DELIS

Corky & Lenny's $$

For more than 50 years, this Jewish delicatessen has supplied Cleveland with its matzo-ball soup, smoked sable fish, potato knishes, and hearty stuffed cabbage dinners. Come early for busy breakfasts of lox, onions, and eggs, challah French toast, and Western omelets with corned beef. Lunches are all about mile-high deli sandwiches, hot turkey and mashed potatoes, and patty melts. For a real Cleveland treat, order your corned-beef sandwich on potato latkes instead of rye bread. You won't be able to stand afterward, but you won't soon forget the experience either. Corky's has a great deli counter for quick take-out orders, deli trays, and baked goods.

MAP 7: 27091 Chagrin Blvd., Beachwood, 216/464-3838, www.corkyandlennys. com; Sun.-Thurs. 7am-9:30pm, Fri.-Sat. 7am-11pm

Nightlife

Downtown.......................106

Ohio City and Tremont...........110

Detroit Shoreway and Edgewater..116

University Circle and Little Italy...117

Cleveland Heights
   and Shaker Heights.............118

Lakewood........................121

Greater Cleveland................123

HIGHLIGHTS

★ **Classiest Place to Lose Your Shirt:** The building that houses the new **Horseshoe Cleveland** used to be a famous downtown department store. Now, instead of selling shirts, it's the site of people losing their shirts on craps, blackjack, and roulette. At least it's a gorgeous setting (page 106).

★ **Best Place to Drink on a Chilly Night:** At **Prosperity Social Club** it's always a good time to enjoy a drink with friends. But thanks to a freestanding wood-burning stove that fills the room with warmth, fragrance, and cheer, wintertime might be the best time of all (page 111).

★ **The Brewery That Made Cleveland Famous:** There are other fantastic breweries in town, but none makes as big of a splash on the beer circuit as **Great Lakes Brewing Co.** Its beers are now sold in more than a dozen states, and the annual release of its Christmas Ale has practically become its own holiday (page 111).

★ **City's Finest Cocktail:** The Ramos gin fizz, as constructed by the pros at **Velvet Tango Room,** tastes like a mix of clouds and Florida sunshine. Built to exacting specifications, the drink contains small-batch gin, orange blossom water, citrus juices, cream, and egg whites. When shaken to bits, it's heaven in a tall glass (page 115).

★ **Most Fun to Have Standing Up:** On many Fridays, **Happy Dog** kicks off the weekend with a polka happy hour that attracts young and old guests, who come for the festive music, free-spirited dancing, and gourmet hot dogs and beer (page 116).

★ **Best Indoor Bar Game:** While we have nothing against pool, darts, or pinball, isn't it time for a change of pace? Folks looking for something new (and old) visit **Stone Mad Irish Pub,** where a full-size indoor bocce court keeps them pleasantly amused all year long (page 116).

★ **Best Small Live Music Venue:** Tucked beneath the canopy of old-growth trees, the converted carriage house at **Barking Spider Tavern** offers a never-ending calendar of live acts performing acoustic rock, folk, blues, and bluegrass. There's never a cover charge; just tip what you like (page 118).

★ **Take a Ride Back in Time:** Step into the **Katz Club** and you'll feel as though you've stumbled onto the bar car of the *Twentieth Century Limited* bound for Grand Central. Reworked from top to bottom, the 1952 Mountain View Diner is now an elegant lounge serving small plates and classic cocktails (page 120).

★ **Best Big Live Music Venue:** Big is relative at **Beachland Ballroom,** a former Croatian social hall with both an intimate tavern and a larger ballroom. Both are used for concerts starring the best touring acts of our day (page 124).

Cleveland didn't score the Rock and Roll Hall of Fame because it is a snoozer of a town. The Moondog Coronation Ball, considered the world's first rock concert, was held here in 1952, attracting tens of thousands of music fans to the old Cleveland Arena. (Granted, the fun was fleeting—the first rock concert quickly devolved into the first rock concert riot.)

Countless performers have emerged from Cleveland garages—or rose to fame thanks to airtime and sold-out performances here. Today, music is as much a part of daily life as it ever was, with countless venues sprinkled throughout town, beckoning fans with live jazz, rock, blues, metal, and alt-country lineups. Some clubs, like the ever-popular Barking Spider Tavern, never have a cover charge, while others, like the well-known House of Blues, often require pricey tickets with service charges to boot. Most venues, however, fall somewhere in between.

Cleveland's long, cold winters seem to spawn new bars by the armload. We locals are fond of hibernating in snug taverns with warm fireplaces, good wine, and hearty grub. While corner bars are far and away the most prevalent dens, Cleveland also is chock-full of wine bars, cocktail lounges, and even a few dance clubs. These days, the top story is beer, whether brewed up fresh and served at a micro (or, in the case of Great Lakes, macro) brewery, or delivered on tap at a growing number of craft beer-themed bars.

If and when spring does finally arrive, locals are eager to move the party outdoors. Restless from a long, slothful season and an ample dose of cabin fever, folks scramble to bars with patios, courtyards, sidewalks, and rooftop decks and stay there until the first snowfall forces them back indoors.

Downtown

Map 1

BARS
Shooter's

Thanks to a massive commercial and residential development project, much of the Flats has been inaccessible to diners and drinkers. That began to change in 2013, when the first phase of the Flats East Bank opened with three new restaurants, an Aloft hotel, and a new office tower. Phase two, which will take place in 2014, will offer even more drinking and dining options. During the summer, there are few better places to unwind with a cocktail and watch the boat traffic cruise up and down the Cuyahoga. An outdoor bar and stage for live music keep this place hopping most nights, but especially so on weekends. To go with the nautical theme, a seafood-centric menu with items like shrimp cocktails, crab legs, and lobster rolls is available all year long. During the off-season, the place slows down considerably, and the patio is all but put to bed.

MAP 1: 1148 Main Ave., 216/861-6900, www.shootersflats.com; daily 11:30am-close

CASINOS
★ Horseshoe Cleveland

The Horseshoe Cleveland is unlike most casinos. For starters, it's in the center of town rather than on some patch of former farmland miles from the city. Second, it's built into the historic Higbee building, a once-famous department store that boasts stunning architectural details throughout the 100,000-square-foot complex. The upscale, attractive urban casino offers 2,100 slot and video poker machines, 119 table games, and a whole floor devoted to live poker play. During busy times, there can be short waits to grab a stool at table games like blackjack and roulette. In addition to a handful of bars, the property has a 400-seat buffet restaurant called The Spread and a small food court with deli, Italian, and Michael Symon's burger bar B Spot options.

MAP 1: 100 Public Sq., 855/746-3777, www.horseshoecleveland.com; daily 24 hours

DANCE CLUBS
Anatomy

If pulsing beats, roped-off VIP seating areas, and A-list crowds sound appealing, this weekend-only nightclub should be on your list. The sharp Warehouse District space attracts sought-after DJs, who in turn attract the well-dressed set. But fickle as club kids are, this place can go from busy to bust on any given night. The best suggestion is to peek through the large front windows to see just what's shaking inside. Regardless, one can always plop down at the sweeping curved bar for a glass of bubbly and wait for the action to come to you.

MAP 1: 1299 W. 9th St., 216/363-1113, www.anatomycleveland.com; Thurs. and Sun. 10pm-2:30am, Fri.-Sat. 9pm-2:30am

Velvet Dog

Men and women of a certain age (young, that is) can't seem to make it through a single weekend without doing the Dog. The Velvet Dog has deservedly earned a reputation as the best place to boogie, and as such, it welcomes the largest and most fashionable crowds. West 6th Street is the Warehouse District's party strip, and this night-club acts like a beacon for fun seekers. The high-tech multilevel club features a Top 40 dance floor, a dimly lit lounge, and the best party roof in town. The place can definitely feel like a meat market at times, but isn't that the point?

MAP 1: 1280 W. 6th St., 216/664-1116, www.velvetdogcleveland.com; Thurs. and Sat. 9pm-close, Fri. 7pm-close

LIVE MUSIC

Peabody's Concert Club

When this storied Cleveland club was located in the Flats, it welcomed every big name that traveled between New York and Chicago, including Pearl Jam, the Red Hot Chili Peppers, and R.E.M. A new location and new management bode well for the venue, now downtown by the Cleveland State University campus. The two-story concert club has three performance stages that range from small and intimate to big and loud. Up-and-coming rock bands still make stops here, and the lineup can include some real gems. This venue is also a favorite of legendary local acts who never fail to attract a following.

MAP 1: 2045 E. 21st St., 216/776-9999, www.peabodys.com; hours vary depending on show

Wilbert's Food & Music

Another club with deep Cleveland roots, Wilbert's has seen its share of superstars. Jeff Buckley, Ryan Adams, Buckwheat Zydeco, and Buddy Guy have all played either here or at the club's previous site. Performing in the modern, spacious, and comfortable club are mainly local and regional blues, jazz, reggae, and roots-rock acts. The venue's site right by Progressive Field makes it a convenient postgame stop for live music. Wilbert's serves food with a Mexican and Southern slant, with items such as quesadillas, burritos, and barbecue ribs.

MAP 1: 812 Huron Rd. E., 216/902-4663, www.wilbertsmusic.com; hours vary depending on show

LOUNGES

Kevin's Martini Bar

Tucked into the basement of **Pickwick & Frolic,** a multidimensional entertainment complex, Kevin's is a Vegas-style lounge with a G-rated personality. Tuxedoed bartenders and kicky cocktail waitresses serve up classic martinis in a retro-chic setting. Bouncy red banquettes, plush drapery, and a glowing bar top make this joint a feast for the senses. Kevin's also features a champagne bar with one of the largest catalogs of bubble bottles in the city. Bartenders here have a few tricks up their sleeves, which, depending on your mood, can be amusing or corny.

MAP 1: 2035 E. 4th St., 216/241-7425, www.pickwickandfrolic.com; Fri.-Sat. 5pm-11pm

Society Lounge

Situated entirely belowground, this new speakeasy finally delivered to the downtown marketplace a much-needed cocktail lounge. The vibe is decidedly Rat Pack, with low lighting, high-backed banquettes, and red velvet sectionals. Walls are gilded with Venetian plasterwork, faux bricks, and rich tapestry. Some 32 feet of hand-painted murals depicting high-society life envelop entire walls. Catering to a more mature demographic, Society offers live jazz, classic and contemporary cocktails, and small plates and desserts.

MAP 1: 2063 E. 4th St., Lower Level, 216/781-9050, www.societycleveland.com; Mon.-Thurs. 5pm-midnight, Fri.-Sat. 5pm-2am

WINE BARS

D'Vine Wine Bar

At times it feels like the staff here is more serious about wine than the clientele, but to each his or her own. This trendy Warehouse District boîte offers a great selection of wine flights, each with four two-ounce pours that adhere to a theme. Grouped by varietal, wine-growing region, or style, the flights are like personal tastings. Exposed brick walls, flickering candlelight, and lofty warehouse ceilings attract couples looking for a romantic getaway. Come early on warm afternoons to snag one of the coveted sidewalk tables. An interesting tapas menu is comprised of enough tasty wine-friendly bites to cobble together a decent meal.

MAP 1: 836 W. St. Clair Ave., 216/241-8463, www.dvinewinebar.com; Mon.-Thurs. 4pm-1am, Fri.-Sat. 4pm-2am, Sun. noon-8pm

clockwise from top left: Fathead's Brewery & Saloon, North Olmstead; Horseshoe Cleveland, downtown; Great Lakes Brewing Co., Ohio City

Ohio City and Tremont Map 2

BARS

ABC the Tavern

This decades-old bar in Ohio City went from largely ignored to hard to ignore thanks to new ownership, who improved the craft beer list, upped the food, and vastly increased attendance. Don't expect much in the way of scenery—just a ruggedly handsome tavern built to stand the test of time. Great pub grub like diner-style burgers and bacon-wrapped hot dogs is served late, making this joint hugely popular with service industry peeps punching out from area restaurants. An old-school bowling machine and an upstairs dartboard add to the authentic saloon-style fun.

MAP 2: 1872 W. 25th St., 216/861-3857, www.abcthetavern.com; Mon.-Fri. 4pm-2:30am, Sat. noon-2:30am, Sun. 4pm-2:30am

Flying Monkey Pub

This welcoming Tremont pub is one of the most handsome drinking establishments around. Two lengthy bars were constructed in mosaic fashioned from a variety of attractive hardwoods. Tables are handcrafted from fine woods too, but these familiar patterns do double duty as chess, checkers, and backgammon boards. A unique belt-driven system spins every ceiling fan in the house with a single motor. Despite the luxe touches, the Monkey is as low-key as they come. That is, until the pleas for the monkey force the little (faux) mascot from his hidey hole, causing the room to erupt in cheers.

MAP 2: 819 Jefferson Ave., 216/861-6659, www.flyingmonkeypub.com; Mon.-Fri. 4pm-2:30am, Sat.-Sun. noon-2:30am

McNulty's Bier Markt

Don't know your *lambics* from your *saisons?* Try them all in this dimly lit beer hall that dispenses some 30 varieties of Belgian and Belgian-style ales on tap—with the appropriate glassware to match—plus an additional 100 or so in bottles. A favorite among hip Ohio City residents, suburbanite pub crawlers, and the odd bachelorette party, the atmosphere here tends to reflect the occupants. Depending on the day or hour, the scene can be quiet and sleepy or bawdy and raucous. But what never seems to change is the top-flight service, matchless beer selection, and super-cool setting. With Bar Cento housed in the same building, good food is just an order away.

MAP 2: 1948 W. 25th St., 216/274-1010, www.bier-markt.com; Mon.-Fri. 4:30pm-2:30am, Sat. noon-2:30am

If you're looking for a laid-back neighborhood bar with decades-old authenticity, look no further than Prosperity. Owner Bonnie Flinner took a 75-year-old shot-and-beer joint and transformed it into a rustic-chic tavern with good food and better drink. There are no hokey themes here, just real folks meeting up for some conversation, occasional live music, and above-average pub grub. A freestanding woodstove adds wintertime charm to the barroom, while a rec room with pool table, antique bowling machine, and classic board games adds a bit of wholesome fun. Come on weekdays 4pm-7pm (Fri. until 6pm) for great deals during happy hour. A garden-style patio is furnished with mid-century modern chairs.

MAP 2: 1109 Starkweather Ave., 216/937-1938, www.prosperitysocialclub.com; Mon.-Sat. 4pm-2:30am, Sun. 4pm-1am

Spotted Owl

The best bars in the world are run by the best bartenders in the world, folks who honestly believe that bars are very special and necessary places. Owl owner Will Hollingsworth is one of those bartenders. For years he's been on a single-minded mission to build the world's most perfect neighborhood bar, and this half-buried Tremont spot is the result of those labors. With a masculine "Massachusetts customs house" feel, this is the kind of cave where you can start your night, end your night, and make the kind of memories with friends that last a lifetime.

MAP 2: 710 Jefferson Ave., www.spottedowlbar.com; Mon.-Sat. 6pm-close

BREWERIES
★ Great Lakes Brewing Co.

Housed in the former home of a seed and feed company, this saloon-style pub is equally famous for its world-class beer and the bullet holes in the vintage bar rumored to have come from Eliot Ness's pistol. To go with those wonderful suds is a menu of hearty pub classics like sausage samplers, burgers, fish-and-chips, and pot roast. Start with an order of the barley pretzels, which are made from spent grains leftover from the brewing process. Beer fans will want to visit on Friday or Saturday afternoon when free brewery tours are offered. Great Lakes operates a biodiesel bus (dubbed the Fatty Wagon) that shuttles diners to Indians games for $1 round-trip. If you're looking for a nice outdoor roost, this place has a great (doggie-friendly) sidewalk patio.

MAP 2: 2516 Market Ave., 216/771-4404, www.greatlakesbrewing.com; Mon.-Thurs. 11:30am-10:30pm, Fri.-Sat. 11:30am-11:30pm

Pub Crawl, Anyone?

Clevelanders love themselves a good pub crawl. Maybe it's the gray skies, chilly night air, or the fact that their pro sports teams always find a way to blow it—locals here spend a lot of time in bars.

Cleveland is blessed with old-fashioned neighborhoods, the kind with a Main Street densely populated with pubs, taverns, saloons, and corner bars. One of the best ways to experience the local color is by working one's way down the block, popping into every single drinking establishment along the way. Better yet, just pick a few that look inviting.

A great way to get to know Tremont is from the inside of a bar. People come from all over to soak up this district's café culture, hitting a procession of galleries, bistros, and bars. Start your trek at **Edison's Pub** (2373 Professor Ave., 216/522-0006, www.edisonspub.com), a cozy den serving great imported beers. Friendly folks, knowledgeable bartenders, and decent pizza make this place a must-

crawl. Next up is the **Flying Monkey Pub** (819 Jefferson Ave., 216/861-6659, www.flyingmonkeypub.com), a handsome tavern filled with handcrafted wood furnishings. The only gimmick here is the monkey mascot that pops out of his hidey-hole late at night. Dive-bar fans will swoon over **Hotz Café** (2529 W. 10th St., 216/771-7004), an old-school Cleveland bar that's been around since 1919. One block west is **Prosperity Social Club** (1109 Starkweather Ave., 216/937-1938, www.prosperitysocialclub.com), a retro saloon popular with every demographic. Folks here take seats at the 1930s bar or, on cold nights, around the blazing wood-burning stove.

What's the sense in paying one's tab and heading to an identical bar down the block? Diversity is precisely what makes Ohio City the pinnacle of pub crawl locales. Start at **Crop Bistro** (2537 Loraine Ave., 216/696-CROP, www.cropbistro.com) for cocktails with a view. Set in a former bank lobby, the restaurant very likely is the

Market Garden Brewery

Ohio City's second brewery behind Great Lakes, this generously sized brewpub seats well over 300 guests in multiple dining rooms, at various bars, and on a gem-like beer garden. Upscale pub grub joins an ever-evolving list of world-class suds, cooked up by an award-winning brewmaster. Thanks to a massive stone hearth, the outdoor beer garden is an all-seasons affair.

MAP 2: 1947 W. 25th St., 216/621-4000, www.marketgardenbrewery.com; Mon.-Thurs. 4pm-2am, Fri.-Sat. 11am-2am, Sun. 10am-3pm

Nano Brew

Little sister to Market Garden Brewery, this lively bar features a teensy one-barrel brewhouse that is prominently displayed in the main room. Watch as award-winning brewmaster Andy Tveekrem and his team use the little system as their sudsy playground, brewing small batches of experimental or less commercial varieties. In addition to those, the bar dispenses two dozen of the best local, regional, and national draft craft beers. Nano's backyard beer garden most dramatic in town, and the bartenders seem to work harder because of it. Beer aficionados have the one-two punch of **Great Lakes Brewing Co.** (2516 Market Ave., 216/771-4404, www.greatlakesbrewing.com) and **McNulty's Bier Markt** (1948 W. 25th St., 216/274-1010, www.bier-markt.com). The former brews and serves matchless American suds in a woodsy pub setting. The latter specializes in Belgian and Belgian-style ales on tap and in bottles. Down the block, **ABC the Tavern** (1872 W. 25th St., 216/861-3857, www.abcthetavern.com) is an old-school saloon with new-school craft beer and an old-timey bowling machine. The later it gets, the wilder this place seems to get. If a contemporary Irish bar sounds tempting, pop into **Old Angle** (1848 W. 25th St., 216/681-5643, www.oldangletavern.com). Set in a renovated hardware store, this pub is not your typical shamrock shack.

Lee Road in Cleveland Heights is a pub crawler's dream. Packed into a short 1,500-foot strip is a wide array of welcoming watering holes. Start at the intersection of Cedar and Lee Roads, near the glowing movie marquee, and work your way south. **Parnell's Pub** (2167 Lee Rd., 216/321-3469) is an Irish-themed sports pub with Guinness on tap, darts in back, and a map of Europe that conspicuously omits England. If it's Tuesday or Thursday, cross the street and head to **Lopez** (2196 Lee Rd., 216/932-9000, www.lopezonlee.com), a trendy Southwestern restaurant. Thanks to half-price margaritas and tequila drinks, this place fills up fast. On the same side of the street a little farther south is **Tavern Co.** (2260 Lee Rd., 216/321-6001). This place changes from family-friendly tavern to locals-only bar as the night progresses. Cap off the night at **Brennan's Colony** (2299 Lee Rd., 216/371-1010), a neighborhood institution that has attracted crowds for decades. On warm nights, make sure to check out the secluded courtyard and bar.

is packed on pleasant days and nights, and the pub-style menu is loaded with creative burgers and snacks.

MAP 2: 1859 W. 25th St., 216/621-4000, www.nanobrewcleveland.com; Mon.-Fri. 4:30pm-2am, Sat.-Sun. noon-2am

DANCE CLUBS

Union Station/Bounce

This gender-bending entertainment complex features a restaurant, dance club, and cabaret. Union Station is an at-times raucous video café that dishes up tasty pub grub, camp-filled TV, and wall-to-wall show tunes. Bounce is the lively dance club, where a diverse crowd shakes it on an elevated circular dance floor. In the cabaret, drag queens keep gay and straight audience members in stitches with over-the-top performances that include stand-up comedy, lip-synching melodies, and spot-on impersonations. A fenced-in parking lot makes coming and going a snap (until it fills up, that is).

MAP 2: 2814 Detroit Ave., 216/357-2997, www.bouncecleveland.com; Tues.-Sun. 5pm-2am

The Spirits of Cleveland

Cleveland has always enjoyed a rich beer-brewing and spirits-distilling tradition. Almost from the moment Moses Cleaveland took his first muddy steps onto the banks of the Cuyahoga River, this town has had an insatiable thirst for suds and hooch.

In more recent history, Great Lakes Brewing Co. in Ohio City was the first microbrewery in the state of Ohio. In the years that followed, the brewery's output climbed from 1,000 barrels of beer per year to a staggering 125,000 barrels per year in 2013. It is now one of the largest breweries in the nation, and beer lovers in 13 states have access to its tasty elixirs.

These days, though, Great Lakes is no longer alone, with places like Buckeye Brewing, Indigo Imp, Fat Heads, Brew Kettle, Rocky River Brewing, Market Garden Brewery, Hansa Brewery, Platform, and Nano Brew all getting in on the action. In short, Cleveland is enjoying a craft-brewing renaissance.

When it comes to spirits, Cleveland is home to Portside Distillery, Cleveland Whisky, Seven Brothers Distilling, and Tom's Foolery, a maker of fine apple brandy, bourbon, and rye. Market Garden is expected to begin distilling soon, too.

While visiting all of these breweries and distilleries is commendable, it certainly isn't advisable. Instead, plan a little pub crawl through Ohio City and you'll be able to sample a good many local brews and spirits. In a short two-block stroll, you can hit four breweries, plus get the opportunity to sample many other freshly made local options.

Start at **Hansa** (2701 Lorain Ave., 216/281-3177), where Lasko, Slovenia's oldest beer, is brewed right here in Cleveland. Next, hit **Great Lakes Brewing Co.** (2516 Market Ave.,

216/771-4404, www.greatlakesbrewing.com), the godfather of Ohio craft beer, where Dan and Pat Conway still produce award-winning craft beers. In addition to a full lineup of widely available varieties like Burning River Pale Ale, Commodore Perry IPA, and Edmund Fitzgerald Porter, beer lovers can enjoy seasonals like Christmas Ale, and pub exclusives that are available nowhere else.

Across the street is **Market Garden Brewery** (1947 W. 25th St., 216/621-4000, www.marketgardenbrewery. com), a sprawling restaurant and brewery with a secret weapon: its head brewer is Andy Tveekrem, who left the top post at Dogfish Head to return to Cleveland. (Interestingly enough, his first gig in the brew world was across the street at Great Lakes.) Grab a seat in the open-air beer garden (year-round thanks to a beefy fireplace) and enjoy a refreshing Pearl Street Wheat or hoppy Cluster Fuggle IPA. There are typically a dozen house beers available, including a Cycle Soda, their version of the German *radler* that combines beer and lemonade.

On the other end of the spectrum— in both geography and ideology—is **Nano Brew** (1859 W. 25th St., 216/621-4000, www.nanobrewcleveland.com). At the far end of the strip, this bar gives new meaning to the term "microbrewery." Owned by the same team behind Market Garden, Nano employs a petite one-barrel system, which is prominently displayed in the bar. The small size gives the brewers the freedom to experiment on recipes not designed for mass appeal. Nano also offers one of the best craft draft selections in the neighborhood, so beer lovers can sample great brews from around the region in one jumping joint.

LOUNGES

Lava Lounge

When this low-key lounge opened in 1999, it was known only to the coolest of cats. These days, it is on most people's radar, but in no way has it lost its cool. More of an anti-club, Lava is for folks who enjoy great tunes without the sweaty gyrations and personal advances. Dark, clubby, and candlelit, the small lounge features martinis, a great beer and wine selection, and vinyl-spinning DJs. There is a 2nd-floor bar and lounge, a small back patio, and a surprisingly good menu that is available late into the night.

MAP 2: 1307 Auburn Ave., 216/589-9112, www.coolplacestoeat.com; Mon.-Sat. 4pm-2:30am, Sun. 7pm-2:30am

★ Velvet Tango Room

Long considered Cleveland's most exclusive speakeasy, Velvet Tango Room no longer qualifies as an underground gem. Featured in glossy national magazines, major dailies, and spirits blogs the world over, it's safe to say that the cat is officially out of the bag. No matter: This 1940s-style lounge is as appealing today as it was yesterday. Tucked inside a plain brick wrapper is an anachronistic world of gracious manners, professional service, and upscale furnishings. Labor-intensive classic cocktails are constructed gram by gram on a scale to ensure consistency. Ingredients are all top-flight, including house-made mixers, fresh-squeezed fruit juices, and cut-to-order garnishes. These drinks require time to create, and they cost twice what one might pay elsewhere, but the finished product makes it all worthwhile. Call ahead to reserve a spot in the private back room.

MAP 2: 2095 Columbus Rd., 216/241-8869, www.velvettangoroom.com; Mon.-Fri. 4:30pm-1am, Sat. 6pm-1am

WINE BARS

Market Avenue Wine Bar

Cleveland's oldest wine bar succeeds because it is a comfortable neighborhood joint that just happens to have an amazing wine selection. The understated charm of the place, with its exposed brick walls, ancient wood floors, and shimmering candlelight, only serves to heighten the appeal of the wine selection. The well-chosen 700-bottle list is loaded with obscure gems, evergreen chestnuts, and drinkable deals, and thanks to their encyclopedic knowledge, the staff can tell you a story about each and every one of them. On any given night, some 75 varieties are available by the glass. There is no hard booze here, but you will find a small but wonderful list of craft beers. Market Avenue shares its picturesque cobblestone alley with Ohio City greats Flying Fig and Great Lakes Brewing.

Absorb the charm from Market Avenue Wine Bar's expansive sidewalk patio.

MAP 2: 2521 Market Ave., 216/696-9463, www.marketavenuewinebar.com; Sun.-Fri. 4pm-1am, Sat. 2pm-1am

Detroit Shoreway and Edgewater

Map 3

BARS

★ Happy Dog

Happy Dog is a prime example of what makes Cleveland special. While developers in other cities take pride in knocking down the old to make room for the new, folks here cling to the past with stubborn determination. You just don't find bars like this elsewhere, save for those ironic replicas built to satisfy urban hipsters. Happy Dog's most impressive feature is its august wooden bar, a 45-stool elliptical behemoth that commands a full third of the room. Original wood-fronted coolers chill the beverages; walls are wrapped in genuine wood paneling; shabby (not shabby-chic) linoleum blankets the floor. The menu at this neighborhood tavern is simple, sort of. You have your choice of either a quarter-pound house-recipe hot dog or a veggie sausage, but with 50 toppings from which to choose, like roasted garlic aioli, pimento mac & cheese and house-made chunky peanut butter, the combinations are virtually limitless. On many Fridays, a rambunctious polka happy hour attracts neighborhood residents, hipsters, and anybody else looking to start the weekend on the right two feet.

MAP 3: 5801 Detroit Ave., 216/651-9474, www.happydogcleveland.com; Mon.-Thurs. 4pm-2:30am, Fri.-Sun. 11am-2:30am

★ Stone Mad Irish Pub

It took owner Pete Leneghan three years and untold dollars to construct this new Irish bar in Detroit Shoreway. What took so long? A stickler for quality craftsmanship, Leneghan made certain that every single element in the place was constructed using the finest materials and methods possible. From the hand-laid cobblestone parking lot and oil-rubbed walnut bars to the stained-glass windows and intricately carved ironwork, this stunningly attractive space is loaded with eye candy. The sizable pub boasts two separate barrooms, a casual dining room with sunken bocce court, and an outdoor courtyard featuring stone-slab tables and a towering four-sided fireplace.

MAP 3: 1306 W. 65th St., 216/281-6500; daily 11am-2am

DANCE CLUBS

Twist

You don't have to be gay to enjoy this diverse neighborhood bar. While gay men definitely make up the majority of the crowd, many in the house are simply there for the good times. Located at the epicenter of Cleveland's gay-friendly district, Twist is more laid-back than many other boy bars. A large main room features a central bar, some soft-seating areas, and loft balconies. A sleek subterranean lounge offers a quiet hideaway for guests hoping to escape the upstairs action. On warm nights, two overhead garage doors are raised high, spreading the party out onto the sidewalk. Affordable martinis, upbeat tunes, and welcoming employees have kept Twist popular for more than 20 years.

MAP 3: 11633 Clifton Blvd., 216/221-2333; Mon.-Sat. 11:30am-2:30am, Sun. noon-2:30am

LIVE MUSIC

Brothers Lounge

A multimillion-dollar renovation of this historic blues club has transformed it into a sleek entertainment complex with neighborhood pub, wine bar, and concert hall. Amish oak flooring, mahogany bars, and a high-tech sound system conspire to create an upscale musical experience not found at most clubs. There is a nightly lineup of local, regional, and national acts, and a great house band that plays every Sunday. Open-mic nights and jam sessions allow others to get in on the action. Don't bother eating elsewhere before or after the show—this place also dishes up some mighty fine grub.

MAP 3: 11609 Detroit Ave., 216/226-2767, www.brotherslounge.com; Mon.-Fri. 11am-2:30am, Sat. 3pm-2:30am, Sun. noon-2:30am

University Circle and Little Italy
Map 4

BARS

The Beer Market

If you are into craft beer and always on the hunt for something new, this entry on the Cleveland market might be worth a visit. A massive roster of more than 500 beers from around the globe means that there's always a unique draft or bottle that warrants further inspection. If the lengthy catalog of liquid assets is intimidating, helpful staffers usually can lend a hand. The Beer Market, while adroit in beer service, leaves the cooking and food service to the other restaurants in the neighborhood. Feel free to bring in or order in.

MAP 4: 11490 Euclid Ave., 216/795-2337, www.the-beer-market.com; Mon.-Fri. 3pm-midnight, Sat. noon-2am, Sun. noon-midnight

LIVE MUSIC
★ Barking Spider Tavern

In an alleyway in the middle of the Case Western Reserve University campus, this laid-back venue requires more than an address and a good map to find. Look for Arabica Café, and then listen for the live acoustic music emanating from a converted carriage house. Performing nightly at this small tavern are singer-songwriter, folk, blues, and bluegrass acts. There is never a cover charge, but guests are encouraged to add to the tip jar as it makes its rounds. On balmy nights, the outdoor picnic tables are filled with well-behaved locals sharing pitchers of beer, many with their dogs in tow.

MAP 4: 11310 Juniper Rd., 216/421-2863, www.barkingspidertavern.com; Mon.-Sat. 2pm-1am, Sun. 1pm-midnight

Cleveland Heights and Shaker Heights

Map 5

BARS
Parnell's Pub

You can't pen a St. Patrick's Day story in Cleveland without including this perennially popular Irish pub. As if the perfect pints of Guinness, bona fide Irish ownership, and a real bristle dartboard weren't enough, this is also the place to go to watch World Cup soccer, regardless of the hour when games are televised. Located directly next door to the Cedar Lee Theatre, this pub makes an ideal pre- or post-flick meet-up spot. A simple menu of deep-fried tidbits offers drinkers enough sustenance to endure a long night of liquid recreation.

MAP 5: 2167 Lee Rd., 216/321-3469; Mon.-Sat. 4pm-2am, Sun. 6pm-2am

Winking Lizard Tavern

This local chain of taverns has grown to more than a dozen locations in about 20 years. Following a formula for success that includes great food and drink served in a comfortable, quirky setting, the Lizard can always be counted on to satisfy a crowd. This home-grown restaurant group also deserves props for electing to reuse vacant properties instead of knocking down and building anew. That means each location has its own unique feel (and a live lizard mascot). This setting once housed the famous Turkey Ridge Tavern, so it's nice to see it getting good use. Expect the bar and dining room to be filled with large parties of college students, sports-obsessed professionals, and buffalo-wing connoisseurs. If you plan on sticking around Northeast Ohio, sign up for the Lizard's legendary World Tour. Simply drink all 100 beers on the list in one calendar year and you'll be the proud owner of a, ahem, jacket vest.

MAP 5: 1852 Coventry Rd., 216/397-8380, www.winkinglizard.com; Mon.-Thurs. 11am-midnight, Fri.-Sat. 11am-1am, Sun. 11am-11pm

BREWERIES

Bottlehouse Brewery

This small-scale brewery in Cleveland Heights has developed into a bona fide neighborhood gathering place. In the back, the owners brew up small batches of pale ale, Kolsch and stout, which are dispensed up front along with bottled beer, craft cocktails, and wine. The family-friendly environment features an open room with picnic tables, pinball machines, and a stage that hosts live music. Bring your own food or order off the menu of house-made pub grub. A sidewalk patio gives beer lovers a place to enjoy the nice weather. Like most breweries, Bottlehouse sells and fills growlers to go.

MAP 5: 2050 Lee Rd., 216/214-2120, www.thebottlehousebrewingcompany.com; Tues.-Sat. 2pm-2am, Sun. 2pm-midnight, Mon. 4pm-1am

LIVE MUSIC

Grog Shop

The original Grog Shop smelled foul, sounded worse, and looked as if it had been designed by a blind architect. Still, when the gritty Grog lost its lease and was forced to start anew, musicians and fans cried in their beers. These days, nobody misses that old club too much thanks to bigger, better, and sweeter-sounding digs. But it's a rock-and-roll club, and this joint is by no means posh. Cement floors, concrete columns, and a growing collection of promo photos and band stickers keep this place real. Owner Kathy Simkoff has a knack for spotting talent early on, and the rock, grunge, and garage bands that break here often move on to greatness.

MAP 5: 2785 Euclid Heights Blvd., 216/321-5588, www.grogshop.gs; hours vary depending on show

Nighttown

Reminiscent of the old-school jazz clubs one used to be able to find in Manhattan, Nighttown is a one-stop shop for killer music, great grub, and sparkling conversation. Named by *Down Beat* magazine as one of the 100 Great Jazz Clubs in the world, this joint snags the biggest names in music as they travel between Chicago and New York. Cleveland Heights is known for its diverse and progressive

NIGHTLIFE CLEVELAND HEIGHTS AND SHAKER HEIGHTS

Smoking Ban

On election day in 2006, Ohio voters passed Issue 5, putting into effect a sweeping indoor smoking ban that extends to all public places and places of employment. This ban applies to all bars, restaurants, and bowling alleys. It may seem strange to walk into a dimly lit corner tavern and not be greeted by a cloud of cigarette smoke, but that's the new reality in Cleveland. If you prefer a cigarette in one hand, many bars have patios that are used simultaneously by puffers and non-puffers alike. Short of that, sidewalks, rooftops, and even fire escapes appear to work just fine.

populace, and this club acts as the neighborhood's living room. An eclectic crowd gathers for dinner shows, cocktails at the bar, or to enjoy a warm night on the roomy patio. Seating for shows is on a first-come, first-served basis, and it's always wise to reserve your ticket in advance.

MAP 5: 12387 Cedar Rd., 216/795-0550, www.nighttowncleveland.com; Mon.-Thurs. 11:30am-midnight, Fri.-Sat. 11:30am-1am, Sun. 10am-midnight

LOUNGES
★ Katz Club

There are other cocktail lounges in Cleveland, but none does such a remarkable job of transporting its guests to another place and time. Step inside the Katz Club and you'll feel as though you've stumbled onto the bar car of the *Twentieth Century Limited* bound for Grand Central. Magnificently reworked from front to back and top to bottom, the 1952 Mountain View Diner is now an elegant cocoon that completely shields inhabitants from the realities outside. The concise menu features classic drinks like Sazeracs, old-fashioneds, and Ramos gin fizzes—all expertly crafted. Martinis and manhattans, in a glorious nod to wilder times, are sold by the pitcher. Snack on fresh-shucked oysters, fine cheeses, or mini latkes with lox and crème fraîche.

1975 Lee Rd., 216/932-3333, www.thekatzclubdiner.com; Wed.-Sat. 8am-1am

WINE BARS
La Cave du Vin

This subterranean cave satisfies both grape and grain lovers thanks to a stellar beer and wine selection. Who needs natural light when you've got a well-selected 500-bottle wine list to brighten the spirits? This dimly lit grotto is frequented by of-age college kids, young professionals on dates, and wine-loving service-industry types who know a good thing when they trip over it. For beer fans, much of the fun comes from plucking one's own from a convenience store-style cooler filled with 200 varieties of fine ale (sorry, Budweiser fans). A small but pleasant menu of wine-friendly snacks is offered to satisfy light appetites.

MAP 5: 2785 Euclid Heights Blvd., 216/932-6411, www.lacaveduvin.com; Mon. 6pm-2am, Tues.-Sat. 5pm-2am, Sun. 7pm-2am

Lakewood   Map 6

BARS
Around the Corner Saloon

As the crowds at this meet-and-greet tavern continued to grow, so too did the bar's footprint. What started out as a one-room corner saloon has ballooned into a multidimensional hot spot with the largest and best drinking patio in Lakewood, graced with a full bar, flat-screen TVs, and amusing Midwestern yard games so there's rarely a good reason to head inside (snow included, thanks to protection and heating). Come on Monday for two-for-one hamburgers or any weekday 3pm-7pm for $5.50 pitchers. A profusion of single guys and girls makes this place hook-up central.

MAP 6: 18616 Detroit Ave., 216/521-4413, www.atccafe.com; Mon.-Thurs. 3pm-2am, Fri.-Sat. 11am-2am, Sun. 9:30am-2am

Five O'Clock Lounge

Like any great neighborhood dive, the Five offers cheap beer, uncomfortable seats, and well-spun rock and roll. Come around happy hour and the crowd is strictly gin-blossomed regulars, noses firmly ensconced in beer mugs. But like the hands on an analog timepiece, the atmosphere here is always shifting. On weekend nights, the better-dressed set scuttles into large round booths, the padding flattened by 70 years of abuse, to while away the night gripping and sipping PBR tallboys. DJs spin a tasty mix of rock, punk, and new wave, and the occasional live band hits the small stage.

MAP 6: 11904 Detroit Ave., 216/521-4906; Mon.-Sat. 2pm-2:30am, Sun. 8pm-2:30am

LIVE MUSIC
Winchester Tavern and Concert Club

The Winchester is a special place. Formerly a bowling alley, the neighborhood tavern and ballroom were designed to emphasize comfort, value, and musical enjoyment. There are seats enough for all who want them, and the bands sound amazing. If you enjoy screeching metal, mosh pits, and beer-soaked fans, the Winchester might not be for you. But if great old acts like Leon Russell, Howard Jones, the Fixx, and the English Beat, served up in a sweet old room, sound like your thing, this place will feel like nirvana. Musicians

Wine Bars Around Town

Cleveland might have a reputation as a beer lover's burg, but that doesn't mean there aren't amazing places for oenophiles to settle in for a glass or bottle of vino. From dark and cozy wood-walled hideaways to airy and contemporary bistros, the range and selection of local wine bars should satisfy all but the biggest cork snobs.

Out in Lakewood, one of the newest spots to join the booming food and drink scene in that neighborhood is **Humble Wine Bar** (15400 Detroit Ave., 216/767-5977, www.humblewinebar.com). Run by the same great folks behind Deagan's Kitchen, Humble puts the wine before all else. The light, airy, and contemporary space was designed to make the place less intimidating to wine newbies. Select from dozens of wines by the glass, including always-fresh kegged varieties, plus 100 more by the bottle.

In addition to a phenomenal cheese and cured meat selection, Humble boasts a prominently displayed wood stone pizza oven that turns out thin and crisp pies.

At last count, **Press Wine Bar** (2221 Professor Ave., 216/566-9463, www.presswinebar.com) in Tremont featured eight wines on tap, giving it one of the largest selections of kegged wine in the city. While no less expensive than wine poured from the bottle, keg wine is considerably more dynamic in flavor and freshness. An even longer wine-by-the-glass and bottle list and an all-Ohio draft beer list have made this one of the busiest bars in the neighborhood. Wine-friendly, chef-driven fare like flatbreads, charcuterie, ale-steamed mussels, and deviled eggs will keep you fueled up in great fashion.

Market Avenue Wine Bar (2521 Market Ave., 216/696-9463, www.mar-

seek this place out because of its size, sound, and appreciative audience. Check the website frequently to see which legends of jazz, rock, rockabilly, alt-country, and bluegrass will be gracing the stage. **MAP 6:** 12112 Madison Ave., 216/226-5681, www.thewinchester.net; hours vary depending on show

WINE BARS

Humble Wine Bar

Run by the same great folks behind Deagan's Kitchen, this Lakewood wine bar puts guests at ease thanks to its easy, breezy contemporary vibe. Gleaming white subway tile is set against warm woods and distressed tin ceilings. On warm days, the entire front of the bar opens up to create a seamless inside/outside space. Select from dozens of wines by the glass, including always-fresh wine on tap, as well as 100 more by the bottle. A small but excellent craft beer list is also available. In addition to a phenomenal cheese and cured meat selection, Humble turns out thin, crisp Neapolitan-style pizzas from its prominently displayed wood stone pizza oven. **MAP 6:** 15400 Detroit Ave., 216/767-5977, www.humblewinebar.com; Tues.-Fri. 4pm-midnight, Sat.-Sun. 11am-midnight

ketavenuewinebar.com) in Ohio City was Cleveland's first wine bar, though when it opened it was across the street where Great Lakes Brewing now has a gift shop. Though the address has changed, little else about the place has—and that's great news. Dark and woodsy, with a decidedly old-world feel, the wine bar is a great alternative to its new, louder, and almost exclusively beer-focused neighbors. A monstrous wine list, a cute sidewalk patio, and serviceable snacks make this joint a fan fave.

D'Vine Wine Bar (836 W. St. Clair Ave., 216/241-8463, www.dvinewinebar.com) enjoys a prime location in the heart of downtown's Warehouse District. As such, it attracts sharp-dressed neighbors and the thirsty after-work crowd. The sharp old structure boasts exposed brick walls, lofty warehouse ceilings, and a sprawling sidewalk patio perfect

for people-watching. D'Vine's wine menu is loaded with well-conceived flights, with tastes of four related. Grouped by grape, region, or style, the flights offer a tasty tutorial on grapes.

Toast (1365 W. 65th St., 216/862-8974, http://toastcleveland.com) is a charming wine bar shoehorned into a 100-year-old storefront in Detroit Shoreway. Six long years in the making, the farmhouse-chic bistro employs homespun elements like mason jars, tea-towel napkins, and rustic wood tables. Staffers don plaid shirts. The wine list is loaded with uncommon gems from the Old World and New, and prices are more than reasonable. Nearly a dozen reds and a dozen whites are available by the glass, with another 30 or so by the bottle. Toast's farm-to-table menu offers seasonal snacks, small plates, and larger meals.

Greater Cleveland   Map 7

BREWERIES
Fat Head's Brewery & Saloon

Longtime award-winning brewer Matt Cole and partners opened up this West Side brewpub, which is loosely affiliated with a pub of the same name in Pittsburgh. Along the way, he built up a thriving microbrewery that was doing so well the company had to build a separate production facility to keep up. Come here to sample brewery-fresh beers like Head Hunter IPA, one of the highest rated IPAs in the nation, Oompa Loompa Chocolate Stout, and Oktoberfest Lager. While you're here, order up a legendary "Headwich," a sandwich that, yes, is roughly the size of your head.

MAP 7: 24581 Lorain Rd., N. Olmsted, 440/801-1001, www.fatheadscleveland.com; Mon.-Thurs. 11am-11pm, Fri.-Sat. 11am-midnight, Sun. 11am-10pm

CASINOS

Hard Rock Rocksino Northfield

For more than 50 years there has been live harness racing at this track about a half-hour south of downtown, where "trotters" pulled two-wheeled "sulkies" around a half-mile course. In late 2013, following a massive renovation, Northfield Park reopened as Hard Rock Rocksino Northfield. In addition to a Hard Rock Cafe, 2,000-seat live music club, and 350-seat comedy club, the complex features 2,300 video lottery terminals. Similar to slot machines and video poker terminals, the games of chance attract gamers of all levels. Because of the way the new gambling legislation was written, only Horseshoe Casino downtown has real table games, slot machines, and poker rooms.

MAP 7: 10705 Northfield Rd., Northfield, 330/467-4101, www.northfieldpark.com; daily 24 hours

Thistledown Racino

This mile-long track about 20 minutes southeast of Cleveland is closing in on 85 years of live thoroughbred racing. In 2013, following an $88 million renovation that saw the arrival of 1,100 video lottery terminals (VLTs), this racetrack officially became a "racino." While you won't find craps, blackjack, or Texas Hold 'Em, you will find a whole host of slot machine-like games that pay out real money. Updated bars and eateries make the entire experience nicer for those betting on the ponies or the machines. There is live racing Friday-Monday May-October, with simulcasted races every day of the week.

MAP 7: 21501 Emery Rd., N. Randall, 216/662-8600, www.thistledown.com; daily 24 hours; admission and parking free

LIVE MUSIC

★ Beachland Ballroom

What once served as a Croatian social hall is now one of the coolest places to catch live music in Ohio. The popular concert venue is comprised of an intimate tavern and a large ballroom, both original to the 1950 structure. Attracted by an eclectic roster of local, regional, and national acts, not to mention the unique setting, live music fans travel here from as far away as Columbus, Pittsburgh, and Detroit. Grab a bite to eat before shows in the tavern, or come back for the amazing weekend brunch. While you're in there, check out the vintage 80-record Rock-Ola jukebox that *Blender* magazine labeled in 2008 as the best in the country.

MAP 7: 15711 Waterloo Rd., Cleveland, 216/383-1124, www.beachlandballroom. com; hours vary depending on show

Arts and Culture

Downtown 128

Ohio City and Tremont 138

Detroit Shoreway
  and Edgewater 139

University Circle and Little Italy . . .142

Cleveland Heights
  and Shaker Heights 145

Lakewood 147

Greater Cleveland 148

Various Venues 149

Look for ★ to find
recommended arts and culture.

HIGHLIGHTS

★ **Best Comedy Club:** Nick Kostis is a brilliant judge of up-and-coming comedic talent, and his club, **Hilarities 4th Street Theater,** is the place to catch it. This upscale 425-seat comedy club attracts the very best touring comics, and the theater is as nice as they come (page 128).

★ **Shakespeare, With a Twist:** The newly renovated historic Hanna Theatre, home to **Great Lakes Theater Festival,** offers a diversity of seating options that range from traditional theater chairs to bar stools (page 137).

★ **Best Reuse of a Trolley Power Station:** In 2013, nationally known art collectors Fred and Laura Bidwell opened the 8,000-square-foot **Transformer Station,** a jewel box of a museum in Ohio City, adding a world-class contemporary art outlet on the west side of town (page 138).

★ **Finest Experimental Theater:** Since the early 1980s, **Cleveland Public Theatre** has produced innovative and adventurous original theater. In fact, the success of this very outfit has in large part triggered the revival of the entire Detroit Shoreway neighborhood (page 140).

★ **Where Art and Architecture Meet:** Designed by London-based architect Farshid Moussavi, the new **Museum of Contemporary Art** in University Circle has forever changed the look of its neighborhood. Brawny, angular, and reflective, the structure is already a local icon (page 144).

★ **Best Damn Band in the Land:** It isn't just locals who fawn all over the **Cleveland Orchestra;** critics in London, Salzburg, and Vienna have hailed the symphony as one of the very best in the world. Check them out at either Severance Hall or Blossom Music Center to hear what the world is talking about (page 145).

C leveland is not a mini New York City. Cleveland-ers do not expect to wake up one morning to learn that their town has become the new Second City. But when one considers the abundance of arts and cultural pursuits available to residents and visi-tors of Northeast Ohio, it is clear that nobody here has cause to complain.

Talent trickles down. And rainmakers like the Cleveland Orchestra, Cleveland Museum of Art, Cleveland Institute of Music, and Cleveland Institute of Art help to create an absolute embar-rassment of riches that even towns like New York and Chicago can't begrudge. With its five stunning vaudeville-era theaters, plus scores of smaller stages, PlayhouseSquare is the second-larg-est performing-arts center in the country. (Sorry, Chicago.) The Cleveland Orchestra has been labeled by many critics as the finest symphony in the world. (Don't feel bad, New York.) The Museum of Contemporary Art now hosts the finest emerging artists in a new multimillion-dollar structure designed by London-based architect Farshid Moussavi, her first U.S. project.

In arts-fueled neighborhoods like Tremont, Little Italy, Detroit Shoreway, and Ohio City, funky new galleries seem to pop up like concertgoers during a standing ovation. Adventurous art fans flock to these lively urban districts for regularly scheduled art walks and gallery hops. These same neighborhoods fill up the social calendar with seasonal block parties, food festivals, and home tours.

Cleveland may not be the richest town in terms of wealth, but when it comes to things that really matter, the town is one of the most prosperous in the Midwest.

Downtown

Map 1

CINEMA

OMNIMAX Theater

That big brown sphere on Lake Erie's shore is not a large egg waiting to hatch; it's the exterior of the Great Lakes Science Center's OMNIMAX Theater. While IMAX films are praised for their scale and richness, OMNIMAX takes the experience to another plane. A six-story wraparound screen surrounds the viewer, creating an extraordinarily immersive experience. The movies shown here are largely the science-museum type, focusing more on education than sheer enjoyment. Also, most are shown only in the middle of the day, making them difficult to schedule around. Still, taking a virtual ride in an F-15 is pretty sweet, especially tilted back at 30 degrees.

MAP 1: 601 Erieside Ave., 216/694-2000, www.glsc.org

Tower City Cinemas

Downtown's only multiplex, this 11-screen theater shows popular first-run fare. While you won't likely catch the latest Woody Allen drama here, you will find slapstick, horror, and superhero megahits. Every March, Tower City Cinemas is the site of the wonderful Cleveland International Film Fest, an 11-day, 140-film extravaganza. Like Cedar Lee Theatre and Shaker Square Cinemas, this theater hosts Bargain Mondays, with $6 tickets and a free fountain drink with any popcorn purchase. Free parking (up to four hours) is available at Tower City Center's parking garage on Huron Road. Present your parking voucher to the box office for validation when you purchase your movie tickets.

MAP 1: Tower City Center, 230 W. Huron Rd., 216/621-1374, www. clevelandcinemas.com

COMEDY CLUBS

★ Hilarities 4th Street Theater

This is the premier comedy club in Cleveland, featuring the best talent in the best setting. Located inside Pickwick & Frolic, a $5 million entertainment complex on East 4th Street, Hilarities attracts every big name in the biz. Owner Nick Kostis has been running comedy clubs in this town since the 1980s, and he has earned a reputation as a brilliant judge of up-and-coming talent. Shows take place in a sharp 425-seat theater, the backdrop of which is a brick

wall left over from the old Euclid Opera House. Before the show, hit
the rustic American restaurant upstairs. After, visit Kevin's Martini
Bar for cocktails.

MAP 1: 2035 E. 4th St., 216/736-4242, www.pickwickandfrolic.com; showtimes
Wed.-Thurs. 8pm, Fri. 7:30pm and 10pm, Sat. 7pm and 9:30pm, Sun. 7pm

The Improv

With venues in about 20 U.S. cities, The Improv is a well-known
comedy club and restaurant. Top touring comedians, rising-star talent, and local favorites confront audiences most nights of the week.
Those who want to secure the best seats in the house must make
dinner reservations, but the wiser choice may be to dine elsewhere
and take your chances on seating. Like every other comedy club
in the world, The Improv charges a little more than they probably
should for drinks.

MAP 1: 1148 Main Ave., 216/696-4677, www.clevelandimprov.com; showtimes
Thurs. 7:30pm, Fri.-Sat. 7:30pm and 10:15pm, Sun. 7pm

CONCERT VENUES

Cleveland Agora

The Cleveland Agora has a rich history that dates all the way back to
the 1960s. The live-music club has been an important force not only
in the Cleveland music scene, but also the national one, breaking
bands too numerous to list. All the great performers have graced
its stages, from Bruce Springsteen and Bob Marley to the Clash and
U2. The music hall is comprised of one large and one small room,
with space for 1,800 and 500 fans respectively. Seating is general
admission for many shows, so get there early if you want to secure
a specific spot. Renovations are underway at the club, including
new LED lighting and two additional box offices. Tickets for shows
can be obtained through **Ticketmaster** (www.ticketmaster.com), or
at the box office Monday-Friday 10am-5pm, later on show nights.

MAP 1: 5000 Euclid Ave., 216/881-2221, www.clevelandagora.com

House of Blues

One of a dozen or so HOBs sprinkled across the United States, the
Cleveland venue was built in 2004. With its considerable might, the
company snags most of the biggest acts that sweep through town.
The large main hall accommodates approximately 1,200 guests,
while the more intimate Cambridge Room, with its modest 120-seat
capacity (350 reception capacity), is better suited to smaller attractions. The compound boasts numerous bars, a full-service restaurant, gift shop, and the exclusive members-only Foundation Room.
Sundays at the House are all about the popular Gospel Brunch,
which features a mile-long buffet and rousing live gospel performance. Tickets for shows can be obtained by phone, online through

Ticketmaster (www.ticketmaster.com), or by stopping by the box office between 10am and 6pm.

MAP 1: 308 Euclid Ave., 216/523-2583, www.hob.com/cleveland

Jacobs Pavilion at Nautica

Pretty as a picture, this sharp urban amphitheater is Jacobs Pavilion at Nautica on the West Bank of the Flats, adjacent to the Nautica entertainment complex, and boasts great views of the river, the bridges, and the passing ships. Largely covered, the roughly 5,000 seats are spread among general-admission floor seats, bleachers, and standing-room areas. Approximately 10 shows per summer come here, ranging from megastars like Dylan to jam bands like Widespread Panic. This snug venue also is ideal for local legends like First Light and Michael Stanley.

MAP 1: 2014 Sycamore St., 440/247-2722, www.livenation.com

Quicken Loans Arena

Known simply as the "Q," Quicken Loans Arena is the permanent home of the Cleveland Cavaliers and Lake Erie Monsters and the temporary home of touring musicians, professional wrestlers, and Olympic gymnasts. Since 2000, the Q has also been the site of the Mid-American Conference (MAC) Men's & Women's Championship Tournaments. Located in the Gateway District, the 20,000-seat arena sits on the southwestern edge of downtown, directly adjacent to Progressive Field. In nasty weather it's good to know that both the Q and Progressive Field can be reached from Tower City and the RTA via protected walkways.

MAP 1: One Center Court, 216/420-2000, www.theqarena.com

Wolstein Center

Cleveland's other main arena is actually part of the Cleveland State University campus. This 14,000-seat venue is home to the CSU Vikings, men's and women's Division I basketball teams. It is also used year-round for major performers like Carrie Underwood, and touring spectacles like the Wiggles. Tickets are available through **Ticketmaster** (www.ticketmaster.com) or at the box office (Prospect Ave. entrance) Monday-Friday, 10am-6pm.

MAP 1: 2000 Prospect Ave., 216/687/9292, www.csuohio.edu/wolsteincenter

GALLERIES
Art Gallery at Cleveland State University

Though this great exhibition space is located on the ground floor of the CSU Art Building, the exhibits are not limited to student shows. In addition to the annual juried student art show, these three galleries present five or six shows per year that explore contemporary political and social themes. The thematically curated exhibits cover

clockwise from top left: Severance Hall in University Circle, home of the Cleveland Orchestra; projector room at Cleveland Institute of Art Cinematheque, University Circle; Capitol Theatre in Gordon Square, Detroit Shoreway

a broad range of mediums and styles from local, national, and international artists. They are recognized by critics as some of the most visually stimulating in town.

MAP 1: 1307 Euclid Ave., 216/687-2103, www.csuohio.edu/artgallery; Mon.-Tues. by appointment, Wed.-Thurs. 10am-5pm, Fri. 10am-8pm, Sat. noon-8pm

Bonfoey Gallery

The Bonfoey has rightfully earned a reputation as one of Cleveland's largest and finest art galleries. Established in 1893, it is certainly the most venerable. Located near PlayhouseSquare, the large space is filled with original 19th-century paintings, signed lithographs, photographs, pastels, glass, and sculpture. Rotating exhibits throughout the year bring in fresh merchandise. The shop also maintains a great selection of original art priced under $500, making it a must-stop on any home-design outing. Come here, too, for appraisals, art restoration, framing, packing, shipping, and installation.

MAP 1: 1710 Euclid Ave., 216/621-0178, www.bonfoey.com; Mon.-Thurs. 8:30am-5:30pm, Fri. 8:30am-5pm, Sat. 9am-noon

Convivium33 Gallery

Set in the nave of a former Roman Catholic church, Convivium33 Gallery at Josaphat Arts Hall is a unique and beautiful space. The architecturally stunning building provides an appropriate backdrop for the works of established local artists. Like the church before it, the gallery and arts center serves to unite the community by presenting meaningful exhibits, hosting important events, and offering studio space to artists. Exhibits are often kicked off with popular Dinner with Art events, where guests feast on gourmet food alongside the artist and his or her work. The gallery keeps regular hours during exhibits; call or check the website for details.

MAP 1: 1433 E. 33rd St., 216/881-7828, www.josaphatartshall.com; by appt.

Front Room Gallery

On the 3rd floor of an industrial-park building complex, Front Room is not front and center in terms of visibility. But this artist-run gallery is ahead of the pack when it comes to finding talented emerging artists on the rise. Seemingly without boundary when it comes to geography and medium, the co-op exhibits work from local, regional, and national artists in disciplines as varied as collage, painting, video, and drawing on found paper. Shows can be solo runs or multi-artist affairs, but they tend to be fresh, current, relevant, and trendy.

MAP 1: 3615 Superior Ave. 4203A, 216/534-6059, www.frontroomcleveland.com; hours vary

SPACES Gallery

Visitors to this 30-year-old artist-run gallery will feast on wildly creative experimental and noncommercial art exhibits from local, regional, and national artists. Through approximately four major shows a year, and spanning every conceivable medium, this leader in contemporary art showcases the talent of emerging and mid-career artists. Much of the art attempts to tackle the most important issues of the day, including political, social, and cultural themes. All events are free and open to the public, and the gallery's lively opening-night parties are some of the best in town. The spaces at SPACES are often rented out for private events, so it is always wise to phone before stopping by.

MAP 1: 2220 Superior Viaduct, 216/621-2314, www.spacesgallery.org; Tues.-Thurs. and Sat. 11am-5:30pm, Fri. 11am-7pm, Sun. 1pm-5pm

Wooltex Gallery

One of the newer and better visual art galleries in the city, Wooltex is roomy, contemporary, and easy to find. Set in an old warehouse that has been converted to live-work space for artists, the gallery never has to search far for talent. The large space serves as a backdrop for high-quality painting, sculpture, video, and installations from largely local artists. Exhibits come and go every month and half or so. Like many other galleries in town, this one is used for private events, so it is always smart to call before visiting.

MAP 1: Tower Press Bldg., 1900 Superior Ave., 216/241-4069, www. thewooltexgallery.com; Mon.-Sat. 11am-3pm

Zygote Press

In its formative stage, this gallery was merely a small printmaking studio for its owners. In little more than a decade, it has developed into the most important nonprofit fine-art printmaking collaborative in the region. Located in an old warehouse in the artistically blossoming Quadrangle District, Zygote Press exhibits a full panoply of printed works of art, including letterpress, waterless lithography, etchings, relief, screen printing, and photo-crossover. Their exhibits feature the work of local, national, and international artists and printmakers.

MAP 1: 1410 E. 30th St., 216/621-2900, www.zygotepress.org; Wed. noon-4pm and 6pm-9:30pm, Sat. noon-4pm, and by appt.

MUSEUMS

Cleveland Police Historical Society and Museum

Cleveland was a city gripped by fear in the mid-1930s as a result of the Kingsbury Run Murders, better known as the "Torso Murders." Over the course of four years beginning in 1934, 13 people were brutally murdered, all of them decapitated, most while they were still breathing. Because most of these victims were unidentified transients, plaster casts, or "death masks," were made of the faces for public viewing in hopes of putting a name with the deceased. Four of these chilling masks are on display at this law enforcement museum, which chronicles the history of the Cleveland Division of Police from its inception in 1866. Roughly 4,000 square feet of space contain thousands of photos, scrapbooks, old police blotters, and artifacts. Learn about Safety Director Eliot Ness and the achievements of the Cleveland Police Department during a guided tour, available by appointment. Stop by the Cop Shop to snag your very own CPD T-shirt or a book about the gruesome Torso Murders.

MAP 1: 1300 Ontario St., 216/623-5055, www.clevelandpolicemuseum.org; Mon.-Fri. 10am-4pm; free

Greater Cleveland Aquarium

In January of 2012, Cleveland added another top regional attraction with the opening of this splashy new aquarium, the first of its kind in the state. Built into the bones of the historic Powerhouse building on the west bank of the Flats, the 70,000-square-foot structure boasts 42 tanks filled with one million gallons of water. The Ohio Lakes and Rivers exhibit educates visitors on local freshwater species that are native to Ohio, including tortoises, catfish, and other local residents. The shark exhibit teems with toothy sharks, eels, and other saltwater sealife. A lengthy 145-foot underwater "Sea Tube" offers an impressive experience, with visitors passing through a tank with more than 5,000 fish. Roughly 300,000 visitors check out the aquarium per year and designs are already in the works to expand the facility. Plan to spend about an hour and a half here.

MAP 1: 2000 Sycamore St., 216/862-8803, www.greaterclevelandaquarium. com; Mon.-Sun. 10am-5pm, closed Thanksgiving and Christmas; $19.95 adult, $13.95 child, $17.95 senior

Money Museum at Federal Reserve Bank

How did we buy things before we had money? Who makes money? Why is a dollar worth a dollar? Answers to these and other cash conundrums are answered most days of the week at this fortress of funds. Designed to teach students and, perhaps, spendthrift adults about what money is, where it comes from, and how to manage it, this museum doesn't exactly sound like a thrill ride, but interactive exhibits help deliver the message in a fun way. For instance, a display on ancient currency shows us that stones, shells, and even cows were once traded as cash (imagine sticking a cow in your purse!). One of a dozen Federal Reserve Banks, the Cleveland office is worth a visit solely to gander at the 12-story Medici-style palazzo designed by the noted firm of Walker & Weeks.

MAP 1: 1455 E. 6th St., 216/579-2000, www.clevelandfed.org; Mon.-Thurs. 10am-2pm, closed bank holidays; free

ARTS AND CULTURE
DOWNTOWN

In 2012, the Rock and Roll Hall of Fame and Museum opened a separate library and archives, the most comprehensive repository of materials relating to the history of rock and roll, including music-related correspondence, concert videos, and financial records. On the campus of Cuyahoga Community College, approximately two miles from the museum, the library gives music scholars access to more than 200 archival collections, including the personal papers of performers, disc jockeys, photographers, journalists, critics, historians, poster artists, collectors, and fans. The collections contain books, sound recordings, video recordings, and individual items like personal letters penned by Aretha Franklin and Madonna, handwritten lyrics by Jimi Hendrix, and rare concert recordings from CBGB in the 1970s. A Rock Hall library card is free (with a valid photo ID) at the library.

MAP 1: 2809 Woodland Ave., 216/515-1956, www.library.rockhall.com; Tues.-Fri. 9am-5pm, Sat. 11am-5pm; free

PERFORMING ARTS

Cleveland Play House

If you're looking for big names and bright lights, this is the theater company for you. Established in 1915, the Play House is one of America's longest-running professional theater companies. Producing a full lineup of popular and dramatic plays from well-established playwrights, the company routinely enjoys packed houses. A recent move to the renovated Allen Theatre complex in PlayhouseSquare has managed to boost already great attendance and sales figures while improving quality and creativity. The popular production of *A Christmas Story,* based on the motion picture based in Cleveland, is an annual tradition that runs from late November through late December.

MAP 1: 1407 Euclid Ave., 216/241-6000, www.clevelandplayhouse.com

DANCECleveland

Dedicated to bringing the very best of modern and contemporary dance to town, DANCECleveland presents the works of nationally and internationally recognized troupes. Performances are held in Akron and in PlayhouseSquare and feature the best touring companies out there, including those of BalletX, Paul Taylor Dance Company, and Cedar Lake Contemporary Ballet. Approximately four to six bookings take place each season, which runs from fall through spring. Tickets are available at the State Theatre box office or by phone.

MAP 1: PlayhouseSquare, 216/241-6000, www.dancecleveland.org

ARTS AND CULTURE

DOWNTOWN

Arts Renaissance on the Cuyahoga

Thanks to progressive-minded industrialists of the last century, Cleveland boasts a rich arts landscape dotted with the likes of the **Cleveland Museum of Art,** the theaters of PlayhouseSquare, and the **Cleveland Orchestra.** But recent changes have boosted to new heights both the stature and reach of the Cleveland arts scene.

The Cleveland Museum of Art has always enjoyed a reputation as one of the premier repositories of fine art, but the museum has gotten bigger, better, and more user-friendly. A multiyear, $350-million renovation and expansion of the museum have left it in the best shape of its 100-year-old life. Begun in 2005, the project celebrated its official grand opening in late 2013.

Both the original 1916 beaux arts building and Marcel Breuer's 1971 addition underwent complete renovations. Two marble and granite wings have been added on. And a massive 39,000-square-foot atrium with a soaring glass ceiling now connects all the spaces. Today's footprint gives the museum 30 percent more gallery space to show off its permanent collection.

To better plan your visit, the museum introduced Gallery One, the largest multi-touch screen in the United States. This 40-foot interactive wall allows visitors to view 3,500 objects from the museum's collection and learn more about their literal and figurative place in the museum. Add to that new fine and casual dining and you see why the museum is operating at a whole new level.

The same can be said for the **Museum of Contemporary Art,** which, given its humble beginnings, has had an even more dramatic rise. For too long, the museum lived in a plain and odd-fitting space far removed from the epicenter of Cleveland culture, University Circle.

That all changed in 2012 when the museum unveiled to the world its stunning new home. Designed by London-based architect Farshid Moussavi, the $27-million, 34,000-square-foot jaw-dropper is garnering serious buzz in the art and architecture sphere. The museum also serves as the cornerstone for the new and growing Uptown neighborhood just steps from the campus of Case Western Reserve University.

In Ohio City, Fred and Laura Ruth Bidwell have restored and expanded an old brick power substation into one of the newest and most talked about contemporary art spaces on the West Side. For half the year, the **Transformer Station,** as it's called, serves as home for the Bidwells' own impressive collection, while the other half of the year it features contemporary art programming from the Cleveland Museum of Art.

These are in addition to a $63.5 million renovation of the **Cleveland Institute of Art** and an ever-growing collection of smaller yet important galleries like **SPACES, Screw Factory, Convivium33,** and **78th Street Studios** that are breathing new life into old neighborhoods.

The Cleveland Institute of Art $63 million expansion is underway with expected completion in September 2015. In addition to updating the institute's McCullough Center with a 79,000-square-foot, four-story addition, the plan also includes a new art gallery and a 300-seat auditorium for the area's nonprofit theater, the Cinematheque.

These are exciting times for the Great Lakes Theater Festival, a company that has been around since the early 1960s and has seen talent the likes of Tom Hanks, Piper Laurie, Hal Holbrook, and Olympia Dukakis. A high-tech overhaul of the historic Hanna Theatre has given this company a striking new home. The reconfigured theater is now an intimate 550-seat space featuring a flexible thrust stage that brings the action right into the laps of audience members. The futuristic stage is appropriate for a company renowned for reimagining classic productions. Unique, too, is the diversity of seating options, ranging from traditional theater chairs and private boxes to more casual lounge and bar seating. Plays are performed in rotating repertory, with shows alternating every few nights. Scheduled performances run from September through June and feature works by Shakespeare, Chekhov, and Sondheim, to name but a few. The Charles Dickens holiday classic *A Christmas Carol* is performed from late November through Christmas.

MAP 1: 1501 Euclid Ave., 216/241-6000, www.greatlakestheater.org; adult tickets range $10-70, are available by phone

PlayhouseSquare

Comprised of five 1920s-era theaters plus numerous smaller performing spaces, PlayhouseSquare is the nation's largest performing-arts center outside of New York City. More than 1,000 shows take place every year, including the best of Broadway, musical acts, opera, literary presentations, and comedy shows. In the 1970s, the five grand vaudeville-era theaters—the Palace, State, Ohio, Allen, and Hanna—were literally moments from the business end of a wrecking ball. Public outcry and strong community involvement not only saved each and every one of them, they eventually brought about the largest theater restoration project of this kind. Saving the best for last, the Hanna received a $20 million makeover in 2008 to transform it into the high-tech home of the Great Lakes Theater Festival, the company that gave Tom Hanks his first big break. PlayhouseSquare is more than just a collection of performance spaces; it is the creative backbone of a district that includes hotels, bars, restaurants, offices, and the home of Cleveland's public radio and television stations. Tickets are available by phone, online, or at the box office in the lobby of the State Theatre, which is open daily 11am-6pm. Smart Seats are available for some performances at a heavily discounted price—ask for them if you don't care where you sit. A nearby parking garage is located at the corner East 15th St. and Chester Avenue. Free 90-minute tours are typically offered the first Saturday of the month, leaving the State Theatre lobby every 15 minutes 10am-11:30am

MAP 1: Euclid Ave., 216/241-6000, www.playhousesquare.org

ARTS AND CULTURE
DOWNTOWN

Ohio City and Tremont Map 2

GALLERIES
Paul Duda Gallery

When you fall in love with this town as deeply as have the locals, come to Paul Duda. This sleek Tremont gallery sells remarkable art photographs of ruggedly handsome Cleveland. Printed in dreamy giclée, an archival ink-jet printing process, images of the Guardians of Transportation, Lake Erie shoreline, and Terminal Tower are mantel-worthy mementos of a fine visit. Vibrant and full-color shots of the skyline, PlayhouseSquare, and Progressive Field will serve as permanent reminders of fun days and nights gone by.

MAP 2: 2342 Professor Ave., 216/589-5788, www.pauldudagallery.com; Thurs.-Fri. 7pm-9pm, second Fri. of the month 6pm-11pm, Sat. noon-9pm

★ Transformer Station

In 2013, nationally known art collectors Fred and Laura Bidwell opened this 8,000-square-foot jewel box of a museum in a building that once housed a trolley car power station, hence the name. The angular, contemporary space features soaring ceilings, clerestory windows, and a beefy and original metal hoist in the center of the room. The exhibits are programmed jointly by the Bidwells and the Cleveland Museum of Art, which long sought a West Side space to show contemporary art. Much of the work—local, regional, national, and international—comes from the Bidwells' own storied collection.

MAP 2: 1460 W. 29th St., 216/938-5429, www.transformerstation.org; Wed., Fri.-Sat. noon-5pm, Thurs. noon-8pm; free

PERFORMING ARTS
Convergence-Continuum

Shattering the theater's fourth wall since 2002, this oddball company is anything but traditional. But with success comes a little more convention—a good thing considering that until recently, the company rarely announced its roster of plays ahead of time. Its stage, called the Liminis, is set in a former garage on the fringes of trendy Tremont and accommodates only 50. Many of the ambitious productions, which run spring through late fall, are performed for the first time in Ohio.

MAP 2: 2438 Scranton Rd., 216/687-0074, www.convergence-continuum.org

Near West Theatre

It's amazing what a few footlights can do for a person. Since 1978, this community theater has changed the lives of more than 15,000

Tremont ArtWalk

Tremont, the Soho of Cleveland, is loaded with artist studios, galleries, boutiques, and bistros. The only problem is, many of the galleries close early or are open only by appointment. That's why the second Friday of each month is a popular day to hit this diverse, walkable neighborhood. Running 6pm-10pm, the **Tremont**

ArtWalk (www.tremontartwalk.org) is an opportunity to hit dozens of locations in a single visit. Numerous shops and galleries open their doors and stay open until late. Better still, many offer free wine and hors d'oeuvres with which to ply customers. If you didn't get enough to eat, stop by any of the trendy restaurants for a proper meal.

children, teens, and adults, many from poverty-stricken families and neighborhoods. By committing to a schedule that is intense, difficult, and ultimately rewarding, participants come out on the other end more confident and with a stronger sense of self. But don't let the grassroots cause delude you; the productions here are as good as any amateur youth theater around. Good news is around the bend, too, as a new 300-seat theater in the emerging Gordon Square Arts District is expected to open in fall 2014.

MAP 2: 3606 Bridge Ave., 216/961-9750, www.nearwesttheatre.org

Detroit Shoreway and Edgewater

Map 3

CINEMA
Capitol Theatre

In 2009, the Capitol Theatre showed its first film in 24 years, following a $7.5 million renovation. The restoration of the 1920s-era vaudeville and silent-movie house was just one aspect of a larger redevelopment of the Gordon Square Arts District, which is home to arts anchor Cleveland Public Theatre and soon Near West Theatre. Now featuring three smaller screens, and run by Cleveland Cinemas, the popular venue shows a mix of popular new releases and indie-minded film fest fodder.

MAP 3: 1390 W. 65th St., 216/651-7295, www.clevelandcinemas.com

GALLERIES
1point618 Gallery

This architecturally stunning storefront in the Gordon Square Arts District contains a 1st-floor art gallery and the offices of an award-winning architect. The gallery, 1point618, holds approximately six to eight shows per year, focusing on contemporary art from regional, national, and international talents. The symbiosis between art and space here serves to somehow elevate both, creating an atmosphere teeming with artistic tension. Stop here before or after dinner at fabulous Spice Kitchen or the fun-spirited Happy Dog.

MAP 3: 6421 Detroit Ave., 216/281-1618, www.1point618gallery.com; during openings and by appt.

Studios at West 78th Street

Just west of the Gordon Square Arts District, this out-of-the-way complex of redbrick buildings has for years attracted artistic types. It was home to *Alternative Press* magazine, as well as a busy recording studio. Now it is developing into an impressive warren of some 40 art galleries, artist studios, and art-services businesses. **Kenneth Paul Lesko Gallery** (216/631-6719, www.kennethpaullesko.com) is a sharp contemporary space that shows fine art, sculpture, and photography. **Kokoon Arts Gallery** (216/832-8212, www.kokoonarts.com) shows the work of "Cleveland School" artists Frank Nelson, Paul Travis, and William Sommer, as well as contemporary American paintings, sculpture, and arresting 2-D computer graphics prints. **Tregoning & Co. (216/281-8626, www.tregoningandco.com)** displays important works of art from notable and established artists. **HEDGE Gallery (216/650-4201)** shows contemporary art in all mediums with a focus on local, emerging talent. The popular and growing "Third Friday" events attract thousands.

MAP 3: Lake Avenue btwn. W. 78th and W. 80th Sts., www.78thstreetstudios.com; hours vary

PERFORMING ARTS

Blank Canvas Theatre

Established in 2011, Blank Canvas Theatre bills itself as a "Theatre For the People." In the artsy 78th Street Studios, the explosive upstart's inaugural season included a sold-out run of the Ohio premiere of *The Texas Chainsaw Musical* and a sold-out run of the Cleveland premiere of *Debbie Does Dallas, The Musical.* The diverse schedule includes dramas, musicals, even sketch comedy shows, and other wildcards geared to make theater fans out of even the most theater-averse guests in the house.

MAP 3: 1305 W. 78th St., Ste. 211, 440/941-0458, www.blankcanvastheatre.com

★ Cleveland Public Theatre

There may be no more important stage in Ohio for experiencing innovative and adventurous original theater. Anchoring the burgeoning Gordon Square Arts District, this public theater opened in 1981 and offers so much more than just modern drama. CPT's groundbreaking performances entertain and inspire an entire community,

Spared from the Wrecking Ball: Cleveland's Great Theaters

Like all cities, Cleveland has blown it by demolishing buildings with great architectural merit. Only in hindsight do civic leaders and city residents typically grasp the value of what's been lost in the name of progress. If not for the work of a few visionary preservationists in the 1970s, Cleveland's PlayhouseSquare would have vanished like so many other architectural gems.

PlayhouseSquare's five opulent theaters opened between 1921 and 1922. Built in the classical style, the Ohio, State, Palace, Allen, and Hanna Theaters boasted expanses of marble, lush hardwoods, hand-painted murals, and extravagant lobbies. For decades these houses entertained pleasure seekers with a variety of vaudeville acts, cinema, and dramatic performances.

In the late 1960s, downtown suffered from a disastrous cocktail of economic distress, suburban flight, and racial disquiet. Shops closed, people fled, and the theaters went dark. Vandals, thieves, and inattention so damaged the shuttered theaters that demolition was all but assured.

Led by Ray Shepardson, a nonprofit called Playhouse Square Association campaigned to save the theaters. Thanks to public and private partnerships, money was raised to not only save the buildings from destruction, but also to begin repairing and restoring them. By the late 1990s, four of the five theaters had been restored to their former glory. In 2008, the last of the five reopened as the stunning new home of the **Great Lakes Theater Festival.** These days, every year more than a million visitors see performances at these venues and scores of smaller performance spaces concentrated in the two-block zone, and the economic overflow can be observed at area restaurants, shops, and hotels.

Walk through PlayhouseSquare on a brisk fall night and it's easy to see what Shepardson worked so hard to preserve. After all, without the arts, where is the beauty of life?

and, in the process, propel it to a better place. From fall through early summer, the calendar is loaded with theatrical gems, many of which are Ohio and regional premieres. On top of the regular roster, special events might include a festival of 10-minute plays, readings of new works by emerging playwrights, and the popular Big Box series of new resident-produced work. Tickets may be purchased by phone or by stopping by the box office Wednesday-Sunday.

MAP 3: 6415 Detroit Ave., 216/631-2727, www.cptonline.org

ARTS AND CULTURE

DETROIT SHOREWAY AND EDGEWATER

University Circle and Little Italy

Map 4

CINEMA

Cleveland Institute of Art Cinematheque

If it weren't for the Cinematheque, obsessive Cleveland film fans would never lay eyes upon some of the finest foreign, classic, and independent movies of our time—or any other, for that matter. As the name suggests, this 600-seat paean to alternative film is on the campus of the CIA, in the Gund Building to be exact. Utilizing deluxe 35-mm projectors, approximately 250 different feature films are shown per year, mostly Thursday through Saturday nights. By September 2015, Cinematheque is expected to be firmly rooted in its new 300-seat theater within CIA's new McCullough Center on Euclid Avenue.

MAP 4: 11141 East Blvd., 216/421-7450, www.cia.edu/cinematheque; most films $9

GALLERIES

Murray Hill School House Galleries

Once a neighborhood schoolhouse, this warren of redbrick buildings now houses upscale apartments, condos, offices, and galleries. The numerous and ever-evolving roster of shops ranges from tiny incubator-sized studios to full-on retail and exhibition spaces. **Juma Gallery (216/721-3773, www.jumagallery.com)** displays handcrafted functional art, plus paintings, ceramics, glass. and jewelry. Beautiful and stirring figurative paintings are available at **Tricia Kaman Studio and Gallery** (216/559-6478, www.triciakaman. com). **Sobella Paper Boutique** (216/229-1333, www.so-bella.com) sells stationery, greeting cards, and custom invitations. These and the other galleries and boutiques in the schoolhouse keep varied hours. Find more information at **Little Italy, Cleveland** (www.little-italycleveland.com).

MAP 4: 2026 Murray Hill Rd., www.littleitalycleveland.com; hours vary

Reinberger Galleries

The Reinberger Galleries are housed in the Gund Building at the Cleveland Institute of Art, which is among the country's top art and design colleges. Billed as the largest college art gallery in Ohio, this 5,000-square-foot exhibition space often features the work of established artist graduates. In addition to displaying the graduate theses of BFA students, and the popular CIA Faculty Exhibition, the galleries present thousands of art and design objects, plus film, video, animation, and art installations. Visitors can look forward to approximately eight shows per year, including the often whimsical and always brash Student Independent Exhibition.

MAP 4: 11141 East Blvd., 216/421-7407, www.cia.edu; summer Mon.-Fri. 10am-5pm, fall-spring Mon.-Thurs. and Sat. 10am-5pm, Fri. 10am-9pm

MUSEUMS

Children's Museum of Cleveland

More than just a rainy-day activity, this hands-on museum will keep the little ones cheerfully engaged come rain or shine. Exhibits endeavor to teach children about science, weather, and Earth's natural water cycle. A tableau walks young urban pioneers through basic skills of the grocery store, bank, and public transportation system. Children under the age of four will enjoy just horsing around in the Big Red Barn-inspired playhouse. Visit Elf Corner, the museum's gift shop, for fun educational toys, books, and games.

MAP 4: 10730 Euclid Ave., 216/791-7114, www.clevelandchildrensmuseum.org; daily 10am-4:45pm; $7

Cleveland Museum of Natural History

History is on display at this fine institute of scientific education. From the moment folks cross the threshold, they are immersed in a world of past, present, and future wonder. Both permanent and visiting exhibits seek to shed light on the mysteries and truths at work in our universe. A mesmerizing Foucault pendulum demonstrates in dramatic, albeit slow, fashion the Earth's rotation on its axis. A 270-pound bob swings on a 32-foot wire, covering six inches of real estate per hour. Fallen dominos mark the passage of time and space. As one might expect of a natural history museum, there are bones, and lots of them. *Australopithecus afarensis,* also known as "Lucy," is our three-million-year-old aunt. A cast of the original skeleton is on display. Dino fans will also discover a tyrannosaur, stegosaur, and "Happy," one of the most complete mounted sauropods on display in the world. A domed planetarium features the amazing SkyScan DigitalSky projector, which can show the positions of more than 5,000 stars, nebulae, and galaxies. Outside the building's walls, visitors can explore a two-acre wildlife center that highlights native Ohio flora and fauna, including bobcats and bald eagles, river otters, and owls. The Blue Planet café serves healthy and delicious lunches every day. Before you leave, stop by the Museum Store to pick your very own "Evolution Happens" T-shirt.

MAP 4: 1 Wade Oval Dr., 800/317-9155, www.cmnh.org; Mon.-Tues., Thurs., and Sat. 10am-5pm, Wed. 10am-10pm, Sun. noon-5pm, closed major holidays; $12 adult, $10 child, student, and senior, planetarium tickets $4 with general admission

In 2013, MOCA completed a monumental move to a new home in University Circle, the epicenter of art in Cleveland. Designed by London-based architect Farshid Moussavi, and built at a cost of $27 million, the gem-like structure has forever changed the look of its new neighborhood. Now the noncollecting museum has more room than ever to showcase risk-taking and provocative visual art from emerging and established artists. Stunning installations, sculptures, paintings, photography, and video are just some of the works that routinely make layovers here. Lectures, readings, films, and performances round out the arts-education programming.

MAP 4: 11400 Euclid Ave., 216/421-8671, www.mocacleveland.org; Tues.-Sun. 11am-6pm, Thurs. until 9pm, closed major holidays; $8 adult, $5 student and senior

Western Reserve Historical Society

Chronicling the history of the Western Reserve, this University Circle institution is comprised of a cultural history museum, an auto and aviation museum, and a research library. In addition to high-profile touring exhibits, the museum holds a bounty of local artifacts, treasuries, and tales from the area once known as the Western Reserve. The Chisholm Halle Costume Collection is one of the top-ranked costume collections in the nation, with some 30,000 garments on rotating display. The Crawford Auto-Aviation Museum displays historically significant automobiles, aircraft, bicycles, motorcycles, and spacecraft, paying special attention to the significant contribution of Northeast Ohio companies. Approximately 150 unique vintage models are on hand. As the principal repository for documents relating to Western Reserve history, the library at WRHS is a popular and important research facility. The fee to park in the museum lot is $5, and $8 during special events, so consider taking public transport.

MAP 4: 10825 East Blvd., 216/721-5722, www.wrhs.org; Tues.-Sat. 10am-5pm, Sun. noon-5pm; $10 adult, $5 child, $9 senior

PERFORMING ARTS

Cleveland Institute of Music

Gifted classical musicians from all over the globe come to Cleveland to study at this world-class conservatory. Those of us who can only dream about such talent flock to this school's matchless concert series. Students, faculty (including many Cleveland Orchestra members), and visiting luminaries perform year-round on the stages of this University Circle institution. Concerts range from solo guitar recitals to full-on string quartets. These days, concertgoers have it better than ever thanks to the stunning Mixon Hall, a 235-seat rectangular glass recital hall. Most concerts are free, and seating for

free concerts is generally on a first-come, first-served basis, though
some passes may be reserved one week ahead of time by phone.
Cameras and recording devices are prohibited.

MAP 4: 11021 East Blvd., 216/791-5000, www.cim.edu; free unless otherwise noted

★ Cleveland Orchestra

There is little contention that the Cleveland Orchestra, under the
leadership of music director Franz Welser-Möst, is one of the finest
orchestras playing anywhere today. Audiences and critics from
New York to Vienna routinely praise the band as sheer musical triumph.
From late September through May, the orchestra performs
at breathtaking Severance Hall. From early July through Labor Day,
the orchestra performs weekend concerts at their summer home,
Blossom Music Center. On a fine summer night, there is nothing
better than spreading out a blanket on the lawn at Blossom to enjoy
some classical music. For decades, the Cleveland Orchestra has
performed a free concert in downtown's Public Square in honor of
Independence Day. The annual event takes place the week of the
Fourth of July, attracts 40,000 people or more, and is capped off
with a rousing performance of Tchaikovsky's 1812 Overture followed
by a fireworks display. Get there early, bring a picnic dinner,
and enjoy one of Cleveland's finest moments.

MAP 4: 11001 Euclid Ave., 216/231-1111, www.clevelandorchestra.com

Cleveland Heights
and Shaker Heights   Map 5

CINEMA
Cedar Lee Theatre

The Cedar Lee shows the very best in first-run independent film.
If it played well at Sundance, chances are good you'll see it on the
marquee of this Cleveland Heights landmark. But it isn't only esoteric
head-scratchers on the schedule; Oscar-worthy Hollywood
fare is also screened here. Cult-movie fans have been coming in
to catch the midnight showing of *The Rocky Horror Picture Show*
since 1998, when the theater began screening it. At the better-than-average
concession stands, you'll find fresh pastries, wraps, coffee
drinks, herbal tea, imported beers, and wine—and popcorn,
of course. Some of the six theaters are roomier than others. Like
Tower City Cinemas and Shaker Square Cinemas, this theater hosts
Bargain Mondays, with $6 tickets and a free fountain drink with
any popcorn purchase.

MAP 5: 2163 Lee Rd., 216/321-5411, www.clevelandcinemas.com

This renovated art deco movie house now features six state-of-the-art theaters that screen major Hollywood releases plus some independent and foreign fare. Located on Shaker Square, the theater is near numerous bars and restaurants, making a dinner-date a breeze. In addition to the typical sugary and crunchy provisions, the concession stand also sells pastries, beer, and wine. Like Tower City Cinemas and Cedar Lee Theatre, this theater hosts Bargain Mondays, with $6 tickets and a free fountain drink with any popcorn purchase.

MAP 5: 13116 Shaker Sq., 216/921-9342, www.clevelandcinemas.com

CONCERT VENUES
Evans Amphitheater

This gem of an urban amphitheater is nestled into a wooded Cleveland Heights park. Wholly invisible to drivers and passersby, the concert venue always delights first-timers (though this is not to say that it doesn't tickle second- and third-timers as well). While small—1,200 under cover, 1,200 on the lawn—Evans Amphitheater draws top-talent artists who crave more intimate settings. The venue is a favorite of singer-songwriters like Lyle Lovett, k.d. lang, and Bruce Hornsby, who seem to make stops here most years. Concerts run from about the middle of June through August. Specials like $2 Tuesdays and free jazz in the afternoon offer amazing shows at amazing prices. The smaller 300-seat Alma Theater is the site of musicals, cabarets, and local acts. Pack a blanket and a picnic, or buy snacks at the concession stand. Though you can't bring in alcohol, you can buy beer and wine inside. Tickets are available through **Ticketmaster** (www.ticketmaster.com), but to save on fees hit the Cain Park box office. This park is also the site of the popular **Cain Park Arts Festival** in July.

MAP 5: Superior at Lee, 216/371-3000, www.cainpark.com

GALLERIES
Heights Arts Gallery

Small but mighty describes this East Side gallery. Run by Heights Arts, a nonprofit community arts organization, the exhibition space focuses largely on the work of local artists. And when it comes to creative talent, residents of Cleveland Heights tend to be unfairly gifted. The gallery puts on five exhibitions a year plus a popular seasonal event: "A Holiday Store" features affordable art gifts by local artists only. Next to the Cedar Lee Theatre, the gallery is a popular pre- and post-film stopover.

MAP 5: 2175 Lee Rd., 216/371-3457, www.heightsarts.org; Mon.-Wed. 10am-5pm, Thurs.-Fri. 10am-9:30pm

Dobama Theatre

For more than 50 years, Dobama Theatre has been a Cleveland Heights performing arts institution, attracting people to its various stages. In 2009, Dobama finally landed a more permanent space at the renovated and expanded Cleveland Heights Public Library. Dobama's mission is to highlight contemporary plays by established and emerging playwrights. Each season Dobama produces five or six plays, the bulk of which are Cleveland, U.S., or world premieres. For a half century, the company has cultivated a reputation for being professional, innovative, and progressive.

MAP 5: 2340 Lee Rd., 216/932-3396, www.dobama.org

Lakewood   Map 6

COMEDY CLUBS

Something Dada

This fast-paced improvisational comedy troupe formed in 1994, making it the longest-running improv show in town. These days, the team operates out of Lakewood's Beck Center for the Arts. Fueled by audience suggestions, however lame they might be, Dada manages to manufacture a roller-coaster ride of laughs. Shows are never the same experience twice.

MAP 6: 17801 Detroit Ave., 216/696-4242, www.somethingdada.com; showtimes Sat. 8pm, average cost $12

GALLERIES

Screw Factory Artists

This rambling brick warehouse, commonly referred to as the Screw Factory, houses dozens of live/work studios and teaching spaces. The building houses more than 30 artist studios and businesses, including those of ceramicists, enamel artists, painters, glassworkers, painters, and mixed-media artists. Hours are kept individually by artist and studio, but exploration is encouraged. Official events are held the first Saturday in May and November, and the popular Last Minute Market, which literally attracts thousands, is held on the third Saturday of December.

MAP 6: 13000 Athens Ave., 216/521-0088, www.screwfactoryartists.com; various and random hours

PERFORMING ARTS

Beck Center for the Arts

In addition to its impressive arts-education programming, the Beck produces a full season of professional theater, including comedies, musicals, and contemporary drama. Roughly eight performances per year are presented from fall through late spring on one of two stages. Recent productions include ambitious takes on *She Loves Me* and *33 Variations.* An equally impressive roster of youth theater is performed by Beck drama students. Make sure you leave a little extra time to wander through the Beck's art gallery, which often is filled with enthralling exhibits.

MAP 6: 17801 Detroit Ave., 216/521-2540, www.beckcenter.org

Greater Cleveland   Map 7

CONCERT VENUES
Blossom Music Center

Built in the late 1960s as the summer home of the Cleveland Orchestra, this amphitheater sees a full range of live-music action from spring until fall. Tucked into Cuyahoga Valley National Park, its setting is one of dense forests, leafy hillsides, and wide-open skies. On a warm summer evening, there is no greater joy than tossing down a blanket and enjoying a picnic under the stars while the orchestra or your favorite band performs. Then again, that night can sour quickly if the clouds darken and the rain falls. Be prepared with tarps, rain gear, and an extra set of dry clothes for the long drive home. Or do what many regulars do: Spring for seats in the covered pavilion as insurance. Traffic in and out of the park can be brutal, so leave plenty of extra travel time.

MAP 7: 1145 W. Steels Corners Rd., Cuyahoga Falls, 888/225-6776, www. clevelandorchestra.com

MUSEUMS
Polka Hall of Fame Museum

Fans of the "happiest sound around" will want to make the short journey to Euclid to visit this museum dedicated to all things polka. Cleveland-style polka has its roots in Slovenian folk music, which was popularized by local musicians such as Frankie Yankovic and Johnny Vadnal. Inside you'll find memorabilia and artifacts from past and present polka stars, including accordions, stage outfits, and photographs. Learn about not just the Cleveland style, but also Chicago, Czech, Slovak, and German. Prominent placement is also devoted to the winners of the annual Polka Hall of Fame awards.

MAP 7: 605 E. 222nd St., Euclid, 216/261-3263, www.clevelandstyle.com; Tues.-Fri. noon-5pm, Sat. 10am-3pm; free

Smart Seats

Looking for an affordable way to catch a show in PlayhouseSquare? Many performances set aside a number of discount tickets that can be purchased ahead of time. These Smart Seats run just $10 apiece, roughly the cost of going to a movie. Simply surf over to www.playhousesquare.org and search for a show that interests you. If the play, concert, or dance listing has the Smart Seats logo under the ticket information, that means there are cheap seats available. You likely will be seated in the rear of the balcony, but at a savings of up to 80 percent off the primo seats, there is little to complain about.

PERFORMING ARTS
Karamu House

Formerly the Playhouse Settlement, Karamu is the nation's oldest African American cultural arts institution. The famous interracial theater company was the site of many Langston Hughes premieres. Under the artistic direction of Terrence Spivey, Karamu is once again electrifying and edifying new generations of theatergoers. While there is no shortage of knee-slapping comedies and musicals, many of the works are serious and thought-provoking examinations of race and culture. The regular schedule runs fall through spring. Tickets are available by phone, online, or at the theater's box office.

MAP 7: 2355 E. 89th St., Cleveland, 216/795-7077, www.karamu.com; $20

Various Venues

PERFORMING ARTS
Apollo's Fire

The *Boston Globe* called Apollo's Fire one of America's leading baroque orchestras. When they are not touring the nation or recording, this professional ensemble moves listeners at home through its calendar of performances. Concerts are held fall through spring at various locations in and around Cleveland and Akron, primarily in large churches. For a bite-size portion of baroque, check the schedule for one of the popular matinee concerts, 45-minute programs geared to young children and antsy adults. Tickets for these and other programs can be purchased by phone or online.

VARIOUS VENUES: 216/320-0012, www.apollosfire.org

GroundWorks Dancetheater

GroundWorks breaks ground by taking risk. The small but professional company's repertory of contemporary dance includes pieces choreographed by artistic director David Shimotakahara as well as works created by various guest choreographers. Performances are scattered about town throughout the year, with appearances at E.J. Thomas Hall in Akron, Cain Park in Cleveland Heights, Lincoln Park in Tremont, and the Akron-Summit County Public Library.

VARIOUS VENUES: 216/691-3180, www.notsoobvious.com; $15-25

Verb Ballets

This contemporary dance company maintains a deep repertory of pieces, many choreographed by former artistic director Hernando Cortez. A self-described curator of expressive movement, Verb "discovers, collects, interprets, and stages choreography that matters." Performances are scattered about town throughout the year, from PlayhouseSquare and Cain Park to Ohio City's Breen Center for the Performing Arts and points south in Akron.

VARIOUS VENUES: 216/397-3757, www.verbballets.org; $10-30

Sports and Activities

Downtown.......................154

Ohio City and Tremont...........162

Detroit Shoreway
and Edgewater 165

University Circle and Little Italy...166

Cleveland Heights
and Shaker Heights.............167

Lakewood.......................168

Greater Cleveland 170

Various Locations.................176

HIGHLIGHTS

★ **Best Way to Get to Know Cleveland:** Longtime guide and gregarious host Karl C. Johnson makes a living showing curious visitors the ins and outs of C-Town. His enlightening and entertaining **Cleveland Tours**—on foot, by car, or aboard Segways—cover all facets of local history, architecture, politics, and sports (page 154).

★ **Best Place to Catch a Foul Ball:** Jacob's Field is now Progressive Field, but this urban ballpark is still tops with local and traveling baseball fans. Home of the Cleveland Indians, **Progressive Field** is consistently ranked among the best places in the major league to watch a game (page 157).

★ **Best Old-School Bowling Alley:** They just don't make bowling alleys like **Dickey's Lanes** anymore, and that's a shame. What this no-frills eight-laner lacks in modern amenities (like electronic scoring), it makes up for in cheap shoes, games, and cocktails (page 163).

★ **Sweetest Spot for Quick Summer Getaway:** Named after the whiskey distilleries that dotted this small peninsula, **Whiskey Island** is adored for its lakeside locale, sand volleyball courts, and casual eatery Sunset Grille. Live music just adds to the island vibe (page 164).

★ **World's Greatest Outdoor Jogging Track:** The **Ohio & Erie Canal Towpath Trail** is an 84-mile gem that winds its way through the beautiful Cuyahoga Valley National Park. With a mostly smooth limestone surface, the path attracts millions of walkers, joggers, and cyclists each year (page 170).

★ **Where to Ride When the Snow Flies:** Mountain bikers flock to **Ray's MTB Indoor Park** because it truly is one-of-a-kind. Inside a 100,000-square-foot warehouse, this remarkably wild indoor bike park is almost as good as the real thing (page 171).

Cleveland sports fans will always envy the teams of Boston, Denver, and Pittsburgh, despite what they say in crowded bars. However, few U.S. cities can support more than one professional sports team, let alone three (five if you count Arena Football and American Hockey League). Add to that a thirst for minor-league outfits and you begin to understand why the courts, diamonds, and fields around town are all active, modern, and centrally located.

Locals don't just watch others enjoy an active lifestyle; the city sits on a Great Lake, is threaded throughout with major rivers and streams, and boasts an "Emerald Necklace" of leafy parks and reservations. Just down the road is a 33,000-acre playground called Cuyahoga Valley National Park. If you are an outdoors enthusiast, Northeast Ohio isn't such a bad place to set up a tent.

More locals are getting around on two wheels than ever before, triggering increased bike lanes, massive group rides, two-wheeled tour groups, and the construction of a new outdoor velodrome.

Visitors are often surprised to learn that Cleveland has beaches—you know, those sandy stretches of coastline perfect for lazing away a warm summer day. In fact, a number of very fine ones dot the North Coast from Toledo to the Pennsylvania border. The ones closest to Cleveland are now stewarded by the good people at the Cleveland Metroparks, meaning they've never been better maintained. All have lifeguards on duty during summer, and most of the parks feature party shelters, picnic areas, grills, playgrounds, and shower facilities.

BOWLING
The Corner Alley

Knocking down pins in rented shoes hasn't looked this cool since Jeff "The Dude" Lebowski did it in his pajamas. This gleaming hipster bowling emporium is right downtown in the hopping East 4th Street area. Combining 16 lanes, computerized scoring, over-size video screens, and comfy lounge areas, this alley is a far cry from the smoke pits found in two-bit shopping centers. The lanes are within a larger complex that features a restaurant, martini bar, and pool tables, and bowlers are waited on hand and foot. Weekend rates can seem steep, but divided by four or six bowlers, it becomes more palatable.

MAP 1: 402 Euclid Ave., 216/298-4070, www.thecorneralley.com; Mon.-Thurs. 11:30am-midnight, Fri.-Sat. 11:30am-2am, Sun. noon-midnight; $35/h on weekends

BICYCLING
Bike Rentals and Sales
Cleveland Bike Rack

The Bike Rack is the city's first full-service bike parking and com-muter center. Located downtown, the center offers secure bicycle parking, individual shower and changing facilities, lockers, bicycle rentals, and minor bicycle repairs. Both adult and children's bikes (cruisers) are available to rent by the hour ($5 for two hours), half day ($15) or full day ($25). Also available are bicycle route maps, brochures discussing points of interest, and event information.

MAP 1: 2148 E. 4th St., 216/771-7120, www.clevelandbikerack.com; Mon.-Fri. 6:30am-7pm, Sat.-Sun. 10am-6pm

GUIDED AND WALKING TOURS
★ Cleveland Tours

For inquisitive groups large and small, longtime guide Karl C. Johnson answers a simple question: What's in Cleveland? Once this curious, gregarious host is through with them, participants will know plenty about Cleveland's rich history, architecture, politics, even sports. Johnson offers tours on foot, by car or van, and even aboard two-wheeled Segways. Two separate three-mile, two-hour walking tours are available: one of downtown, the other through Ohio City. The downtown tour covers notable spots like the Arcade, Cuyahoga County Courthouse, Terminal Tower, and Old Stone Church in deeply intimate fashion. In Ohio City, Johnson not only guides folks past grand Victorian homes, he tells tales about occu-pants past and present. The tour works its way through the West

Side Market, past old brewers' mansions, and along church-dotted lanes. Narrated and escorted Segway tours last one hour and require a brief instructional introduction.

MAP 1: 230 Huron Rd., Ste. 100.31, 216/394-0095, www.clevelandsegwaytours. com; by appt.; $60 up to four people, $15 additional person

Goodtime III

If it weren't for the *Goodtime III,* tens of thousands of locals and visitors would never get to view Cleveland from the water, which many assert is her best side. In the 50-plus years that the *Goodtime* has motored these waterways, that view has only improved. Passengers still journey up the Cuyahoga River, past the remnants of the city's mighty industrial past. But the landscape is cleaner, brighter, and more varied than ever before, with attractive new condos, promising development, and actual wildlife. Shutterbugs are afforded some of the very best vantage points from which to capture Cleveland's skyline and its matchless assortment of bridges. The sheer romance of the setting inspires a number of couples to wed aboard this 1,000-passenger ferry each summer. Various tours are offered from Memorial Day through the end of September, including narrated lake and river cruises, lunch and dinner-dance cruises, and the ever-popular rush-hour party cruise. Prices range from $20 for the adults-only dance cruise up to $50 for the dinner cruise. Reservations are always recommended.

MAP 1: E. 9th St. Pier, 216/861-5110, www.goodtimeIII.com; $20-50

Trolley Tours of Cleveland

The clang, clang, clang of Lolly the Trolley is a familiar sound for locals, who for years have observed these bright red open-air carriages shuttle the curious about town. Despite the hokeyness factor, these trolleys provide a wonderful perspective on a city that often obscures its assets, with seasoned guides weaving historical, architectural, cultural, and political tidbits into a memorable excursion. General one- and two-hour tours hit the major sights of North Coast Harbor, Warehouse District, Ohio City, PlayhouseSquare, Millionaire's Row, and University Circle, while numerous specialty tours focus on Little Italy and Lake View Cemetery, ethnic markets of Cleveland, unique churches about town, and the trail of Eliot Ness. Tours, which leave from the Powerhouse at Nautica entertainment complex in the Flats, take place year-round, but occur more frequently from Memorial Day to Labor Day. It is required that all customers reserve a spot by calling in advance. Also, children under five are not permitted on the two-hour tour.

MAP 1: 2000 Sycamore St., 216/771-4484, www.lollytrolley.com; one-hour tour $11 adult, $8 child, $10 senior; two-hour tour $17 adult, $12 child, $16 senior

GYMS

YMCA of Greater Cleveland

The YMCA operates about a dozen branches in Northeast Ohio, including a lovely and convenient location just 20 blocks east of Public Square. In return for a membership, visitors have access to individual fitness assessments, certified trainers, even massage therapists. There are free weights, cardio machines, racquetball and basketball courts, and a swimming pool. Add to that roster of amenities a hot tub, sauna, and steam room, and you'll wonder why folks bother to spring for pricey health clubs. Members have the right to use facilities at every other Greater Cleveland YMCA.

MAP 1: 2200 Prospect Ave., 216/344-0095, www.clevelandymca.org; Mon.-Fri. 5:30am-9pm, Sat. 7am-5pm, Sun. 10am-5pm; adults $55 per month, plus onetime $100 registration fee

PARKS

Cleveland Public Library Eastman Reading Garden

This semi-secluded urban park has the feeling of a secret garden. Wedged between the broad shoulders of the Main Library and the Louis Stokes Wing, the space is buffered from wind, noise, and prying eyes. Yet open to the busy main streets on either end, the garden is still connected to the city around it. Beyond a pair of heavy bronze gates, the lovely open-air park unfolds gradually. Leafy trees and sturdy sculpture provide the bones, while a graceful fountain, designed by the Ohio-born artist behind Washington, DC's Vietnam Veterans Memorial, cascades gently in the background. On warm summer days, the garden is a favorite lunch spot for office workers itching to escape their desks.

MAP 1: 325 Superior Ave. NE, 216/623-2800, www.cpl.org

ROWING AND KAYAKING

Western Reserve Rowing Association

Adults, college students, and high school athletes come here to learn how to row from some of the best talent around. Classes range from basic fundamentals programs to pro-level competitive rowing, and they take place on the Cuyahoga River. Fun and social summer and fall rowing leagues are very popular for both casual and serious scullers. The WRRA also fields teams at many regional and national regattas, offering truly competitive scullers an opportunity to test themselves against a larger field. Learn-to-row classes cost $45 and take place throughout spring, summer, and fall. Check the website for dates, fees, and information.

MAP 1: 1003 British St., www.westernreserverowing.com

Chief Wahoo: The Mascot Controversy

Go to the season's opening baseball game at Progressive Field and you'll likely encounter some angry folks. No, these are not fans grumbling over the price of a cold beer; they are Native Americans protesting the use of Chief Wahoo, the Cleveland Indians mascot. There is little doubt that this caricature, with its red skin, toothy grin, and feathery headgear, is an offensive stereotype to many people. Like that of the Washington Redskins mascot, the image stirs up a robust discussion about race, free speech, and the slippery issue of intent. Team history would have people believe that the character was meant to honor the first American Indian in pro baseball, not to disparage any particular group. Regardless, teams have so much tradition wrapped up in a name, logo, and merchandise that change is difficult to accomplish.

SPECTATOR SPORTS
Baseball
★ Progressive Field

If there is anything better than spending a glorious summer afternoon at the ballpark, don't tell the 40,000 or so happy souls at Progressive Field. Consistently selected as one of the best places in the major league to watch a game, this park, which is home to the **Cleveland Indians,** will make a baseball fan out of just about anybody. When it was unveiled in 1994, this park was known as Jacob's Field—or simply, "The Jake." In 2008, Progressive Insurance purchased the naming rights, leaving fans without a suitable nickname. Unlike the Indians' previous home at cavernous Cleveland Municipal Stadium, which they shared with the pro football team, Progressive Field is strictly a ball field. Its location in the heart of downtown makes it a true urban field of dreams. And when they built it, people came. Cleveland fans filled the venue between 1995 and 2001, creating a sellout record of 455 home games in a row that remained unmatched until the Red Sox surpassed it in 2008. During those years the Indians ruled the Central Division, making it to the playoffs every year and the World Series twice. After disappointing seasons from 2001 to 2004, the Indians began rebuilding under the leadership of GM Mark Shapiro and skipper Eric Wedge. In 2007, the team beat the New York Yankees to become American League Division champs, only to come up one win shy of the World Series. There's newfound hope under GM Chris Antonetti, who made big moves, like hiring Terry Francona, who led the Boston Red Sox to two World Series victories.

The fan-friendly facility features comfortable seats, generous legroom, and angled seating that provides unobstructed sight lines of the field. Spectators have great views not only of the players, but also the downtown skyline and one of the largest full-color video displays in American professional sports. Tours of the park are offered throughout the season and numerous Team Shops sell all manner of official gear. Newly created Heritage Park, located in center field, is home to the Indians Hall of Fame and other historical exhibits. Fans who want to try to get autographs of their favorite players may attempt to do so up to 45 minutes before game time in Sections 125-134 and 169-175.

About 80 home games are played April-September. Tickets can be purchased at the Progressive Field box office, though **Ticketmaster** (www.ticketmaster.com), or from unofficial scalpers who prowl the area before and during every game. Bring a hat, wear sunscreen; some seats are in full sun.

MAP 1: Corner of E. 9th St. and Carnegie Ave., 216/420-4487, www.indians.com

Basketball
Cleveland Cavaliers

For their inaugural year in the NBA, 1970, the Cavs amassed the worst record in the league. Things wouldn't improve much until 1976, when the team made it to, but lost, the Eastern Conference Finals. Following a very sad period in Cavs history known as the "Ted Stepien Years," the team ultimately rebounded under new ownership, coaching, and talent. The late 1980s and early 1990s were good to Cleveland basketball fans, with a number of consecutive years of playoff appearances and a shot at the Eastern Conference Championship. This being Cleveland, we'll let you guess how that one turned out.

The basketball gods smiled upon Cleveland in 2003, when the Cavs' first-pick choice in the NBA Draft netted a high school phenom by the name of LeBron James. Under the leadership of coach Mike Brown, "King James" and company would make it all the way to the Eastern Conference Finals in just three years. It would take four years, however, for the team to claim the title of Eastern Conference Champions. That year, 2007, the Cavaliers reached the NBA Finals for the first time in their 37-year history only to be swept by the San Antonio Spurs in four games. We all know what happened next, with LeBron taking his talents to South Beach.

In Cleveland, the Cavaliers play about 40 games October-April at Quicken Loans Arena, a 20,000-seat venue downtown. Tickets are available through **Ticketmaster** (www.ticketmaster.com), or, preferably, through **Flash Seats** (www.cavs.flashseats.com), an online ticket exchange.

MAP 1: One Center Court, 800/820-2287, www.nba.com/cavaliers

Cleveland State University Vikings

For those who prefer the unsullied action of college sports, the Cleveland State University Vikings play a full roster of men's and

Cleveland Sports: Hope and Heartache

Year after year, die-hard Cleveland sports fans pin their hopes and dreams on a championship run only to have their hearts torn asunder by a last-minute calamity. And those are the good years; most leave no hope for a championship run whatsoever. Despite having three professional sports teams, locals have had little to cheer about since 1964, when the Browns won a pre-Super Bowl championship. The Indians haven't clinched a national title since Harry Truman was president. And the Cavaliers? Don't get us started.

It's not as if Cleveland teams haven't been close. There have been times when the Browns, Indians, and Cavs each have put together such miraculous seasons that little stood between them and sweet, sweet victory. But even as Cleveland fans rooted on these teams each and every step of the way, they prepared themselves for the ultimate, inevitable disappointment. This might seem like pessimism, but to Cleveland sports fans, it's just the painful reality.

Ask locals about "The Drive," "The Fumble," "The Shot," or "The Decision" and watch as their faces sag into a familiar contortion of woe. These phrases might sound like simple game plays, but in truth they represent the heartbreaking moments that forever scarred generations of Clevelanders.

All the 1987 Browns had to do to reach the Super Bowl was prevent John Elway and the Denver Broncos from scoring all the way from their own two-yard line with a little over five minutes left to play in the game. Instead, Elway managed to march his team in a 15-play drive all the way to the end zone to send the game into overtime. We know what happened then.

Against all odds, the Browns managed to make it back to the AFC Championship Game the following season, only to face off against the Denver Broncos. With less than two minutes to play in the game, Cleveland needed a touchdown to tie the game. No problem, since they drove the ball all the way down to the eight-yard line. Bernie Kosar's handoff to Ernest Byner was clean, and it looked like the running back would take the ball in for a game-tying touchdown. Instead, he fumbled the ball on the goal line; Denver recovered it and went on to win the game.

Starring in "The Shot" was basketball superstar Michael Jordan. In Game 5 of the NBA Playoffs, Cleveland led the Chicago Bulls by one point. The series was tied 2-2, so whichever team won the game moved on to the semifinals. With just 3.2 seconds left in the game, the ball was inbounded to Jordan for one quick shot. He made it, clinching both the game and the series.

On July 8, 2010, during a live public broadcast dubbed *The Decision*, LeBron James famously told the breathless world that he was "taking my talents to South Beach," dashing all hopes for a Cavs championship anytime soon.

While lacking a catchy tagline like the others, the Indians' 1997 loss to the Florida Marlins in the 11th inning of the seventh game of the World Series ranks up there with the saddest moments in Cleveland sports. Others include blowing a 3-1 lead over the Boston Red Sox in the 2007 ALCS, losing to the Oakland Raiders in the 1981 AFC Playoff Game, and the Cavs getting swept by the San Antonio Spurs in their first-ever NBA Finals appearance in 2007.

After decades of wrenching heartache, you'd expect Cleveland sports fans simply to abandon hope altogether. But that's not the case. After a few weeks of inconsolable crying, fans here stand up, brush it off, and say, "Wait till next year."

women's collegiate sports, including basketball, swimming, soccer, and softball. Men's basketball is without question the most closely followed. The Vikings, under the direction of coach Gary Waters, are fast becoming a team to watch in NCAA Division I ball, playing in the Horizon League. Meanwhile, in 2007 the women's basketball team made their first trip ever to the NCAA Tournament. Basketball games are played at the Wolstein Center and tickets are available at the Wolstein Center box office or by calling 216/687-4848. For more information on all CSU sports action, visit the website.

MAP 1: Wolstein Center, 2000 Prospect Ave., www.csuvikings.com

Football
Cleveland Browns

Cleveland is a football town. If you don't believe it, head over to the Municipal Parking Lot early in the morning on a brutally cold winter day. The scene one is likely to find will look as if an entire Jimmy Buffet concert was airlifted from Key West to the North Pole. Tailgaters get up early, brave traffic, and fight for spots just for the privilege of pre-partying with like-minded fans before games. Sure, alcohol plays a big part. But even the most sober Clevelanders can't help but get swept up in the passion of the pigskin. Einstein said that the definition of insanity is doing the same thing over and over again and expecting different results. Einstein obviously wasn't a Browns fan. Despite backing a team that has never even made it to the Super Bowl, Browns fans, game after game, year after year, merrily return to the scene of the crime.

Apart from three years in the late 1990s when team owner Art Modell, a name uttered only in the darkest of corners, moved the Browns to Baltimore, Cleveland has had a football team to support since 1946. And at many times, a very good one at that. The Browns have 15 former players in the Pro Football Hall of Fame, a number that is around the fifth-highest in the league. Names like Jim Brown, Otto Graham, Paul Warfield, and Ozzie Newsome will be instantly recognizable to even the most casual of fans. In the late 1980s quarterback Bernie Kosar led the team to the AFC Championship game, only to be defeated by John Elway and the Denver Broncos on a 98-yard march down the gridiron that will forever be known simply as "The Drive." As Cleveland fate would have it, the following year's AFC Championship game—*against the Broncos*—ended in a loss as the result of a fumble on the three-yard line. That play, by the way, is now called "The Fumble."

Regardless of who ultimately gets the start, come rain, shine, or Lake Effect snow, you can bet that 73,000 fervent fans will fill FirstEnergy Stadium every home game. Built in 1999, the modern stadium offers unobstructed views of the field and places fans closer to the action. Tickets are not cheap, and are not easy to get. For the truly rabid Browns fans, a bleacher section known as the Dawg Pound, located at the east end zone, is home to hooting, hollering, and, yes, woofing. No matter where you end up sitting, it is imperative that you dress as if you were preparing to scale Mt. Everest. Completely open to the elements, the stadium can be quite insufferable for the ill-equipped. Again, alcohol helps.

Fans don't have to wait until the first game to inspect their team. Training camp normally opens in mid- to late July at a training facility in Berea, Ohio, not too far from downtown. All practices are open to the public and free of charge.

Eight regular-season home games are played September-December. Tickets for games can be purchased through **Ticketmaster** (www.ticketmaster.com) or the online ticket exchange **Viagogo** (www.viagogo.com).

MAP 1: 100 Alfred Lerner Way, 440/891-5050, www.clevelandbrowns.com; $75-300 and higher depending on the opposing team and position in the playoff race

Cleveland Gladiators

When former Browns quarterback and Cleveland sports legend Bernie Kosar relocated the Arena Football League's Gladiators from Las Vegas to Cleveland, he all but promised a postseason appearance in the first year. Considering that the team's record the prior year was a dismal 2-14, it was a bold statement to be sure. To get there, Kosar retooled the team and hired a new coach. In 2008, the team's first year in Cleveland, the Gladiators came up one win shy of the ArenaBowl. Under the leadership of coach Mike Wilpolt, and behind the arm of quarterback Ray Philyaw, the squad went 9-7 in the regular season, and beat Orlando in the wild-card round and Georgia in the division round. They lost the AFL National Conference title game to Philadelphia. In fitting tribute, coach Wilpolt was selected Arena Football League coach of the year. The 18-game season runs early March through late July, with nine home games played at Quicken Loans Arena. Attendance averaged just over 8,000 people per game in 2013. Tickets are available at www.clevelandgladiators.com, www.ticketmaster.com, and the Quicken Loans Arena box office.

MAP 1: One Center Court, 216/420-2222, www.clevelandgladiators.com; $10-85

Hockey
Lake Erie Monsters

Pro hockey fans can enjoy the fast-paced puck action of the Lake Erie Monsters, a team in the American Hockey League and affiliated with the NHL's Colorado Avalanche. Home games are played in Quicken Loans Arena, with roughly 40 dates between mid-October and mid-April. During the team's inaugural 2007-2008 season, they averaged a more-than-respectable 6,000 fans per game. The season closer drew some 15,400 spectators, the largest that year in the American Hockey League. Tickets can be purchased at the Quicken Loans Arena box office, all **Ticketmaster** (www.ticketmaster.com) locations, or by calling 866/99-PUCKS (866/997-8257).

MAP 1: One Center Court, 866/997-8257, www.lakeeriemonsters.com

Ohio City and Tremont
Map 2

BICYCLING
Bike Rentals and Sales
Joy Machines Bike Shop

Opened in 2011, this neighborhood bike shop is just one of the many bike-related businesses to spring up in Ohio City and beyond in direct response to the upsurge in two-wheeled transport. This full-service shop carries bike brands like Surly, Jamis, Linus, Torker, Redline, Pake, and Xtracycle, but will also build a bespoke bike for those who prefer to go that route. This is also the place to grab light-duty items like helmets, locks, and lights, while the handy bicycle pumps and wrenches are perfect for quick tune-ups.

MAP 2: 1836 W. 25th St., 216/394-0230, www.joymachinesbikeshop.com; Mon.-Sat. 11am-7pm, Sun. noon-6pm

Ohio City Bicycle Co-Op

For bike rentals close to downtown, you can't beat Ohio City Bicycle Co-Op. This great nonprofit organization awards free bikes to kids who spend a little time learning about bike repair and safe cycling. In addition to selling surplus bikes, the agency rents quality bikes, which helps fund their Earn-a-Bike program. Bikes for rent come in two classifications: normal and performance. For getting around town, the collection of older road and mountain bikes should fit the bill. Racers or off-roaders will want to go with a higher-end performance model. Rates are about $7 per hour, $25 per day, and $75 per week for the basic bike, and approximately twice that for a performance bike. Cash or check deposits are required and range from $50 to $2,000.

MAP 2: 1823 Columbus Rd., 216/830-2667, www.ohiocitycycles.org; Thurs. 5pm-9pm, Sat. noon-4pm

BOWLING

★ Dickey's Lanes

We wish all bowling alleys were more like Dickey's, a no-frills eight-laner just south of Tremont. What you won't find here are tipsy bachelorette parties, electronic scoring, or even pinsetters that work 100 percent of the time. What you will find are passionate neighborhood bowlers, cheap games, and sharp pencils. A dimly lit lounge dispenses cheap cocktails and a random selection of good and not-so-good beers, served up with a smile and story by the owners. When you're in that bar, ask one of the owners to flick the switch that illuminates the intricate scale model of the entire bowling alley, built entirely out of wooden matchsticks. It's just one of the surprises that await first-time visitors to this dated Cleveland treasure.

MAP 2: 3275 W. 25th St., 216/741-9774; Mon.-Sun. noon-2am; $2.50 per game, $2 for shoes

GUIDED AND WALKING TOURS

Veterans Memorial Bridge Tour

Judging by the steady increase in attendance at these rare tours, interest in the past grows stronger every year. Though Cleveland's streetcar lines and subway stops have been dormant since 1954, vestiges of those times remain hidden in plain view. While the main platform of the Detroit-Superior (Veterans Memorial) Bridge was and is devoted to auto traffic, the lower level once linked the east and west sides of town via trolley tracks and tunnels. Three times a year, usually on the Saturdays before Memorial Day, Independence Day, and Labor Day, the Cuyahoga County Engineer's Office opens up the 2nd level for self-guided tours. There, in a sort of elevated grotto, visitors can enjoy a modest museum dedicated to Cleveland's outmoded transportation system. While the ephemera are cool, it's the views out and down that tickle the most.

MAP 2: W. 25th St. and Detroit Ave., 216/348-3824, www.publicworks. cuyahogacounty.us; 9am-3pm on tour days; free

PARKS

Fairview Park/Kentucky Gardens

This two-acre patch of organic earth is home to some 130 community gardens, each no larger than 20 feet by 20 feet. For nearly six decades, Ohio City residents have provided food for their families by tilling in this urban oasis. Neighbors pay as little as $6 a year for their plots, but must work to maintain common spaces, which include mature fruit trees, working beehives, and ripening compost piles. It's best to visit this park in summer and fall, when gardeners are busy tending to their pint-size farms, absolutely teeming with colorful life.

MAP 2: Franklin Blvd. at W. 38th St., 216/288-3211, www.kentuckygardens.com; dawn-dusk

Seductively elusive, this 20-acre park is so close you can prac-tically touch it. But good luck actually getting there. Located where the Cuyahoga River spills into Lake Erie, this park is lit-erally a mile from Public Square. To get here, though, requires a series of navigational machinations that seem to thwart most would-be visitors. That's perfectly fine with the regulars, how-ever, who worship this tiny park as if it were the last unsullied strip of land in the world. Named after the whiskey distilleries that dotted the peninsula in the 1830s, the park has become one the newest gems gracing the North Coast. Permanent volleyball courts draw local sports clubs, while the **Whiskey Island Marina's Sunset Grille** (216/631-1813, www.whiskeyislandmarina.com) is beloved by boaters and landlubbers looking for a seaside restau-rant. Bird-watchers come here for the wildlife and shutterbugs for the matchless views of the Flats, city skyline, and Lake Erie. Even architecture fans come here, to gaze at the fading shell of an abandoned Art Moderne-style coast guard station. For detailed directions, visit the website.

MAP 2: 2800 Whiskey Island, www.wendypark.org; dawn-dusk

YOGA
Vision Yoga & Wellness

Housed in the 150-year-old Heil's Block Building in the heart of Ohio City, Vision has quickly become a neighborhood essential. Thanks to vaulted ceilings, arched windows, exposed brick, and local fine art, the studio is airy, relaxing, and comfortable. In ad-dition to individual and group yoga and fitness classes, Vision of-fers therapies such as massage, acupuncture, Reiki, and Thai yoga massage. A full calendar of workshops like Restorative Yoga and Couple's Massage offer instruction.

MAP 2: 1861 W. 25th St., 216/348-1111, www.visionyoga.net; classes 7 days a week

Detroit Shoreway and Edgewater

Map 3

PARKS

Lakefront Reservation

Formerly known as Edgewater State Park, this lakefront park and beach was recently taken over from state control by the locally run Metroparks. That's great news for the walkers, joggers, bicyclists, kite-flyers, sunbathers, and anglers who frequent this prominent park just a few miles from the hustle and bustle of downtown. Long suffering from insufficient amenities and management, the park is in line for some major improvements. The property is comprised of two main areas, an elevated bluff and a lake-level beach. Amateur and professional shutterbugs flock to the bluff for unrivaled city, lake, and sunset views. Walkers, joggers, and bicyclists crisscross the park on paved pathways, while anglers drop lines off nearby piers and break walls. Don't ignore this park in winter, when frozen ocean spray creates dramatic natural sculptures along the shore. As fun as this park can be during the day, it's best to hightail it on out come dusk.

Some 1,500 feet of sandy beachhead attract families, bookish loners, and anglers, who drop their lines off nearby piers and break walls. Walkers, joggers, and bicyclists crisscross the park on paved pathways, which connect the area to nearby neighborhoods.

If you can tolerate the near-freezing water temps, Lake Erie can actually provide a pretty decent **winter surfing** experience. Winter's steady winds whip across the lake, stirring up waves that routinely hit the 10-foot mark. Swells as large as 20 feet have been reported. Only a fool would hit these waters without a wetsuit, and it's wise to grab your longest, fattest board for increased buoyancy. Edgewater certainly isn't the O.C.'s Newport Beach, and for that, Cleveland's cultish surfers can be thankful. You better hurry up, though; once the lake freezes, it's either Cali or wait 'til next year.

MAP 3: 6500 Memorial Shoreway, 216/881-8141, www.clevelandmetroparks.com

YOGA

There's No Place Like OM

Not very long ago, a studio that offered classes in chanting, meditation, and yoga had as much chance of survival in Detroit Shoreway as did a sushi restaurant. Well, the sushi restaurant still hasn't arrived, but There's No Place Like OM has garnered the support of the community and then some. Proprietor and instructor Buck Harris endeavors to unite body, mind, and spirit into a sort of harmony that is often impossible in the "real world." In this studio, regardless of yogic prowess, we are all brothers and sisters. Sisters, however, are not welcome at every class. Buck's surprisingly popular Buck Naked Yoga is for men only. And as the name implies, it is practiced without the confinement of clothing. OM my!

MAP 3: 5409 Detroit Ave., 216/409-4161, www.clevelandyoga.net

University Circle and Little Italy

Map 4

PARKS

Rockefeller Park

Tucked into an otherwise unforgiving neighborhood, Rockefeller Park is a leafy 130-acre swath that links University Circle and Lake Erie. Mostly hugging Martin Luther King Jr. Boulevard, the park contains walking paths, tennis courts, picnic areas, playgrounds, and basketball courts. Gorgeous arched bridges move city traffic from one side to the other. The park is perhaps most widely recognized as the home of the **Cultural Gardens** (www.culturalgardens. org), some three dozen sculptural gardens dedicated to ethnicities that have made Cleveland their home. In the India Garden, there is a striking bronze statue of Mahatma Gandhi mid-stride, clutching his walking stick. Time and poverty have not been kind to the many statues, monuments, and sculptures that form the centerpiece of the gardens. Some have been stolen for scrap, were tagged by gang members, or have fallen to the ravages of weather and neglect. But others are in the midst of repair, which is good news for fans of outdoor sculpture. Located here, too, is the **Rockefeller Park Greenhouse** (750 E. 88th St., 216/664-3103, www.rockefellergreenhouse.org), a year-round conservatory boasting lush tropical fruit plants, exotic orchids, and formal gardens. The greenhouse is also a great place to park when visiting the Cultural Gardens as it is free and close. It is important to note that while largely safe during the day, the area surrounding Rockefeller Park is nowhere to hang out after dark.

MAP 4: 690 E. 88th St., www.city.cleveland.oh.us

YOGA

Cleveland Yoga

Cleveland Yoga, long known for its exceptional teachers, recently added this contemporary studio in University Circle. They offer a vast variety of workshops and classes geared for beginners and seasoned pros, including teacher training.

MAP 4: 11461 Euclid Ave., 216/291-7122, www.clevelandyoga.com

Cleveland Heights and Shaker Heights

Map 5

PARKS

Horseshoe Lake Park

Some of the many assets that attract residents to Shaker Heights are its green spaces. Deliberately laid out in the early 1900s as a garden community, the East Side suburb boasts numerous recreational gems, and Horseshoe Lake Park is one of them. Near the preservation-minded Nature Center at Shaker Lakes, this park shares a similar stance on the environment. Elevated boardwalks fashioned from recycled materials weave through wetlands, simultaneously protecting the natural habitats while providing visitors a keen vantage point. Paved trails offer walkers, joggers, and bicyclists a safe route around the park, while nearby dirt paths wind their way through forests, ravines, and fields. Bird-watchers come here for the rich diversity of songbirds, waterfowl, and predators. Stone-clad shelters feature fireplaces and plenty of space to celebrate.

MAP 5: South Park Blvd. at Park Dr., www.shakeronline.com

YOGA

Atma Center

This warm and welcoming studio in Cleveland Heights has been introducing stiff novices to the practice of yoga for more than 15 years. Free introductory classes are a regular occurrence here, where patient instructors promote holistic health practices. Atma offers a complete range of classes, from the basic fundamentals to lengthy and intensive multi-week programs. New moms and moms-to-be can enlist in pre- and postnatal stretching classes that incorporate breathing and meditation. The on-site bookstore stocks a full catalogue of yogic studies materials, required reading for some of the more serious programs. Check the website for classes, times, and prices.

MAP 5: 2319 Lee Rd., 216/371-9760, www.atmacenter.com

Lakewood

Map 6

BOWLING

Mahall's Twenty Lanes

A beloved Lakewood institution for 90 years, this 20-lane bowling alley has been given a second life thanks to new management with fresh ideas. For starters, the bar has been updated with a whole new menu of craft beers and specialty cocktails. New food service features hip takes on burgers and tacos, while guest chefs and food trucks mix things up. Live music, often with multiple acts, attracts bowlers and non-bowlers alike. Bowlers had better know how to score a frame the old-fashioned way, because there are no machines to do it for you. Low-tech scoring translates into affordable bowling.

MAP 6: 13200 Madison Ave., 216/521-3280, www.mahalls20lanes.com; games around $3, shoes $2

ICE-SKATING

Halloran Ice Skating Rink

What this rink lacks in luxury it makes up for in sheer curiosity. Run by the City of Cleveland's Department of Parks and Recreation, Halloran is one of the only outdoor refrigerated rinks in the region. In summer, the ice melts and the spot is opened up to roller skaters. Winter skating begins in October and runs until spring. If you don't mind weaving your way through exuberant youths, this rink can offer a nostalgic charm that borders on romantic. And because the fees are quite cheap, this trip will leave you with plenty of cash for that après-skate dinner-date.

MAP 6: 3350 W. 117th St., 216/664-4187, www.city.cleveland.oh.us; Mon.-Sat. except holidays; $1.25 including rental fees

Serpentini Arena

Formerly Winterhurst Ice Rink, this popular Lakewood city rink has been leased by a private operator and received about $1 million in improvements. With two ice rinks, the arena is busy most days of the week with open skating, drop-in freestyle, youth hockey, and speed skating. The arena is also home to four separate high school varsity ice hockey teams. The facility is open year-round and offers lessons, rentals, and concessions. Hours vary by day, week, and month, so check the website before dropping in.

MAP 6: 14740 Lakewood Heights Blvd., 216/529-4400, www.serpentiniarena.com; $6, less for Lakewood residents

PARKS

Lakewood Off-Leash Dog Park

This great off-leash doggie park is off Valley Parkway, in the Rocky River Reservation of the Cleveland Metroparks. The fenced-in area takes up two-thirds of an acre and features mature trees, gravel surfaces, waste-bag dispensers, and water stations for both canines and humans. A double-gated entrance gives owners an opportunity to unleash the hounds safely. So they don't harass the big guys, dogs smaller than 25 pounds have their own fenced-in area. No aggressive dogs—or people—are welcome.

MAP 6: 1699 Valley Pkwy., www.lakewooddogpark.com

ROWING AND KAYAKING

41° North Kayak Adventures

Paddlers of all skill levels will find what they're looking for at this great local outfitter. For beginners, 41° offers paddling courses taught by certified instructors. Those with even the littlest bit of paddling experience can sign up for an unforgettable sunset kayak tour, which takes participants into North Coast Harbor along Lake Erie's shore, right by the Rock and Roll Hall of Fame. More adventurous half-, full-, and multiday trips are also available to those who make arrangements ahead of time. More advanced paddlers can rent their own rig and glide into Lake Erie alone or with friends. The rental center is at the Boat Barn in the Rocky River Reservation of the Cleveland Metroparks, just south of the public boat ramps and marina. Dress appropriately.

MAP 6: Rocky River Reservation, 1500 Scenic Park Dr., Lakewood, 866/529-2541, www.kayak41north.com; rentals Memorial Day weekend through October, $15 per half hour to $50 full day

YOGA

Puma Yoga

This welcoming, intimate, and warm studio provides a peaceful, noncompetitive environment for those who wish to learn and practice vinyasa alignment-based yoga. The instructors provide the kind of individual attention that ensures effective and safe learning. In addition to group classes, Puma offers private instruction, workshops, and teacher training.

MAP 6: 15602 Detroit Ave., 216/221-6265, www.pumayoga.net

BEACHES

Headlands Beach State Park

Clear across town in Mentor, this beach is the largest in the entire state, boasting a mile-long stretch of natural sand perfect for people-watching and navel-gazing. During summer, the beach attracts scores of folks from throughout the region, all eager for a little vacation close to home. Bird-watchers flock to adjacent Headlands Dunes State Nature Preserve, a native dune environment that sees a steady stream of migratory birds.

MAP 7: 9601 Headlands Rd., Mentor, 440/257-1331, http://parks.ohiodnr.gov

Huntington Beach

Tucked into the posh West Side communities of Bay Village and Rocky River, and within the Huntington Reservation of the Cleveland Metroparks, this small but well-maintained beach is one of the most active in the area. In addition to picnic shelters with charcoal grills, a concession stand operated by local favorite Mitchell's Ice Cream dispenses chilly treats all summer long.

MAP 7: Lake Rd. at Porter Creek, 216/635-3200, www.clevelandmetroparks.com

BICYCLING

Bike Rentals and Sales

Century Cycles

To experience as much of the scenic Ohio & Erie Canal Towpath Trail as possible, a bike is pretty much a necessity. Of course, most folks don't make a habit of traveling with their bikes in tow, and that's where Century Cycles comes in. In the heart of the Cuyahoga Valley National Forest, in the charming town of Peninsula, this great cycle shop rents bikes for use on the trail. Riders with little ones can also rent kiddie trailers that attach to the rear of the bike. Best of all, the shop is literally steps from the towpath. Credit card are required for a security deposit.

MAP 7: 1621 Main St., Peninsula, 800/201-7433, www.centurycycles.com; Mon.-Thurs. 10am-8pm, Fri.-Sat. 10am-6pm, Sun. noon-5pm, rentals $9 per hour

Bike Trails

★ Ohio & Erie Canal Towpath Trail

When completed, this monumental path will stretch 101 miles from downtown Cleveland to New Philadelphia, following the path of the historic Ohio & Erie Canal. Already, some 80 miles of level crushed-limestone path attracts millions of walkers, joggers, and bike riders per year. Pick up the trail south of town in Valley View and follow it as it winds its way through beautiful Cuyahoga Valley National Park. The scenery along the path, which hugs and at times crisscrosses the Cuyahoga River, is simply amazing. Old canal locks and mile markers can be spotted, as can dense forests, fertile wetlands, and varied wildlife. Stop off at numerous visitors centers along the way to view historical and natural exhibits. Riders of all skill levels can enjoy this smooth trail. For those who have bit off a bit too much and are now dreading the journey back, the **Cuyahoga Valley Scenic Railroad** (www.cvsr.com) is a lifesaver. Flag down the train at any boarding station, hop on with your bike, and ride as far as you want for $3. Check the website for train times.

MAP 7: 11 trailheads within Cuyahoga Valley Nationl Park, www.nps.gov/cuva

Mountain Biking
Ohio & Erie Canal Reservation Mountain Bike Trail

Hats off to the Cleveland Area Mountain Bike Association that built and maintains this single-track trail minutes from town at the Ohio & Erie Canal Reservation of the Cleveland Metroparks. Although it is just a two-mile loop, riders swear it feels longer thanks to a nice switchback pattern down the face of a wooded hillside. Given the terrain, which leaves little room for error, the trail is best for intermediate riders. This park connects with the Towpath Trail, making it easily accessible to riders. If it has recently rained and the trail is muddy, riding is forbidden.

MAP 7: Grant Ave. at E. 49th St., www.clevelandmetroparks.com; dusk-dawn

★ Ray's MTB Indoor Park

Ray's is the only attraction of its kind anywhere on the globe. Now approaching 100,000 square feet of indoor mountain bike nirvana, this remarkable place just keeps growing and growing. Inside a cavernous warehouse about five miles west of downtown, Ray's features separate courses geared to beginner, intermediate, and expert riders. Race down narrow paths, around steeped embankments, through obstacle courses, over bumpity bridges, and into the air courtesy of vertical jumps. Riders come from all over the country to check out the rad madness.

MAP 7: 9801 Walford Ave., Cleveland, 216/631-7433, www.raysmtb.com; Mon.-Fri. noon-10pm, Sat.-Sun. 9am-10pm; winter only; weekday $21, weekends $27

CROSS-COUNTRY SKIING, ICE-SKATING, AND SNOWSHOEING
Kendall Lake Winter Sports Center

Tucked deep within Cuyahoga Valley National Park, a cozy stone-and-chestnut shelter serves as the nucleus of winter activities in the park. In addition to the breathtaking scenery, the lodge offers cross-country ski instruction, equipment rental, and priceless information. Sign up for a weekend cross-country ski lesson on your skis or theirs, followed by a vigorous miles-long expedition down the Towpath Trail. For a slower, simpler pace, don a pair of rented snowshoes and head into the majestic backcountry. When nearby Kendall Lake is adequately frozen, take your ice-skating to the great outdoors. Don't have your own skates? No problem, the shelter rents them. Even if you prefer to pull on nothing more than a pair of hiking boots, come to this lodge for maps, hot chocolate, and like-minded companionship. Call for snow and ice reports before you visit.

MAP 7: Truxell Rd., Peninsula, 216/524-1497, www.nps.gov/cuva

GOLF

Shawnee Hills Golf Course

Shawnee Hills offers golf for players of all skill levels, making it one of the most versatile of the Cleveland Metroparks' seven public courses. Beginners and pros alike can sharpen their short game on the zippy little 9-hole, par-3 course. More advanced players, meanwhile, will likely gravitate to the 18-hole 6,200-yard course that features rolling terrain and unforgiving water hazards. Perhaps the most difficult hole of all Metroparks courses, #4 is a tree-lined uphill 469-yard par-4 dogleg left that was converted from a par 5. The course also has a pro shop, snack bar, cart and club rental services, practice putting green, and driving range. It's located in the Bedford Reservation.

MAP 7: 18753 Egbert Rd., Bedford, 440/232-7184, www.clevelandmetroparks.com

Sleepy Hollow Golf Course

This great Stanley Thompson-designed course opened in 1925 as a private country club. Today it is a part of the Cleveland Metroparks system, which runs seven public courses in and around Cuyahoga County. Considered brutally challenging yet also surprisingly beautiful, this 18-hole 6,700-yard course plays downhill and uphill, with and against the prevailing winds. Some holes play easier than others for that reason. Hole #2 is a long 240-yard par 3. The longest hole, #4, is a 590-yard par 5. In 2012, Sleepy Hollow was ranked *Golfweek Magazine*'s No. 1 municipal course in Ohio and No. 23 in the country. Golfers will find a pro shop, snack bar, cart and club rental services, practice putting green, and driving range. It's located in the Brecksville Reservation.

MAP 7: 9445 Brecksville Rd., Brecksville, 440/526-4285, www. clevelandmetroparks.com

Cleveland Velodrome

In August of 2012, the **Cleveland Velodrome** (5033 Broadway Ave., http://clevelandvelodrome.org) opened in the Slavic Village neighborhood just south of the city. The 166-meter Olympic-style bicycle racing track is the only one of its kind between the East Coast and Chicago. The outdoor steel-and-wood track, which features 50-degree banked turns and 15-degree banked straightaways, is open to riders of all skill levels.

All first-timers must attend a Track 101 class to learn about track safety, track etiquette, and to acquire the necessary technical skills. The class is free and open to riders of all ages. The next level up is Track 201, which covers basic track racing skills.

Riders can use their own bikes only if they fit the requirements, otherwise there are single-speed, fixed-gear track bikes for rental for both kids and adults ($10). Season passes ($200) and day passes ($15) are available. The track is open May through September, weather permitting.

GUIDED AND WALKING TOURS
Cuyahoga Valley Scenic Railroad

One of the longest scenic railroads in the nation, the CVSR stretches a full 51 miles, from just south of Cleveland all the way down to Canton. And "scenic" is the operative word. For much of the journey, the tracks bisect the majestic Cuyahoga Valley National Park while hugging the Cuyahoga River and paralleling the popular Towpath Trail. Passengers ride in authentic climate-controlled coaches built in the 1950s. More than just a tour train, the railroad is a key resource for visitors to the valley. Many hop aboard just to travel to their favorite park spot, while bicyclists take advantage of the popular bike-and-ride program, which offers them and their rig a $3 lift back home. But you don't need to bike, hike, or climb to enjoy this train. Sign up for a lengthy scenic expedition through the park and watch as nature unfolds outside your window. The lush forests, wetlands, and prairies of the park teem with flora and fauna. White-tailed deer and wildflowers, songbirds and snapping turtles, cattails and coyotes—it's all on display in the valley. The trains operate all year long and offer dozens of different excursions, from midwinter charmers to evening wine-tasting trips. Without question, this railroad is one of the brightest gems in Northeast Ohio. Check the website for more information.

MAP 7: 7600 Canal Rd., 800/468-4070, www.cvsr.com

ROCK CLIMBING
Cleveland Rock Gym

For nimble-fingered folks itching to scamper up a wall, this indoor climbing gym will more than satisfy the urge. What once was a light-industrial warehouse in Euclid has been converted into a more-than-acceptable winter substitute for rock climbing. The facility is comprised of 30-foot top-rope walls and numerous bouldering areas, some featuring near-horizontal overhangs. Climbers who have no prior experience must make reservations for an introductory class. Those with enough knowledge to pass a basic belay test, however, are free to plan their routes up the tall walls. A one-day pass is around $12, a five-day pass is $45, and a one-month pass is $60.

MAP 7: 21200 St. Clair Ave., Bldg. B3, Euclid, 216/692-3300, www. clevelandrockgym.com; Mon.-Fri. 4pm-10pm, Sat.-Sun. noon-6pm; one-day pass around $12, five-day $45, one-month $60

SKATEBOARDING
Chenga World
Folks with real wheels—a car, that is—will want to make tracks to this monster indoor park, a couple miles from Cleveland Hopkins International Airport. Skaters, BMX riders, even bladers seem to peacefully coexist here thanks to the sheer magnitude of the place. There are plenty of ramps, rails, wall rides, verts, and jumps offering numerous paths and lanes through the park. Since it is owned by flatlander Scott Powell, you know you'll have plenty of open space to practice your spins, stalls, and hops. An on-site pro shop is well stocked with merch for that last-minute repair or a brand-new deck. Helmets are required and can be rented for about $5 a day. Folks under 18 years of age need a release signed by a parent.

MAP 7: 14700 Snow Rd., Brook Park, 216/433-7588, www.chenga.cc; Mon.-Fri. 4pm-10pm, Sat. 1pm-10pm, Sun. noon-7pm; around $10 for an all-day pass

SKIING, SNOWBOARDING, AND TUBING
Alpine Valley Ski Resort
Located smack-dab in the middle of the Snowbelt, Alpine Valley gets pounded by snowfall. With average yearly totals around 120 inches, the resort receives double that of Boston Mills and Brandywine. While compact, this charming resort has the look and feel of a quaint little ski village. But modern features like state-of-the-art snowmaking machines, a snow-tube park, and Ohio's longest half-pipe keep this place popular with winter enthusiasts. There are 11 trails covering 72 skiable acres, with a range of easy, moderate, and difficult runs. Lessons, equipment rental, and food service is available. Check the website for months, days, and hours of operation.

MAP 7: 10620 Mayfield Rd., Chesterland, 440/285-2211, www.alpinevalleyohio. com; adult lift passes $30-35 full day and $27 half day, complete equipment rental package about $25, tubing $15 for two hours

The sister resorts of Boston Mills and Brandywine might not offer the best skiing in the country, but they do provide a surprisingly good downhill experience. And their location just 20 miles from town makes them all the more appealing. Combined, the two parks boast 18 trails covering 88 skiable acres. Both offer a nice mix of bunny runs, intermediate trails, and challenging black diamonds for skiers and snowboarders. When Mother Nature isn't cooperating, snow-making machines keep the slopes in business. Well-synchronized chairlifts can shuttle 20,000 skiers an hour while preventing overcrowding of the slopes. Boston Mills and Brandywine are two separate parks five minutes apart by car. Lift tickets and passes are valid at both, however, since they are owned by the same company. Lessons, equipment rental, and food service are available at both resorts, while inner tubing is offered only at Brandywine. Check the website for months, days, and hours of operation.

MAP 7: 7100 Riverview Rd., Peninsula, 330/657-2334, www.bmbw.com; lift passes about $43 full day and $38 evening beginning at 3:30pm, complete equipment rental package about $30

TOBOGGANING
Mill Stream Run Reservation
Twin refrigerated chutes whisk adventurers 70 feet down and 1,000 feet out on toboggans built for four. This seasonal tradition kicks off the day after Thanksgiving and runs through the first weekend in March. Apart from really warm or really wet days, the chutes are open Thursday through Sunday and holidays. Be prepared to hike up 110 steps to the top to earn your exhilarating 15-second descent. Riders must be at least 42 inches tall and wear mittens or gloves. When you've had enough of the frosty free falls, head into the chalet to enjoy the warm glow of two fireplaces and a large-screen television.

MAP 7: Cleveland Metroparks, 440/572-9990, www.clevelandmetroparks.com; $4 one-ride ticket, $10 pass for multiple runs

Various Locations

BICYCLING
Bike Rides and Tours
Critical Mass
On the last Friday of each month the bicycling community in Cleveland congregates and then collectively sets off en masse for these popular group rides. Critical Mass bike rides take place in more than 300 cities around the world to demonstrate and celebrate biking, educate others, and engage with like-minded individuals. Depending on the weather, these rides can attract anywhere from a few hundred riders all the way up to 1,000. Check the website for the location of the next meet up.

VARIOUS LOCATIONS: www.clevelandcm.wordpress.com

Cleveland Cycle Tours
If you have the itch to ride on a 15-person party bike, this tour company is for you. This fully pedal-powered vehicle can be rented by the group for neighborhood tours, pub crawls, or anything else you can think of. It's been spotted frequently in Ohio City, where it takes its riders from brewery to brewery.

VARIOUS LOCATIONS: 440/532-9995, www.bikecct.com

Bike Trails
Cleveland Metroparks All-Purpose Trails
Cleveland Metroparks maintains more than 100 miles of paved, all-purpose trails for bicycling, walking, jogging, and inline skating. They have more than a dozen different reservations scattered around town, so a trailhead is never too far away. A short drive from downtown is Rocky River Reservation, which features a scenic 13-mile stretch of all-purpose trails that sometimes follows the Rocky River. Though not directly connected, another nine miles of all-purpose trail through Mill Stream Run Reservation can easily be accessed by a short ride along Valley Parkway, adding up to a very enjoyable 22-mile route. Other particularly picturesque rides can be found at the North and South Chagrin Reservations.

VARIOUS LOCATIONS: www.clemetparks.com

GUIDED AND WALKING TOURS
CityProwl
Jennifer Coleman recalls how exciting it was as a child to explore the nooks and crannies of her downtown. Now an adult, Coleman has figured out a way to share that excitement with other residents and visitors. Through her website, CityProwl.com, Coleman

Fishing

Lake Fishing

Lake Erie offers anglers some serious fishing opportunities, with championship walleye and tasty yellow perch coming in at the top of the list. However, those without their own boat have relatively few options when casting for dinner. The easiest and cheapest is simply dropping a line in the water off a pier or breakwall. Edgewater State Park is a popular site for shore-bound anglers, offering a generous fishing pier. A little east of town is the **East 55th Marina** (5555 N. Marginal Rd.), another nice spot to spend a few hours casting. The next most economical alternative is to hop aboard a party boat, sometimes called a "head boat" because passengers are charged per head. Unlike pricey charter boats, head boats accept singles and couples for a modest fee. One of the few to depart from within the city, **Discovery Dive Charters** (16975 Wildwood Dr., 216/481-5771, www.wildwoodmarina.com) operates out of Wildwood State Park Marina, just a few miles east of downtown. **Trump-Tight Fishing Charters** (216/581-7619, www.trump-tight.com) charges between $400 and $500 for a full day of fishing, departing from nearby E. 72nd Street. For a totally unique fishing experience, consider signing up for an evening or nighttime walleye trip in the spring with **FishCrazy Charters** (216/408-0404, www.fishcrazycharters.com). The evening trip runs most days 5pm-11pm, while the weekend-only night trips run 11:30pm-5am. Rates are about $400 for up to five people.

Regardless of which option he or she chooses, every angler must possess a current Ohio Fishing License, available through the **Ohio Department of Natural Resources** (www.ohiodnr.com) or at bait shops near the docks. Cost is $11 for a one-day license, $19 for a year. When fishing, it is imperative to bring an ice-filled cooler to protect your catch. Many of the better charter companies will provide one for you. Also, be prepared for the weather.

River Fishing

The well-stocked rivers and streams of Northeast Ohio provide some of the best steelhead trout fishing in the country. Fly fishers from throughout the Midwest make their way to Lake Erie tributaries from fall through spring hoping to catch and release one of the most beautiful sport fish of all. The rivers that offer the best fishing are the Rocky, Chagrin, and Grand, though gaining access isn't always easy due to private-property restrictions. The Rocky River and Mill Stream Run Reservations of the Cleveland Metroparks enjoy miles of access to the Rocky River, making those parks a favorite destination for anglers. On the other side of town, the North and South Chagrin Reservations provide access to the bountiful Chagrin River. When it comes to fly-fishing for steelhead, sometimes it's best to call in the pros. Professional guides know the rivers better than anybody, and they will take you to the fish. Plus, many offer lessons in casting before setting out. One guide of note is **Chagrin River Outfitters** (440/247-7110, www.chagrinriveroutfitters.com), which charges about $275 for a half day.

offers free downloadable audio tours for use in any MP3 player. Each covers about a mile in distance and takes around 40 minutes to complete. Loaded with historical, architectural, and anecdotal information, the tours are an easy, cheap, and entertaining way to squeeze more into a leisurely stroll. At least five different

Hunting

Ohio's dense forests, lush wetlands, and grassy prairies provide the ideal breeding ground for a whole host of elusive game. Depending on the season, Ohio hunters might be after white-tailed deer, wild turkey, waterfowl, squirrel, grouse, pheasant, quail, and coyote. It would take an entire chapter to cover the myriad rules, laws, and restrictions that govern hunting in Ohio, with each game having its own season dates, bag limits, and check-in requirements. For up-to-date information on hunting, visit the **Ohio Department of Natural Resources'** website (www.ohiodnr.com), which has a wealth of resources on the topic. It goes without saying that a hunting license is required for most pursuits.

downtown tours, or prowls, are available, including ones covering Public Square, the Warehouse District, and the old arcades. Simply visit the site, download the file, print out a map, and make your way to the starting point.

VARIOUS LOCATIONS: www.cityprowl.com

PARKS

Cleveland Metroparks

Fortunately for the residents of Greater Cleveland, early city and county leaders had the foresight to set aside some ground for conservation, education, and recreation. Cobbling together patches of land, the park board ultimately assembled a remarkable chain of parks and connecting boulevards that encircled the whole of Cuyahoga County. This ribbon of green space largely follows the waterways of the Rocky River, Chagrin River, Big Creek, Chippewa Creek, Tinkers Creek, and Euclid Creek. On a map, this patchwork of parks looks like a leafy necklace around the neck of Lady Cleveland, hence the Metroparks' nickname, the Emerald Necklace. In 2013, the Metroparks entered into a long-term lease with the City of Cleveland to manage the city's six lakefront parks as well. Combined, the Metroparks' 18 reservations cover more than 22,000 acres of dense forest, wetland, prairie, ravines, lakes, and streams. The activities available within the park system are seemingly endless, including (just to name a few) hiking, biking, swimming, fishing, golfing, cross-country skiing, birding, tobogganing, and geocaching, not to mention visiting the Zoo and RainForest. In addition to all the standard recreational opportunities, Metroparks' ambitious Institute of the Great Outdoors offers skill-based courses in survival, fly-fishing, backpacking, canoeing, kayaking, and so much more. Throughout the entire year, captivating events are held at the reservations' various lodges, shelters, and nature centers. Folks assemble for moonlit owl walks, fall foliage strolls, and marshy reptile hunts. It would not be hyperbole to claim that one could spend the rest of his or her life taking advantage of the park's gifts without ever tapping them out. Begin to explore them on the Metroparks website.

VARIOUS LOCATIONS: 216/635-3200, www.clevelandmetroparks.com

SPECTATOR SPORTS
Roller Derby
Burning River Roller Girls

Fans of the fast-paced sport of roller derby have a friend in the Burning River Roller Girls, Cleveland's first all-female flat-track derby league. The league consists of six teams of elbow pad-clad bruiser babes that jam, block, and pivot their way around an 88-foot oval track. Points are scored for each player lapped on the opposing team. Half the fun is just reading the names on the scorecard: EnemyLou Harris, Rainbow Fright, and Social Batterfly sound like nightmares on wheels. Matches are lively, fun, and chock-full of kitsch. They are played monthly from March through August at various locations around town. Tickets can be purchased online by visiting the website.

VARIOUS LOCATIONS: www.burningriverrollergirls.com; $12-22

SWIMMING POOLS
City of Cleveland

The City of Cleveland operates about 22 indoor and outdoor swimming pools throughout the city. All of the outdoor pools follow the seasonal schedule listed above. Many neighborhood pools offer learn-to-swim programs in addition to general open swim time. Check the city website for locations around town.

VARIOUS LOCATIONS: 216/664-3018, www.city.cleveland.oh.us; mid-June-mid-August, Wed.-Sun. noon-7:30pm

ULTIMATE FRISBEE
Cleveland Disc Association

Cleveland-based devotees of the fast-moving sport of Ultimate Frisbee are blessed to have the organizing talent of the CDA. Literally hundreds of players and dozens of teams play in competitive spring and summer leagues at parks and school ball fields all over town. There is even a winter league, played indoors at a domed sports complex, for those who never want the fun to stop. The summer action culminates with the annual No Surf in Cleveland Tournament, a monster two-day event that draws players and teams from all across the region. For those who have always wondered what Disc was all about, simply check the website to find out where the next matches will be held.

VARIOUS LOCATIONS: www.cleveland-disc.org

Shops

Downtown.......................183

Ohio City and Tremont 186

Detroit Shoreway and Edgewater. .191

University Circle and Little Italy...196

Cleveland Heights
    and Shaker Heights.............197

Lakewood........................202

Greater Cleveland 205

It is not too difficult in Cleveland to find places to part with one's hard-earned cash. Stroll through any of the city's most popular neighborhoods and you're likely to unearth a treasure trove of independent shops, many found no place else on Earth. Tremont and Little Italy each boast scores of galler-

ies and boutiques stocking one-of-a-kind fashions, fine art, and funky accessories. Coventry Road in Cleveland Heights is a stroller's dream, dotted with incense-filled import shops, used record depots, and wacky novelty-filled toy stores. Lorain Avenue running from Ohio City into Detroit Shoreway has more vintage, antiques, and secondhand shops than a sane shopper can visit in a single weekend. West 25th Street just west of downtown is a patchwork of ethnic shops, hidden gems, and bin-filled thrift stores.

Numerous universities in the area seem to keep the demand for books strong, as reflected by a relatively high number of new and used bookstores. Fans of old vinyl and comics have a friend in C-Town, as do lovers of handcrafted specialty foods. Perhaps it's the cold winters, but folks here appear to enjoy holing up with a good book and a dish of fine chocolates.

Cleveland's proximity to the East Coast means that trend-conscious shoppers have little trouble finding a great pair of designer jeans, a hot bag, or the perfect little black dress. Upscale malls like Eton Chagrin Boulevard and Beachwood Place contain not only the best national retailers, but a surprisingly fresh crop of indie boutiques. And when getting dolled up for that night on the town, guys and gals have their pick of top-talent salons and spas for their

HIGHLIGHTS

★ **Best Place to Catch 216 Fever:** With the motto "Spreading Cleveland pride one T-shirt at a time," **CLE Clothing Co.** is like a team shop for the entire city. This upbeat downtown retail store sells all manner of Cleveland-themed clothing, books, and gifts (page 183).

★ **Most Exotic Grocery Store:** Cleveland's AsiaTown neighborhood continues to grow, but almost since the beginning, **Tink Holl** was there to serve its homesick community. This sizable Asian grocery has everything from chopsticks to golden roast duck (page 185).

★ **Where to Support Your Beer-Brewing Habit:** Home brewers come to the **Cleveland Brew Shop** in Tremont not just for equipment, ingredients, and supplies, but also instruction, encouragement, and camaraderie. First-timers can sign up for a beer brewing 101 class (page 186).

★ **Best Place to Discuss Kerouac: Visible Voice Books** owner Dave Ferrante can discuss Boho lit with the best of them. And because his shop is just 2,200 square feet, he likely has the time and inclination to do so (page 186).

★ **Finest Chocolates:** Willy Wonka has nothing on Amanda Montague. At her urban confectionary emporium, **Lilly Handmade Chocolates,** she crafts delicious works of art from fresh ingredients. Handmade truffles, bars, and candies all seem to come with a golden ticket (page 189).

★ **Best Source for New-Old Things:** The folks at **Reincarnation Vintage Design** don't just resell old stuff, they transform it into cool new home furnishings. Visit this two-level New York-style loft showroom to see what's currently on display (page 195).

★ **Weirdest, Wackiest, Nerdiest Novelties:** Coventry Road has always been home to eccentrics. Thanks to **Big Fun,** those wack-doodles have a shop to call their own. For decades, Big Fun has tickled us silly with its cosmic collection of vintage toys, campy gifts, and nerd-approved clothing (page 199).

★ **Best Used Vinyl Shop:** When a shop features a cat named Vinyl, its owners must be music-obsessed. The friendly folks at **Music Saves** are indeed serious about the selection of used indie rock, but about everything else they are refreshingly genial (page 205).

★ **Best Place to Sweat:** Apart from the neighborhood around it, little has changed at the **Russian-Turkish Baths** since it opened in the late 1920s. Known simply as "the Schvitz," this is where in-the-know men come to steam, sweat, kibbutz, drink, and eat steak (page 208).

★ **If You've Gotta Go to the Mall…:** Most malls are as unique as a McDonald's hamburger. But **Eton Chagrin Boulevard** is loaded with scores of independent fashion-forward shops found nowhere else. This is also where you'll find Michael Symon's B Spot burger bar (page 209).

mani, pedi, or waxing. Even the furriest of Clevelanders—the dogs and cats, that is—seem to have at their disposal the finest in grooming, day care, and overnight boarding.

Downtown Map 1

GIFT AND HOME
★ CLE Clothing Co.

With the motto "Spreading Cleveland pride one T-shirt at a time," this upbeat downtown retail store is like a team shop for the entire city. Adjacent to Positively Cleveland, the city's visitor's bureau, CLE Clothing sells all manner of Cleveland-themed clothing, books, and gifts. It doesn't take an urban sociologist to see that more and more locals are proud to call themselves Clevelanders, and they're expressing their civic pride with T-shirts emblazoned with 216, the local area code, or sayings like "Vacation in Cleveland." Stop in here for great gifts like stickers, coasters, beer koozies, key chains, hoodies, and more.

MAP 1: 342 Euclid Ave., 216/736-8879, www.cleclothingco.com; Mon.-Sat. 11am-9pm, Sun. noon-6pm

The Only Cleveland Store

When you want to take a little piece of Cleveland back home, this unabashedly passionate souvenir shop in Tower City Center will fill your shopping bags. As the area's only authorized retailer for the Rock and Roll Hall of Fame, Cleveland Museum of Art, and Cleveland Museum of Natural History, this store will make short work of your gift list. This likely is the only place in the world that stocks Rock Hall guitar picks, Cleveland Browns pennants, authentic Stadium Mustard, and beautifully framed skyline photos all under the same roof. Returning Clevelanders nostalgic for the "good old days" can score items bearing long-gone celebrities like Mr. Jingeling and Ghoulardi.

MAP 1: 230 W. Huron Rd., 216/241-2011, www.theonlyclevelandstore.com; Mon.-Sat. 10am-7pm, Sun. noon-5pm

Surroundings Home Décor

Urban pioneers looking to furnish their modern downtown lofts know to come here for all manner of sleek home furnishings. Like many of the condos it outfits, Surroundings is housed in an open-plan Warehouse District showroom with support columns and exposed HVAC systems. A favorite of designers, architects, and consumers alike, the gallery stocks high-end European lines for both home and office, with numerous pieces for every room, need, style, and budget. This is also the place to come for the latest in lighting technology and design. For those who lack a sharp eye, Surroundings offers interior design consultation.

MAP 1: 850 W. St. Clair Ave., 216/623-4070, www.shdecor.com; Tues.-Fri. 11am-6pm, Sat. noon-6pm

HEALTH AND BEAUTY
Marengo Luxury Spa

Within the Hyatt Regency at The Arcade, Marengo is one of the only full-service luxury day spas in the downtown area. The plush digs strike the right tone for a half or full day of premium pampering. While a tad pricey, the services offered are top-notch and professionally administered. Massage services include those geared specifically to pregnant woman and sore-muscled athletes. Men's and women's facials, manicures, and waxing are available here, as are traditional hair cutting, coloring, and styling services. This dreamy spa is popular with wedding parties getting their makeup and up-dos before the big event.

MAP 1: 401 Euclid Ave., 216/621-4600, www.marengospa.com; Mon.-Fri. 10am-7pm, Sat. 9am-6pm

PETS
Cleveland MetroBark

MetroBark's location and hours make it popular with East Side commuters, who drop off their charges on the way to work and pick them up on the way home. The facility has begun boarding dogs, but the method—sending them home with an employee—may not sit well with some parents. Pets who spend the day romping in the 6,000-square-foot indoor and 14,000-square-foot outdoor pens come home good and tired, meaning they are less likely to chew your new Jimmy Choos. Grooming is limited to a quick bath and towel dry. Campers must be at least three months old, nonaggressive, and current with their vaccinations.

MAP 1: 3939 Payne Ave., 216/881-3644, www.metrobark.com; Mon.-Fri. 6:30am-7pm; approx. $13 half day, $20 full day

SHOPPING CENTERS AND MALLS
5th Street Arcades

Formerly the Colonial Arcade, one of two beautiful and historic downtown arcades built around the turn of the 20th century, 5th Street Arcades now houses an eclectic and evolving mix of shops, boutiques, and restaurants. Along with anchor tenants like Pour Coffee, Vincenza Pizza, and Colossal Cupcakes, new shops and galleries will cycle in and out in somewhat incubator fashion, with successful ones hopefully growing roots. Newer shops include Bliss Books (indie bookseller), Bright Green Gift Store (organic gifts and decor), and Sushi 86 (restaurant). Soulcraft Gallery is a showroom for locally manufactured furniture, with more than a dozen Cleveland furniture designers displaying their work. In the summer, a farmers market occasionally pops up, as do events and after-work get-togethers, all catering to the growing downtown residential market.

MAP 1: 530 Euclid Ave., 216/583-0500; hours vary by store

Tower City Center

You may not find the latest fashions at this mall, which is in the belly of the Terminal Tower, but that doesn't mean it should be wholly overlooked. When built, the mall was stocked to its gleaming glass roof with world-class stores. These days, the selection is more commonplace than one-of-a-kind, with the likes of Bath & Body Works, Foot Locker, and Johnston & Murphy. Chic et Mode and The Cleveland Store are here, as is a multiscreen movie theater, food court, and numerous kiosks. Morton's Steakhouse and Hard Rock Cafe call this mall home. And kids still go gaga over the majestic central fountain, which spouts water in rhythmic and dramatic sequences. Tower City Cinemas is the site of the Cleveland International Film Fest in March.

MAP 1: 230 W. Huron Rd., 216/623-4750, www.towercitycenter.com; Mon.-Sat. 10am-7pm, Sun. noon-5pm

SPECIALTY FOODS

★ Tink Holl

This granddaddy of Asian groceries carries a dizzying array of imported products, frozen foods, fresh produce, and live seafood. Home cooks come here for hard-to-find greens like pea shoots, baby bok choy, and Chinese mustard greens. Unsweetened soy milk is ground fresh on-site, and the copper-colored roast ducks that hang behind glass are sold by the half or whole. Asian snacks like fresh-fried shrimp chips are sold by the bag, and the on-site restaurant Szechuan Gourmet is one of the best in town. There are other Asian markets in town, but this one manages to combine the best of all of them under one roof.

MAP 1: 1735 E. 36th St., 216/881-6996; daily 9:30am-8pm

Ohio City and Tremont Map 2

ARTS AND CRAFTS
★ Cleveland Brew Shop

This truly is a one-stop shop for all your beer and winemaking needs, and it caters to an ever-growing and passionate base of skilled hobbyists. In addition to stocking quality equipment, fresh ingredients, and helpful literature, this friendly Tremont shop holds regularly scheduled classes for beginners and others. Complete beer kits bundle up everything a brewer will require to whip up a batch of American pale ale or a Belgian tripel.

MAP 2: 2681 W. 14th St., 216/574-2271, www.clevelandbrewshop.com; Tues.-Fri. 11am-7pm, Sat. 10am-5pm

Glass Bubble Project

Chances are you've never experienced a gallery like this one. It's an absolute blast—with a blast furnace, to boot. Tucked into a cramped garage, which itself is secreted behind a block of buildings, Glass Bubble Project is a glassblowing studio run by remarkable—and remarkably peculiar—artists. An open-studio policy means that visitors can stroll in anytime and catch the artists dipping blowpipes into glory holes. (That's glassblowing lingo, by the way.) Impromptu demonstrations are fine for most, but the Bubble also offers private lessons, easily scheduled with a phone call. Gift ideas abound, from one-of-a-kind blown-glass bowls and glassware to Christmas ornaments and found-art sculpture.

MAP 2: 2421 Bridge Ave., 216/696-7043, www.glassbubbleproject.com; Mon.-Sat. 10am-6pm, Sun. 11am-4pm

BOOKS AND MUSIC
★ Visible Voice Books

At this sweet little indie bookstore in hip Tremont, fine literature shares shelf space with a vast collection of pop culture titles. The eclectic catalog is hand chosen by owner Dave Ferrante and it strongly reflects his personal tastes, which lean toward the bohemian and erudite. At 2,200 square feet, the store is small enough to lavish individual attention yet large enough to accommodate approximately 7,000 titles. Kerouac fans will find here not just words on a page but a kindred beatnik spirit of adventure as well. Bonuses include frequent poetry readings and book signings, a large local author section, plus a wine bar and alfresco courtyard for sipping. Live acoustic music is also on tap some nights.

MAP 2: 1023 Kenilworth Ave., 216/961-0084, www.visiblevoicebooks.com; Tues.-Thurs. noon-8pm, Fri.-Sat. noon-9pm

Evie Lou

After years spent writing about fashion for the Cleveland *Plain Dealer*, former style editor Kim Crow opened this chic women's clothing shop in the hip Tremont neighborhood. While style is first and foremost on her mind, it's really the comfort of her customers that drives her and her store. The shop sets out to prove that style and comfort are not mutually exclusive, dishing up the latest trends in eminently wearable fabrics. Though the shop carries a wide range of brands and designers, Crow keeps the ever-rotating stock down to a manageable size so as to not overwhelm her clients.

Map 2: 2509 Professor Ave., 216/696-6675, www.evielou.com; Mon.-Wed. 11am-7pm, Thurs.-Sat. 11am-8pm, Sun. noon-4pm

Pinky's Daily Planner

Designer and sewer extraordinaire Stephanie Fralick calls her shop a "modern clothes-closet for spirited girls." The peculiar name Pinky's Daily Planner refers both to Fralick's Tremont boutique and her line of playful and distinctive skirts and dresses. In addition to those on display, many garments are made-to-order based on past and current collections, or simply custom-made from scratch. Pinky's also carries fashions from independent designers rarely represented in the region. The look is decidedly retro-meets-modern, with throwback-inspired threads mingling with gently worn vintage pieces. This "closet" is also stocked with belts, boots, bags, and bling.

MAP 2: 2403 Professor Ave., 216/402-2536, www.pinkysdailyplanner.com; Fri. 6pm-10pm, Sat. noon-10pm, other hours by appt.

GIFT AND HOME

Banyan Tree

In a neighborhood littered with boutiques, Banyan Tree rises to the top of the pack thanks to its well-edited and ever-evolving catalog of inventory. Blessed with a keen eye for fashion, home decor, and accessories trends, the owner has created one of the best go-to places for appreciated gifts. Once purchased, those gifts are lovingly and fashionably wrapped at no charge. Sleek and modern, this urban shop carries handmade textiles, season-appropriate designer garments, vintage jewelry, and funky home furnishings. Sorry, no kitschy postcards or T-shirts here.

MAP 2: 2242 Professor Ave., 216/241-1209, www.shopbanyantree.com; Mon.-Wed. 11am-7pm, Thurs.-Sat. 11am-9pm, Sun. 11am-4pm

Johnnyville Slugger

Owner John Smatana calls his products "man sticks," and that's about as accurate a descriptor as you'll likely get. Since 2011, he has been making custom baseball bats at this colorful Ohio City storefront. He'll engrave just about anything on a baseball bat that's been stained just about any color under the sun. Sports teams, universities, motorcycle brands, and rock bands are just some of the common themes. All the work is done in house, much of it behind a glass wall allowing visitors to watch. If you're in the market for "the best gift in the history of the world (for under $200)"—Smatana's words, not ours—then run the bases over to this clubhouse.

MAP 2: 1826 W. 25th St., 216/470-4838, www.johnnyvilleslugger.com; Mon.-Sat. noon-7pm

Room Service

This popular Ohio City shop has a little bit of everything, but all of it is selected for its modern and quality design. Shoppers will find an ever-changing variety of goods that range from men's and women's apparel to home decor items, to gifts and stationery. The design-minded owners have a knack for keeping abreast of the hippest, most up-to-date trends and finding the products that best represent those trends. They also go out of their way to stock locally made clothing, crafts, and art. Cleveland-themed T-shirts can be purchased here along with hilarious cards and gift items.

MAP 2: 2078 W. 25th St., 216/696-6220, www.rscleveland.com; Mon.-Sat. 11am-6pm, Sun. 11am-5pm

Something Different

When tooling around the West 25th Street area of Ohio City, make a quick detour into this wildly eclectic shop. Slightly chaotic and cramped, Something Different carries all manner of gifts, souvenirs, fashions, jewelry, even toiletries, some admittedly more "different" than others. Knickknacks abound, like colorful glassware, greeting cards, and wine carriers. But fine art and sculpture can be found here, too, and the gallery is a great outlet for local artists. Reasonable price points and complimentary designer gift wrapping add to the allure of this fun diversion.

MAP 2: 1899 W. 25th St., 216/696-5226, www.somethingdifferentgallery.com; Mon. and Wed.-Sat. 10:30am-6pm

HEALTH AND BEAUTY

Zen Metro Spa

This stylish urban salon is adored by some of this city's trendiest residents, who come for world-class talent, services, and product. Spread across three long and narrow floors is a full-service salon and spa offering everything from color and cuts to manicures and waxings. Spa services such as facials, massages, and salt glows are provided on the lower level. Owner Rob Torma has been in the salon business for more than 20 years, and he has assembled a professional team that seems obsessed with making people look and feel their absolute best.

MAP 2: 1870 W. 25th St., 216/939-1760, www.zenmetrospa.com; Tues.-Thurs. 10am-8pm, Fri. 10am-6pm, Sat. 10am-5pm

SPECIALTY FOODS

Campbell's Sweets Factory

For years, Campbell's operated a popular stand down the street at the West Side Market. That was then, as they say, as the company has grown to the point that even this adorable retail sweets factory no longer can keep up with demand. Old and new fans of Campbell's gourmet popcorn—available in dozens of flavors, including the cheese-caramel Dichotomy—chocolate-covered pretzels and Oreos, and fluffy and flavorful cupcakes make regular pilgrimages here to satisfy their cravings. An open kitchen and front display window offer behind-the-scenes views of the action. If that's not enough, tours of the entire operation are also offered.

MAP 2: 1979 W 25th St., 216/574-2899, www.campbellssweets.com; Mon.-Thurs. 10am-7pm, Fri.-Sat. 9am-7pm

Hansa Import Haus

Inside a kitschy faux-Swiss chalet, Hansa Import Haus provides a culinary lifeline for Cleveland's sizable German immigrant population. This quirky gingerbread shop has survived for more than 40 years thanks to its deep selection of German, Swiss, and Austrian imports, ranging from hard-to-find spreads, meats, and cheeses to harder-to-find beers, including Bavarian smoke beer. Rows of store shelving sag beneath the weight of enough cookies, cakes, and chocolates to make even the most stoic national weep with longing. And if that homesickness becomes too unbearable, there is an on-site travel agency to book a hasty return visit.

MAP 2: 2717 Lorain Ave., 216/281-3177, www.hansaimporthaus.com; Mon.-Sat. 9am-5:30pm

★ Lilly Handmade Chocolates

At this urban confectionery emporium owner and culinary school grad Amanda Montague transforms the world's finest chocolate into handmade truffles, bars, and candies. Like delicious works of art, the sweets are nearly as much fun to look at as they are to gobble. Chocolate rich in cocoa butter is paired with fresh ingredients like pistachio, raspberry, Vietnamese cinnamon, even lemongrass or bacon, to create treats that leave a lasting impression. Done up in hot pink and black, the shop would not be out of place on L.A.'s Melrose Avenue. Lilly also stocks chocolate-friendly wine and beer, such as champagne, big reds, dessert wines, and Belgian-style ales, making it a one-stop shop for gluttonous epicures.

MAP 2: 761 Starkweather Ave., 216/771-3333, www.lillytremont.com; Tues.-Sat. noon-7pm, Sun. 10am-2pm

Market at the Fig

Chef Karen Small, who runs the wonderful Flying Fig bistro next door, transformed a seldom-used private dining room into a sleek gourmet retail marketplace. The European-style shop offers a deft mix of prepared foods, made-to-order sandwiches, specialty retail products, and beer and wine. Come here for a light breakfast, amazing chef-designed sandwiches, and heartier dinner-friendly fare. Also on hand are charcuterie, artisanal cheeses, house-made pastries, breads, pickles, and jams. Come here after a visit to the West Side Market to grab a nice bottle of wine and some snacks for the room.

MAP 2: 2523 Market Ave., 216/241-4243, www.theflyingfig.com; Tues.-Fri. 11am-8pm, Sat. 10am-8pm, Sun. noon-7pm

VINTAGE AND ANTIQUES

Deering Vintage

With some three decades in the retail fashion industry, the owner of this stylish Ohio City resale shop knows what she likes and what she doesn't like. She specializes mainly in clothing and accessories from the 1970s and older but will make exceptions for fabulous newer pieces. Recently spotted items here have come from designers such as Geoffrey Beene, Bonnie Cashin, YSL, Dior, Bobbie Brooks, Young Edwardian, and other lesser known (and less expensive) manufacturers.

MAP 2: 1836 W. 25th St., 216/274-1211, www.deeringvintage.com; Mon.-Sat. noon-8pm

Elegansia

Owner Eva Cirjak combs through countless tag sales, estate sales, and flea markets so you don't have to. All you have to do is amble into her elegant, modern, and well-organized store and spend like it's 1969. Among the gently worn designer and vintage women's clothing lucky shoppers will unearth labels from Gucci, Giorgio Armani, and Lilly Pulitzer. Vintage gowns from Yves Saint-Laurent and Emilio Pucci go fast. Shoppers won't find basic needs here, but if you don't dawdle, you might score that one-of-a-kind ostrich cape that Cirjak just got in.

MAP 2: 1810 W. 25th St., 216/274-1116; Mon.-Sat. 12:30pm-5:30pm

Open Air in Market Square

Like a New York City flea market, this weekly summer gathering attracts enthusiastic bargain hunters and accidental tourists. Though one is not very likely to score a future family heirloom, as much of the stock falls into the bric-a-brac category, there are plenty of interesting, kitschy, and just plain odd items up for sale. In addition to the requisite candles and incense, used vinyl and CDs, beaded jewelry and textiles, there is original art and photography, homemade soaps, and vintage clothing. One vendor fashions light-switch plates from recycled roofing slate, while another sells all manner of eyeball art. Live music, food, and community outreach stations add even more character to this exuberant neighborhood block party where locals and their dogs catch up with their mates and playmates.

MAP 2: Market Square Park, corner of Lorain Ave. and W. 25th St., 216/781-3222; Memorial Day weekend-Labor Day weekend Sat. 10am-4pm

Unique Thrift

Part of a small Midwest chain of thrift stores, Unique feels a lot like a Salvation Army. This location is large, bright, and occasionally messy, but those with a keen eye and a soft touch can score anything from a rare LP to a bunny-plush cashmere sweater. Shoppers will find a wealth of clothing, furniture, tableware, and outdated electronics. Visit on Monday for a 25-50 percent discount on every item in the store. Unique's off-label use is as the best source for last-minute Halloween costumes. Oh, the horror.

MAP 2: 3333 Lorain Ave., 216/631-0205, www.uniquethriftstore.com; Mon. 7am-9:30pm, Tues.-Thurs. and Sat. 9am-9pm, Fri. 9am-9:30pm, Sun. 11am-7pm

Detroit Shoreway and Edgewater

Map 3

BOOKS AND MUSIC

Bent Crayon Records

You won't find Top 40 music at this focused West Side shop. What you will find is scads of experimental, techno, house, left field electronic, drone, noise, post-punk, African dub, bass, and forward-thinking rock music. Obscure labels and imports draw a select demographic to be sure, but for these fans, Bent Crayon is a lifesaver. Don't know your emo from your trance? No problemo—the enthusiastic staffers will not only point you in the right direction, they'll likely pop some on the sound system for an auditory explanation.

MAP 3: 1305 W. 80th St., Ste. 216, 216/221-9200, www.bentcrayon.com; Tues.-Sat. 11am-6pm, Sun. noon-5pm

Guide to Kulchur

Guide to Kulchur is an indie-minded book, magazine, and periodicals shop run by husband-and-wife team Lyz Bly and R. A. Washington. A large emphasis here is placed on fanzines (zines), and the operators hope to amass thousands of local, national, and international zines. More important, they hope to usher in the next generation of those writers with their co-op workshop for zines, handmade books, small pubs, chapbooks, and other printed ephemera. Look to this spot, too, to host writers, artists, and intellectuals to discuss the weighty topics of the day.

MAP 3: 1386 W. 65 St., 216/644-0095; Tues.-Thurs. 1pm-8pm, Fri. noon-1am, Sat. noon-9pm, Sun. noon-6pm

Hausfrau Records

At just around 400 square feet, Hausfrau Records can hardly be classified as a mega record store—or mega anything for that matter. But what this all-vinyl shop lacks in size it more than makes up for in spunk. Owner Steven Peffer manages to unearth and display vintage and not-so-vintage LPs and 45s in the genres of rock, punk, jazz, soul, and synth. Thanks to fair pricing and a keen eye, the owner moves through inventory (much of it obscure) at a steady clip. This spare, almost utilitarian store is immediately adjacent to Capitol Theatre, making a natural pre- or postshow stop.

MAP 3: 1388 W. 65th St., 216/394-5171; Tues. 1pm-7pm, Wed.-Sat. 1pm-8pm

CLOTHING

Christophier Custom Clothier

When the time comes to man-up in terms of fashion—you know, swap the snarky tees for a big-boy suit—shoppers would do well to visit Maurice Christophier. For years, this well-dressed haberdasher has outfitted clients in timelessly classic apparel, much of it custom made, all of it flawlessly tailored. Bespoke shirts and suits are this shop's bread and butter, but a guy can also pick up a smart off-the-rack blazer and a pair of the world's most comfortable khakis. To finish the polished look, this West Side boutique maintains an unmatched collection of socks, belts, and cuff links.

MAP 3: 9308 Clifton Blvd., 216/961-5555, www.christophier.com; Tues.-Fri. 10am-5:45pm, Sat. 10am-4pm

Yellowcake Shop

Designer and artist Valerie Mayen gained national recognition as a contestant on Season 8 of *Project Runway*. Inspired by Cleveland's vibrancy and growing fashion scene, Mayen decided to permanently take root in her adoptive city by opening this shop on the near west side of town. Like the old-fashioned dessert, Yellowcake clothing is classic and sweet. The garments are designed here, made here, and sold here. Mayen creates bold and colorful women's clothing, classic yet updated menswear, and fun and festive children's clothing. Since inception, Yellowcake has contributed five percent of its profits to a charitable organization that supports the relief of hunger, homelessness, and poverty.

MAP 3: 6500 Detroit Ave., 216/236-4073, www.yellowcakeshop.com; Wed.-Fri. 1pm-8pm, Sat. noon-6pm, Sun. 1pm-6pm

PETS
Pet-Tique

This smallish near-west shop is filled to the rafters with—you guessed it—dog and cat supplies galore. Going well beyond the usual grab bag of treats, toys, and embarrassing clothing, Pet-Tique stocks a fabulous array of breed-specific dog-training books, the latest and greatest pet mags, and a full line of try-to-understand-your-cat books. Bring Fido and Tabby in for a romp around the tiled space, allowing them to pick out their own schwag. Cool sunglasses? Check. Spiky collar? Check. New lead? Check. Clean up in aisle five? Check.

MAP 3: 10906 Clifton Blvd., 216/631-2050, www.pettique.com; Mon.-Fri. 10am-8pm, Sat. 10am-6pm, Sun. 11:30am-4pm

VINTAGE AND ANTIQUES
The Cleveland Shop

Around since 1979, The Cleveland Shop is one of the oldest and best-known vintage shops in the region. The store's claim to fame is authentic period costumes, which it both sells and rents. Folks looking to get dolled up for a Victorian murder mystery or hippie-themed love-in know to come here for their getups. While half the fun is the hunt, The Cleveland Shop makes it easy to snag the booty thanks to its tidy arrangement and wonderful service. Located in the Gordon Square Arts District, this secondhand shop is first with bargain hunters.

MAP 3: 6511 Detroit Ave., 216/228-9725, www.clevelandshop.com; Tues.-Fri. 11am-6pm, Sat. 11am-5pm

Flower Child

Shoppers keen on a particular vintage era have it easy at Flower Child thanks to period-specific displays, which are arranged precisely as they might have been at department stores decades ago. This super-popular multiroom shop moves through inventory quickly, meaning that frequent visits net frequent scores. Expect furniture, clothing, jewelry, lighting, and accessories from the 1930s through the 1970s, all artfully displayed. A great source for mid-century furniture, vintage jewelry, including Bakelite and men's cuff links, and all manner of floor, wall, and ceiling lighting.

MAP 3: 11508 Clifton Blvd., 216/939-9933, www.flowerchildvintage.com; Mon., Wed., and Thurs. noon-7pm, Fri.-Sat. noon-8pm, Sun. noon-5pm

clockwise from top left: 5th Street Arcades, downtown; Music Saves, Collinwood; CLE Clothing Co., downtown

Annoyed by the quality of modern furniture, Caley Coleff would scout out older pieces to customize and sell to a few friends and family. Business picked up, and she upgraded to this colorful neighborhood shop. While the location has changed, the system has not: Coleff still scouts out interesting used furniture (much of it plucked from the proverbial trash heap) before applying her own bold designs onto it. In addition to bar stools, dressers, and armoires, there are smaller items like lamps, signs, and tableware. Brisk business means that items are constantly being replaced with new (old) stuff.

MAP 3: 11102 Detroit Ave., 216/221-8221; Tues.-Wed. noon-7pm, Thurs.-Sat. noon-5pm

Lorain Avenue Antiques District

This ragtag collection of thrift, consignment, antiques, and restoration shops has long been a magnet for steely-eyed bargain hunters. Loosely centered around West 78th Street, the stores range from filthy dustbins to New York-style lofts. There is never a dearth of architectural salvage, from stately wooden fireplace mantels and stained-glass windows to porcelain pedestal sinks and claw-foot tubs. Don't miss Suite Lorain for vintage collectibles, Antique Gallery at the Bijou for Arts and Crafts furnishings sold in an old theater, and Reincarnation Vintage Design for everything from farmhouse chic to mid-century modern. This urban landscape is better suited to the self-assured explorer than the high-maintenance mall-walker. For the truly adventurous, a stop at Steve's Lunch for cheap, delicious, and potentially addictive chili dogs is an absolute must anytime of day or night.

MAP 3: Lorain Ave. btwn. W. 65th St. and West Blvd., www.discoverlorainave.com; hours vary but many shops open only Wed.-Sun. noon-5pm, see website for more information

★ Reincarnation Vintage Design

Owner Ron Nicolson doesn't just resell old furniture, he repurposes it into hip home furnishings and accessories. By staying abreast of the latest home decor trends, Nicolson and wife Cyndy know what to look for while traveling their never-ending circuit of estate sales, auctions, antiques swaps, and demo sites. An old wooden door is transformed into a funky dinette table; a long-forgotten industrial workbench becomes a stainless-steel kitchen island; galvanized wire conveyor belting is segmented into durable and distinctive doormats. This two-level New York-style loft showroom is a must-visit when hitting the antiques and resale shops of Lorain Avenue.

SHOPS
DETROIT SHOREWAY AND EDGEWATER

Being open only on weekends allows him time to find new cool stuff, says Nicolson.

Suite Lorain

Easily one of the best vintage shops in Cleveland, Suite Lorain is 8,000 square feet of retro fun. The former bowling alley digs are an appropriate setting for the well-tended collection of clothing, home furnishings, small appliances, and accessories from the 1920s through the mid-20th century. Numerous vendors keep the place uber-stocked with cool kitsch and collectibles, including old records, magazines, and posters. A favorite among designers, touring musicians, and fashion-savvy ladies, this West Side shop knows the difference between trash and treasure.

University Circle and Little Italy

Map 4

CLOTHING

Anne van H. Boutique

Owner Anne van Hauwaert describes her salon as "the most international boutique this side of New York." She is being modest. Her art gallery-like shop in University Circle would be at home not just in the Big Apple, but also Los Angeles, Montreal, or Brussels, the owner's home turf. Well-traveled shoppers come here for Anne's own sleek fashions as well as those from other top European designers. Truly wearable, the clothes feature bold, artistic prints, modern cuts, and high-quality fabrics. Vintage fans may score an old Pucci, Dior, or Gaultier. Stunning jewelry, bags, shoes, scarves, and hats are also sold here.

Cleveland Heights and Shaker Heights

Map 5

ARTS AND CRAFTS

Fine Points

Knitters and crocheters make journeys short and long to come to this distinctive shop. Inside this charming Victorian house on artsy Larchmere Boulevard is a kaleidoscope of today's hottest fibers, yarns, and textiles. Shoppers can purchase yarn to go, commission a one-of-a-kind garment, or snag one of the owner's handcrafted knit fashions. The boutique also stocks a full panoply of knitting supplies, including books, patterns, needles, and accessories. Newbies can sign up for an informal class here to learn the ropes, so to speak.

MAP 5: 12620 Larchmere Blvd., 216/229-6644, www.finepoints.com; Tues.-Sat. 11am-6pm, Sun. noon-5pm

Passport to Peru

Coventry was hippie central in the 1960s, and this store is a lasting legacy of those heady times. Incense fills the air and permeates all manner of imported merchandise, from downy alpaca sweaters and hats to trippy-dippy tie-dyes. Long the go-to source for Birkenstocks and Naot sandals, Passport is also a gift-hunter's best friend. Fine ethnic jewelry, embroidered handbags, wooden wind chimes, and natural skin drums are just a sliver of the hippie-chic schwag on tap. Grab an incense burner and satchel of sticks for the road. It'll keep fresh the memory of Coventry's rich past.

MAP 5: 1806 Coventry Rd., 216/932-9783; Mon.-Sat. 11am-8pm, Sun. noon-5pm

Utrecht Art Supplies

Sure, this store is not unique to Cleveland. But when Cleveland Institute of Art students need to stock up on quality art supplies, they come to the Mayfield Road outpost of this great chain. Utrecht carries one of the largest inventories of oil, acrylic, and watercolor paints, plus the canvases, brushes, and easels to go with them. Sculpture artists will find numerous types of clay and stone and the implements to carve them. Simply painting a dorm room? Come here for tapes, straight edges, and templates to get the job done right. Curious about a specific genre? Grab an instructional manual and, perhaps, change your destiny.

MAP 5: 2768 Mayfield Rd., 216/371-3500, www.utrechtart.com; Mon.-Fri. 9:30am-7pm, Sat. 10am-6pm, Sun. noon-5pm

BOOKS AND MUSIC

Loganberry Books

Established in 1994, this cozy book nook specializes in children's and illustrated books, women's history titles, and art and architecture tomes. Along with these genres, plus popular fiction, shoppers can find used rare books, including leather-bound first editions. Fans of traditional bookstores will adore Loganberry, which sports warm oriental rugs, wood floors, and row upon row of open shelving. Loganberry's popular "Stump the Bookseller," a web service where readers post often-sketchy details in hopes of identifying an old favorite book, has been featured in the *New York Times* and on NPR. Strong Bindery, an outfit that restores and repairs old books, is on-site.

MAP 5: 13015 Larchmere Blvd., 216/795-9800, www.loganberrybooks.com; Mon.-Wed. 10am-6pm, Thurs.-Fri. 10am-8:30pm, Sat. 9am-6pm

Mac's Backs Books

It makes sense that Mac's carries works by adult-comic artists like Harvey Pekar and Robert Crumb: Both authors spent formative years tooling around this bohemian neighborhood. This delightfully cramped tri-level shop has an unrivaled selection of literary journals, hard-to-find magazines, classics, and nonfiction. Those looking for a lighter read can pore over thousands of new and used fiction, mystery, and science fiction titles. Equal parts town hall and bookseller, Mac's is the site of frequent neighborhood meetings, readings, discussions, and workshops.

MAP 5: 1820 Coventry Rd., 216/321-2665, www.macsbacks.com; Mon.-Thurs. 10am-9pm, Fri.-Sat. 10am-10pm, Sun. 11am-8pm

Record Revolution

This Coventry Road institution boasts a basement filled with new and used vinyl and CDs. The underground setting suits the shop to a T considering the place was ground zero for the cultural revolutions that erupted some five decades ago. Vestiges of that counterculture remain today, largely in the form of all manner of smoking paraphernalia, incense, and hippie clothing. Young alternative types visit the main-floor boutique to stock their wardrobes with funky vintage clothing, jewelry, and accessories. Rounding out the inventory are obscure rock videos, posters, and DVDs.

MAP 5: 1832 Coventry Rd., 216/321-7661; Mon.-Sat. 11am-9pm, Sun. noon-7pm

CLOTHING

Gentleman's Quarters/Frog's Legs

Style-conscious men and women have been coming to this upscale clothier for some 40 years. Stocking mostly high-end European fashions, the Larchmere store caters less to hipsters than to

Comics in Cleveland

From Mr. Natural to Superman, Cleveland has had a hand in creating some of the most lasting comic characters. More recently, Cleveland has served as ground zero for the latest comics-themed Hollywood blockbusters, with both *The Avengers* and *Captain America: The Winter Soldier* being filmed in the 216. And judging by the comic book and novelty shops in town, people around here prefer to never grow up.

Jerry Siegel and **Joe Shuster** were just kids when they met at Glenville High in Cleveland. But these whiz kids soon found themselves writing and illustrating comics, including those of the popular Doctor Occult, for big-time mags like *New Fun*. Despite a few earlier failed attempts, Siegel and Shuster finally sold a story they had been working on for years about a mild-mannered reporter with superhuman abilities. In 1938, Superman debuted on the cover of Issue #1 of *Action Comics*. The Man of Steel soon found his way into newspapers, radio programs, television shows, motion pictures, and, if you can believe it, a Broadway musical.

In the 1960s, Coventry Road in Cleveland Heights was a counterculturist's dream. The bohemian strip with a tie-dye vibe was home to **Harvey Pekar.** With the neighborhood as his backdrop, he began writing his curmudgeonly autobiographical comic *American Splendor.* The long-running strip was adapted into a successful film of the same name starring Paul Giamatti.

One of Pekar's earliest illustrators was **R. Crumb,** a friend who would go on to create such infamous characters as Fritz the Cat and Mr. Natural. Crumb's sexually and politically charged comics made him the darling of the antiestablishment crowd. And who can forget the lovable *Calvin and Hobbes,* penned by the famously shy native Bill Watterson.

To browse thousands of new and used comic books, locals hit **Carol & John's Comic Book Shop.** This mom-and-son operation has been chugging along for almost 25 years thanks to superhuman customer service and personal attention. Coventry Road is still comic central thanks to **Big Fun,** a novelty shop for the kid in all of us. Vintage toys, zany collectibles, gag gifts, hipster clothing, and plenty of comic book-themed fun packs this amazing mindtrip of a store.

upwardly mobile hautesters. An in-house tailor will make sure that those new threads from Italy, France, Sweden, and Germany fit like a glove. Frog's Legs, the women's accessories shop within GQ, carries custom jewelry, purses, and scarves.

MAP 5: 12807 Larchmere Blvd., 216/229-7083; Tues.-Thurs. 11am-7pm, Fri. 11am-6pm, Sat. 10am-4:30pm

GIFT AND HOME
★ Big Fun

For those among us who refuse to grow up, Big Fun offers relief in the form of cool stuff and kinship. It's hard to not act a wee bit juvenile perusing the over-the-top greeting cards, gag gifts, and campy 1980s TV lunchboxes. Old is new here, with a monster selection of vintage toys, retro candy, and nerd-friendly clothing. Atari T-shirts,

Star Wars collectibles, and an entire section devoted *The Wizard of Oz* (look for the spinning model of Dorothy's farmhouse) are just some of the things kitsch shoppers will find here. Grab a seat in the old-timey photo booth and leave with a strip of black-and-white memories. Big Fun truly is big fun. There is also a second location in Lakewood.

MAP 5: 1814 Coventry Rd., 216/371-4386, http://bigfunbigfun.com; Mon.-Thurs. 11am-8pm, Fri.-Sat. 11am-10pm, Sun. 11am-7pm

City Buddha

Follow the Buddha's teachings and you may buy nothing here but a carved wooden Buddha. But where's the fun in that? Like a street bazaar airlifted from Indonesia, this fragrant shop deals in imported exotica, mostly from Southeast Asia. Jammed with handmade furniture, hand-carved figurines, hand-painted pottery, and hypnotically beautiful textiles, City Buddha makes home design easy, cheap, and fun. What began as an open-air stand over a decade ago is now a bustling Coventry Road shop frequented by hippies, yuppies, and well-heeled travelers. As the Buddha might say, "Fill your mind with compassion, but fill your home with really cool stuff."

MAP 5: 1807 Coventry Rd., 216/397-5862, www.citybuddha.com; Mon.-Thurs. noon-8pm, Fri. noon-9pm, Sat. 11am-9pm, Sun. noon-7pm

duoHOME

At this smart-dressed storefront shoppers will find a selection of sophisticated yet comfortable furnishings, mostly in traditional, transitional, and modern styles. A full line of carefully chosen lifestyle products and accessories will doubtless brighten one's home while adding affordable functionality to boot. Come here for DIRT sootless soy candles, stylish ARCHITEC kitchenware, and colorful adjustable scatter tables. The "duo," by the way, comes from the store's dual personality as both retail shop and interior design studio, which is run by the owners in the back.

MAP 5: 3479 Fairmount Blvd., 216/651-4411, www.duohome.com; Mon.-Sat. 10am-5:30pm, Thurs. until 7pm

HEALTH AND BEAUTY

Quintana's Barber Shop

Owner Alex Quintana takes the art—and he does consider it an art—of barbering very seriously. His domain is a charming renovated colonial in Cleveland Heights, divided upstairs and down by his barbershop and his wife's day spa. Guys looking for a great cut, or possibly a close shave, would do well to book a chair here. Look for the spinning barber pole, then head inside for a cup of hot coffee, a stack of great mags, and a pleasantly masculine environment. Call the same number to book a massage, facial, or waxing.

MAP 5: 2200 S. Taylor Rd., 216/321-7889, www.quintanasbarbershop.com; Tues.-Thurs. 8am-8pm, Fri. 8am-6pm, Sat. 8am-4pm

KIDS

Playmatters Toys

Indie-minded parents who like to sidestep the big-box chains love this small homegrown toy shop. Like the other four Northeast Ohio locations, the Shaker Square outpost is best known for educational and classic toys. Playmatters holds its own against the giants by offering high-quality products and great customer service. Replacing the sea of plastic play palaces are nontoxic wooden toys, snuggly plushies, and hard-to-find retro games. Thanks to plenty of hands-on displays and fully functional models, kids have just as much fun shopping as they do buying. But Playmatters' tagline is "Toys that teach, challenge, and inspire," so you know you'll find a million new ways to enlighten the little ones.

MAP 5: 13214 Shaker Sq., 216/752-3595, www.playmatterstoys.com; Mon.-Sat. 10am-6pm, Sun. noon-5pm

PETS

Coventry Cats

Notwithstanding the name, this Coventry Road shop features a cornucopia of both dog and cat paraphernalia. They don't stock live animals, but they do carry a fine selection of holistic pet food, toys, clothing, and bedding. Deck out your pooch in a new collar, some winter booties, maybe the latest Halloween costume. Jewish or not, your feline will look sharp in a stylish yarmulke. If he or she deserves it, buy your kitty friend a stash of fresh catnip and a cat-friendly video to groove on, featuring frolicking mice, birds, and squirrels. Good dogs get meaty rawhides, annoying squeaky toys, and fresh-baked goodies.

MAP 5: 1810 Coventry Rd., 216/321-3033; Mon.-Sat. 10:30am-8pm, Sun. noon-5pm

VINTAGE AND ANTIQUES

Heide Rivchun Conservation Studios

This Larchmere shop has a dual identity. It is the site of owner Heide Rivchun's renowned furniture conservation and restoration business, and it is the storefront where she displays her wonderful collection of antiques for sale. Stocking fine furniture largely from the 18th and 19th centuries, as well as striking architectural items, the store is popular with designers, decorators, and informed homeowners. Old globes, full fireplace mantels, stained-glass windows, portly earthenware casks—these are just some of the unique items on hand.

MAP 5: 12702 Larchmere Blvd., 216/231-1003, www.conservationstudios.org; Mon.-Fri. 9am-5pm, Sat. 10am-4pm

Lakewood

Map 6

BOOKS AND MUSIC

Carol & John's Comic Book Shop

This mom-and-son operation is approaching the 25-year mark thanks to its super-friendly, customer-oriented approach to sales. The owners pledge to read everything they stock so as to provide an honest, informed opinion when asked to do so. Anybody interested in new and used comics will have a field day at this tidy, well-organized shop, with weekly deliveries of both big-name and small-run publications. While at its heart a hard-core comic depot, Carol & John's also stocks a nice selection of graphic novels, action figures, posters, and apparel. As it is in a West Side strip mall, there is plenty of easy and free parking.

MAP 6: 17462 Lorain Ave., 216/252-0606, www.cnjcomics.com; Mon.-Fri. noon-8pm, Sat. 10am-7pm, Sun. noon-5pm

My Mind's Eye Records

Vinyl junkies rejoice at the sight of this jam-packed Lakewood shop. Two rooms house an ever-changing catalog of new and used LPs, CDs, and DVDs. Hard-core music fans know to stop by regularly for the best chance to snag a rare gem, especially in the early-heavy-metal and garage-rock genres. Dusty collections from the recently departed seem to arrive daily. If we didn't know better, one might assume store owner Charles Abou-Chebl had a hand in the process. But no, he merely dispenses an encyclopedic knowledge of music trivia while possessing an almost stereotypic indie-record-store persona. Heck, it's a joy to shoot the breeze with the dude, whether shopping or not.

MAP 6: 16010 Detroit Ave., 216/521-6660, www.mymindseyerecords.com; Mon.-Sat. noon-9pm, Sun. noon-7pm

HEALTH AND BEAUTY

Reagle Beagle

If it weren't for the Beagle, hairy dudes would be roaming the streets of Cleveland like Bigfoot's kin. This men's-only "hair saloon" specializes in manscaping services for those men who are less than enthusiastic about visiting girly salons. Seduced by cold beer, fruity wine, and a pinball machine, among other dude-tastic diversions,

Walk All Over Waterloo

This blue-collar, ethnic neighborhood nine miles from downtown Cleveland is emerging as one of Cleveland's latest comeback stories. On the shores of Lake Erie, this is one of the few communities with actual, affordable access to one of the region's best treasures. Accessible housing, a grassroots arts movement, and an increasing number of restaurant and retail options are combining to turn Collinwood into one the city's next hot neighborhoods.

Guided by one of the city's most fervent arts organizations, Waterloo Arts, this close-knit community has taken bold steps of late to attract artists, who increasingly are being priced out of bigger (and prohibitively expensive) markets. Grant programs help artists buy or rehab homes in the area, support their work, and promote the efforts in a national marketing campaign.

The primary gallery in the area is **Waterloo Arts Gallery** (15605 Waterloo Rd., 216/692-9500, www.artscollinwood.org), run by the local arts organization. Others in the area include **Waterloo Studios** (15316 Waterloo Rd., 216/383-8002), **Waterloo 7 Studio** (10513 Waterloo Rd., 239/293-9548, www.schmidtsculpture.com), **Miller Schneider Gallery** (16008 Waterloo Rd., 440/715-0603), and **Satellite Gallery** (442 E. 156th St., 216/621-6644, www.lorennaji.com).

On the first Friday of every month, **Walk All Over Waterloo** invites people to explore the area's art galleries, restaurants, and shops, which keep their doors open a little later. Each year in June, the **Waterloo Arts Fest** attracts approximately 5,000 attendees, who come for art and stay for the live music, food, and fun.

One of the country's top live-music venues, the **Beachland Ballroom,** has been hosting the best touring talent in an old Croatian social hall in this neighborhood since 2000. Those deep musical roots have led to the launch of two great record shops, **Music Saves** (15801 Waterloo Rd., 216/481-1875, www.musicsaves.com) and **Blue Arrow Records** (16001 Waterloo Rd., 216/486-2415, www.bluearrowrecords.com), which offers an extensive collection of LPs and 45s from the 1950s to today.

Going hand in hand with vinyl record shops, of course, are shops featuring vintage and eclectic clothing and accessories. That's precisely what's on display at **Star Pop** (15813 Waterloo Rd., 216/965-2368, www.starpopcleveland.com), **This Way Out** (15711 Waterloo Rd., 216/458-1156), and **Native Cleveland** (15813 Waterloo Rd., 216/383-5196, www.nativecleveland.com).

The increased foot traffic in the area has led to a mini restaurant boom, of sorts, with a handful of new options. **Blitz BBQ** (15710 Waterloo Rd., 216/692-9775) dishes up slow-smoked meaty goodness while **Callaloo Cafe** (15601 Waterloo Rd., 216/926-4673) offers an authentic taste of the Caribbean. But for a soul-satisfying taste of the old country, hit the **Slovenian Workmen's Home** (15335 Waterloo Rd., 216/481-5378) every Friday 3pm-8pm for one of the best fish fries in town.

guys easily relinquish their superfluous eyebrow, neck, and back hair. Each styling station boasts its very own flat-screen so the cord to SportsCenter never needs to be severed. Sign up for the popular House Cut, a veritable menagerie of postpubescent primping. Plus a shoeshine!

MAP 6: 17617 Detroit Ave., 216/228-9677, www.thereaglebeagle.net; Mon.-Fri. 10am-8:30pm, Sat. 9am-5pm, Sun. noon-4pm

KIDS

Paisley Monkey

This homegrown Lakewood children's boutique started as an on-line business before graduating to a small retail shop and then graduating once again to a larger shop. They've done so by offering unique products from more than 120 manufacturers. There literally are thousands of fun and colorful gift items, like toys, books, clothing, music, baby gear, and cloth diapers. The owners go out of their way to stock high-quality products that are sustainably made and often made in the United States.

MAP 6: 14417 Detroit Ave., 216/221-1091, www.paisleymonkey.com; Tues.-Fri. 11am-8pm, Sat. 10am-5pm

PETS

Inn the Doghouse

If you're looking for a place to stash your pooch for an hour, afternoon, or evening, this well-run doggie day care and boarding facility is a godsend. The lucky dogs have their run of a roomy 7,200-square-foot indoor playpen with an attached 1,600-square-foot outdoor facility. Boarded dogs spend the days with the day-campers before retiring to their suites for dinner and a nap. While here, dogs can sign up for grooming services like a brush and blow, nail clipping, and, er, anal gland expression. Proof of current vaccinations is required.

MAP 6: 1548 W. 117th St., 216/651-0873, www.innthedoghouse.com; approx. $14 half day, $22 full day, $35 overnight

SPECIALTY FOODS

Geiger's Clothing & Sports

At this 75-year-old shop, a guy can walk in and purchase a fashionable necktie, a ridiculously flimsy Speedo, and a pair of cross-country skis. (Let's just hope he doesn't wear them all home.) Despite this seemingly slapdash approach to haberdashery, Geiger's has earned a serious reputation as the place to go to get your skis edged, your tennis racket restrung, and your snowboard waxed baby-smooth. Look good as you play hard in apparel by North Face, Patagonia, and Marmot, all available here. Folks visiting during winter might be happy to learn that this Lakewood shop rents skis, snowboards, and snowshoes by the day and weekend. (Speedo not included.)

MAP 6: 14710 Detroit Ave., 216/521-1771, www.shopgeigers.com; Mon.-Thurs. 10am-8pm, Fri.-Sat. 10am-6pm

VINTAGE AND ANTIQUES

Play it Again, Sam

There has been an undeniable uptick in the demand for old-school vinyl records, and few shops have been positioned to take advantage of that trend as well as Play it Again, Sam. This West Side institution doesn't sell records, but a bewildering selection of vintage two-channel stereo equipment. Audiophiles come here for both new and used tuners, preamps, receivers, turntables, cassette recorders, CD players—even reel-to-reel tape recorders. If you have a vinyl collection in need of a little TLC, bring it here for a trip through Sam's deep-cleaning machine. Those old platters will come out looking and sounding as good as new.

MAP 6: 14311 Madison Ave., 216/228-7330, www.playitagainsam.com; Mon.-Tues. and Thurs.-Sat. 10am-6pm

Greater Cleveland   Map 7

BOOKS AND MUSIC
★ Music Saves

Though the name might lead you to believe otherwise, Music Saves does not specialize in Christian rock. What this shop does carry is new and used indie rock, in all its blessed forms. Down-to-earth civility is a rare find at many indie record shops, where vast stores of knowledge often can come across as dweeby condescension. Everything here, from the fat cat named Vinyl to the very flexible closing time, is refreshingly genial. In artsy Collinwood, the store is bright, festive, and outfitted with comfy furniture. While dedicated largely to vinyl—hence the feline's moniker—Music Saves also deals in CDs and music-related DVDs. Stop here before concerts at the nearby Beachland Ballroom. Not only can you buy the performers' tunes; you can buy your tickets to the show.

MAP 7: 15801 Waterloo Rd., Cleveland, 216/481-1875, www.musicsaves.com; Tues.-Thurs. noon-9pm, Fri.-Sat. noon-10pm, Sun. noon-4pm

CLOTHING
Kilgore Trout

For decades, Kilgore Trout has been recognized as one of Cleveland's finest menswear providers. These days, women don't just tag along to help outfit their guys; they come to build their own wardrobes. With exclusive lines like Tory Burch and Catherine Malandrino, it's clear why. This handsome East Side boutique is flush with 10,000 square feet of top-quality men's and women's clothing and accessories. In addition to scrupulously tailored suits by Ermenegildo Zegna, men can find belts, cuff links, English-made socks, and fine shaving products. Gals go gaga over Paul Smith bags, Yummiglass jewelry, and Diptyque perfumes and scented candles.

MAP 7: 28601 Chagrin Blvd., Woodmere, 216/831-0488, www.kilgoretrout.com; Mon.-Sat. 10am-6pm, Thurs. until 8pm

Chagrin Falls: Worth the Trip

It might take a good 35 minutes to reach Chagrin Falls from downtown Cleveland, but the destination makes the journey worthwhile. Reminiscent of a quaint New England town, this charming burg boasts a village square (triangle, actually), bustling Main Street, and the namesake waterfalls. Make the trip in mid-October and you might never again pine for a fall foliage trip to New Hampshire.

Wear comfortable shoes and you can easily hit all the popular spots on foot. Park your car near the centrally located square and you'll even be able to drop off shopping bags as they accumulate.

Every small town needs an independent bookstore, and in Chagrin Falls it's **Fireside Book Shop** (29 N. Franklin St., 440/247-4050, www. firesidebookshop.com). For 50 years, this cozy bookshop has kept locals well informed thanks to its new and used titles. Fireside also carries an uncharacteristically large selection of children's toys, puzzles, and games. Music buffs make the trek to **Warren Henry Music** (49 W. Orange St., 440/247-0300, www.warrenhenry-music.com) for high-quality musical instruments (especially guitars), sheet music, books, and accessories.

Chagrin Falls residents take pride in their lovely Western Reserve-style homes, and they have no shortage of shops to keep them well furnished. **Simpatico** (8 E. Washington St., 440/247-3116, www.simpaticoliving. com) offers high-end home furnishings, lighting, and art, including 100 percent sustainable and nontoxic furniture.

At **Three Home** (477 Industrial Pkwy., 440/247-8425, www. threehome.net), shoppers will find eclectic, one-of-a-kind, and hard-to-pigeonhole home furnishings and accessories, much of it falling in the architectural salvage category. Shabby-chic freaks are in heaven upon entering **White Magnolia** (46 N. Main St., 440/247-5800), an airy shop loaded with trend-conscious treasures. Antique crystal chandeliers, Parisian textiles, and architectural-salvage items adorn this roomy boutique; the in-store bakery turns out

Knuth Shoes

Knuth sells shoes, no surprise there. They've got gals well covered when it comes to sandals, sneaks, slides, slings, and stilettos. But this trendy women's fashion boutique goes well beyond footwear, providing one of the sharpest selections of clothing and accessories. Styles run the gamut from young and flirty to classy and sophisticated. All the hottest brands are represented here, with lofty prices to match the au courant threads. Smart shoppers swear by the sales, though, which make room for new inventory by slashing prices. Shopping for someone else? Knuth is a great source for last-minute gifts, with a glut of hip bags, hats, sunglasses, and jewelry.

MAP 7: 30619 Pinetree Rd., Pepper Pike, 216/831-1116, www.knuths.com; Mon.-Wed. and Fri.-Sat. 10am-6pm, Thurs. 10am-8pm

delish cupcakes. For those with more traditional tastes, **Chagrin Antiques** (516 E. Washington St., 440/247-1080) stocks high-end collectibles like 19th-century English furniture, rare jewelry, and porcelain.

Clothes-obsessed ladies can lose track of entire afternoons in Chagrin Falls. **Juicy Lucy** (31 W. Orange St., 440/247-5748, www.juicylucya-clothingstore.com) attracts women from all over the region thanks to its high-end collection of New York and European fashions and jewelry. **Nola True** (15 N. Franklin St., 440/247-8980) caters to a slightly younger clientele with its fresh and current fashions. The more sophisticated gal hits **Find Me!** (24 N. Main St., 440/247-3131, www.findmecha-grinfalls.com) to shop for clothing, shoes, and accessories in an elegant antique setting. Men are well taken care of at **Cuffs** (18 E. Orange St., 440/247-2828, www.cuffsclothing.com), an old-fashioned gentlemen's outfitter housed in a brick 19th-century home. When Cuffs customers tire of shopping for timeless Italian, French, and American designs, they can enjoy a glass of wine at the in-store wine bar. If you prefer to purchase an entire bottle, stop by **Chuck's Fine Wines** (23 Bell St., 440/247-7534, www.chucksfinew-ines.com) for matchless selection and service.

You can't travel to Chagrin Falls and not stop for an ice cream cone at **Jeni's Splendid Ice Creams** (67 North Main St., 440/247-2064, www.jenis.com) or popcorn at the old-timey **Popcorn Shop** (53 Main St., 440/247-6577, www.chagrinfall-spopcorn.com), both perched above the falls. For a full meal, hit **Rick's Cafe** (86 N. Main St., 440/247-7666, www.rickscafeandcatering.com) for burgers and ribs or **Umami Asian Kitchen** (42 N. Main St., 440/247-8600, www.umamichagrinfalls.com) for seafood-heavy Pacific Rim cuisine.

To turn your day trip into an overnight stay, book a room with a fireplace at the charming **Inn of Chagrin Falls** (87 West St., 440/247-1200, www.innofchagrinfalls.com).

HEALTH AND BEAUTY

Scott Metzger Systems

Run by nationally renowned hairdresser Scott Metzger, this salon likely contains more talent behind the chairs than any other in the region. As former creative director for Vidal Sassoon, Metzger was literally the hairdresser to the stars, with his work appearing on the covers of *Rolling Stone* and *People* magazines. Hip, hot, and relevant, the cuts are both in demand and pricey at this warm and sophisticated salon. While Metzger gets about $175 for his time, other stylists are more reasonably priced at about $60.

MAP 7: 3628 Walnut Hills Rd., Beachwood, 216/464-8822, www.scottmetzgersystems.com; Wed., Fri., and Sat. 10am-5pm, Tues. and Thurs. 10am-6pm

★ **Russian-Turkish Baths**

Known simply as "The Schvitz," this old-school bathhouse remains virtually unchanged since it opened in the late 1920s, when Jewish fathers took their sons for a steam before the start of the Sabbath. Today it serves as a sort of underground men's club, a place where buddies of all religions meet up after work for a steam, a rub, and a steak. Though it's called the Schvitz, the real draw here is the steak, which is cut to order on an old band saw before getting a good broil and dousing of chopped garlic. Men eat in bedsheets, sip ice-cold beer, and *kvetch* about women and work. Would-be patrons will not find a listing for the place in the phonebook, and the club is in a dicey part of town, so it is wise to come with a regular who knows the way.

MAP 7: E. 116th St. and Luke Ave., Cleveland, 216/561-0578; hours vary; Oct.-Apr.

KIDS

Nicky Nicole

This oh-so-hip kid's boutique sells merchandise for girly girls aged 4-14, stocking tie-dyed tees, designer jeans, and hot bags. The selection here is varied enough, says management, to appeal to "soccer players, drama queens, fashion mavens, and equestrians." Just as you'd expect for a tweener glam fest, the vibrant shop is pink, sparkly, and cheerful, making it the perfect roost for a Webkinz party, dress-up bash, or plain-old shopping spree. Killer service lands Nicky Nicole on numerous "Best Of" lists.

MAP 7: 28601 Chagrin Blvd., Woodmere, 216/464-4411, www.nickynicole.com; Mon.-Sat. 10am-6pm, Thurs. until 8pm, Sun. noon-5pm

PETS

Barkley Pet Hotel and Day Spa

With amenities like daily linen service, dips in the pool, and nightly tuck-in tummy rubs, pooches at this posh doggie hotel and day spa truly have it better than at home. The 15,000-square-foot state-of-the-art complex can comfortably board 150 dogs and 18 cats. Accommodations range from poolside villas to quiet private suites with plasma TVs. Owners can ogle their babies 24 hours a day via webcam. Barkley also offers cage-free doggie day care, grooming services, and wellness treatments such as hydrotherapy and acupuncture. Over the top? Best save that question for Fido.

MAP 7: 27349 Miles Rd., Orange Village, 440/248-2275, www. thebarkleypethotel.com; Mon.-Fri. 7am-7pm, Sat. 9am-5pm, Sun. 11am-4pm

SHOPPING CENTERS AND MALLS

Beachwood Place

It may be a mall, and it may be loaded with mostly chain stores, but Beachwood Place still ranks as one of the premier shopping destinations in Ohio. Where else will shoppers find under one glorious roof H&M, bebe, Lucky Brand, and BCBG? Origins and Sephora are here, as are L'Occitane and Lush Cosmetics. Gap, Pottery Barn, and Banana Republic are anchored by Saks Fifth Avenue, Nordstrom, and Dillard's. Far from just another depressing indoor mall, Beachwood Place is bright, airy, and surprisingly cheerful.

MAP 7: 26300 Cedar Rd., Beachwood, 216/464-9460, www.beachwoodplace. com; Mon.-Sat. 10am-9pm, Sun. noon-6pm

Crocker Park

Encompassing 12 "city" blocks, Crocker Park is much more than just a shrine to capitalism; it is becoming a bona fide village. People actually choose to live at this mall, snatching up apartments and condos so as to be close to the Gap and MAC Cosmetics. Seemingly every major chain store is present here, including Abercrombie, Guess, Talbot's, J. Crew, and Victoria's Secret. On warm days, the cafés along "Main Street" throw open their doors and arrange alfresco seating on the generously proportioned sidewalks. A few indie spots like 87 West wine bar and Hyde Park steak house can be found among the chains.

MAP 7: 25 Main St., Westlake, 440/871-6880, www.crockerpark.com; Mon.-Sat. 10am-9pm, Sun. 11am-6pm

★ Eton Chagrin Boulevard

Rarely does a mall get a second chance. But when developers added on to this fading mall, essentially giving it more of a street-side feel, they infused it with fresh life. Today, the mall has grown into an attractive indoor/outdoor multiplex boasting numerous independent clothing shops, most not found elsewhere. This is where you'll find Kilgore Trout, Nicky Nicole, Audrey's Sweet Threads, and Bonnie's Goubaud—all unique to this locale. Restaurants like Michael Symon's B Spot and the nuevo Latino spot Paladar, along with Trader Joe's, make this a destination for foodies. This center is also home to the Genius Bar at a new Apple Store.

MAP 7: 28601 Chagrin Blvd., Woodmere, 216/591-0544, www.etonchagrinblvd. com; cost varies by shop and restaurant

Legacy Village

Euphemistically billed as a "lifestyle center," Legacy Village is essentially an outdoor mall. But built at a cost of $150 million, at least it is an attractive outdoor mall. Constructed to resemble a faux Main Street setting, complete with centrally located village green, the 80-acre complex boasts monster attractions like Crate & Barrel and Restoration Hardware. Popular chain restaurants like The Cheesecake Factory, The Melting Pot, and California Pizza

The antithesis to a suburban lifestyle center, Hingetown is both a shopping destination and an urban movement. With the conversion of a sleepy, underutilized redbrick building in Ohio City, developer Graham Veysey has activated a portion of Cleveland that, while optimally located, has long been ignored. Dubbed "Hingetown" because of the way it links—or acts as a hinge between—existing Cleveland assets like Ohio City's Market District, Gordon Square Arts District, and the Warehouse District, the mini-development has helped energize an entire neighborhood.

Over the course of just a few short months, this "collective of creatives" saw the arrival of multiple small, independent start-ups, all of which opened in the renovated Striebinger Building at W. 29th and Church Streets. Those businesses include **Cleveland Tea Co.** (440/346-9922), a high-end tea company; **Beet Jar Juice Bar** (330/233.7383), a vegan and raw foods café; **Kutya Rev Ohio City Dog Haven** (216/215-8895), a holistic pet supply store; **Harness Cycling Studio** (216/785-7746), an indoor cycling studio; and **Jukebox** (216/543-7074), a music-forward bar and lounge.

"We're getting people who are the poster people for Cleveland's renaissance," Veysey told the local media. "People in their 20s and 30s starting their own businesses."

These shops complement new but already thriving draws in the immediate area like Rising Star Coffee Roasters and the Transformer Station art gallery. The renovated residential space on the upper floors of the Striebinger Building joins significant new apartment and condo construction taking place in the neighborhood to help alleviate the massive pressure on the urban residential market.

Whatever Veysey has done is working. Throughout the summer and fall, open-air concerts held on blocked-off city streets attract hundreds of residents ranging in age from bike-riding hipsters and stroller-pushing parents to empty-nest urban transplants. Hingetown has truly woken up a formerly sleepy pocket of the city.

Kitchen are represented. While mostly stocked with national brands, the mall has a couple local shops like Contessa Gallery and Picciones' Jewelers.

MAP 7: 25001 Cedar Rd., Lyndhurst, 216/382-3871, www.legacy-village.com; Mon.-Thurs. 10am-8pm, Fri.-Sat. 10am-9pm, Sun. noon-6pm

SPECIALTY FOODS

b.a. Sweetie Candy Company

With some 300,000 pounds of candy on stock at all times, it's safe to assume that this confection warehouse can satisfy any sweet tooth. Around since the 1950s, Sweetie has grown into a major player in the candy wholesale business, buying and selling ridiculous amounts of the stuff. Lucky for sugar junkies, they also run a retail shop, well stocked with the same dizzying array of treats, including a pretty awesome Pez display. With rows and rows of bulk, retro, and hard-to-find gems like Moon Pies and Mary Janes, this place is like the Sam's Club of sourballs.

MAP 7: 7480 Brookpark Rd., Cleveland, 216/739-2244, www.sweetiescandy.com; Mon.-Sat. 10am-8pm, Sun. 11am-5pm

Gallucci's Italian Foods

When Gust Gallucci came to Cleveland in the early 1900s, he joined an already large and growing Italian population who longed for authentic products from their homeland. So, in 1912, he opened the first Italian and imported foods store, which later moved to this location. Still family owned and operated, this jam-packed store boasts a meat and cheese counter, a pastry counter, a prepared foods section, and shelves and shelves of Italian foods, wines, and packaged items. This is where people come for sliced prosciutto, real parmigiano reggiano cheese, pizza dough, tomato sauce, pasta, and cannoli shells. During lunch, nearby workers stream in for hearty, homemade meatball sandwiches, lasagna, and deep-dish pizza by the slice.

MAP 7: 6610 Euclid Ave., Cleveland, 216/881-0045, www.tasteitaly.com; Mon.-Fri. 8am-6pm, Sat. 8am-5pm

The Sausage Shoppe

Anthony Bourdain knows his smoked meats, and made sure to visit this Cleveland institution while filming an episode of his award-winning Travel Channel show *No Reservations*. As old-school as a hand-powered eggbeater, this Old Brooklyn butcher shop sells German-style meats cured in the traditional old-world fashion. Shops like this, where meats are ground and mixed by hand—with zero preservatives, fillers, or additives—and smoked on premises, are literally a dying breed. Come with a cooler and load up on 15 kinds of bratwurst, garlic bologna, fresh or smoked liverwurst, killer beef jerky, and natural-casing wieners. You may never again come this close to porcine perfection.

MAP 7: 4501 Memphis Ave., Cleveland, 216/351-5213, www.sausageshoppe.com; Wed. 10am-3pm, Thurs. 10am-4pm, Fri. 9am-6pm, Sat. 9am-3pm

Hotels

Downtown 215

Ohio City and Tremont 220

University Circle
   and Little Italy 222

Cleveland Heights
   and Shaker Heights 225

Lakewood 226

Greater Cleveland 226

PRICE KEY
$ Less than $150 per night
$$ $150–250 per night
$$$ More than $250 per night

Greater Cleveland is blessed with enough brand-name hotels, independent inns, charming bed-and-breakfasts, and budget-minded hostels so that every budget, style preference, and location requirement can be met with relative ease. Thanks to massive new development projects like the Global Center for Health Innovation and convention center, the Horseshoe Casino, and Flats East Bank, downtown is seeing its first new hotel boom in ages. By 2015, 800 new rooms should be online in the city center alone.

Apart from those downtown, there are a pair of new hotels in University Circle and a sporty new hostel in Ohio City. Those join a predictably large contingent of rooms near Hopkins International Airport, and an even larger fleet of hotels in suburban Beachwood, of all places. Some areas, like Tremont, Lakewood, Detroit Shoreway, Cleveland Heights, and Shaker Heights are largely devoid of inns.

The good news, though, is that downtown's central location makes it a fine jumping-off point for most major sights, attractions, and neighborhood visits. If you don't have a car, it makes sense to examine the public transportation system before booking a room.

CHOOSING A HOTEL

For most business and pleasure visits, a downtown address is the most logical option. And downtown is manageable enough in size that lodging decisions need not be based solely on proximity to a sight, event, or organization. Options range from very basic budget

HIGHLIGHTS

★ **Best Hotel Bar with a View:** Step outside the XYZ Lounge in the new **Aloft Cleveland Downtown** and you'll be perched above the Cuyahoga River with views of the city skyline. It's a great place to enjoy a mojito and the setting sun (page 215).

★ **Finest Reuse of a Really Old Mall:** The Arcade is likely the most magical interior space in Cleveland, and now you can sleep there. One hundred years after it was built, the attractive Victorian atrium was converted into the sharp-dressed **Hyatt Regency at The Arcade.** At least now those gargoyles have something to guard come nightfall (page 218).

★ **Schmanciest Lobby:** Carved of marble pulled from the same quarry as Michelangelo's *David,* the central fountain in the lobby of the **Renaissance Cleveland Hotel** is truly a work of art. The rest of this grand entrance hall is nothing to sneeze at either (page 218).

★ **Most Modern Hostel:** Banish notions of dank hostels with rentable sheets. The new **Cleveland Hostel** is a contemporary if spare 60-bed inn in the middle of bustling Ohio City. Bike rentals, a communal kitchen, and a rooftop patio make this the perfect urban perch (page 220).

★ **Best Jazz Club Turned Hotel:** One would be hard pressed to find a more interesting backstory than that of **DoubleTree by Hilton,** also referred to as the Tudor Arms Hotel. Built in 1933, the 12-story Gothic Revival building originally was the fashionable Cleveland Club. Later, it was the Tudor Arms, a popular jazz club (page 222).

★ **Best Bed for Bicyclists:** The **Inn at Brandywine Falls** is tucked into Cuyahoga Valley National Park, literally steps from its namesake falls. Better yet, the lengthy and scenic Towpath Trail is only a mile and a half from the front door (page 228).

inns on the fringes of town to ritzy four-star gems right on Public Square. How you ultimately decide will likely be a combination of availability, location, budget, and occasion. Two buddies cycling across the United States might not require the same level of comfort and service as, say, that honeymooning couple from Albuquerque. When staying downtown and traveling by car, it almost always makes financial sense to find overnight parking outside the hotel.

Despite the fact that 2.5 million people visit University Circle each year, it used to be a chore to track down a decent room there. That's no longer the case thanks to a pair of new hotels, which join the two large InterContinental hotels near the Cleveland Clinic campus and a few smaller inns. RTA's speedy HealthLine Rapid Transit buses connect downtown and University Circle like never before.

Due to its bounty of charming century homes, Ohio City has developed a happy little cluster of bed-and-breakfasts. A handful of well-run inns can be found within blocks of one another, and each offers the sort of personality and personal attention that fans of the genre seek. A contemporary new hostel (not a youth hostel) in the heart of Ohio City has become an instant hit with budget-minded travelers or just those who appreciate "experiencing" rather than just visiting a new city.

There are options for those who prefer to stay close to the airport, Cleveland Metroparks, Cuyahoga Valley National Park, or Chagrin Falls.

Downtown

Map 1

★ Aloft Cleveland Downtown $$

Aloft Cleveland Downtown, a boutique brand from Starwood Hotels & Resorts, opened this contemporary 150-room hotel in the summer of 2013. It is part of the Flats East Bank development that overlooks the Cuyahoga River and includes hotel, office, and restaurant properties. The hotel is about a 15-minute walk from Public Square and directly accessible from Hopkins International Airport via RTA's train service. Aloft hotels are consistently ranked among the best in terms of design, technology, and service. A second-floor bar and common space features 24-hour pantry and patio boasting great downtown views. Free hotel-wide wired and wireless high-speed Internet access, and electronics charging stations in all rooms are ideal for tech-focuses travelers.

MAP 1: 1111 W. 10th St., 216/400-6469, www.starwoodhotels.com

Brownstone Inn $

If you are the sort of budget-minded traveler who appreciates personal attention and doesn't bristle at the thought of conversing with other guests, consider booking a stay at the Brownstone Inn. Run by the impeccable Robin Yates, this 19th-century Victorian bed-and-breakfast has charm and personality to spare. The lovingly restored town house offers five rooms, two of which feature sitting areas. All but one has its own bath. Breakfast is taken in the formal dining room, where other visitors might be on hand to share their recent sightseeing experiences. If not, you can count on the amiable Yates to recommend the very best sights, restaurants, and shopping excursions. If all else fails simply pore over the accumulated maps and tourist literature. The Brownstone is a short five-minute drive from downtown on an oft-traveled thoroughfare into town. While far from bustling, the immediate neighborhood is mostly safe, quiet, and worry-free. Access to all major highways is a few blocks away. To find this attractive inn, simply look for the massive elm tree, which is one of the oldest living specimens in the region.

MAP 1: 3649 Prospect Ave., 216/426-1753, www.brownstoneinndowntown.com

Comfort Inn Downtown $

If you're searching for a basic hotel at a great rate, the Comfort Inn Downtown may be the best option. Situated just blocks from Public Square, this hotel is far cheaper than its location would have you believe. Granted, the bargain-basement rates tend to attract a more boisterous crowd, including those visiting for rock concerts and sporting events. Invest in a good pair of earplugs, however, and your stay may indeed be comfortable. Included in the rate is complimentary continental breakfast, wireless Internet, and local phone calls.

MAP 1: 1800 Euclid Ave., 216/861-0001, www.choicehotels.com

Hilton Garden Inn $$

If you're in town to catch a Cavs or Indians game, it's tough to book a room much closer to the action. In fact, you can see Progressive Field from many of Hilton Garden Inn's 240 guest rooms. Prices tend to fluctuate alongside the activity at the nearby stadiums and arenas, starting as low as $100 and climbing to $200 and up. To save some cash, check the website for packages built around sporting events, museum passes, and musical performances that include breakfast, parking, and admission. Like most modern hotels, this one offers complimentary high-speed Internet and a microwave, refrigerator, and coffeemaker in every room. There are also a casual restaurant, fitness center, and small pool on-site. Located adjacent to highway on-ramps, this hotel provides easy access into and out of the city.

MAP 1: 1100 Carnegie Ave., 216/658-6400, www.hiltongardeninn.com

clockwise from top left: Cleveland Hostel, Ohio City; Hyatt Regency at The Arcade, downtown; Clifford House Bed and Breakfast, Ohio City

Holiday Inn Express Hotel and Suites $

Perhaps the best union of location, price, and good looks, this Holiday Inn Express often pleasantly surprises first-time guests who are expecting a plain-vanilla property. In a retrofitted 19th-century bank, the hotel may be one of the most architecturally striking Holiday Inns around. From the gorgeous former bank lobby to the spacious, high-ceilinged rooms, nothing is standard-issue budget hotel. Guests can choose between single rooms or suites, but all have free high-speed Internet, a minifridge, and a coffeemaker, while some even boast hardwood floors and whirlpool tubs. Stays also include free hot breakfast, access to the recently renovated fitness center, and use of a game room with pool tables and pinball machines. For killer views, request rooms on the upper floors of this 15-story building. The hotel is conveniently located six blocks from Public Square.

MAP 1: 629 Euclid Ave., 216/443-1000, www.ihg.com

★ Hyatt Regency at The Arcade $$

In 1999, Hyatt spent approximately $60 million to retrofit the upper floors and adjoining towers of the stunning 1890 Arcade into a comfortable, modern hotel. Most rooms are generously proportioned and feature vaulted ceilings, original artwork, and stellar views of either the Arcade or the city. Guests enjoy wireless Internet access, a fitness center, and easy access to the Arcade's shops, services, and restaurants. This hotel is conveniently located near the East 4th Street entertainment district.

MAP 1: 420 Superior Ave., 216/575-1234, www.cleveland.hyatt.com

Marriott Downtown at Key Center $$

One of Cleveland's premier accommodations, this 25-story, 400-room property is attached to Key Tower and within easy walking distance to FirstEnergy Stadium, the Rock and Roll Hall of Fame, and the Great Lakes Science Center. Upscale all the way, with prices to match, this sharp hotel has undergone a $10 million renovation. Rooms all boast top-of-the-line bedding, flat-screen TVs, wireless Internet access, CD players, and updated bathrooms. Guests have use of an indoor pool, sauna, and fitness center, and an on-site restaurant serves breakfast, lunch, and dinner. The hotel also features a bar, snack shop, and loads of meeting and banquet space. For special occasions, consider booking one of the luxurious guest suites with spectacular city views.

MAP 1: 127 Public Sq., 216/696-9200, www.marriott.com

★ Renaissance Cleveland Hotel $$$

Originally opened in 1918 as the Cleveland Hotel, this beaux arts gem exudes opulence, grace, and beauty. More reminiscent of a major museum than a hotel lobby, its entrance hall features a soaring barrel-vaulted ceiling, massive marble fountains, and high arched windows that perfectly frame the city outside. The upmarket address right on Public Square comes with a price, of course, with rates generally ranging from $140 to $475 depending on the size of the room or suite. After a long day touring the city, settle into the classy Lobby Court Bar for a classic cocktail. Also in this 500-room property are a wonderful French bistro, an indoor pool, and a well-stocked fitness center. With the RTA located just steps away, transportation to and from the airport, University Circle, and Shaker Square could not be simpler.

MAP 1: 24 Public Sq., 216/696-5600, www.marriott.com

The Ritz-Carlton ❸❸❸

While admittedly below par compared to others in this illustrious hotel chain, The Ritz-Carlton Cleveland still deserves props for service, elegance, and location. Though some rooms could use updating, the hotel's common areas sparkle with sophistication, and the in-room amenities are close to what one might expect of the Ritz, with marble tubs, terry robes, and the matchless Muse restaurant and ritzy Lobby Lounge. Located just off Public Square, the Ritz is close to public transportation and has covered access to both Quicken Loans Arena and Progressive Field. Adjacent Tower City Center is no Rodeo Drive, but the physically attractive mall has more than enough diversions to kill a few hours of downtime. To ease those lofty prices, explore the hotel's packages, such as the Fresh Market package, which includes a chef-guided tour of the West Side Market followed by a meal constructed from those just-purchased items.

MAP 1: 1515 W. 3rd St., 216/623-1300, www.ritzcarlton.com

Westin Cleveland Downtown ❸❸❸

Cleveland's newest hotel is set to open its doors in April 2014. That's when the Westin Cleveland by Starwood Hotels will unveil its 500-room gem in the heart of the city. A dated Crowne Plaza hotel recently underwent a $64 million renovation that transformed it into a swank urban retreat. A hop, skip, and jump from the Rock and Roll Hall of Fame, FirstEnergy Stadium, and the convention center, its location is prime for both pleasure and business travelers. Upscale rooms, a massive fitness center, a chef-driven restaurant, and top-notch Westin amenities combine to form a first-rate home away from home.

MAP 1: 777 St. Clair Ave. NE, 216/771-7700, www.starwoodhotels.com

HOTELS
DOWNTOWN

Wyndham Cleveland at PlayhouseSquare ⑤⑤

A recent top-to-bottom overhaul freshened up this already attractive downtown hotel. In addition to the upscale public areas, spacious guest rooms, and attentive staff, this hotel boasts a stellar location in the heart of PlayhouseSquare. Just steps from the theaters, the hotel makes a stress-free home base for seeing shows in the area. The hotel's position on Euclid Avenue also makes trips to University Circle via the HealthLine an absolute breeze. Rooms feature comfy beds, high-speed Internet access, and Herman Miller desk chairs. A high-quality restaurant and bar mean that guests needn't leave the building for a decent pre- or post-curtain meal.

MAP 1: 1260 Euclid Ave., 216/615-7500, www.wyndham.com

Ohio City and Tremont   Map 2

★ Cleveland Hostel ⑤

In 2012, the same year that the West Side Market celebrated its 100th birthday, a brand-new hostel opened up down the block in a 100-year-old building. Both events were greeted with consummate joy and appreciation. No neighborhood has evolved as rapidly and significantly as Ohio City has done in a few short years, and the birth of this contemporary hostel is proof of that. Owner Mark Raymond has created a haven for budget-minded travelers who enjoy getting to know their hotel mates. A common area with fridge and kitchen means that guests can shop at the market and cook up their own meal. A rooftop patio gives them a great place to enjoy that meal with stunning views of the city skyline. There are 60 beds in rooms that range from fully private with a bathroom to shared accommodations. Prices per night start as low as $30. On-site bike rental and proximity to RTA's light-rail make this a great home base from which to explore near and far.

MAP 2: 2090 W. 25th St., 216/394-0616, www.theclevelandhostel.com

Clifford House Bed and Breakfast ⑤⑤

Innkeeper Jim Miner describes his house as eclectic—and that may be an understatement. Built in 1868, added onto in 1890, and renovated in the 1970s, the structure features architectural elements as varied as Tuscan, Queen Anne Victorian, Georgian Colonial, and Louis XIV. Despite the mishmash, the result is a cozy home with space enough for privacy. Accommodations range from a single room that shares a bath to a self-contained mother-in-law suite ideal for longer stays and families. A private 3rd-floor suite includes a queen bed, private bath, and fridge. The inn also features wireless

Stone Gables Bed and Breakfast $$

Partners Richard Turnbull and James Hauer spent years restoring the 1883 Queen Anne Victorian that is now Stone Gables Bed and Breakfast. With 6,000 square feet of living space, this charming inn boasts two suites and three rooms, each with king beds, private baths, and wireless Internet. Breakfasts are gourmet, with fresh fruit, eggs Benedict, and French toast the order of the day. Turnbull takes his job as innkeeper seriously and provides guests with local maps, travel info, and recommendations for area restaurants and galleries. This bed-and-breakfast is family-, gay-, and pet-friendly.

MAP 2: 3806 Franklin Blvd., 216/961-4654, www.stonegables.net

University Circle and Little Italy
Map 4

Cleveland Clinic Guesthouse $$

Budget-minded families with loved ones receiving treatment at the Cleveland Clinic are this 230-room hotel's bread and butter. The location is every bit as close to the health-care facility as the nearby InterContinental hotels, but the short- and long-term room rates are considerably more affordable. Renovations have given this property a much-needed face-lift, but guests looking for luxury would do well to stay elsewhere. For longer stays, make sure to request a room with kitchenette and fridge. Stays do include free parking and Internet access in the lobby.

MAP 4: 9601 Euclid Ave., 216/707-4200, www.guesthouseclevelandclinic.com

Courtyard by Marriott $$

This brand-new Courtyard by Marriott is situated in the heart of University Circle, making it convenient for travelers planning to hit the museums, explore Little Italy, visit local universities, or tend to those requiring care at University Hospitals or the Cleveland Clinic. This contemporary 155-room hotel features a crisp wood-trimmed lobby with computer-friendly stations, 24-hour convenience market, and quick-service bistro. There is an on-site pool and fitness center, business center, and an outdoor terrace with gas fire pit. Complimentary high-speed Internet access is available throughout the property.

MAP 4: 2021 Cornell Rd., 216/791-5678, www.marriott.com

★ DoubleTree by Hilton $$

One would be hard pressed to find a more elegant, attractive hotel in Cleveland than the DoubleTree by Hilton, also referred to as

The Bed-and-Breakfasts of Ohio City

The singular arrangement of restored Civil War-era homes, a walkable neighborhood with a wealth of attractions, and proximity to downtown and public transportation has made Ohio City fertile ground for bed-and-breakfasts.

Despite its petite size, this picturesque neighborhood boasts three privately operated urban inns, each with its own charms, quirks, and stories to tell. Less than a mile from Public Square, Ohio City is close to downtown's major offerings. But the area's narrow lanes, leafy canopies, and distinctive architecture can make it feel a million miles—and years—away from big-city life. The neighborhood's main drag of W. 25th Street, the neighborhood's main drag is loaded with enough bars, restaurants, and shops to keep one pleasantly occupied for days (and nights). A nearby light-rail stop makes for a breezy trip to the airport, downtown, or points east.

The largest of the bed-and-breakfasts is **Stone Gables,** a roomy Queen Anne Victorian with a welcoming double-stair front porch and festive color scheme. Partners Richard Turnbull and James Hauer do triple duty as hosts, chefs, and tour guides at this gay-friendly inn. Bridge Avenue is one of the most aesthetically pleasing stretches of Ohio City, and it is home to two of the area's four inns. **J. Palen House,** the relative newcomer, gracefully straddles the line between antiquity and modernity. Long a flophouse, the 1872 Victorian features original floors, doors, and stained-glass windows. Yet, it also boasts wireless Internet, a fully outfitted business center, and an eager-to-please innkeeper. Additional nearby properties now provide even more overnight options, and there's even talk of the innkeepers opening a nearby bistro. Just around the corner, **Clifford House** might be the homiest inn of them all. Innkeeper Jim Miner lives here with his pets, and there is nothing like a warm slobber from a happy puppy to remind us why we sidestepped that big, anonymous hotel in the first place.

Internet and cable. Miner, who lives on-site, has a dog and a cat, so those with relevant allergies should take note.

MAP 2: 1810 W. 28th St., 216/589-0121, www.cliffordhouse.com

J. Palen House ⑤⑤

Ohio City's newest bed-and-breakfast, J. Palen House seems to try a little bit harder to please its guests. Once a 14-room flophouse, the main 1872 Victorian structure has been gently converted into a comfortable three-suite urban inn. Thankfully, architectural highlights like original parquet wood floors, pocket doors, and a two-story stained-glass window have withstood multiple remodels. While historic touches remain, including the quirky skeleton-style room keys, modern amenities like guest-controlled thermostats, wireless Internet, and a fully outfitted business center make this inn a best-of-both-worlds proposition. In the morning, chat with houseguests over fresh-squeezed orange juice, stuffed French toast, and Belgian waffles. Additional nearby properties have provided even more options for B&B-loving travelers. Free off-street parking.

MAP 2: 2708 Bridge Ave., 216/664-0813, www.jpalenhouse.com

the Tudor Arms Hotel. Built in 1933, the 12-story Gothic Revival building originally was the fashionable Cleveland Club. Later, it was the Tudor Arms, a popular jazz club. After years of neglect, the property was restored at a cost of $22 million and reopened as this hotel. It's about halfway between downtown and the East Side neighborhoods of Shaker and Cleveland Heights. Drop-dead beautiful ballrooms here attract countless weddings and celebrations. An on-site Mediterranean restaurant, plush rooms, and complimentary high-speed Internet access make this a fine choice for long and short stays.

MAP 4: 10660 Carnegie Ave., 216/455-1260, www.doubletree3.hilton.com

Glidden House $$

For forays into the cultural playground that is University Circle, there may be no better jumping-off point than the Glidden House. Once you park your car at this 1910 French Gothic mansion, you can rely solely on foot power to get to the orchestra, museums, and institutions that dot the circle. Located on the campus of Case Western Reserve University, the inn also is convenient for appointments at the school. If there is a consistent complaint about the Glidden House, it is that some rooms do not live up to the grandeur of the building's exterior and common areas. In fact, some rooms have little more appeal than a standard chain experience. As at many off-brand hotels, rooms, suites, and experiences can vary widely. A continental-style breakfast buffet is served each morning in a lovely interior chamber. Check the hotel's website for various packages that combine a room with theater tickets and museum passes.

MAP 4: 1901 Ford Dr., 866/812-4537, www.gliddenhouse.com

InterContinental Hotel and Conference Center $$

It's understandable that travelers have difficulty making sense of the InterContinental hotels situation in Cleveland, since there are two separate properties located five blocks apart on the Cleveland Clinic campus. The far grander sibling in this hotel family is unquestionably the InterContinental Hotel and Conference Center. Completed in 2003 at a cost of around $100 million, this luxury 330-room hotel wows visitors from the get-go thanks to a 3,000-piece granite mosaic world map that serves as the lobby floor. Modern, well-appointed rooms feature high-speed Internet connections, 27-inch flat-screen televisions, minibars, coffeemakers, and CD players. The on-site fitness center is equipped with state-of-the-art cardiovascular and strength-training machines, plus locker rooms, showers, and sauna. Hungry guests can dine at the world-class Table 45 or the more casual North Coast Café. Of course, as the style, service, and amenities rise, so too does the price. Rooms

CouchSurf Your Way to a Good (and Free) Night's Rest

Clevelanders have always been generous, and despite economic challenges, the city is among the most philanthropic in the nation. So it's no surprise that so many locals participate in the **CouchSurfing Project.**

The CouchSurfing craze helps to remove financial barriers from domestic and international travel, but that's not all. Participants open up their homes to travelers, asking for nothing in return apart from a thank-you. Many go well beyond simply providing a roof, offering to pick folks up from public transport, preparing a home-cooked meal, and showing guests around the city. The benefits, in addition to the cash savings, are a more personal experience, heightened cultural exchange, and quite possibly a new friend.

A recent search of Cleveland members offering a free stay resulted in thousands of hits. The list includes people with such occupations as paramedic, chef, student, teacher, journalist, photographer, and musician. They are young and old, male and female, attached and single. The only universal quality among them seems to be a spirit of adventure, philanthropy, and camaraderie.

Surf your way over to www.couchsurfing.com to read more about this fun and frugal way to travel.

at this hotel are consistently more expensive than those at the Suites, with rates ranging from $200 to $300 and up per night. Both InterCons are less than two miles from University Circle, Case Western Reserve University, and Little Italy. Downtown is about a 10-minute drive away.

MAP 4: 9801 Carnegie Ave., 216/707-4100, www.ihg.com

InterContinental Suites Hotel $

Around since 1999, the InterContinental Suites Hotel is the older and smaller of the two InterContinentals. It also tends to be the more economical option. Room rates typically hover in the $150 range. Guests can expect mostly one- and two-bedroom suites with all the usual amenities, including high-speed Internet access, refrigerators, microwaves, and coffeemakers. This hotel also features a newly renovated fitness center, contemporary restaurant, and festive bar with outdoor patio. Both InterCons are less than two miles from University Circle, Case Western Reserve University, and Little Italy. Downtown is about a 10-minute drive away.

MAP 4: 8800 Euclid Ave., 216/707-4300, www.ihg.com

University Circle Bed and Breakfast $

"This is not the romantic-getaway-type bed-and-breakfast," admits innkeeper William Bowman. "You won't find hot tubs in all the rooms." What you will find at University Circle Bed and Breakfast is a clean, professional, and well-placed inn less than a mile from University Circle's major cultural attractions. As a short-term corporate-stay facility, the renovated century home is popular with professionals visiting the nearby universities, hospitals, and institutions. Typical guests here stay about a week and some even come from overseas. Rates include breakfast, wireless Internet, and free off-street parking. Additional accommodations are available at Bowman's sister operation, **The Place on Larchmere** (12404 Larchmere Blvd., 216/721-8968, www.larchmerehouse.com) near Shaker Square.

MAP 4: 1575 E. 108th St., 216/721-8968, www.ucbnb.com

Cleveland Heights and Shaker Heights

Map 5

The Alcazar $

Modeled after a similar Alcazar hotel in St. Augustine, Florida, this historic Cleveland Heights landmark exudes architectural charisma. The building's remarkable five-story pentagonal shape frames a sequestered urban garden. Whether spending the night here or not, folks in the vicinity would be wise to poke their heads into the grand lobby to catch sight of the mosaic stone floor, extraordinary Spanish tile work, and fishpond with fountain. As is the case with the nearby Glidden House, rooms sometimes have a tough time living up to the expectations created by the building's exterior and common areas. Today's Alcazar guests are a mix of frugal pleasure travelers, short-term business guests, and long-term independent senior residents. Rooms range from bare-bones efficiency to fully furnished multi-bedroom suite. The Alcazar is just steps from a main street lined with a coffee shop, bookstore, wineshop, and restaurants. Nighttown, one of the world's best jazz supper clubs, is less than a block away.

MAP 5: 2450 Derbyshire Rd., 216/321-5400, www.thealcazar.com

Lakewood Map 6

Days Inn $

Lakewood is a beautiful tree-lined community about five miles west of downtown. When it comes to commercial lodging, however, options are few. For the price, this Days Inn offers a clean, comfortable, and efficient place to rest your head. No, it's not the Ritz, and yes, it can get noisy, but this locale provides a decent home base for exploring Cleveland and its western suburbs. Included in the cut-rate price is complimentary continental breakfast, free wireless Internet, free off-street parking, and cable, making it a sensible, albeit nondescript, temporary address.

MAP 6: 12019 Lake Ave., 216/226-4800, www.daysinn.com

Emerald Necklace Inn $

If plans call for hitting the bike paths of the Rocky River Reservation, consider this inn your cozy home base. Literally steps from the park, this charming Victorian bed-and-breakfast is close to golf, tennis, fishing, and cross-country skiing. Or simply enjoy the inn's impeccable gardens and surrounding green space. The inn offers guests a choice of three rooms, all with private bath, some with views of the lush Cleveland Metroparks. Stays include complimentary full breakfast, free wireless Internet, and off-street parking. Have the staff pack a picnic lunch for your travels through the park. Better yet, arrange to have an in-room massage waiting when you return. Reminiscent of days gone by, the snug little country inn also runs a tea parlor that is open to the public.

MAP 6: 18840 Lorain Rd., Fairview Park, 440/333-9100, www. emeraldnecklaceinn.com

Greater Cleveland Map 7

Cleveland Airport Marriott $

When an early flight out of town awaits, it might be wise to stay near the airport. This nicely appointed Marriott is five minutes from Hopkins International, and the hotel offers a free round-the-clock shuttle service. While nothing to write home about on the outside, this 370-room property is actually quite attractive inside. There is an elegant terrazzo lobby, a restaurant featuring local, handcrafted cuisine, a lounge, indoor pool, and 24-hour fitness center. The comfortable guest rooms all offer wireless Internet service, crisp new linens, and a workstation outfitted with an

ergonomic chair. Not only is this location situated by the airport,
it is close to the I-X Center and a highway that offers a straight shot
to downtown.

MAP 7: 4277 W. 150th St., Cleveland, 216/252-5333, www.marriott.com/cleap

The Club at Hillbrook 💲💲

Mention Hillbrook Club to most East Siders and you're bound to
receive some oohs and ahhs. The tony private club is in the densely
forested Chagrin River Valley, and it is the preferred wedding site
of the area's wealthiest socialites. But you needn't be a Rockefeller
to experience this 40-room English Tudor mansion. The Hillbrook
Inn allows guests to live like a member for a fraction of the cost.
Included with a night's stay is access to the private dining room,
swimming pool, fitness center, and tennis courts. Approximately
seven different suites are available, each with private bathrooms
and wireless Internet. Most feature original architectural accents
like leaded-glass windows, black-walnut moldings, and stately fireplaces. A continental breakfast is included in the price of the room.

MAP 7: 14800 Hillbrook Dr., Chagrin Falls, 440/247-4940, www.clubhillbrook.com

Embassy Suites Cleveland Rockside 💲

Independence is a popular stop for business travelers; the city includes a thriving economic corridor home to numerous Northeast
Ohio companies. Situated at the crossroads of I-77 and I-480, the
location also puts travelers about 15 minutes from downtown and
10 minutes from the airport. Like other Embassy Suites, this one
features a roomy central atrium around which are the balconied
hotel floors. Rooms in the all-suite hotel include separate spaces
for sleeping and living, with an additional sleeper sofa, armchair,
and TV. Rooms offer wired high-speed Internet access, while wireless access is available for a nominal fee. All stays include a full
breakfast, nightly Manager's Receptions with free snacks and beverages, and complimentary transportation to the airport. Other
amenities include an indoor pool, fitness center, business office,
and free parking.

MAP 7: 5800 Rockside Woods Blvd., Independence, 216/986-9900, www.
embassysuites.com

Hampton Inn Beachwood 💲💲

There are times when staying in the eastern suburbs just makes
sense. Perhaps you are visiting family or friends who reside in
Beachwood, Pepper Pike, or Shaker Heights. Or maybe you want
to hit the shops of Beachwood Place, Eton Chagrin Boulevard, or
Legacy Village. With the Hampton Inn you know you'll find re-
liable comfort, service, and value. All 139 rooms feature cushy
Hampton beds, complimentary high-speed Internet access, and

cable TV. Included with the price of the room is Hampton's complimentary breakfast buffet. The modern hotel has a business center, indoor swimming pool, whirlpool spa, and fitness center. Travel to downtown is a snap thanks to nearby highway access.

MAP 7: 3840 Orange Pl., Beachwood, 216/831-3735, www.hamptoninn.com

★ Inn at Brandywine Falls ⑤⑤

This 165-year-old farmhouse estate is tucked into the Cuyahoga Valley National Park, literally steps from scenic Brandywine Falls, a 65-foot gem. Guests who book a room or suite at this charming inn likely do so because they plan on taking advantage of the wealth of recreational pursuits in the area. The Towpath Trail and Cuyahoga Valley Scenic Railroad are both about a mile and a half from the front door. Ohio's best ski resorts are around the corner. And Blossom Music Center, the summer home of the Cleveland Orchestra, is just down the road. Rooms range from cozy 2nd-floor nooks to spacious suites with wood-burning Franklin stoves. Vertically gifted guests are advised to avoid the low-ceilinged Anna Hale's Garret. Despite the historical nature of the house and property, all rooms feature private baths and free wireless Internet.

MAP 7: 8230 Brandywine Rd., Sagamore Hills, 888/306-3381, www. innatbrandywinefalls.com

Inn of Chagrin Falls ⑤⑤

Though only 35 minutes from downtown Cleveland, Chagrin Falls has enough charms to warrant an overnight stay. Situated around the town's village square are scores of independent boutiques, galleries, shops, and restaurants, not to mention the namesake waterfall. Granted, as the town's only hotel, the Inn of Chagrin Falls has a bit of a lock on the local lodging. But this graceful Western Reserve building has charms all its own. Many of the 15 rooms boast gas fireplaces, and some of those also have a whirlpool tub. Guests can expect a certain country-style decor, and the finishes may not be the most up-to-date. But calm, comfort, and service seem to make up for the inn's lack of panache.

MAP 7: 87 West St., Chagrin Falls, 440/247-1200, www.innofchagrinfalls.com

Excursions from Cleveland

Akron and Vicinity 235

Ashtabula County 244

Lake Erie Islands and Vicinity 251

Amish Country 263

HIGHLIGHTS

★ **Best Place to See Chuck Close Up Close:** The renovated **Akron Art Museum** has one of the most impressive collections of 20th-century art. Fans of Chuck Close's large-scale photorealistic paintings can ogle at his mesmerizing *Linda* here as well as works by Andy Warhol and Frank Stella (page 235).

★ **Most Complete Collection of Super Bowl Rings:** Gridiron fans make the pilgrimage to Canton from points afar to wallow in the memorabilia at the **Pro Football Hall of Fame.** The museum's Super Bowl Room contains collectibles from every championship game played to date (page 237).

★ **Longest Covered Bridge in America:** Ashtabula County is home to 17 covered bridges, including **Smolen-Gulf Bridge,** the longest in the United States. Bridge buffs come here to admire the craftsmanship and charm of these handsome overpasses (page 244).

★ **Most Interesting Souvenir from the Ice Age:** When a massive glacier rubbed its way across the northern tip of Kelleys Island about 18,000 years ago, it etched striking **Glacial Grooves** into solid bedrock. Measuring 10 feet deep, 35 feet wide, and 400 feet long, the furrows are remnants of the Pleistocene Ice Age (page 256).

★ **Most Appropriate Place to Scream:** Thanks to its matchless collection of the world's tallest, fastest, and steepest roller coasters, **Cedar Point Amusement Park** is consistently heralded as the world's best amusement park. Hop on Top Thrill Dragster to zip to a speed of 120 miles per hour before climbing to a height of 420 feet (page 259).

★ **Best Place to Buy a Goat:** When farmers need to buy livestock, they head to the **Kidron Auction.** This lively Amish Country auction is open to the public, making the weekly event a popular, albeit unconventional tourist attraction (page 264).

Ohio is a state of remarkable contrasts. Tucked alongside metropolitan areas like Cleveland, Akron, and Columbus is the world's largest Amish community. A day or two spent exploring these scenic back roads is like a trip back in time. Jimmy Buffett may have Key West, but North Coasters have Put-in-Bay, an island town with similar hedonistic sensibilities that attracts a million revelers each summer. And thanks to peculiar microclimates, scores of modern winemakers continue to set up shop along the southern shores of Lake Erie, where they produce intensely flavored fruit and high-quality wines—and cozy tasting rooms to sample them in.

PLANNING YOUR TIME

While visits to Akron, Ashtabula County, and Amish Country can conceivably be accomplished as part of a day trip, spending the night at any of these destinations will allow you to more thoroughly delve into the local color. Along these same lines, it's more than doable to enjoy Cedar Point Amusement Park in a there-and-back trip. But visits to the Lake Erie Islands, which require a round-trip ferry ride from the mainland, are best coupled with an overnight stay.

As for which trip is best for you, let the destination be your guide. Thrill ride fanatics travel great distances to spend the day at Cedar Point, where the tallest, fastest, longest, and scariest roller coasters consistently garner national acclaim. Families with children should seriously consider spending the night in the area, where

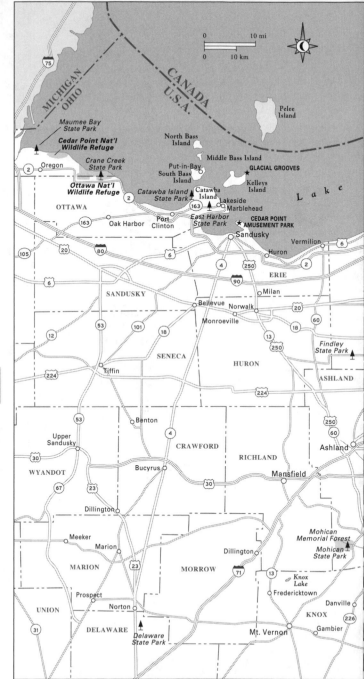

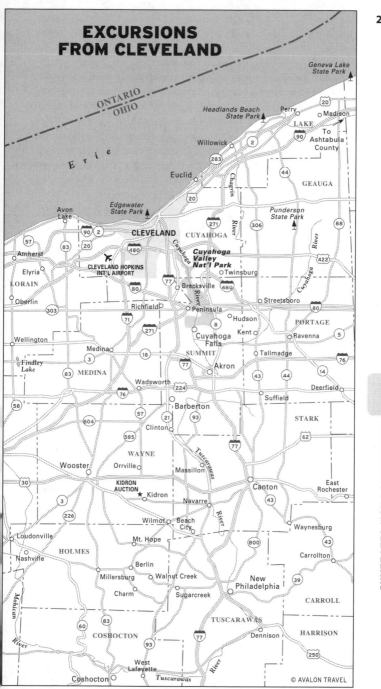

EXCURSIONS FROM CLEVELAND

Geneva Lake State Park

ONTARIO
OHIO

Erie

Headlands Beach State Park

Perry
Madison

Willowick

LAKE

To Ashtabula County

Euclid

GEAUGA

Avon Lake

Edgewater State Park

Punderson State Park

CLEVELAND
CUYAHOGA

Amherst

CLEVELAND HOPKINS INT'L AIRPORT

Cuyahoga Valley Nat'l Park

Twinsburg

Elyria

LORAIN

Oberlin

Richfield

Brecksville

Streetsboro

Peninsula

Wellington

Hudson

Kent

PORTAGE

Ravenna

Medina

Cuyahoga Falls

SUMMIT

Tallmadge

Findley Lake

MEDINA

Akron

Wadsworth

Suffield

Barberton

STARK

Clinton

Wooster

WAYNE

Orrville

Massillon

KIDRON AUCTION
Kidron

Navarre

Canton

East Rochester

Wilmot

Beach City

Waynesburg

Loudonville

Mt. Hope

Nashville

HOLMES

Berlin

Walnut Creek

Carrollton

Millersburg

New Philadelphia

Charm

Sugarcreek

CARROLL

Mohican River

TUSCARAWAS

HARRISON

COSHOCTON

Dennison

West Lafayette

Coshocton

Tuscarawas River

© AVALON TRAVEL

kid-friendly attractions like Kalahari Waterpark and African Safari Wildlife Park will keep the little ones thoroughly entertained for hours on end.

While Put-in-Bay and South Bass Island get most of the attention, Kelleys Island is equally adored for different reasons. About 300 residents call this four-square-mile island home year-round. The rest of population are weekend and summertime visitors from the mainland. Popular activities here are sunbathing, swimming, fishing, boating, and hiking ecologically diverse nature preserves. Of course, there are also bars and restaurants here as well to enjoy a nice dinner or nightcap. The Lake Erie islands shut down after Labor Day, so make sure to schedule your visit between Memorial Day and early October to enjoy the festive atmosphere.

Lovers of fine wine and finer scenery should head east to Ashtabula County, the official capital of the Ohio wine industry. Dozens of wineries and tasting rooms dot the picturesque landscape, and most drives include passages across postcard-worthy covered bridges. This excursion is likely best for adult couples looking to slow down, get off the grid, and savor Ohio's finest wines and, perhaps, fall foliage.

Amish Country is at its peak in the fall, when the leafy rural landscape changes color from verdant green to crimson and gold. It is also the busiest time here, when shops, restaurants, and hotels all get crowded. Children will get a kick out of seeing horse-drawn buggies share the road with "English" automobiles, while the massive Lehman's Hardware is a veritable treasure chest of old-timey products, gifts, and toys.

Art and/or sports fans should plan the short trip south to the Akron/Canton region. To gridiron fanatics, the Pro Football Hall of Fame in Canton is a bucket list topper, where the whole of professional football history is on display for die-hard fanatics to peruse and absorb. Not far from the Hall is the Akron Art Museum, one of the best repositories for 20th-century art in the region, with particularly close attention paid to postmodern painting, photorealism, surrealism, and pop art.

Akron and Vicinity

Akron, located a short drive south of Cleveland, presents travelers with a number of enticing attractions. Smaller and more manageable than Cleveland, the city can assuredly be the site of a wonderful day trip. But an overnight stay will accommodate a more vigorous exploration of the city's treasures. Art fans will doubtless plan a stopover at the Akron Art Museum, while minor league baseball buffs will want to take in an Akron Aeros game at lovely Canal Park. Garden and architecture aficionados absolutely must discover the grandeur of Stan Hywet Hall. If there are football fans in the group, a stop in Canton to explore the Pro Football Hall of Fame on the way to or from Akron is required.

SIGHTS

Akron Aeros

Many fans of America's favorite pastime hold minor league ball in higher regard than the big leagues. Citing cheaper outings, a more manageable setting, elevated player passion, and better in-park promotions, true baseball fans are wild about the minors. As the Cleveland Indians' AA affiliate, the **Akron Aeros** (300 S. Main St., 330/253-5153, www.akronaeros.com, $10 reserved, $9 bleachers) outfit is a proving ground for the big-brother team to the north. And the Aeros' home, newly built **Canal Park,** is an absolute gem of a ballpark. Designed by the same firm behind Progressive Field and Camden Yards, the park is modern, intimate, and integrated within its downtown environment. The park seats 9,000 and treats fans to the largest freestanding scoreboard in the minor leagues. The 70-game home season runs from early April through August. Single-game tickets can be purchased over the phone, online, or in person at the box office.

★ Akron Art Museum

To much fanfare, in 2007 the 85-plus-year-old **Akron Art Museum** (1 S. High St., 330/376-9185, www.akronartmuseum.org, Tues.-Sun. 11am-5pm, Thurs. until 9pm, $7 adult, $5 senior and student) unveiled the opening of the new John S. and James L. Knight Building, which combines with an original 1899 structure to more than triple the size of the gallery. Upon its debut the ultramodern glass-and-steel edifice was the talk of the art and architecture world. With "floating" gallery spaces and exaggerated cantilevered overhangs, the contemporary building rivals its contents for attention.

While smaller than many major museum holdings, Akron's 3,700-work collection is a tightly curated sampling of important 20th-century art, with particularly close attention to postmodern

Why Canton Is Home to the Football Hall of Fame

By the 1900s, organized football had become a popular American pastime. Many cities fielded teams, but they largely remained individual entities. Ohio was a particular hotbed of football activity, with numerous teams spread throughout the state. In 1920, the American Professional Football Association (now the NFL) was founded in Canton with 11 teams in the league. Football legend Jim Thorpe was selected as president. Five of the league's teams were from Ohio, including the Canton Bulldogs, Cleveland Tigers, and Akron Professionals. In 1961, the City of Canton made an official bid to the NFL to be the site of the hall. Acceptance soon followed, and the Hall of Fame opened to the public two years later.

painting, photorealism, surrealism, and pop art. Chuck Close's mesmerizing *Linda* is here, as is Andy Warhol's *Elvis* and Ohio-native Elijah Pierce's *The Wise and Foolish Virgins and Four Other Scenes*. Works by Frank Stella, Claes Oldenburg, and Donald Judd are also on display. Akron Art Museum also maintains a choice photography collection, with whole galleries devoted to the medium. Ironically, cameras are prohibited in the galleries.

American Toy Marble Museum

While spherical marbles were made as far back as 5,000 years ago, Akron was the site of the first mass-produced clay marble. Big deal, right? Well, Akron's American Marble & Toy Manufacturing Co. didn't just manufacture marbles, it created an affordable children's toy that swept across the landscape like a whirling dirt devil. At its peak in the late 1800s, the factory was cranking out a million orbs a day, making it the first mass-producer of toys in the nation. Located on the very site of that old marble factory is the **American Toy Marble Museum** (200 S. Main St., Lock 3 Park, 330/869-5807, www.americantoymarbles.com, Sat. 10am-1pm, free), a shrine to all things round and roly. Here, visitors can track the evolution of the game, the toy, and the craft that is marbles. Kids can even pick up the sport and play for "funsies." The museum is also the site of a popular annual marbles tournament.

Blossom Music Center

Fans of the Cleveland Orchestra might consider adding an amphitheater visit to their summer Akron excursion (or building an Akron itinerary around a trip to Blossom). Built in the late 1960s as the summer home of the symphony, the **Blossom Music Center** (1145 W. Steels Corners Rd., Cuyahoga Falls, 888/225-6776, www.clevelandorch.com) is tucked into the leafy Cuyahoga Valley National Park. Pack a picnic and a blanket and find a space on the sweeping lawn to enjoy the orchestra under the stars. To insure a dry night, it might be wise to invest in sheltered pavilion seats. Blossom is also the site of rock, country, and alternative music performances spring to fall.

Hale Farm & Village

Want to show your children what life was like before cell phones, computers, and refrigerators? **Hale Farm & Village** (2686 Oak Hill Rd., Bath, 800/589-9703, www.wrhs.org, Memorial Day-Labor Day Wed.-Sat. 11am-5pm, Sun. noon-5pm, $14.50 adult, $7.50 child, $12.50 senior) is a town trapped in the mid-1800s, when things like electricity, automobiles, and iPhones were still a few years down the road. This living history museum employs historical interpreters dressed in period costume to recount the story of the Western Reserve, the Civil War years, and life in the middle of the 19th century.

The land originally belonged to Jonathan Hale, a Connecticut farmer who relocated in 1810 to the Western Reserve. Today, skilled artisans demonstrate the very same techniques used to construct the buildings, tools, and crafts of Hale's day. Brick makers fire air-dried bricks the old-fashioned way; blacksmiths forge farm and household implements by hand; glassblowers keep Ohio's rich glass-making history alive. In fact, at the farm you can buy primitive handblown glass objects in their characteristic amber, cobalt, and green tints.

Inventor Now Museum & Store

In 1995, a well-established inventors museum relocated from the U.S. Patent and Trade Office in Alexandria, Virginia, to Akron, Ohio. The **Invent Now Museum & Store** (221 S. Broadway St., 800/968-4332, www.invent.org, Tues.-Fri. 10am-4pm, free) features 2,000 square feet of state-of-the art multimedia and exhibits that celebrate invention and human creativity. Exhibits change annually. One recent exhibit called *Inventive Eats: Incredible Food,* encompassed food-related highlights, patents, innovations, and trademarks. A museum shop features innovative products and themed apparel.

★ Pro Football Hall of Fame

For more than 45 years, the Canton-based **Pro Football Hall of Fame** (2121 George Halas Dr. NW, 330/456-8207, www.profootballhof. com, daily 9am-5pm, Memorial Day-Labor Day daily 9am-8pm, $16 adult, $10 child, $13 senior) has been attracting gridiron fans with its shrine to the legends of the game. This museum of football history has expanded four times to accommodate its growing collection and its burgeoning attendance figures. In fact, the Hall of Fame recently completed the largest expansion and renovation project in its history, done in time to celebrate the museum's 50th anniversary in 2013. The property grew from 85,000 square feet to 118,000 square feet, with an additional 37,000 square feet renovated.

Nearly a quarter of a million visitors travel to sleepy Canton, Ohio, to pay tribute to football's past and present superstars. Most popular on the must-see list likely is the Hall of Fame Gallery, where bronze busts of all enshrinees are on permanent display. Cleveland Browns fans might want to bypass the Super Bowl Room, which exhibits memories and memorabilia from every championship played to date.

Real football fans strive to attend the annual Pro Football Hall of Fame Enshrinement Festival, a days-long event that includes the Enshrinement Ceremony, dinner, parties, and the NFL Hall of Fame Game. Tickets are hard to come by, so phone early (888/310-4255).

Stan Hywet Hall

Akron's **Stan Hywet Hall** (714 N. Portage Path, 330/836-5533, www. stanhywet.org, Apr. 1-Dec. 31 Tues.-Sun. 10am-4:30pm, $8 adult, $4 student, more for tours) is widely considered one of the finest examples of Tudor Revival architecture in the region. The moniker (pronounced STAN HEE-WIT) is Old English for "stone quarry," a fitting name for this stunning American country estate built in 1912 by F. A. Seiberling, founder of Goodyear Tire & Rubber. Akron's only National Historic Landmark, the magnificent manor house, outbuildings, and gardens are open to the public for self-guided and guided tours.

The Manor House alone boasts 21,000 panes of glass, 23 fireplaces, and 65 rooms. Guided one-hour tours take visitors throughout the house, paying special attention to the Great Hall, Music Room, and Billiards Room. Well preserved and brimming with original fixtures, furnishings, and priceless antiques, the house was a model of modernity when it was completed. Tours begin on the hour most days.

While considerably smaller than its original 1,000 acres, the lush estate surrounding the home is filled with botanical treasures. Perched on the precipice of the Cuyahoga Valley, the 70 acres feature English and Japanese gardens, an apple orchard, and a stately birch tree allee. Throughout the year, the grounds are the site of outdoor theater, musical performances, and food and wine festivals. Check the website for special events.

RESTAURANTS

In the heart of downtown Akron, **Crave** (59 E. Market St., 330/253-1234, www.eatdrinkcrave.com, Mon.-Thurs. 11am-10pm, Fri. 11am-11pm, Sat. 5pm-11pm, $12-30) is a boldly contemporary bistro that specializes in eclectic, affordable comfort food. The menu features a raft of creative small plates, sandwiches, and entrées. Wildly unconventional-sounding combinations invariably work to create unforgettable tastes. Cumin-scented fried pickles, Guinness-glazed steak skewers, and sour cherry-infused duck breast are just some of the 50 or so dishes available on the all-day menu. Wine and beer fans will dig Crave's lengthy and equally affordable roster of great finds. When booking a table, it might be helpful to know there is an airy dining room, a long communal table, and a lively barroom, so choose accordingly.

From the curb, the **Diamond Grille** (77 W. Market St., 330/253-0041, Mon.-Fri. 11am-11pm, Sat. 5pm-midnight, $25-35) looks more like a shuttered shot-and-a-beer joint than a popular steak house. In fact, if it weren't for the dimly illuminated neon sign, you'd swear the place was toast. But this clubby Akron landmark is beloved precisely for that understated elegance. This is where professional golfers like Tiger Woods and Vijay Singh come to protein-load before hitting the links at nearby Firestone Country Club. Nationally recognized as the place to be for stiff martinis, thick slabs of prime beef, and, perhaps, a heaping serving of nostalgia, the Grille can be tough to get into on a busy night, so call in advance. And don't expect cushy leather banquettes when you do score a table—the interior matches the exterior. As one might expect, the food's not cheap, with steaks priced well north of $30. To sample this anachronistic steak sensation, you can leave the charge cards at home: The Grille accepts only cash.

Any way you slice it, **Luigi's** (105 N. Main St., 330/253-2999, www.luigisrestaurant.com, Mon.-Thurs. 11am-2am, Fri. 11am-4am, Sat. 4:30pm-4am, Sun. 4pm-2am, $9-11) is an Akron institution. Since 1949, folks have been coming here for what many believe is the city's best pizza, lasagna, and Italian comfort food. The setting is casual, lively, and fun, with walls of old black-and-white photos to keep you occupied during the (sometimes lengthy) wait for a table. Readers of the comic *Funky Winkerbean* will recognize Luigi's as the uncanny inspiration behind Montoni's, a recurring location owing to the cartoonist's fondness for the place. Perhaps unique to this family-run eatery are the late-night hours, which on Friday and Saturday stretch well into the next morning. Bring cash or a bank card; Luigi's doesn't accept credit cards (but there is an ATM machine on-site).

For more than 80 years, **Swenson's Drive-In** (658 E. Cuyahoga Falls Ave., 330/928-8515, www.swensonsdriveins.com, Mon.-Sun. 11am-1am, $2-3) has been filling the hearts and bellies of burgers fans, who makes pilgrimages here for soul-satisfying food. Now with multiple locations, these old-school drive-ins feature curbside ordering and delivery of wonderful diner-style burgers, fries, and milk shakes. The Galley Boy—a double cheeseburgers with two special sauces—is a house favorite, as are the onion rings and thick and creamy shakes.

The **West Point Market** (1711 W. Market St., 800/838-2156, www.westpointmarket.com, Mon.-Sat. 8am-7pm, Sun. 10am-5pm) has blossomed from a third-generation grocery store into a world-class specialty foods market, with more than 25,000 square feet of wine, cheese, meat, seafood, produce, prepared foods, and bakery departments. With the market as its larder, it is no surprise that the quality of food served at the in-store **Beside the Point Café** ($6-15) is impressive in its own right. Diners can expect an upscale cafeteria-style operation featuring house-made soups, create-your-own salads and sandwiches, and hearty home-style comfort foods. Beverage choices include fine beer and wine by the glass.

NIGHTLIFE

With a name like **69 Taps** (370 Paul Williams St., 330/253-4554, www.69taps.com, daily 4:30pm-2:30am), it is no stretch to assume that this bar stocks a nice selection of draft ales and lagers. And it does—69 of them to be precise. While not exceptional in its range, the list includes plenty of tasty suds. This unpretentious bar is a favorite of young professionals and of-age college students who flock here for the daily happy hours featuring $2 drafts. Plenty of TVs, a couple pool tables, and a foosball table give this den a mild sports-bar feel, but it rarely gets as rowdy as the others.

For something a little more polished, hit the popular (and cheekily named) **Office Bistro and Lounge** (778 N. Main St., 330/376-9550, www.theofficebistro.com, Mon.-Thurs. 11am-11pm, Fri. 11am-1am, Sat. 4pm-1am, Sun. 10am-8pm). Great starters and small plates join martinis, specialty cocktails, and craft beers in this upscale lounge.

Wine lovers adore **750 ml** (2287 W. Market St., 330/794-5754, www750mlwines.com, Mon.-Thurs. 11am-10pm, Fri.-Sat. 10am-midnight), a cozy wine bar with a laid-back vibe. Numerous high-quality wine selections can be had at 750 ml, with approximately 10 reds and 10 whites by the glass, and 800 by the bottle. A limited food menu offers up salads, small plates, flatbreads, and desserts.

SHOPS

Don Drumm Studios and Gallery

Artist Don Drumm has made a name for himself by pioneering the use of cast aluminum as an artistic medium. His distinctive sculptures have been commissioned by fans worldwide, but Ohio natives appear to be most smitten. Art lovers flock to **Don Drumm Studios and Gallery** (437 Crouse St., 330/253-6268, www.dondrummstudios.com, Mon.-Fri. 10am-6pm, Sat. 10am-5pm), home to two wonderful galleries that showcase works not just by Drumm but also

clockwise from top left: bikes for rent on Kelleys Island; horse-drawn carriages parked at an Amish auction, Berlin; Pro Football Hall of Fame, Canton

some 500 other North American craftspeople, artists, and designers. To wipe out your holiday gift lists in one fell swoop, come here to shop the huge inventory of handcrafted jewelry, glass, crafts, and sculptures. Large alfresco courtyards are stocked with unique outdoor home accessories like wind chimes, water fountains, and sculptural wall hangings.

Hartville MarketPlace and Flea Market

Roughly halfway between Akron and Canton, the **Hartville MarketPlace and Flea Market** (1289 Edison St., Hartville, 330/877-9860, www.hartvillemarketplace.com, Mon., Thurs.-Sat. 9am-5pm) is a 100,000-square-foot building stuffed to the rafters with more than 100 independently owned and operated 10-foot-by-10-foot shops. For the sheer sake of brevity we'll simply call the variety staggering. While live animals are no longer proffered here, shoppers can still walk away with pet-related items like treats and collars. Vendors come and go, but you can always count on finding books, clothing, antiques, cheese, fudge, nuts, coins, jewelry, sports memorabilia, and hardware. There is an equally large outdoor flea market, arranged on more than 20 acres of blacktop, that bursts with additional vendors during the summer months (though it is open year-round). When you're hungry for some biscuits and gravy, sidle on over to Sarah's Grille, the on-site restaurant.

Harry London Candies

Chocolate lovers might want to pull off I-77 for an emergency confection on the way to or from the Akron-Canton area. **Harry London Candies** (5353 Lauby Rd., N. Canton, 800/321-0444, www.londoncandies.com, Mon.-Sat. 9am-6pm), founded by a steelworker turned chocolatier, has been handcrafting fine candies in the European tradition since 1922. This shiny new chocolate factory and retail shop sells more than 500 varieties of sweets, from truffles and pralines to peanut butter joys and dark chocolate-covered pretzels. One-hour factory tours are offered Monday-Friday 10am-3pm. Reservations are required and can be made by phone.

HOTELS

Set inside a magnificent 1923 Tudor Revival mansion, the **O'Neil House** (1290 W. Exchange St., 330/867-2650, www.oneilhouse.com, $75-200) is not your run-of-the-mill bed-and-breakfast. Once the home of William O'Neil, founder of Akron's General Tire Company, the museum-quality residence now offers discerning travelers a choice of four glorious suites, each with private bath. The 19-room property boasts oak-paneled walls, leaded-glass windows, and oriental rug-clad wood floors. Gourmet breakfast, served in a lovely sunroom, is included in the room price. Innkeeper Gayle Johnson maintains pets of her own, so none are welcome.

For a clean, comfortable, convenient, and affordable night's stay just outside Akron, the **Courtyard by Marriott Akron** (100 Springside Dr., www.marriott.com, $140-190) is a good bet. The 75 guest rooms include all the usual amenities, including wireless Internet, coffeemakers, and large TVs. Food and beverages, including a breakfast buffet, are served in the lobby Bistro. There is an indoor pool, whirlpool, and fitness center.

PRACTICALITIES
Tourist Information

The **Akron/Summit Convention & Visitors Bureau** (77 E. Mill St., 330/374-7560, www.visitakron-summit.org, Mon.-Fri. 8am-5pm) is inside the John S. Knight Center, Akron's convention center. By phone, online, or in person, the CVB helps potential visitors with all aspects of their trip, including accommodations, planning excursions, suggesting attractions, and locating discounts.

You'll find the **Canton/Stark County Convention & Visitors Bureau** (222 Market Ave. N., 800/552-6051, www.cantonstarkcvb.com, Mon.-Fri. 8:30am-5pm) inside the Millennium Centre office building in downtown Canton. Or simply visit the website, which has all the information a visitor to Stark County might need when planning a short or extended stay in the area.

For information on a host of Ohio sights, attractions, and activities, contact the **Ohio Division of Travel and Tourism** (800/BUCKEYE, www.discoverohio.com).

Media

The main daily newspapers in the Akron/Canton region are the *Akron Beacon Journal* (www.ohio.com) and the *Canton Repository* (www.cantonrep.com).

Getting There

From Cleveland, getting to Akron and Canton is a relatively straight shot south on I-77. Akron is approximately 45 minutes by car, while Canton is closer to an hour and 10 minutes. Many frugal travelers to Akron, Canton, and Cleveland choose the **Akron-Canton Airport** (888/434-2359, www.akroncantonairport.com) over Cleveland Hopkins International Airport because of cheaper fares and fewer hassles. Discount carriers like **AirTran** (800/247-8726) and **Southwest** (800/435-9792) operate flights from here. For less than $25, travelers can hop a **Greyhound** (www.greyhound.com) in Cleveland and travel south to either city.

Getting Around

A traveler abandoned in Akron or Canton without wheels could manage, but it would be difficult to experience all these cities had to offer. Many of the attractions listed in this section are miles apart, and neither city has the most comprehensive public transportation system. Plus, it would be hard to move from one city to the other. Do yourself a favor and rent a car or hire a **cab** (City Yellow Cab, 234/542-3941; Akron Checker Cab, 330/376-5555) if you really want to experience both cities.

Ashtabula County

A short ride east from Cleveland lands travelers in one of the most scenic patches of the state. Out here, there is a closer connection to the landscape, with much of the tourist industry hinging on proximity to Lake Erie. Geneva on the Lake is a century-old lakeside resort, complete with old-time strip, cozy rental cottages, and family-friendly activities. Ashtabula County boasts 170,000 farmed acres, and agritourism is big business. Farm stands dot the scenic country lanes, and corn mazes and apple orchards fill the fields. There are 17 covered bridges in this one county, elevating a pleasant autumn drive to an unforgettable experience. And when it comes to wine, this northeastern corner of the state is king. Thanks to the moderating temps of Lake Erie, wine grapes thrive here, and the wine they produce is no joke. An overnight stay is recommended, especially when enjoying multiple wineries!

SIGHTS

Adventure Zone

Kid fun is priority one at **Adventure Zone** (5600 Lake Rd., Geneva on the Lake, 440/466-3555, www.adventurezonefun.com, Memorial Day-Labor Day daily 11am-10pm, weekends only May and Sept.), a family-friendly entertainment center. Pay-as-you-go attractions like go-karts, climbing walls, batting cages, a restored merry-go-round, and a rather challenging 18-hole minigolf course will keep the little ones occupied for hours. Open for over a decade, this independently owned and operated amusement center takes pride in its cleanliness, its well-mannered staff, and the affordability of entertainment. Adults can rent street-legal golf carts here to cruise up and down the famous Geneva on the Lake strip.

★ Smolen-Gulf Bridge

They are still building **covered bridges** in Ashtabula County, if you can believe that. The latest, the Smolen-Gulf Bridge, is the longest covered bridge in the United States at 613 feet. For those keeping track, that makes 17 covered bridges in the county, more than any other in Ohio. Most are far older than the Smolen-Gulf, with some dating all the way back to 1867. Bridge fans come to admire the craftsmanship of the various construction methods, which include Pratt truss, Howe truss, and Town lattice designs. Self-guided auto tours of the bridges are very popular, especially in the picturesque autumn months. The routes are well marked and maps can be obtained by contacting the **Ashtabula County Covered Bridge Festival** (25 W. Jefferson St., 440/576-3769, www.coveredbridgefestival.org). Paddlers might choose to experience the bridges from below while cruising along the lovely Grand River. Contact **Raccoon Run Canoe Rental** (1153 State Rd., Harpersfield, 440/466-7414, www.raccoon-runcanoerental.com) to rent a canoe or kayak for a two- to eight-hour trip. One flat fee includes equipment, shuttles to and from drop-off points, flotation devices, river maps, litter bags, and safety demonstrations. They are open May through October.

Geneva on the Lake

Ohio's oldest summer resort district **Geneva on the Lake** (800/862-9948, www.visitgenevaonthelake.com) has, since the turn of the 20th century, enticed well-heeled vacationers from nearby cities to take in the beaches, burgers, and big bands. While "progress" has tarnished some of this historic town's old-timey charm, there is still plenty to do, see, and enjoy in and around this lakefront village. Charming cottages and bed-and-breakfasts still dot the shoreline, along with glitzy new hotels and condos. Like a Jersey Shore midway, the famous strip is lined up and down with fast-food snack bars, ice-cream parlors, arcades, bars, and nightclubs. Cars, motorcycles, and golf carts prowl the road in search of adventure, camaraderie, and entertainment. The **Cove** (5326 Lake Rd., 440/466-8888) is the strip's oldest rock-and-roll joint, with live music all weekend long, while the **Swiss Chalet** (5475 Lake Rd., 440/466-8650) is geared more toward the Top 40 set. All summer long, Geneva on the Lake is home to seasonal festivals, outdoor concerts, flea markets, and celebrations. Most businesses, sights, and attractions keep different hours depending on the season, so it is wise to call before visiting. Check the visitors bureau's website for detailed information.

Geneva State Park

This 700-acre **lakefront park** (4499 Padanarum Rd., 440/466-8400, www.ohiodnr.com) offers a wealth of recreational pursuits. There is a 100-yard sandy beachhead, boat marina, ramps for launching watercraft into Lake Erie, and numerous all-purpose trails that snake through the terrain. The park is popular with hunters, cross-country skiers, and anglers who fish for walleye, yellow perch, and even salmon. Stop by the park's **Geneva Marina** (440/466-7565) to

Ohio Wine

It surprises folks to learn that Ohio winemakers produce great wine. And not just the sickly sweet stuff, either. Currently, there are more than 100 licensed wineries in the state. Each year they produce more than 750,000 gallons of wine valued at $75 million. Most have tasting rooms and welcome visitors to sample the latest vintages.

In 1860, Ohio led the entire nation in wine production. Growers learned early on that areas near Lake Erie enjoyed unique microclimates that provided long growing seasons. Wineries were first established on the Lake Erie Islands, but soon they began popping up along the entire southern shore of the lake. This area was long referred to as the Lake Erie Grape Belt.

Prohibition shuttered most Ohio wineries. And when production did again become legal, most operations set up shop in California. But over the years there has been a steady resurgence in Ohio grape growing, and new wineries continue to open throughout the state. Most are located along Lake Erie in Northeast Ohio, where long, dry autumns give the grapes plenty of time to mature and ripen.

Ohio has a deserved reputation for producing sweet wine, and many wineries do still concentrate on those styles. Catawba, a domestic variety first planted in the 1820s, is still a popular choice for sweet-wine fans. But more and more, sophisticated winemakers are planting classic European varietals such as cabernet franc, chardonnay, and pinot noir, which thrive in the cool climate. The wines these vintners make routinely earn awards and garner national attention.

While visiting all 100 wineries would be admirable, most people choose to arrange more reasonable expeditions. The Ohio Wine Producers Association has divided the state into six wine-producing regions, each with its own wine trail. Stretching from Cleveland to the Pennsylvania border is the **Lake Erie Vines and Wines Trail,** a strip of 40 some wineries. To sample some great juice, visit Markko Vineyard, Tarsitano Winery, and Harpersfield Vineyard. When hunger strikes, stop by the lovely Ferrante Winery & Ristorante for Italian fare or the uber-casual Hil-Mak's Seafood for killer fried lake perch.

If you are in the area over the first weekend in August, consider hitting **Vintage Ohio** (www.visitvintageohio.com), a huge wine and food festival held at Lake Metroparks Farmpark.

get your fishing license, bait and tackle supplies, and boating accessories. When you've reached your daily limit, come back and take advantage of the marina's fish-cleaning services. For overnight visitors to the area, the park offers campsites and cedar cottages, and is also the site of the Lodge at Geneva on the Lake, a well-appointed 100-room hotel.

Kiraly's Orchard

If it's autumn when you visit Northeast Ohio, stop by **Kiraly's Orchard** (6031 S. Ridge West, Ashtabula, 440/969-1297, Aug.-Oct. daily 9am-5pm) to pick your own apples straight from the tree. Yellow delicious, granny smith, rome, fuji, and other varieties are grown on-site in the family's 70-acre orchard. Apples are typically ready for harvest beginning early September and running through October. Bring your own bags and the apples cost about $16 a bushel, roughly the size of a clothes hamper. The retail shop also sells already-picked apples, fresh apple cider, and other seasonal produce. The farm grows its own peaches, nectarines, and plums as well.

Lake Metroparks Farmpark

Agrarian-minded parents may wish to make a stopover at **Lake Metroparks Farmpark** (8800 Chardon Rd., Kirtland, 800/366-3276, www.lakemetroparks.com, daily 9am-5pm, closed major holidays, $6 adult, $4 child, $5 senior) on their way to or from Ashtabula County. At this 235-acre working farm, city folk can experience all manner of country life, from milking a cow to enjoying a wagon ride or corn maze. Demonstrations cover such agricultural activities as sheepherding, cheese making, maple syrup tapping, and crop harvesting. More than 50 breeds of livestock, including a dozen endangered breeds, are on hand to inspire future PETA members. Solar- and wind-power exhibits show off the future of sustainable energy production. A farmers market selling locally grown produce runs here June through October. Many other interesting seasonal events take place throughout the year.

WINERIES

Hugging the southern shore of Lake Erie is a microclimate ideally suited to growing wine grapes. The lake's accumulated heat from summer provides warm autumn breezes that extend the grape-growing season well into fall, giving the fruit the opportunity to fully ripen. Ohio is one of the top 10 wine-producing states in the nation, and the lush Grand River Valley is home to more than half of the state's vineyard acres. Like other wine-producing regions, this one is filled with wineries offering tastings, bottle sales, and winery tours. A day or two spent exploring the numerous wineries that populate the landscape is time very well spent. Call ahead as hours change by vineyard, season, and day of the week.

Debonne Vineyards (7743 Doty Rd., Madison, 440/466-3485, www.debonne.com) is one of the oldest, largest, and most commercially successful wine producers in the state. The 110-acre vineyard produces riesling, chardonnay, pinot gris, and cabernet franc. Debonne also produces ice wine, which is unique to very few regions in the world. Vidal Blanc grapes are left on the vine to freeze, then they are immediately picked and pressed, and the highly concentrated nectar transforms into a deliciously sweet dessert wine. The large, modern facility offers tours and tastings year-round, and an outdoor grill serves food in the summertime. Throughout the year are activities include hot-air-balloon races, Sunday jazz concerts, car shows, and wine and food festivals.

At 18 acres, **Harpersfield Vineyard** (6387 Rte. 307W, Geneva, 440/466-4739, www.harpersfield.com) is a moderately sized estate winery, but it boasts charm in spades. Come during winter and you'll sample the vineyard's fine wines by the fireside in the rustic tasting room. Imagine sipping gewürztraminer, pinot noir, and late-harvest pinot gris as fresh-baked baguettes are plucked from the wood-fired brick oven. Gourmet cheeses and specialty foods are also served in the tasting room, and there is live entertainment during summer weekends.

Markko Vineyard (4500 S. Ridge Rd., Conneaut, 800/252-3197, www.markko.com) just may produce the finest estate-grown wines in Ohio. In fact, their chardonnay and riesling can hold their own against any in the country. Using European vinifera grapes rather than the more popular (and hardy) French-American hybrid grapes was a risk these winemakers were willing to take to make great wine. The employment of a unique vine trellis and canopy system has allowed the grapes not only to survive but flourish, resulting in world-class wines.

Charming **Tarsitano Winery** (4871 Hatches Corners Rd., Conneaut, 440/224-2444, www.tarsitanowinery.com) is just four miles from the Pennsylvania border, putting it squarely in the picturesque Conneaut Creek growing region. This boutique-style winery maintains just 17 acres of vineyards, but it produces about a dozen different wine varieties. Sample the cabernet sauvignon and chardonnay to taste their best work. An on-farm café is open Thursday-Sunday year-round.

For more information on Ohio wineries visit **Ohio Wine Producers Association** (www.ohiowines.org).

RESTAURANTS

Eddie's Grill (5377 Lake Rd., Geneva on the Lake, 440/466-8720, daily 11am-11pm Memorial Day-Labor Day, $3-6) is rightly famous for its killer cheeseburgers, foot-long chili dogs, and fresh-cut fries. The popular 1950s-style diner features open-air counter service, indoor booths with personal jukeboxes, and youthful servers. This place gets super crowded on warm summer nights, but things move quickly. Bring cash or a bank card for the nearby ATM. No credit cards are accepted.

Just down the road from the scenic Harpersfield covered bridge is **Ferrante Winery & Ristorante** (5585 Rte. 307, Harpersfield, 440/466-8466, www.ferrantewinery.com, hours vary by month, $11-20), an amiable winery and restaurant. Complementing the house-made wines are hearty Italian-style specialties. Pizza, pasta, and chicken and veal dishes rule the menu, and many are made with the winery's award-winning vintages. During summer, a sprawling outdoor patio overlooking the vineyards is host to live music, wine-tastings, and light meals. A large gift shop stocks wine and wine accessories.

Folks trek to the Ashtabula Harbor for swimmingly fresh fried perch dinners at **Hil-Mak's Seafood** (449 Lake Ave., Ashtabula, 440/964-3222, www.hilmaks.com, Tues.-Sat. 11:30am-2:30pm and 5pm-10pm, $10-18). Because Hil-Mak's also operates a fish market, the restaurant has access to a full roster of local and regional seafood. They don't do fancy here; what they specialize in is great clam chowder, perch sandwiches, fried clams, crab cakes, and onion rings. Seafood aficionados will swear they were dining on the East Coast instead of the North Coast.

When you've had all you can take of the touristy crowds, slip away to the comforting embrace of the **Old Mill Winery** (403 S. Broadway, 440/466-5560, www.theoldmillwinery.com, Mon.-Thurs. 3pm-9pm, Fri. 3pm-midnight, Sat. 1pm-midnight, Sun. 1pm-9pm, $12-17). This cozy neighborhood winery and restaurant treats everybody like regulars, mainly because most of them are. Tucked into a big old red mill, the restaurant grills up a mean steak, but the house favorite is assuredly the loaded wineburger, topped with bacon, mushrooms, and grilled onions. A little snow in winter doesn't stop the intrepid chefs at Old Mill from grilling outdoors all year long. There are live bands most weekend nights.

HOTELS

If you want to be close to the summer action at Geneva on the Lake, **The Eagle Cliff Inn** (5254 Lake Rd. E., 440/466-1110, www.beachclubbandb.com, $119-149) places you squarely in the thick of things. Directly on the strip, this elegant inn is steps from Lake Erie and provides easy access to Ashtabula County's best assets. Listed on the National Register of Historic Places, the faithfully restored inn offers six rooms with private baths. Bed-and-breakfast guests take their full breakfast in the parlor or from the comfort of the inn's gracious front porch. The inn also runs the more budget-friendly **Beach Club Cottages,** well-appointed efficiencies located behind the house.

Built at a cost of close to $20 million, the **Lodge at Geneva on the Lake** (4888 Rte. 534, 866/806-8066, www.thelodgeatgeneva.com, $100-250) is on the grounds of Geneva State Park but operated by the county. This hotel is the natural choice for travelers who prefer modern amenities over country charm. The 100-room complex offers guests numerous lodging choices, ranging from comfortable standard rooms to premium lake-view rooms with balconies. Multiroom suites are ideal for families. An outdoor pool and kid zone are open during summer, while a glass-enclosed pool and hot tub are available year-round. Other amenities include a great game room, fitness center overlooking Lake Erie, and massage services.

Rent a bike from the lodge and hit the trails that hug the Lake Erie shoreline. Folks traveling with pets will be happy to know that the lodge offers pet-friendly rooms with direct access to a grassy expanse.

Romantic getaways are the order of the day (and night) at **Peggy's Bed and Breakfast** (8721 Munson Hill Rd., Ashtabula, 440/969-1996, www.peggysbedandbreakfast.com, $119-140). Tucked into a leafy landscape, Peggy's one and only cottage is nothing if it isn't private. The snug environment features a full kitchen, loft bedroom, two fireplaces, patio, and screened porch. Breakfast is delivered in the morning right to your residence. And we're not talking cereal and toast: Peggy offers her guests a full menu of gourmet options, including cream caramel French toast, corned-beef hash, and corn muffins with pecans and maple syrup. The location is ideal for hitting the trails, wineries, covered bridges, or Lake Erie shore, and you can even borrow one of Peggy's bikes.

Looking like a vintage city hall transplanted from New England to Geneva, the stately Western Reserve-style building that houses the **Polly Harper Inn** (6308 S. River Rd., 440/466-6183, www.pollyharperinn.com, $95-155) sits proudly atop a bluff in the scenic Grand River Valley. The location is idyllic for winery visits, as the inn literally overlooks vineyards and is close to dozens more. This countrified bed-and-breakfast offers three suites, all with private baths and gas fireplaces. Enjoy the rustic beauty of the nearby Grand River courtesy of a scenic trail that winds right behind the inn.

PRACTICALITIES
Tourist Information

Information and maps of Ashtabula County covered bridges can be obtained by contacting the **Ashtabula County Covered Bridge Festival** (25 W. Jefferson St., 440/576-3769, www.coveredbridgefestival.org).

The **Ashtabula County Convention & Visitors Bureau** can be reached by calling 800/337-6746 or going to www.visitashtabulacounty.com.

For information on Geneva on the Lake, contact **Visit Geneva on the Lake** (800/862-9948, www.visitgenevaonthelake.com).

For information on Ohio's wine industry, wine-related events, and wine-trail maps, contact the **Ohio Wine Producers Association** (800/227-6972, www.ohiowines.org).

Media

Read the ***Ashtabula Star Beacon*** (www.starbeacon.com) for local news and current events. **Gazette Newspapers** (www.gazettenewspapers.com) publishes a number of community newspapers throughout the county, including the *Ashtabula County Gazette, Jefferson Gazette, Pymatuning Area News, Shores News,* and *Valley News.*

Getting There

Expect a nonstop drive from downtown Cleveland to Geneva on the Lake to take just over an hour. The trip is easily accomplished by taking I-90 to OH 2 to US 20. **Greyhound** (www.greyhound.com) has a station in Ashtabula at 1520 Bunker Hill Road (440/992-7550).

Getting Around

Serious cyclists can get along just fine on a good bike (depending on the weather, of course), but others will likely need a car to move about since major sights and attractions are miles apart. Two taxi companies operate in the area, **Premier Transportation** (440/466-1515) and **City Taxicab** (440/992-2156), and are available for inter-county trips.

Lake Erie Islands and Vicinity

Just an hour west of Cleveland is an entirely different landscape. From Memorial Day until Labor Day, typically sleepy lakeside communities transform into seasonal hot spots, teeming with pleasure boaters, nature-loving day-trippers, and hard-partying souls. Comprised of mainland towns like Sandusky, Lakeside, Marblehead, and Port Clinton, and islands such as South Bass and Kelleys, the Lake Erie Islands region is a magnet for summer fun. The epicenter of this party is assuredly Put-in-Bay, but Cedar Point in Sandusky is no slouch either. To reach South Bass and Kelleys Islands you'll need to ride a ferry from the mainland, making a day trip impractical. Many businesses in the area are seasonal, so check before planning a stop.

SOUTH BASS ISLAND

Home to rowdy Put-in-Bay, South Bass Island often is described as the Key West of the North Coast. While downtown is indeed party central, the island can be extremely accommodating to families, especially during the week and away from downtown. But many come to South Bass precisely for the no-holds-barred party atmosphere, and they are rarely disappointed.

Sights

If you enjoy the cold comfort of caves, consider a visit to **Crystal Cave** (978 Catawba Ave., 419/285-2811, www.heinemanswinery. com, tours daily early May-late Sept., $6 adult, $3 child), thought to be the world's largest geode. The 55-degree chamber is lined with sky-blue celestite crystals, some sticking out a full foot and a half, and it feels like you're walking through the inside of a paperweight. Non-gemstone fans may not see what all the fuss is about, but crystal collectors might just call this place mecca. When the tour is through, visit the attached **Heineman Winery,** which has been making wine for over a century. Tours of the winery are offered, and wine and grape juice tastings are held in a picturesque garden.

Rising 352 feet above Lake Erie, **Perry's Victory and International Peace Memorial** (93 Delaware Ave., Put-in-Bay, 419/285-2184, www. nps.gov/pevi, daily late Apr.-mid-Oct., limited or no hours the rest of the year, $3 adult, free child) is a conspicuous landmark on the shoreline. Established in honor of those who fought in the Battle of Lake Erie during the War of 1812, from the top the monument offers visitors views of the islands, Michigan, and Ontario. The memorial is now a national park, and on weekends uniformed rangers do history demonstrations capped off by the firing of flintlock muskets.

Parents in search of a surefire way to occupy the kids should plan a visit to **Perry's Cave Family Fun Center** (979 Catawba Ave., 419/285-2283, www.perryscave.com, daily May-Sept., weekends only Apr. and Oct.). This family entertainment center is jam-packed with enjoyable time-killers. Best among them is the War of 18 Holes miniature golf course, which peppers kids with historical facts about the War of 1812 and Commodore Perry along the way. The rather challenging course is surrounded by mature trees and winding (faux) streams. If you can differentiate between a swallowtail and a lacewing you might really enjoy the Butterfly House. This 4,000-square-foot butterfly aviary houses more than 500 different varieties of exotic butterflies. For help identifying the species, tap the knowledge of the helpful staff. Kids can strap into a harness and tie onto a safety rope at the 25-foot climbing wall. Varying degrees of difficulty ensure that even the most novice climber should be able to have some degree of success. Pan for gemstones at the Gemstone Mining Sluice, stop by the Antique Car Museum, or spelunk in Perry's Cave: There is no shortage of low-impact fun at this place. Because each attraction is separately priced, the fees can quickly add up. To get your money's worth it might make sense to purchase an Island Fun Pack from **Lake Erie Islands Regional Welcome Center** (800/441-1271).

Restaurants

Praised equally for its waterfront views and lobster bisque, the **Boardwalk** (341 Bayview Ave., 419/285-3695, www.the-boardwalk. com, Memorial Day-Labor Day daily noon-8pm, weekends only in Apr. and Oct., $6-18) is one of the most popular dining and entertainment spots on the island. Enjoy views of the harbor boat traffic from elevated decks. Meals are casual, affordable, and delicious, and include live Maine lobster, shrimp, and that island-famous bisque. Live music and dancing keeps this joint jumping well into the night.

Frosty's Bar (252 Delaware Ave., 419/285-3278, www.frostys. com, Memorial Day-Labor Day daily 7am-1am, weekends only in Apr. and Oct., $8-19) is busy morning, noon, night, and late-night thanks to a full slate of tasty offerings. Many island-hoppers start their day here with eggs Benedict or a big plate of blueberry pancakes made with fresh fruit. Others start with a Bloody Mary to clear away the cobwebs. Frosty's pizza has been a Put-in-Bay staple for over 50 years.

Put-in-Bay is more famous for the drinks and depravity than good grub, but that doesn't mean you can't score a decent platter of fish. **Goat Soup and Whiskey** (820 Catawba Ave., 419/285-4628, daily Memorial Day-Labor Day, $15-35) seems to validate the maxim that states the farther from the main strip you go, the better the food and service. A half-mile from the harbor, the Goat is laid-back, family-friendly, and committed to putting out quality fare. Get the perch tacos, flour tortillas stuffed with fresh-fried fish, cabbage slaw, and house-made taco sauce. Cocktails here benefit from fresh-squeezed fruit juices, a rarity in these parts.

Nightlife

Depending on what sort of crowds you can handle, the **Beer Barrel** (441 Catawba Ave., 419/285-7281, www.beerbarrelpib.com, mid-Apr.-Oct.) and the **Roundhouse Bar** (60 Delaware Ave., 419/285-2323, www.theroundhousebar.com, daily 11am-1am mid-Apr.-Oct.) are notorious nightspots. As such, they can be insufferably loud, crowded, and crass. But given the right time of day and proper frame of mind, they also can be riotously fun. Typically, weekend nights are the craziest times. Beer Barrel claims rights to the world's longest permanent bar, a commendable 400-footer that if placed on its end would best Perry's Memorial. Both bars play host to some of the finest island musicians, so check the schedules to see if Mike "Mad Dog" Adams or Pat Daily is on tap to play.

Festivals and Events

Plan well ahead if you intend to visit South Bass Island for its popular **Christmas in July** weekend. Hotels, bed-and-breakfasts, and campgrounds fill up early and fast, and some ferry companies require proof of lodging before you can come aboard. But book in advance you'll enjoy a wild weekend filled with Christmas-themed entertainment, anachronistic holiday decorations, and bachelorettes in Santa caps. Look for it in late July.

South Bass Island takes on a whole new charm come October, and many people elect to delay their visit until then so as to enjoy Put-in-Bay sans the crowds. Hence the popularity of mid-October's

clockwise from top left: Stan Hywet Hall, Akron; grapes on the vine in Ohio Wine Country; Put-in-Bay harbor, South Bass Island

Recreation

There is little sense visiting the walleye capital of the world only to leave the fishing to everybody else. Get a group of five or six together and contact **Put in Bay Charter Fishing Service** (419/341-2805, www.putinbaycharterfishingservice.com) for a half or full day of chartered boat fishing. All you need to bring is cash, an Ohio fishing license, and a cooler full of snacks: Captain Bruce will handle the rest. Packages range from $450 to $600 and include all bait, tackle, and equipment. Fish cleaning is extra. If you prefer to travel the waterways without a guide, call the folks at **Put-in-Bay Watercraft** (419/285-2628, www.pibjetski.com) to rent fishing and powerboats, personal watercraft, and kayaks. They are located within South Bass Island State Park.

Hotels

Host to one million visitors per year, South Bass Island has as many lodging options as there are tastes. From pitching a tent to renting a multiroom luxury cottage, the sleep of one's dreams is easy to land given a little advance planning.

Folks looking for a slower pace and quainter setting should book a night's stay at the **Anchor Inn** (500 Catawba Ave., 419/285-5055, www.anchorinn.info, $79-220). This 1917 bungalow boasts classic front-porch charm and gracious hospitality. Close to the action but far enough away to be peaceful, this romantic getaway is popular with couples, honeymooners, and mature travelers. Lovely gardens attract a multitude of migratory birds and provide a delightful spot for the day's included breakfast. This bed-and-breakfast offers three guest suites with private baths. One has its own balcony overlooking the gardens.

Stay at the **Grand Islander Hotel** (432 Catawba Ave., 419/285-5555, www.grandislanderpib.com, $100-290) if you want a lively pool scene: Splash! is billed as the world's largest swim-up bar. While we can't verify that boozy factoid, we can promise you a pirate ship (with a bar) and an on-site Vegas-style nightclub (without gambling). Comfortable if not glamorous lodging is the order of the day here, but most guests could care less where they pass out after a long night of fun. This festive complex is not exactly what one might call kid-friendly, though during the week things tend to be on the mild side.

Got a crowd? Book a suite at the **Put-in-Bay Resort** (439 Loraine Ave., 888/742-7829, www.putinbayresort.com, $150-850) and you and seven friends can sleep comfortably. This hotel's three-bed grand suite features a living room, kitchenette with refrigerator, wet bar, and private bath with bathtub. Rates range from $150 for a standard room up to $850 for a multiroom suite.

KELLEYS ISLAND

If South Bass Island is the Key West of the North Coast, then Kelleys Island is Sanibel. A slower pace and more nature-centric pursuits attract families looking for a true island getaway. Bird-watchers flock here in spring and fall to catch the migratory bird scene. Anglers and water-sports enthusiasts spend hours in and around the lake. Honeymooners and amorous couples hole up in romantic Victorian inns. The above is not meant to imply that Kelleys Island is a snooze; a party is always happening somewhere.

Sights

Caddy Shack Square

In downtown Kelleys Island is Caddy Shack Square, a complex with family entertainment, shopping, and food and drink. This is where folks can rent bikes and golf carts, play 18 holes of miniature golf, hit the arcade, or relax with a massage. If you're searching for a souvenir or gift, try the **Booga Shack,** which sells original island wear. No need to divulge what the **Flip Flop Shop** sells. Dessert fans swear by the hand-dipped cones at **Dipper Dan's Ice Cream Stand,** while caffeine junkies line up for a fix at the incomparable **Erie Island Coffee Co.**

★ Glacial Grooves

Trek to the northern tip of the island to see what effects a little ice can have on solid bedrock. Sometime near the tail end of the Pleistocene Ice Age, a massive glacial sheet rubbed its way across this stretch of North America, leaving behind an otherworldly landscape. These deeply etched **Glacial Grooves** (419/797-4530, dusk-dawn, free), some 10 feet deep, 35 feet wide, and 400 feet long, are striking illustrations of nature's potent force. The immediate area is fenced off, but a walkway takes visitors close to the action, which likely took place 18,000 years ago.

Kelleys Island State Park

While partiers flock to nearby South Bass Island, nature lovers gravitate to Kelleys. One of the major draws is **Kelleys Island State Park** (920 Division St., 419/797-4530, dusk-dawn, free), a 677-acre park in the north-central portion of the island. Six miles of hiking trails wind sightseers past scenic lake views and through beautiful nature preserves. Take the one-mile North Shore Loop trail to enjoy shoreline vistas, blooming wildflowers, and, in spring and fall, an anthology of migratory birds that use the island as a stopover point in their travels. Bring a towel and plop down at the sandy beach or drop a fishing line into the lake from a pier. Looking for something a little more high impact than pier fishing or birding? Contact **Kelley's Island Kayak Rental** (419/285-2628, www.kelleysisland.info) within the park to rent your own craft.

Restaurants and Nightlife

At night, **Bag the Moon** (109 W. Lakeshore Dr., 419/746-2365, daily in season, $9-14) turns into a rambunctious saloon, where folks go gaga for booze-filled strawberries with whipped-cream topping. During the day, however, Bag the Moon is a family-friendly restaurant serving reasonably priced American fare. Come here to start your day with one of the best breakfasts on the island. Popular meals include corned-beef hash and strawberry-stuffed pancakes.

Enjoying a handcrafted microbrew on the shores of Lake Erie is a singular joy. **Kelleys Island Brewery** (504 W. Lakeshore Dr., 419/746-2314, www.kelleysislandbrewpub.com, daily in season, $14-19) brews great small-batch beer just yards from the lake, and a pet-friendly patio means you don't have to enjoy a pint in solitude. Come here for a satisfying lunch of burgers, brats, and beer. For dessert, there are fantastic root beer floats and milk shakes. If you have an action-packed morning planned, call ahead to order the Wake and Bake, a pot of hot coffee and a half-dozen muffins packed up to go with all the fixings.

More than just a restaurant, **Kelley's Island Wine Co.** (418 Woodford Rd., 419/746-2678, www.kelleysislandwine.com, daily in season, $8-12) is really a family-friendly entertainment destination. Set apart from downtown, the spacious setting has room enough for volleyball courts, horseshoe pits, and plenty of alfresco dining. The wine, like most produced in the area, leans toward the sweet and rosy variety. But the straightforward food seems to be liked by all. Great pizzas, pastas, fish skewers, and steak are served by a gracious staff.

For some odd reason, the Brandy Alexander is the official drink of Kelleys Island, and the **Village Pump** (103 Lakeshore Dr., 419/746-2281, www.villagepump.com, daily Mar.-Dec., $9-15) is the official supplier. This historic building once housed a post office and then the town gas station, hence the name. On a prime summer weekend, this homey tavern might serve 3,000 hungry guests, an eclectic mix of locals, island-hoppers, and families. Favorites here include textbook fried lake perch, home-style specials, and those addictive ice cream-infused Brandy Alexanders.

Festivals and Events

South Bass has its wild Christmas in July, while Kelleys throws the more family-friendly **IslandFest.** The event kicks off with dancing, parades, and craft fairs and culminates with a rousing fireworks display. If you plan on visiting the island around the end of July when this popular weekend-long party takes place, you'll want to plan well ahead.

Hotels

Scenic Lakeshore Drive is sprinkled with attractive Victorian homes. Few are as graceful as **A Water's Edge Retreat** (827 E. Lakeshore Dr., 800/884-5143, www.watersedgeretreat.com, $200-280), a three-story beauty that houses a luxury bed-and-breakfast. The impeccable inn offers six suites with private baths and views of Lake Erie, Cedar Point, and Marblehead Lighthouse. Book a sailing trip on the owner's 35-foot yacht or just kick back with a glass of wine on the sweeping front porch. Prices include a gourmet hot breakfast, use of a bicycle, and a discount on golf-cart rentals.

Campers have it made on Kelleys Island. **Kelleys Island State Park** (920 Division St., 419/746-2546, $25-100) offers numerous shaded campsites, many with electric hookups. For something a little more out of the ordinary, put in a reservation for one of the park's yurts. These large circular canvas tents provide a nice middle ground between roughing it and luxury. Each has a kitchen, living area, and private bath.

MAINLAND

You don't have to hop a ferry to enjoy the mainland communities of Lakeside, Port Clinton, Marblehead, and Sandusky. Home to major tourist attractions and out-of-the-way finds, these seaside locales buzz all summer long with activity.

Sights

African Safari Wildlife Park

We assume camels don't drive, but judging by the way these beasts of burden inspect automobiles at **African Safari Wildlife Park** (267 Lightner Rd., Port Clinton, 800/521-2660, www.africansafariwild-lifepark.com, daily late May-early Nov., hours and admission vary), you'd swear they were in the market for a new ride. This 100-acre wildlife preserve is a must-do adventure for families with children. During the drive-through portion of the park, animals literally poke their heads inside the car to snack on grain and carrots. Gentle zebras, alpacas, camels, and elands all approach the cars, absolutely thrilling the youngsters within. A walk-through portion has a number of other animal-related activities, including pony and camel rides. Pig races are a popular daily diversion. Come to the park early, bring your own carrots (much cheaper than at the park), and leave the Ferrari at home—cars routinely endure bumps, occasional bruises, and plenty of slobber. Check the website for "carload" discounts.

Thanks in no small part to its collection of the tallest, fastest, steepest roller coasters, **Cedar Point Amusement Park** (1 Cedar Point Dr., Sandusky, 419/627-2350, www.cedarpoint.com, daily mid-May-Aug., weekends only Sept.-Oct., $55 at gate, $45 online, $10 parking) is widely recognized as the world's best thrill park. Top Thrill Dragster zips to a speed of 120 miles per hour before climbing to a height of 420 feet. The newest ride, GateKeeper, is the tallest, fastest, and longest wing roller coaster in the world. Maverick, is a mile-long ride through canyons, dark tunnels, and around embankments. Tamer children's rides, live entertainment, and food options abound at this massive 370-acre amusement park. To avoid the longest lines, try scheduling your visit between Sunday and Wednesday. It is helpful to know that rides do shut down due to rain, high winds, or lightning, and no, rain checks and refunds are not awarded. Next to Cedar Point is **Soak City** (daily late May-Aug., $29 adult, $16 child under 48" and senior), an 18-acre water park with dozens of waterslides, a sizable wave pool, inner tube river rides, and sun-soaked spots for kicking back. Season passes, Ride & Slide tickets good for both Cedar Point and Soak City, and AAA passes all can save considerable money on admission.

Kalahari Waterpark

One of three in the nation, the 880-room African-themed **Kalahari Waterpark** (7000 Kalahari Dr., Sandusky, 877/525-2427, www.kalahariresort.com/ohio, Sun.-Thurs. 10am-9pm, Fri.-Sat. 10am-10pm, $49) is Ohio's largest indoor/outdoor water and adventure park. Regardless of the weather outside, families can hit the beach all year long at this ginormous all-in-one entertainment complex. A FlowRider offers surfable waves everyday; the Zip Coaster is a wet-and-wild roller coaster; a 12,000-square-foot wave pool keeps the swells steady despite the tide. An equally enjoyable outdoor water park, open Memorial Day through Labor Day, adds a whole new dimension of fun come summertime. Hotel stays include admission to the parks.

Marblehead Lighthouse

The view from the top of **Marblehead Lighthouse** (110 Lighthouse Dr., Marblehead, 419/734-4424, www.dnr.state.oh.us, tours late May-mid-Oct., free) includes Kelleys Island, South Bass Island, and the beautiful Sandusky Bay. This landmark lighthouse has guided sailors since 1822, making it the oldest continuously operated lighthouse on the Great Lakes. Selected for inclusion on a U.S. postage stamp, the classic form rises to a height of 65 feet and is one of the most photographed structures on the lake. The picturesque grounds also make a great location for a family picnic, filled with scenic vistas, room to relax, and massive stones that kids can scramble up and over. An old lighthouse keeper's house now serves as a museum operated by the Marblehead Lighthouse Historical Society. It is open whenever the tower is open.

Restaurants

For more than 20 years, **Chez Francois** (555 Main St., Vermillion, 440/967-0630, www.chezfrancois.com, Tues.-Thurs. 5pm-9pm, Fri.-Sat. 5pm-10pm, Sun. 4pm-8pm, closed Jan.-mid-Mar., $34-44) has offered incomparable French cuisine in a romantic post-and-beam structure. Classics like escargot, veal sweetbreads, and beef Wellington are freshened up by seasonal ingredients and matchless execution. The restaurant maintains a dress code (jackets for men, no flip-flops, etc.), but the more casual riverfront café serves the same food without the fuss. Pleasure boaters can tie up at the nearby **Vermilion Public Guest Docks** (440/967-7087).

In an area festooned with fried-fish shacks, **Jolly Roger Seafood House** (1737 E. Perry St., Port Clinton, 419/732-3382, mid-Feb.-late Nov., Sun.-Thurs. 11am-8:30pm, Fri.-Sat. 11am-9:30pm, $5-12) stands out for its quality, consistency, and value. Baskets overflowing with fresh-fried perch, walleye, onion rings, and hush puppies stream out of this busy little kitchen. As it should be, Jolly Rodger is a no-frills operation, with disposable plates, plastic cutlery, and paper napkins.

Know going in that **Mon Ami** (3845 E. Wine Cellar Rd., Port Clinton, 800/777-4266, www.monamiwinery.com, daily, hours vary by season, $21-30) has changed considerably since its days as a quaint winery restaurant. This operation seems to grow each year, making it one of the busiest attractions in the region. Depending on the season, visitors can expect crowds of hungry day-trippers lining up for the popular all-you-can-eat buffet. Folks in search of peace, quiet, and romance would do well to pick out a spot in the dining room, while those looking for a party should make a beeline to the Chalet, a massive bar area with live entertainment. Mon Ami shines on warm summer nights as the food and party spill outdoors.

Festivals and Events

Times Square has its fancy-schmancy LED-powered crystal ball. Port Clinton has a 20-foot-long, 600-pound fiberglass walleye named Wylie. Each New Year's Eve, the tiny town of Port Clinton doubles in size from 6,000 to 12,000 when enthusiastic crowds brave frigid temps to experience the **Walleye Drop** (Madison St. in downtown Port Clinton, www.walleyemadness.com). Festivities begin at 3pm and climax at the stroke of midnight, when Wylie makes the plunge from his comically large rod and reel. Like a

Hotels

With the rugged good looks of a northwestern lumberjack, **Great Wolf Lodge** (4600 Milan Rd., Sandusky, 888/779-2327, www.great-wolflodge.com, $150-350) is a wilderness-themed resort and indoor water park. The 271-suite hotel is loaded with family-friendly attractions and activities. There are two casual restaurants, game arcades, a rock climbing wall, and fitness center, not to mention one of the largest indoor water parks in the nation. In the summer, an outdoor pool joins the list.

If you want a short two-minute walk to Cedar Point, stay at the historic **Hotel Breakers** (1 Cedar Point Dr., Sandusky, 419/627-2350, www.cedarpoint.com, $150-350). This beachside hotel is on Cedar Point Peninsula and features two outdoor pools, an indoor pool, and beach access. Prices can vary widely based on room size and location within the complex, so do your research before booking. Guests get to enter the amusement park an hour before the general public, making roller-coaster lines short and sweet.

Lakeside is an enlightened community of progressive types—a true chautauqua where seasonal residents seek to nurture mind, body, and spirit through intellectual, cultural, and recreational pursuits. Many summertime visitors own pricey Victorian cottages, but travelers can simply book a room at **Hotel Lakeside** (150 Maple Ave., Lakeside, 866/952-5374, www.lakesideohio.com, Memorial Day-Labor Day $80-200), a 130-year-old landmark. Sign up for lectures, seminars, and classes at nearby Lakeside or simply unwind on the hotel's gracious porch and take in the views.

PRACTICALITIES
Tourist Information

For more information on Lake Erie's shores and islands, contact the **Lake Erie Shores & Islands Welcome Center** (419/625-2984, www.shoresandislands.com). Other helpful websites include the **Port Clinton and Put-in-Bay Travel Guide** (www.portclinton.org), the **Put-in-Bay Chamber of Commerce** (419/285-2832, www.put-in-bay.com), and **Kelleys Island Chamber of Commerce** (419/746-2360, www.kelleysislandchamber.com).

Media

Check out the *Sandusky Register* (www.sanduskyregister.com) and *Port Clinton News Herald* (www.portclintonnewsherald.com) for up-to-the-minute news and information in the area.

Dig up a copy of Norman Hills's *A History of Kelleys Island, Ohio* originally published in 1925, for a historical look at Kelleys Island.

Islands

If you've got your own boat, just punch 41° 39' 15" N, 82° 49' 15" W into your GPS to find Put-in-Bay, otherwise you'll need to hop a ferry. The *Jet Express* (800/245-1538, www.jet-express.com, $17 one-way) is the fastest way to the islands, but it is also the most expensive. The *Jet Express* departs from two locations: Port Clinton and Sandusky. The **Kelleys Island Ferry** (510 W. Main St., 419/798-9763, www.kelleysislandferry.com, $8 one-way) goes back and forth between Marblehead and Kelleys Island. **Miller's Boat Line** (800/500-2421, www.millerferry.com, $6 one-way) operates a ferry between Catawba and South Bass Island. Free overnight parking makes this option a great choice.

Regardless which option you choose, make sure you are familiar with the ferry's return schedule before booking passage; some operate later than others.

Mainland

To get to Sandusky, Marblehead, Lakeside, and Port Clinton from Cleveland, simply take I-90 west to OH 2 west. **Greyhound** (www.greyhound.com) will drive you from Cleveland to Sandusky for about $15 with advanced purchase.

Getting Around

The preferred modes of transportation on Kelleys and South Bass Islands include golf carts, mopeds, bicycles, and stumbling. Wise visitors know to leave their cars on the mainland. To rent a golf cart on South Bass Island contact **Delaware Golf Carts** (266 Delaware Ave., 419/285-2724, www.putinbayrentals.com), which rents four-, six-, and eight-person gas-powered carts by the hour, day, or week. Prices range from $50 to $100 a day based on cart model and day of the week. For bicycles stop by **Island Bike & Cart Rental** (419/285-2016, www.perryscave.com) as you disembark in downtown Put-in-Bay. This outfitter stocks nice-quality singles, tandems, trailers, and tag-alongs for around $15 a day.

On Kelleys Island, contact **Caddy Shack Rentals** (Caddy Shack Sq., 419/746-2518, www.caddyshacksquare.com) or the **Casino Restaurant & Marina** (104 Division St., 419/746-2773, www.kelleysislandcasino.com) for a full range of bike and golf-cart rentals. Call for pricing and to reserve in advance.

To move from South Bass Island to Kelleys Island and vice versa, contact *Jet Express* (800/245-1538, www.jet-express.com).

Amish Country

The world's largest Amish community resides in a five-county area of rural Ohio, and Holmes County is home to about half of them. A day or two spent exploring the scenic back roads of this unspoiled landscape can be pure magic. Filled with blazing red barns, fertile fields, and horse-drawn buggies, the scene is one visitors often cherish for a lifetime. Despite what you may have read or heard about the Amish, they are a graceful, gentle community that welcomes visitors into their villages, shops, and even homes. They support themselves largely by crafting furniture, foodstuffs, and handicrafts that they sell to "English" folk like you and me. Make sure to explore the historic Main Streets of Millersburg, Berlin, and Charm. Autumn, when visitors are treated to the tail end of the harvest, colorful fall foliage, and cooler temps, is the busiest time in Amish Country. Most Amish businesses are also closed on Good Friday, Thanksgiving, and Christmas. In Amish Country, Sunday is a day of rest and worship. Some stores, attractions, and restaurants are closed, but you can always find a place to eat or shop in Millersburg or Berlin.

SIGHTS

Amish & Mennonite Heritage Center

Your very first stop in Amish Country should be the **Amish & Mennonite Heritage Center** (5798 County Rd. 77, Berlin, 877/858-4634, www.behalt.com, Mon.-Sat. 9am-5pm, June-Oct. Fri.-Sat. 9am-8pm). Start with an informative video on the local Amish and Mennonite community, then immerse yourself in *Behalt,* a 265-foot cyclorama, or cylindrical panoramic painting. Observers standing in the middle have a 360-degree view of the painting, which depicts the heritage of the Amish people from 1525 Zurich to the present day. This is a good place to stock up on area maps, brochures, and books about the Amish written by the Amish.

Ohio Hot Air Balloons

Hot-air balloons seem uniquely suited for scenic Amish country. **Ohio Hot Air Balloons** (800/611-1298, www.balloonridesoverohio.com, $250 adult, $150 child) entertains brave souls with an unforgettable trip over a lush rural landscape. Drift lazily above Amish farms as awestruck children wave and give pursuit with barking dogs in tow. Fall is the best time, when leaves change from green to yellow, orange, and fire-engine red. The one-hour flights include a postflight celebration. Sunrise and sunset flights are available. Bring along a camera for once-in-a-lifetime shots.

Negotiating Amish Buggies

Holmes County is Amish Country, and this picturesque rural region looks, sounds, and smells different from any other place on Earth. The Amish believe in simplicity, hard work, and religion, and their old-fashioned customs are designed to foster strong family bonds. Because they eschew modern technologies like automobiles, the Amish travel by horse and buggy.

Almost every road in Holmes County is a designated National Scenic Byway, and motoring along these gorgeous country lanes is a thing of beauty. But beauty quickly can turn to tragedy when a fast-moving car collides with a slow-moving buggy. Buggies travel at speeds of just five miles per hour and seemingly can appear out of nowhere. Drive slowly and cautiously at all times, but especially at night and when approaching a hill. And if you do approach a buggy, do not tailgate or honk, which can spook the horse. Simply pass by slowly, making sure to leave plenty of room between car and buggy. Keep in mind that it is considered disrespectful to stare, take photographs, or enter someone's private property.

★ Kidron Auction

When a farmer needs to buy or sell a farm animal, he visits his local livestock auction. Lucky for you, the experience is open to the public. The oldest and largest livestock auction in the state, the **Kidron Auction** (4885 Kidron Rd., Kidron, 330/857-2641, www. kidronauction.com, Thurs.) has been in operation from 1924, with weekly events since 1932. Farmers or the just plain curious are welcome to sit in and observe the lively action. The event opens with a hay and straw sale at 10:15am before moving on to dairy cattle, feed pigs, sheep, and goats. Get here early to grab a good seat in the selling ring; it fills up fast.

Scenic Drives

One of the most enjoyable things to do in Amish Country is to take a leisurely drive on the many scenic back roads and byways that crisscross the area. It is here that you'll get the best glimpses of everyday life in one of the most beautiful and peaceful places on Earth.

Ohio Route 39 runs east and west through the heart of Amish Country. You can pick it up in Dover, which is exit 83 off of I-77 coming south from Cleveland. Working west you'll pass through the towns of Sugarcreek, Walnut Creek, Berlin, and Millersburg. Smaller side trips can include a short venture south on Rt. 557 to the aptly named village of Charm, north on Rt. 241 to Mt. Hope, and south on County Road 68 (also known as Port Washington Road) to Baltic.

Labeled as the first trail in the nation to accommodate riders and Amish buggies, the scenic **Holmes County Trail** (www.holmestrail.org) runs for miles and miles, with a few gaps here and there. When completed, the Holmes County Trail will run the 29 miles between Fredericksburg to Killbuck, passing right through Millersburg. When combined with the nearby Mohican Valley Trail and Kokosing Gap Trail (complete with 370-foot-long covered bridge), a biker can cover some 50 miles of scenic trailway through America's heartland.

Tree Frog Canopy Tours

Ohio's longest, fastest, and highest zipline tour is about nine miles south of Amish Country. More accurately, **Tree Frog** (21899 Wally Rd., 740/599-2662, www.treefrogcanopytours.com, daily 8am-5pm, $75) is a "canopy tour" because in addition to ziplines, the adventure includes suspension bridges and a few short rappels through the treetops.

Yoder's Amish Home

Eli and Gloria Yoder have made a living by sharing with outsiders the unique culture of their Amish past. They open their 116-acre **Yoder's Amish Home** (6050 Rte. 515, Millersburg, 330/893-2541, www.yodersamishhome.com, mid-Apr.-Oct. Mon.-Sat. 10am-5pm, $5 adult, $3 child) to visitors and along the way convey interesting facts about the history and lifestyle of the Amish people. Tour a 120-year-old barn constructed in the old-fashioned peg-and-beam design. The barn is filled with bunnies, lambs, horses, and puppies. Take a ride around the farm in a horse-drawn buggy ($3.50 adult, $2 child).

RESTAURANTS

The granddaddy of Amish restaurants, **Amish Door** (1210 Winesburg St., Wilmot, 888/264-7436, www.amishdoor.com, Mon.-Sat. 7am-8pm, $10-15), has been serving stick-to-your-ribs comfort food for more than 30 years. What began as a small eatery has ballooned into an entire complex, complete with dining, shopping, and lodging. Dinners are filling, fabulous, and wallet-friendly. The menu is loaded with Amish kitchen classics like meat loaf, roast turkey, and chopped steak. Folks travel miles out of their way to tuck into plates of "broasted" fried chicken. Dinners include salad bar, vegetable, real mashed potatoes with gravy, and stuffing. If that doesn't push you over the edge, stop by the amazing bakery on your way out this Amish door.

For traditional Swiss, Austrian, and Amish cuisine, hit **Chalet in the Valley** (5060 OH 557, Millersburg, 330/893-2550, www.chaletinthevalley.com, Tues.-Sat. 11am-8pm, closed Jan.-mid-Mar.,

$9-17). Since it's next to Guggisberg Cheese, it is only natural that one of the house specialties is bubbly cheese fondue. Move on to one of five different schnitzel entrées or the Amish sampler overloaded with roast beef, ham, fried chicken, mashed potatoes, and gravy. Cap off the meal with fresh-baked fruit pie. This is hearty home-style comfort at its best.

When you've had your fill of old-country dining, head to **South Market Bistro** (151 S. Market St., 330/264-3663, www.southmarketbistro.com, Tues.-Sat. 11am-2pm and 5:30pm-10pm, $16-30) in nearby Wooster. Tucked into the fertile farmland of Wayne County, South Market Bistro attracts diners from as far afield as Cleveland and Columbus with its sustainable, seasonal cuisine. A full three-quarters of the food served in this cosmopolitan bistro comes from local farms and producers, including the meat, poultry, and dairy. I guess you could call the place Wooster's answer to Chez Panisse.

SHOPS

Calling themselves "The Grandma of bulk foods," the **Ashery Country Store** (8922 OH 241, 330/359-5615, Mon.-Sat. 8am-5pm) specializes in bulk sales of spices, nuts, candy, dried fruit, pasta, and baking supplies. This old-fashioned general store stocks more than 1,200 items, with a matchless inventory of spices, cheese, meats, and fresh-baked goods. Home cooks and bakers used to high grocery-store prices will be in happy disbelief when they shop at the Ashery.

About two miles from downtown Berlin, in the picturesque Doughty Valley, **Guggisberg Cheese** (5060 OH 557, Millersburg, 800/262-2505, Apr.-Dec. Mon.-Sat. 8am-6pm, Sun. 11am-4pm, Jan.-Mar. Mon.-Sat. 8am-5pm) is home to the original Baby Swiss. Founded by a cheese maker of Swiss origin, the factory and retail store stocks a vast array of dairy and meat products, plus imported Swiss cuckoo clocks. Buy a four-pound wheel of the cheese that made Guggisberg famous, or select others from the amazing variety of distinctive cheeses. On weekday mornings visitors can peek through a window to watch cheese being made.

Concerned that the Amish community would begin to have trouble finding the nonelectric tools they needed to survive, in 1955 Jay Lehman founded **Lehman's Hardware** (1 Lehman Cir., Kidron, 330/857-5757, www.lehmans.com, Mon.-Sat. 8am-5:30pm). Of course, it isn't just the Amish who crave old-fashioned, high-quality nonelectric merchandise. Survivalists, environmentalists, victims of natural disasters, and nostalgia buffs all have needs that are satisfied by this amazing store. Filled with anachronistic items like wood-burning cook stoves, steel-cut nails, wooden wheelbarrows, and American-made children's toys, the 32,000-square-foot retail store is quite the adventure. Ironically, it is now the Amish themselves who are stocking the store with their high-quality handmade products.

Folks who relish the homey atmosphere of a bed-and-breakfast while enjoying the amenities of a contemporary hotel will appreciate the **Barn Inn Bed & Breakfast** (6838 County Rd., Millersburg, 877/674-7600, www.thebarninn.com, $110-220). Clean, comfortable, and gracious, the inn offers 11 well-appointed rooms, all with private entrances, private baths, and wireless Internet. Rooms also include a full country breakfast. The location is ideal for exploring Amish Country, and the innkeepers will be glad to provide guests with recommendations.

Set on a 70-acre farm overlooking scenic Holmes County, **The Charm Countryview Inn** (3334 State Rt. 557, 330/893-3003, www. charmcountryviewinn.com, $100-145) is an ideal bed-and-breakfast option just a few miles from the aptly named village of Charm. All 15 guest rooms have private baths, queen-size beds, solid oak furniture, and handmade quilts. Home-cooked breakfasts, prepared by Amish and Mennonite cooks, are served family style.

Perched on a hilltop overlooking the beautiful Holmes County countryside, **Holmes with a View** (3672 Township Rd. 154, Millersburg, 877/831-2736, www.holmeswithaview.com, $135-245) truly does offer stellar vistas. Stacked into a trio of unique round buildings, six circular suites come fully equipped with kitchen, living, and dining areas, gas fireplace, whirlpool tub, and entertainment center. The location is close to many Amish Country sites, yet the inn is sheltered away in a quiet corner of the county.

The serene and stunning **Inn and Spa at Honey Run** (6920 County Rd. 203, Millersburg, 800/468-6639, www.innathoneyrun.com, $120-320) fits well into its attractive landscape. Surrounded by 70 natural acres, this private retreat offers a number of wonderful accommodations. The Main Lodge has rooms with views of nearby bird feeders that attract a wealth of avian activity. In the unique earth-sheltered Honeycomb, guests stay in rooms carved into a hillside. Small families or couples looking for solitude will appreciate the cabins, which are tucked into the woods and feature a kitchen, living area with stone fireplace, and whirlpool tub. The spa's topnotch therapists and world-class treatments are worth a visit to Honey Run on their own.

PRACTICALITIES
Guided Tours and Maps

Why don't Amish wear mustaches? How can you tell if the Amish are married? Do they pay taxes, serve in the military, vote, or go to college? These are just a few of the questions answered on the **Amish Heartland Tours** (330/893-3248, www.amishheartlandtours.com), a locally run company that dates back to 1993. They offer a wide range of informative and captivating excursions, from half-day trips to overnight adventures. Participants are granted entry into private Amish homes for dinner, taken for a ride in a horse-drawn buggy, or whisked away on a narrated drive through the back roads of Amish Country. This outfit will even custom design a multiday voyage, with all arrangements for lodging, meals, and attractions mapped out in advance.

The next best thing to a well-versed insider is a good map. When in Amish County, pick up a copy of the **Amish Highways and Byways Map,** which is available at most shops for around $4. (Or visit www.experience-ohio-amish-country.com to order one in advance.) This invaluable resource contains detailed maps of Holmes County, Millersburg, Berlin, Walnut Creek, and Sugarcreek, allowing tourists to get lost on out-of-the-way back roads without ever really getting lost.

Tourist Information

There are a number of particularly helpful organizations and websites to give you a hand in planning your visit to Amish Country. Perhaps the best recourse is the **Holmes County Chamber of Commerce** (877/643-8824, www.visitamishcountry.com). Their website is jammed with all sorts of wonderful info on area sights, shops, restaurants, hotels, and maps. While not an official tourism site, **Experience Ohio Amish Country** (www.experience-ohio-amish-country.com) is one of the best out there, especially when it comes to detailing the Amish way of life. It is written by passionate fans of the area. Also check out www.berlinohio.com and www.millersburgohio.com.

Getting There

Holmes County is about 80 miles south of Cleveland. There are any number of ways to get here, but the best combination of direct and scenic is to go south on I-77 until you hit Dover. From here you can travel west along scenic Route 39, which passes through the most visited villages and towns of Sugarcreek, Berlin, and Millersburg.

Getting Around

While rural Holmes County has plenty of scenic country roads, it has zero interstate highways. Getting around requires a car or bike and a very good map. (GPS wouldn't hurt either.) Towns, attractions, and sights are spread apart by miles of farmland, making an automobile or motorcycle one's best bet for experiencing as much as possible.

Background

The Setting.....................270

History 272

Government.....................275

Economy.........................276

People and Culture...............278

The Setting

GEOGRAPHY AND CLIMATE

The dominant natural feature of Cleveland isn't land but water. Lake Erie, the southernmost of the Great Lakes, occupies a none-too-subtle position due north of the city. The lake's freshwater supports local industry, sustains sport fish populations, irrigates regional crops, flows through kitchen faucets, and falls as winter precipitation. Yet, despite the importance and proximity of this sizable body of water, Clevelanders largely ignore it. It isn't their fault: A shoreline freeway thwarts easy access, a municipal airport gobbles up prime real estate, and exclusive marinas snub the masses.

The city's second most defining physical feature is likely the Cuyahoga River, which slices through town, dividing Cleveland into two distinct and distinctive sides. To locals, east and west are not merely points on a compass, they are lifelong labels affixed at birth. Here, you are either an East Sider or West Sider, and as such possess a certain assemblage of stereotypical characteristics, accurate or otherwise. In the old days, it was rare for folks to venture from one side to the other, as odd as that sounds. These days, those traditions are as outdated as the aforementioned stereotypes.

Much fuss has been made of Cleveland's weather, but apart from the six months of winter (okay, that's a joke), the region possesses a fairly typical continental climate. Spring can provide a loathsome late-season snowfall before warming up to a seasonable 70 degrees by June. Summers are hot, occasionally humid, and punctuated by spectacular thunderstorms. Don't worry, they pass through briskly, leaving cooler, clearer, and drier weather in their wake. Fall is Cleveland's most brilliant season, boasting warm, dry days, crisp, cool evenings, and a backdrop of luminous fall foliage. In Northeast Ohio, smart brides skip the June wedding in favor of early October. Winters start slower around here than in other parts of the Midwest thanks to the lake, its accumulated warmth acting as a sort of down blanket. Cleveland's impressive snow totals can be blamed—or credited, depending on one's point of view—on a phenomenon know as the Lake Effect. As cold arctic air passes over the relatively warm lake water, it picks up evaporated moisture and dumps it as shovelfuls of snow on area driveways. The largest snow accumulations occur well south and east of downtown in an area appropriately dubbed the Snow Belt, but rare are the occasions when road crews don't immediately clear it from the streets.

Lake Erie Mirage Effect

Imagine standing on the banks of Lake Erie in Cleveland and suddenly the Canadian shore comes into perfect view, as though the 50-mile divide had been whittled down to one mile. A rare optical phenomenon known as the Lake Erie Mirage Effect can do just that, making buildings, cars, and even people seem like they were close enough to reach out and touch.

Mirages occur all the time. Whether it's the proverbial oasis in a desert or a shimmering highway on a sun-soaked day, the optical trickery is the result of light refracting as it passes through layers of variously heated air. But while highway mirages are an everyday occurrence, the Lake Erie Mirage is not. Still, there have been numerous reports by people on both sides of the lake who have experienced this remarkable spectacle.

During an atmospheric inversion, cold dense air hovers near the lake's surface and warm air floats in layers above. As light travels through these layers, it refracts, or bends, acting like a magnifying lens that brings distant objects into clear view. So if you find yourself by the water's edge on a calm day, glance across the lake; you may just spot a Canadian flag.

ENVIRONMENTAL ISSUES

In many ways, the environmental challenges faced by Cleveland and Cuyahoga County mirror those found elsewhere in the nation. Unchecked urban sprawl has seen the creation of numerous exurban communities, along with the requisite big-box shopping centers, all at the expense of once-fertile farmland. What do we have to show for all that progress? How about lengthy commutes, increased air pollution, and deteriorating inner-ring neighborhoods and infrastructure. Add to that Cleveland's proximity to coal-fired power plants, soot and sulfur dioxide-spewing steel mills, and other heavy industry and you get a city with elevated levels of ozone and particle pollution.

But the news is not all bad. Ambitious downtown development projects and a renewed interest in urban living show promise in stemming the outward migration and already are bringing thousands of new residents into the city center. Better still, many of these new structures are taking advantage of ecoconscious green-building techniques. The recently completed $200 million HealthLine links Public Square and University Circle, Cleveland's two most dynamic employment centers, with a shiny fleet of environmentally friendly hybrid-electric buses. Bike lanes allow nearby commuters to pedal to work. And a recent national study recognized Cleveland as one of the country's most walkable cities, with special nods to the neighborhoods of downtown, Ohio City, Tremont, and Detroit Shoreway.

Cleveland was the butt of innumerable jokes when, in 1969, the Cuyahoga River burst into flames thanks to layers of oily industrial runoff. That shameful fire brought national attention to environmental issues everywhere, eventually leading to the passage of the Clean Water Act. While nobody dips their canteen into the Cuyahoga, wastewater treatment improvements have brought the river within accepted water-quality standards, and it's not uncommon to spot snapping turtles, great blue herons, and red-tailed hawks along the banks. Lake Erie, once a pea-green cesspool of fetid decay, is far cleaner, clearer, and teeming with sport fish. There are still water-quality issues, and swimmers are cautioned to keep apprised of no-swim advisories at area beaches (check www.ohionowcast.info), but even those appear to be decreasing from year to year.

Best of all, perhaps, is a 2008 study that recorded wind speeds off Lake Erie's shoreline as well above those necessary to support energy-producing turbines. Such promising reports could very well translate into jobs, clean energy, and a progressive new image for Cleveland.

History

Long before there were the Cleveland Indians there were Indians in Cleveland. The area's first settlers, members of various Native American tribes, gave the twisty, turny Cuyahoga River its name: Cuyahoga is the Indian word for "crooked river." In 1796, Moses Cleaveland departed his vessel at the mouth of that very river to begin surveying the Western Reserve, a three-million-acre tract of land governed by Connecticut. In the process, he established the city that would become the territory's capital. Cleaveland became Cleveland, anecdotal lore will have one believe, when the village newspaper dropped the "a" in order to squeeze the name onto the paper's masthead.

The swampy Flats on either side of the Cuyahoga River, which served as a trading post and pioneer hangout, soon became the epicenter of commerce and industry. It was on the banks of this river that Cleveland generated its fortunes, with steel mills, shipyards, oil refineries, breweries, and assembly plants springing up like shiitakes. The Ohio & Erie Canal opened up Cleveland and the interior of Ohio to the Ohio River and points east and west, providing a massive new market for its goods. The rapidly developing city was the first to employ electric streetlights, streetcars, and traffic signals. Cleveland was the site of the first automobile sale and offered free home mail delivery before any other U.S. city.

John D. Rockefeller, "the richest man in America," transformed the Flats into the nation's oil capital. By the late 1800s, Standard Oil controlled most of the nation's refining capacity. Rockefeller's unlawful monopoly was broken up soon after the turn of the 20th

Mad Butcher of Kingsbury Run

When two boys playing in the Kingsbury Run area of Cleveland stumbled across a decapitated body, it was the beginning of a citywide reign of terror that would last for years. What police discovered when they arrived on the scene was not one but two decapitated bodies.

It was September of 1935, and over the next three years a dozen other victims would turn up, all decapitated and most dismembered. The Mad Butcher of Kingsbury Run, as he would soon be called, was one of the most depraved serial killers in our nation's history. Officially, the case has never been solved, despite having Eliot Ness in charge of the investigation.

When Ness accepted the job of Cleveland Safety Director, he intended to focus on greed, corruption, and fraud. But soon, the lawman found himself in charge of quelling one of the most heinous killing sprees in history. He personally interviewed witnesses, placed 20 of his best officers on the case, and rounded up every bum in Kingsbury Run for questioning.

Because the heads and hands were removed from the bodies, identifying the victims was nearly impossible. Many remain nameless to this day. In an attempt to indentify one of the last victims, Ness ordered a plaster cast be made of the severed head. This "death mask" was then displayed during the 1936 Great Lakes Exposition, a Cleveland-based World's Fair that attracted four million visitors in a single summer. Nobody recognized the face. This mask and three others are on display at the Cleveland Police Historical Society and Museum.

As a profile emerged, it was believed police were looking for a killer with a firm grasp of anatomy and a private place to perform the messy business. Butchers, hunters, and even doctors were considered likely suspects. But an almost complete lack of clues made finding him extremely challenging.

Attention soon turned to Dr. Frank Sweeney, a big, strapping man who grew up in the Kingsbury Run area and had an alcohol problem. Despite overwhelming confidence that Sweeney was the killer, a lack of direct evidence prevented a conviction. Two days after he was interrogated, Sweeney voluntarily admitted himself to a hospital. The murder spree stopped at the same time.

century, but his largesse lives on in named buildings, parks, and through generous donations and endowments.

By 1920, Cleveland was the nation's fifth-largest city. That same year the Cleveland Indians defeated the Brooklyn Dodgers to win the World Series, no doubt helped along by the first unassisted triple play in a world championship game. Despite the nationwide Depression, Cleveland, for two summers in 1936 and 1937, hosted the elaborate Great Lakes Exposition. Similar in size and scope to a World's Fair, the event saw the construction of 200 art deco-style buildings stretching from Public Square to the lakefront. Literally millions of people traveled from far and wide to experience exotic cultures, theatrical performances, and spectacular attractions. Billy Rose's Aquacade was a floating extravaganza filled with singers, dancers, and swimmers, including Olympic gold medalist Johnny

Weissmuller. General Electric debuted the nation's first 50,000-watt lightbulb, a glowing achievement to be sure.

Following its peak in 1950, Cleveland's population began a slow and steady decline. Industrial production waned, white residents fled the city for neighboring suburbs, and the once-mighty Flats conflagrated into a national disgrace. Racial unrest visited many U.S. cities in the 1960s, and Cleveland was not immune. For six days in 1966, the 20-block neighborhood of Hough was the scene of fires, gunplay, and looting. When all was said and done, four were dead and another two dozen severely injured. Just one year later, however, Carl Stokes was elected as the first black mayor of a major U.S. city. His victory made the cover of *Time* magazine.

Cleveland's darkest days, perhaps, were in the late 1970s, when it became the first major U.S. city since the Depression to default on its financial obligations. Yet, by the bicentennial celebrations of 1996, the "Mistake on the Lake" had begun its transformation into "The New American City." Ambitious new downtown projects saw the construction of three new professional sports venues, a state-of-the-art science center, and the Rock and Roll Hall of Fame. The Flats was reborn, this time as a nationally recognized adult playground with nightclubs, restaurants, and brewpubs. Offering more than just something to do on a weekend, this compilation of civic triumphs buoyed the spirit of an entire city, signaling brighter days ahead. Some were even calling it a renaissance.

As present-day Cleveland deals with the serious issues of employment, education, inner-city crime, and balancing the books, ambitious new projects once again point to a brighter future. Since its completion in 2008, the RTA HealthLine Bus-Rapid Transit has spurred more than $4 billion in supplemental development up and down its nine-mile run along Euclid Avenue. The Cleveland Clinic, University Hospitals, Case Western Reserve University, and scores of other University Circle start-ups continue to generate cutting-edge jobs in biotech at an unprecedented pace. Presently, there is a mini-boom of downtown residential and commercial projects, including a green-lighted $500 million makeover of the east bank of the Flats. A new convention center and medical mart may someday get built, which will showcase medical devices, inventions, and discoveries.

Government

Cleveland is the county seat of Cuyahoga County, Ohio's most populous county as of the last census, with almost 1.3 million residents. The historically progressive district has voted Democrat in all but one presidential election since the 1960s. Despite a record 227,000-vote advantage over President George W. Bush in the 2004 election, John Kerry went on to lose the state of Ohio, and thus his bid for the White House. Many in politics contend that voting irregularities in Ohio clinched Bush's victory in the Electoral College. Some will go so far as to say that Bush, with help from then secretary of state Kenneth Blackwell, flat out stole the election. Issues included the use of outmoded punch-card voting machines, the purging of tens of thousands of eligible voters from the rolls, the refusal to process new voter registration cards, understocking likely Democratic polling sites with voting machines, and barring people from voting in the wrong precinct. The story ends on an even more troubling note when, against state and federal law, two-thirds of Ohio's 2004 ballots were lost or destroyed, making it impossible to ever fully determine the accuracy of that year's vote count. (No, folks in Cuyahoga County are *not* over it.) Vowing reform, the incoming Democratic secretary of state Jennifer Brunner forced the resignation of numerous Board of Elections officials.

BACKGROUND
GOVERNMENT

Every city has problems that shape and define it; Cleveland and Cuyahoga County seem to be suffering from governmental bloat that threatens to drag the entire region down. Thanks to 200 years of business as usual, the 16 counties that make up the economic region known collectively as Northeast Ohio have become a fragmented web of independent cities, villages, and townships, most with their own school system, city hall, and police and fire station. This redundancy in service has lead to an aggregate cost of government that has risen at a level more than twice the rate of inflation. These days, the watchword on local editorial pages is "regionalism." Leaders, finally seeing the negative effects on the region's economy that this unchecked waste causes, have begun endorsing plans for reform. By consolidating services, surrendering some autonomy, and coming up with appropriate tax-sharing strategies, the region may yet work its way out of the muck, mire, and mess of the status quo. On a slightly smaller scale, equally fervent attempts are being made to reform Cleveland's overstuffed city council. With 21 members representing just 445,000 residents, the council employs more members than those of Cincinnati and Columbus combined. In predictable fashion, most of the aforementioned governing bodies agreed that the ideas are so beneficial they warrant further study.

Lately, however, bright spots in local government are eclipsing a less-than-stellar recent history. After a years-long FBI probe uncovered massive county corruption and landed numerous politicians and business leaders in jail, county residents voted to abolish a commissioner system in favor of a charter government with an elected county executive and an 11-member county council. With transparency and accountability now the watchwords, people once again have confidence in their elected officials.

Economy

If you look in the right places, there is plenty to be optimistic about when it comes to the economic future of Cleveland and Northeast Ohio. Despite its Rust Belt roots, the region is fast becoming a hotbed of high-tech activity in the areas of health care, bioscience, information and health-care technology, and alternative energy solutions. While overall employment in manufacturing has undoubtedly taken a hit, the industry still accounts for about a fifth of the jobs in the region. But these days, in addition to rolling out steel, rubber, and automobile parts, area factories are beginning to focus on next-gen polymers, innovative medical devices, and tomorrow's fuel cell components.

Spurred on by initiatives like the Third Frontier Project, a 10-year $1.6 billion cash infusion, and grants from the Cleveland Foundation, one of the country's most generous philanthropic organizations, area institutions continue to expand and spin off new start-ups. Between 2007 and 2011, 226 Greater Cleveland companies collectively attracted $961 million from venture capitalists and angel investors. That activity represents a 133 percent increase in deals and a 26 percent increase in dollars when compared to the previous five years. Technology leaders like NASA Glenn Research Center, Case Western, Cleveland State University, and Parker Hannifin are helping to cultivate a "green-collar" workforce centered on the field of renewable energy. The state is poised to become a leader in fuel cells, biofuels, and wind-turbine-component manufacturing.

HEALTH CARE AND EDUCATION

Cleveland is home to top hospitals, medical schools, and universities such as the Cleveland Clinic, Case Western Reserve University, and University Hospitals, and it appears that health care is becoming the economic engine of this ship. The epicenter of this activity is University Circle, a one-square-mile cluster of cultural, educational, and medical institutions. The district is the second-largest employment center in Cleveland. Each day, approximately 40,000 people go to work at 50 or so organizations, pulling down a collective $850 million per year. But that epicenter might be shifting downtown as the city gears up for the opening of the Global Center for Health Innovation, a massive showcase for the latest in health-care technology, education, and commerce.

In addition to being among the most respected health-care facilities in the world, the Cleveland Clinic is an economic powerhouse, with revenues topping $4 billion annually. The immense hospital system employs 39,000 people, making it Ohio's second-largest private employer. It even maintains its own police force. The Clinic continues to expand its Midtown footprint, steadily replacing deserted brownfields and neglected warehouses with new medical buildings and parking garages. Built at a cost of over $600 million, The Miller Family Pavilion and the adjacent Glickman Tower are the latest additions to the sprawling campus. Meanwhile, on the main campus of nearby University Hospitals, the 375,000-square-foot Seidman Cancer Center opened in spring 2011, setting a new standard of care for cancer treatment.

LEGAL

Home to the founding offices of Jones Day, Squire, Sanders & Dempsey, Baker Hostetler, and Thompson Hine, among other firms, Cleveland has long been a legal powerhouse. There are over 10,000 registered attorneys in Greater Cleveland, giving the region a lawyer density on par with Chicago, Atlanta, and New York. The legal profession is one of the city's largest employment sectors, following closely behind health care and education.

FINANCIAL

Up until the recent economic meltdown, Cleveland was home to two of this nation's biggest banks, National City and KeyCorp. Early advances in steel, oil, and auto industries, coupled with favorable banking laws, turned Cleveland into a major financial center. Finance still plays a major role in the local economy, with one of the country's 12 Federal Reserve Banks, plus sizable offices for money giants JPMorgan Chase and Fifth Third, calling Cleveland home.

FORTUNE 500

Northeast Ohio is home to a number of Fortune 500 companies, including Progressive Insurance, Goodyear Tire, Eaton Corporation, Sherwin-Williams, KeyCorp, and American Greetings.

EUCLID CORRIDOR PROJECT

Cleveland suffered terribly from the foreclosure crisis, with as many as 12,000 homes vacant in and around Cleveland neighborhoods. But thanks to one massive infrastructure project, there is some good news to counter the bad. Greater Cleveland Regional

Transit Authority's $200 million undertaking saw the rehabilitation of seven miles of Euclid Avenue, paving the way for speedy transit service along dedicated bus lanes between Public Square and University Circle. According to some estimates, close to $4 billion is being invested along the refurbished HealthLine route. Piggybacking off those sporty new buses, streetscapes, and transit stations are renovated apartment buildings, fashionable restaurants, and fresh tech start-ups. Ever-expanding Cleveland State University, which is bisected by Euclid Avenue, is spending $300 million alone on new academic buildings and student housing.

LOOKING AHEAD

Water helped make Cleveland an industrial powerhouse decades ago, and it may play an even more important role in the city's economic future. While Southern and Southwestern U.S. cities are battling over access to freshwater, Ohio, along with seven other U.S. states and two Canadian provinces signed the Great Lakes Compact. The Great Lakes-St. Lawrence River Basin Water Resources Compact was then signed into federal law, preventing thirsty outsiders from diverting water from the Great Lakes, the largest source of freshwater outside the polar ice caps. As freshwater becomes an increasingly sought-after resource, one necessary for business and development, not to mention that thing called life, some foretell a reverse migration back to Midwestern cities with access to that water.

People and Culture

Roughly equidistant from Chicago and New York City, Cleveland is described as the point where the East Coast meets the Midwest. The city is close enough to the heartland to reap the hospitable sensibilities of that region—hence the saying: "Winters here may be harsh, but never the people." Quick jaunts to the Big Apple are easy as pie, creating locally a demand for the same products, fashions, restaurants, and nightlife enjoyed out of town. Cleveland's best-of-both-worlds situation translates to hurried commuters, dressed to the nines, stopping to point a misguided soul in the right direction.

If any word accurately describes the people of Greater Cleveland, it is diverse. After the initial settling of transplanted British colonists, Cleveland enjoyed numerous waves of ethnic-specific immigration. By the late 1800s, a full 10 percent of the population was Irish. Most lived in Ohio City and worked at the docks unloading cargo. A comparatively larger contingent of German immigrants followed, some coming from as near as Pennsylvania, others straight from the motherland. Other significant migrations included large contingents of Italians, Russians, Jews, Slovenians, Slovakians, Poles, Hungarians, and Ukrainians. Much later, the city welcomed Asian immigrants, specifically Chinese, Korean, and Vietnamese, but also Thai, Laotian, and Indian. Hispanics came in equally impressive numbers too. Walk into the West Side Market on a busy Saturday morning and you might be able to pick out a dozen different languages.

Cleveland's present-day population is just under a half million, down about 8 percent from the late 1990s. The city suffered its biggest losses in the 1970s, when almost 25 percent of its residents fled town, many simply relocating to suburban environs. Today, the five-county Greater Cleveland area contains well over two million people, making it one of the most densely populated regions in the country.

There are signs that this outward migration may slow, even reverse, in the coming years. Massive new investment in University Circle-area hospitals, spurred by a surging knowledge economy, coupled with a mini-boom of downtown housing projects, show promise in stemming the tide.

THE ARTS

Cleveland has always been a leader in the cultural arts. Its impressive collection of world-class institutions would be a boon for a city of any size, let alone one of only a half million. Supported by a long-standing tradition of generous arts philanthropy, the city's theaters, museums, music ensembles, dance companies, and independent galleries enjoy a relatively strong footing despite rocky economic times.

For close to 100 years, the Cleveland Museum of Art has been regarded as one of the finest repositories of visual art in the world. Generous donations and a sizable endowment have made possible the recently completed eight-year, $350 million expansion and renovation. For just as long, the Cleveland Orchestra—"the Best Band in the Land," according to *Time* in 1994—has regaled listeners from its majestic perch in Severance Hall. Established at the same time, the Cleveland Play House was the nation's first professional theater company. PlayhouseSquare is the second-largest arts district in the country, bested only by New York's Lincoln Center. All five of the district's 1920s-era theaters have been carefully restored.

University Circle, just one square mile, contains the country's greatest concentration of cultural and educational institutions. In addition to Severance Hall and the Cleveland Museum of Art, the dense enclave is home to the Botanical Garden, Western Reserve Historical Society, Museum of Natural History, Institute of Music, Institute of Art, and the Children's Museum. The Museum of Contemporary Art is presently building there a multimillion-dollar showcase for cutting-edge art. Many of these institutions are enjoying financial support thanks to a voter-backed cigarette tax, with 1.5 cents per cigarette going to numerous arts and cultural organizations.

Now in its fourth decade, the Cleveland International Film Fest is a 12-day event featuring more than 180 films and 165 shorts from 60 countries. As many as 90,000 viewers attend screenings at Tower City Cinemas. The IngenuityFest returns annually with a weekend-long celebration of art and technology, filling the lakeshore with live and interactive exhibits in visual art, music, dance, and video.

Art has and continues to be a driving force in the resurrection of urban neighborhoods. Tremont is buoyed by a vast array of independent galleries, studios, and boutiques, and its monthly ArtWalks keep the area's shops, restaurants, and bars hopping year-round. Little Italy has carved a sort of double-sided niche for itself, with art and food sharing equal billing. Up-and-comer Detroit Shoreway can credit theater as one the main reasons for its present-day resurgence.

Cleveland has music in its blood, plain and simple. The "Rock and Roll Capital of the World" loves its live music, and countless clubs around town regularly attract yesterday's, today's, and tomorrow's hottest acts. Meanwhile, the Rock and Roll Hall of Fame attracts everybody else, with millions flocking to the museum to take a stroll down musical memory lane.

All of these quality-of-life amenities combine to create a city that is vibrant, relevant, intelligent, and fun, which is one of the reasons Cleveland regularly finds itself near the top of lists ranking livability, literacy, and places to raise a family.

FESTIVALS AND EVENTS
Winter
Brite Winter Fest
Launched in 2010 by a few friends who thought Cleveland needed an outdoor festival in the dead of winter, **Brite Winter Fest** (www. britewinter.com) has grown like the proverbial downhill snowball. After 800 crazy people showed up to an out-of-the-way urban park the first two years, the event was moved to the Market District in Ohio City, where the festival has grown to a staggering 10,000 attendees. Held in mid February, the event features outdoor art installations, 50 bands and live performances across 8 stages, and fun-spirited games like the 24-foot giant wooden skeeball. Of course, the neighborhood bars and restaurants make ideal places to warm up over a hot cup of bourbon.

With about 90,000 people attending some 300 films over an 11-day period, the **Cleveland International Film Fest** (Tower City Cinemas, 877/304-3456,www.clevelandfilm.org, cost varies) is an absolute whirl of activity. Screenings take place all day in multiple theaters at Tower City Cinemas. Bona fide film-fest fans know to get their program guide well in advance so as to map out a plan of attack. The March event always kicks off with an opening-night film and gala, followed by approximately 180 feature-length films and 170 short subjects from more than 60 different countries. Numerous filmmakers are personally on hand to lead post-flick Q and-A sessions. Attending the festival for the first time can be a little overwhelming. The best strategy is to look over the program guide, select the movies you'd care to see, and buy tickets in advance. Short of that, it is wise to get to the cinema early to avoid being shut out. Tickets can be purchased in the lobby of Tower City Cinemas, online, or by phone and cost $14, less for 10-packs and members of the Cleveland Film Society. If you self-parked in the Tower City lot, make sure to get your parking voucher validated at the cinema box office.

Cleveland WinterFest

Thousands choose to get into the holiday spirit by attending **Cleveland WinterFest** (Public Sq., www.downtowncleveland.com, free), an annual downtown celebration. Festivities take place in Public Square on the first Saturday after Thanksgiving. A number of family-friendly events occur throughout the day in and around the square, but the real party kicks off with the holiday tree lighting at dusk. Depending on the weather, the parade of vintage horse-drawn carriages that follows can look like a scene ripped from a Currier and Ives print. Fire trucks, fife and drum corps, and marching bands also boisterously work their way around the square. The night is capped off by a spectacular fireworks display.

St. Patrick's Day Parade

The Cleveland Irish community is large and proud. How else do you explain an outdoor parade in the middle of March attracting upward of 375,000 people? With roots stretching clear back to 1867, Cleveland's **St. Patrick's Day Parade** (Superior Ave., www.cleveland-sirishparade.org, free) is one of the largest and oldest of its kind in the nation. The parade steps off at 1pm on March 17; if the holiday falls on a Sunday, start time is 2pm. More than 10,000 participants take part in the march, which works its way down Superior Avenue from East 18th to Public Square. Get to the parade route early to secure a good vantage point to watch the seemingly never-ending line of marching bands, Irish dancers, drill teams, military units, civic clubs, waving politicians, and local celebrities. Because this event is held in March, the weather can be wildly unpredictable. As the Boy Scouts say, "be prepared."

Spring
Cleveland Asian Festival
In just a handful of years, **Cleveland Asian Festival** (AsiaTown, www. clevelandasianfestival.org, free) has grown from an interesting neighborhood gathering to one of the most widely attended cultural events of the year, attracting close to 50,000 over a weekend. Intended to celebrate Asian Pacific Heritage Month, and spread over two days in May, the festival features outdoor stages hosting local musicians, martial arts demonstrations, Taiko drummers, and a traditional Asian fashion runway show. Also on the annual billing are the crowd favorite Lion and Dragon dances, foods from multiple Asian and Pacific Island cultures, and a pop-up marketplace offering diverse wares from handmade clothing to household goods.

Dyngus Day Cleveland
After attending the Dyngus Day festivities in Buffalo, which attract upward of 60,000 people each year, Justin Gorski decided that Cleveland needed its very own. Often described as the Polish version of Mardi Gras, **Dyngus Day** (Gordon Square Arts District, www.clevelanddyngus.com, free) always takes place on the Monday after Easter. The event is a traditional pagan holiday that began as a celebration of the rites of spring, but has evolved into just another reason to skip work and have fun. The event, only a handful of years old, has already grown from 1,500 people to more than a few thousand. The bash includes an Accordion March, the traditional crowning of Ms. Dyngus, and live polka music and dancing at neighborhood bars.

Great American Rib Cook-Off
A Memorial Day tradition for close to 25 years, the **Great American Rib Cook-Off** (Jacobs Pavilion at Nautica, 216/622-6558, www.fox8. com/rib, $8 adult, free child under 12) kicks off summer with a carnivorous celebration of smoke, fire, meat, and music. For four days in May, some of the nation's best pit masters gather at Jacobs Pavilion at Nautica to show off their barbecue prowess and compete for the titles of "Greatest Ribs," "Greatest Sauce," and "People's Choice." Wander the festival and sample St. Louis-style ribs, pulled pork, and barbecue chicken from some serious talent. Keep an eye out for former Cleveland Browns star Al "Bubba" Baker, who smokes the real deal at his popular Avon restaurant Bubba's Q. The admission price does not include food and beverage tickets, which are swapped for the real deal. Keep in mind that prices for ribs and

other food items can be steep. Admission does include loads of free entertainment, including local, regional, and national music acts.

Rite Aid Cleveland Marathon

Started in 1978, the **Rite Aid Cleveland Marathon** (800/467-3826, www.clevelandmarathon.com, free) is one of the oldest continuously held footraces in the nation. More than $20,000 in prize money is awarded to the winners of the men's and women's marathon, half-marathon, and 10K races. Of course, the 20,000 or so athletes who compete each year do so for bragging rights, not cash. The relatively flat 26.3-mile course takes runners past such notable landmarks as the Rock Hall, Great Lakes Science Center, Cleveland Browns Stadium, and through Ohio City, PlayhouseSquare, and University Circle. Even if you've never donned a pair of sneakers in your life, consider coming down for the party. In good weather, massive and enthusiastic crowds gather along the course and at the finish line (E. 9th St. and St. Clair Ave.) to cheer on the runners.

Tri-C JazzFest

This annual 10-day **Tri-C JazzFest** (216/987-4444, www.tri-c.edu, cost varies) is the largest music festival in Ohio and the largest educational jazz festival in the country. The popular event, now more than 30 years in the making, begins in April and takes place at numerous venues throughout town. Local, national, and international jazz artists not only perform, but teach, compose, and inspire the next generation at workshops, clinics, and lectures. Tickets for the concerts range in price. Check the Tri-C website for schedules, performance, events, and ticket information.

Weekend in Ohio City

For more than 20 years, the popular springtime **Weekend in Ohio City** (Market Ave. and W. 25th St., 216/781-3222, www.ohiocity.org, $130 Evening in Ohio City, $20 Ohio City Home Tour) has showcased the slow, steady, and undeniable renaissance of this blossoming urban neighborhood. The umbrella event entitled Weekend in Ohio City is comprised of Evening in Ohio City, a progressive food-and wine-tasting that moves guests from house to house, and Ohio City Home Tour, the main event. Art, architecture, and history buffs—not to mention the unabashedly nosey—have the opportunity to snoop into a dozen or so lovingly restored late-19th-century Victorians, Italianates, and Colonials. It's spread across a sizable distance, so attendees can either stroll from home to home or hop aboard one of the ever-circulating trolleys. Many in attendance make the wise decision to take a midday break at one of the local eateries for a quick bite and much-earned refreshment. Evening in

Ohio City tickets move quickly, but Ohio City Home Tour tickets can be purchased the day of the event.

Summer
Burning River Fest

Stewarded by the green-tinged Great Lakes Brewing Co., the **Burning River Fest** (Coast Guard Station on Whiskey Island, www.burningriverfest.org, $10 presale, $12 day of event, free child under 12) is more than just another occasion to party. Held annually in July, the fest is all about living responsibly. Important issues such as ecological conservation, environmental protection, historic preservation, and sustainable use of waterways are tackled through numerous exhibits, discussions, and demonstrations. Despite the lofty message, some 11,000 folks find plenty of reasons to smile at this bio-minded block party. Top chefs are on hand to whip up sustainably harvested meals. Bands play on three separate stages. Kids are entertained by face painting and biodegradable balloon animals. And for thirsty adults, there are always buckets of ice-cold locally brewed beer.

Cain Park Arts Festival

Held annually the second full weekend in July, the **Cain Park Arts Festival** (Superior Rd. at Lee Rd., 216/371-3000, www.cainpark.com, $5) is a top-rated juried arts event that runs Friday through Sunday and features the visual art of some 150 artists. Over the course of a weekend, more than 60,000 visitors will stroll the wooded grounds of Cain Park exploring original works of art, including paintings, watercolors, photography, sculpture, ceramics, and jewelry. Accompanying the art show is a full complement of adult and family entertainment at nearby Evans Amphitheater and Alma Theater. Local restaurants also set up shop and provide the fuel for an afternoon of delicious spending.

Cleveland Pride Parade and Festival

In 2013, the **Cleveland Pride Parade and Festival** (Voinovich Bicentennial Park, 216/226-0004, www.clevelandpride.org, free, donations welcome) celebrated its 25th anniversary, making it one of the longest-running Pride events in the country. You certainly needn't be lesbian, gay, bi, or transsexual to enjoy this fantastically festive day. Normally held in late June, the event kicks off with a wild parade to Voinovich Park, where an all-day party ensues. Multiple stages feature top-talent musicians and entertainers, while rallies and speeches preach messages of tolerance and acceptance. Revelers can quench their thirst in a lakeside beer garden and sate their hunger at numerous food stands. Also, look for Pride-related events all weekend long at area gay bars such as Twist. Step off takes at Voinovich Park kicks off at 1pm.

Clifton Arts & Musicfest

What started as a small neighborhood block party some 25 years ago has blossomed into a full-fledged arts and music festival attracting close to 40,000 revelers per year. Only slightly smaller than the renowned Cain Park Arts Festival, **Clifton Arts & Musicfest** (Clifton Blvd. at W. 117th St., 216/228-4383, www.cudell.com, free) features the works of about 120 different artists in every conceivable genre. Long regarded as one of the more free-spirited neighborhoods, Clifton knows how to throw a bash. A full lineup of live music covers most tastes, from rock and blues to reggae and funk. Scores of restaurants dish up local specialties and community and civic organizations offer craft activities for the little artists in the group. Look for this event around the third Saturday in June.

Feast of the Assumption

Technically, the **Feast of the Assumption** (Mayfield Rd. at Murray Hill Rd., 216/421-2995, www.littleitalycleveland.com, free) celebrates the ascension of the Virgin Mary. Practically, it is an occasion to party like the characters on the *Sopranos*. This annual four-day blowout begins solemnly enough, with Mass followed by a procession of the Blessed Virgin through Little Italy. The real party hits the streets at night, when literally thousands descend upon the narrow lanes of this old-world neighborhood. Main attractions, apart from the booze, include authentic Italian treats like sausage-and-pepper sandwiches, creamy gelato, and delicious cannoli. Back-alley charity casino games tucked into smoky tents have a delightfully illicit feel to them. The festivities end with a bang thanks to a rousing fireworks display. Look for the event in mid-August.

North Union Farmers Market

The **North Union Farmers Market** (216/751-7656, www.northunion-farmersmarket.org, free) operates approximately eight seasonal markets throughout Greater Cleveland, mostly between July and October (see a complete listing of locations, dates, and times on the website). All are authentic producer-only markets, meaning that all food sold is actually grown, raised, or produced in the region by those who peddle it. Depending on the time of year, shoppers are likely to find fresh greens, radishes, garlic, tomatoes, corn, grass-fed beef, foraged wild mushrooms, homemade goat cheese, honey, bread, farm-raised shrimp, free-range poultry, and edible flowers. Without question, the oldest and best market in the bunch is the one held on Saturday mornings at Shaker Square, beginning around the middle of April and lasting well into December. A smaller indoor market even lasts through winter. In midsummer, the Shaker market teems with activity. Young couples sip coffee purchased from one of the nearby cafés and casually shop for dinner. The city's top chefs, including Doug Katz from Shaker Square's fabulous Fire Food & Drink, shop for the evening's specials. Other chefs give demonstrations on how to cook with local ingredients. Performers provide a musical backdrop. To get the best selection, it is always wise to go early; many items sell out well before the noon closing time. Always make a complete lap before purchasing anything, as another producer may have something slightly better, cheaper, or sweeter. Bring cash, preferably small bills, and bags to cart your items home. Oh, and leave the dogs at home; they aren't welcome here.

OneWorldFest Cleveland

Established in 2013, the new **OneWorldFest Cleveland** (Cleveland Cultural Gardens, www.clevelandoneworldfestival.com, free) is an annual multicultural celebration of music, arts and food appropriately located in the Cleveland Cultural Gardens of Rockefeller Park along MLK Jr. Drive and East Boulevard. Launched by serial arts entrepreneur James Levin, who also birthed Cleveland Public Theatre and IngenuityFest, the daylong festival will honor and celebrate all nations and cultures. From noon to dusk, several stages and venues will feature performers presenting a wide variety of cultural displays that represent Cleveland's 100-plus nationalities, many of which have a dedicated garden in the park. Expect an interesting mix of ethnic foods and beverages. The free event is held in late August.

Parade the Circle

University Circle's signature summer event **Parade the Circle** (216/707-5033, www.clevelandart.org, free) is not focused around a specific holiday, but on artistic expression, creativity, and the rich diversity of the neighborhood. The centerpiece of the event is the parade, which begins at noon and features a psychedelic pageant of whimsical costumed marchers. Approximately 2,000 people take part, some dressed as giant puppets, some towering over the crowd on stilts, and others taking spots on imaginative floats. Entertainment before and after the parade ranges from African dance and classical music to storytelling and puppet shows. The Circle Village area on Wade Oval is loaded with family-appropriate arts and crafts, food, and festivities. Typically held the second Saturday in June, the parade and subsequent activities can attract 60,000 people in nice weather. Grab your spot along East Boulevard or Wade Oval Drive by noon to enjoy the show.

Taste of Tremont

Of all the summer neighborhood festivals, **Taste of Tremont** (Professor Ave., 216/575-0920, www.tasteoftremont.com, free) pretty much has a lock on the "best food" category. Tremont is home to many of Cleveland's best restaurants, and most are on full display at this boisterous block party. Cordoned off from Literary Road to Jefferson Avenue, Professor Avenue turns into a blocks-long street party, capped off with a celebratory open-air beer garden. Sample the specialties of more than 20 local restaurants, most of which are dished up personally by the chefs. Live bands perform throughout the day, as do various and sundry roaming entertainers. Many of the super-cool galleries and boutiques extend their hours to coincide with the festival. The Taste of Tremont usually runs noon-8pm around the third Sunday in July.

Wade Oval Wednesdays

On Wednesday evenings from June through August, folks gather on beautiful **Wade Oval** (216/707-5033, www.universitycircle.org, free) for free outdoor concerts, movies, and entertainment. This family-friendly event—simply referred to as WOW!—features local bands that play reggae, jazz, blues, and rock. Food, beer, and wine are sold on-site, and local artisans set up booths to sell their crafts. Many of University Circle's major cultural attractions offer extended evening hours that coincide with WOW! events, making it easy to plan a civilized night on the town. Concerts usually run 6pm-9pm.

Weapons of Mass Creation Fest

Launched in 2010, **Weapons of Mass Creation Fest** (Gordon Square Arts District, www.wmcfest.com, cost varies) is part creative conference, part music festival, and 100 percent unique. The grassroots annual event was started by advertising and marketing agency principals with designs on making Cleveland a creative powerhouse. During the day, folks attend talks by speakers and designers from inside and outside the region. At night, they hit local clubs to hear music. The talks tackle subjects like design, entrepreneurship, and pursuing happiness through creative endeavors. Recent events have featured 20 speakers, 20 designers, and 30 bands. All of it is centered in the Gordon Square Arts District. Tickets are required for most talks and shows.

Fall

Cleveland National Air Show

If it's Labor Day in Cleveland, you can be sure to hear the roar of the U.S. Navy's Blue Angels F/A-18s as they prowl the skies for the **Cleveland National Air Show** (Burke Lakefront Airport, 216/781-0747, www.clevelandairshow.com, cost varies). As the show's headline act, the Angels perform a one-hour choreographed flight presentation each day. Other major tactical demonstrations include those of the Air Force's F-15 Eagle, F-16 Fighting Falcon, Navy's F/A-18F Super Hornet, and the Ohio Air National Guard's C-130 Hercules support aircraft. Look skyward, too, for amazing airborne acts like Cold War dogfights, biplane barnstorming, and the Army's Golden Knights precision parachute team. Other attractions on the grounds include an F/A-18 flight simulator, numerous planes for viewing and cockpit picture-taking, and educational displays from NASA Glenn Research Center. Expect also the typical assortment of overpriced fair food and beer. Gates open Saturday morning, with shows running 10am-5pm Saturday, Sunday, and Monday. Parking at the Municipal Parking Lot is expensive, so consider carpooling or taking RTA's Waterfront Line to East 9th Street, which leaves a relatively short walk to the area. Or simply do as thousands of others do: Find a spot along the shoreline and watch the action for free. General admission and reserved box seating tickets are available at the gates the day of the show, by phone, or online.

IngenuityFest

IngenuityFest (Lakefront docks 32 and 30, north of First Energy Stadium, 216/589-9444, www.ingenuitycleveland.com, free) is billed as the fusion of art and technology. That's as precise a definition as one is likely to get when it comes to this free-flowing, high-concept, avant-garde celebration of interactive art. As far from a stodgy museum experience as one can possibly get, Ingenuity takes place in more than 120,000 square feet of warehouse space at the shipping docks in Cleveland harbor. The warehouses provide plenty of indoor exhibition space, but many more exhibits and events take place outdoors along the lakefront. With surprises at every turn, even in the strangest of places, Ingenuity is an interactive feast for a creativity-loving mind. Look for it in late September.

Oktoberfest

Fans of German food, beer, music, and even dogs will want to set aside some time over Labor Day weekend for **Oktoberfest** (Cuyahoga County Fairgrounds, 164 Eastland Rd., Berea, 440/348-0960, www.bereaoktoberfest.com, $10 adult, free child under 12), a celebration of all things Deutschland. From the ceremonial tapping of the keg to the very last "pah" of the oompah-pah bands, this popular seasonal attraction really does have something for everybody. Massive tents are erected to house the steady stream of performers, making this a rain-or-shine event. Music spans the generational divide, with polka, swing, disco, and rock. Food is provided by some of the most authentic German restaurants in the region. Beer is free-flowing and plentiful in the Bier Garden. One of the most eagerly anticipated events is the wiener-dog race, where vertically challenged dachshunds lumber their way down a 40-foot track in hopes of snagging the trophy. Parking is free all weekend.

Sparx City Hop

Billed as Ohio's largest art walk, **Sparx City Hop** (216/736-7799, www.downtowncleveland.com) unites the efforts of more than 50 independent galleries into a weekend-long celebration of art and culture. Typically held around the third weekend of September, Sparx organizes a network of trolleys to link the major art districts in Tremont, Little Italy, University Circle, and downtown. Not only is the goal to spark interest in local art, but to stimulate excitement about these urban neighborhoods on a smaller, more intimate level. Over the Saturday and Sunday events, galleries and nearby retail shops extend their hours of operation. Satellite art exhibits, mini-festivals, and musical performances also take place at various locations over the course of the weekend. Brightly marked bike paths were recently added to the proceedings, making it easier to pedal one's way from gallery to gallery.

Year-Round

Cleveland Flea

Inspired by the Brooklyn Flea, a few creative and determined Clevelanders started the hip monthly **Cleveland Flea** (St. Clair Superior, www.theclevelandflea.com, flea is free, dinner and classes vary) in 2013. Intended to inject life into a lesser activated corner of urban Cleveland, the Flea sets up in various locations within the St. Clair Superior neighborhood, including ethnic meeting halls, parking lots, and alleyways. The organizers hand select a variety of local vendors who sell original crafts, furniture, vintage items, even home-baked foods. Maker classes held in a nearby space teach attendees how to do everything from raise urban chickens and brew beer to make a terrarium. Along with the monthly markets, there is also a pop-up dinner, cooked by a local chef and served in a vacant storefront, an urban farm, even a bank lobby. Second Saturdays 9am-4pm.

Pop Up City

Like the proverbial Jell-O on a wall, **Pop Up City** (www.popup-cleveland.com) is tough to pin down. But this arts-centric organization's wild and spontaneous pop-up experiences are well worth the investigation. Temporarily plugging the idle gaps in a shrinking city, Pop Up uses abandoned structures and vacant spaces as its canvas of choice. A neglected downtown storefront is transformed into a bustling bazaar filled with eager shoppers seeking artsy wares. The roof of an industrial building is transformed into an elegant open-air restaurant serving local sustainable cuisine. A pedestrian overpass is inhabited by storytellers, artists, and musicians. One particularly exuberant midwinter event took place on a barren stretch of riverbed and featured ice art, snowboarding, and a bonfire. Check the website periodically for updates.

Essentials

Getting There .292

Getting Around 293

Tips for Travelers 297

Health and Safety 299

Communications and Media 300

Getting There

Cleveland is serviced by a major international airport, a Greyhound bus terminal, an Amtrak station, numerous interstate highways, and a turnpike, making travel to and from the city a relative breeze.

BY AIR

Cleveland Hopkins International Airport (CLE, 216/781-6411, www.clevelandairport.com) is the largest commercial airport in Ohio, serving around nine million passengers annually. Most major airlines and regional jets operate into and out of the airport. CLE is a major hub for United Airlines (800/864-8331, www.united.com,), often making that airline the best and most affordable option. Other major carriers include **Delta** (800/221-1212, www.delta.com), **Northwest** (800/225-2525, www.nwa.com), **Southwest** (800/435-9792, www.southwest.com), and **U.S. Airways** (800/428-4322, www.usairways.com).

CLE offers more than 320 daily nonstop flights to more than 80 destinations, with direct international service to cities in England, France, Mexico, and Canada. The busiest times at the airport are between 6am and 7:30am, and between 4:30 and 6:30pm. Parking is available 24 hours a day, 365 days a year in short- and long-term garages.

Ground transportation to downtown Cleveland is cheap, easy, and efficient thanks to a light-rail service that transports passengers from an airport train station directly to Public Square. The **Greater Cleveland Regional Transit Authority** (216/566-5100, www.riderta.com) Red Line operates Monday through Saturday approximately every 15 minutes from 4:29am until 7:45pm, and approximately every 20 minutes from 7:45pm until 1:05am. On Sunday, the train operates from 4:32am until 1:14am. The train costs $2 for the one-way trip and takes approximately 25 minutes to travel from the airport to downtown.

To hail a cab, travelers need to make their way to the taxi stand located at the southern end of the lower-level baggage claim area. The journey to town takes between 20 and 30 minutes and costs approximately $40. Most area hotels offer complimentary shuttle service to and from the airport, and like the taxi cabs, the shuttles are accessed on the lower-level baggage claim area. Call your hotel from the lower-level courtesy phones to verify service times.

To arrange private ground transportation, call **Hopkins Transportation Service** (800/543-9912). The company offers door-to-door service for all travelers, including those with disabilities.

BY CAR

Those traveling by car from the south will enter Cleveland either via I-71 or I-77. Those traveling from the east or west will approach the city via I-90. The trip from Columbus clocks in at around 2.5 hours; the trip from Chicago can be completed in just over five; those traveling from Pittsburgh should expect to land in C-Town in just over two hours; while Detroiters can look forward to a 2.5-hour journey.

BY TRAIN

Cleveland is serviced by **Amtrak** (200 Cleveland Memorial Shoreway, 216/696-5115, www.amtrak.com), but arrival and departure times are anything but convenient. The *Capitol Limited* runs daily between Washington DC, and Chicago, stopping in Cleveland around 3am. The *Lake Shore Limited* travels daily between Chicago and New York City, stopping in Cleveland around 6am.

BY BUS

Travelers can leave the driving to Greyhound by visiting what once was a flagship hub for the bus line. Built in 1948, the **Greyhound terminal** (1465 Chester Ave., 216/781-0520, www.greyhound.com) is one of the finest examples of Streamline Moderne design in the nation. The terminal is conveniently located downtown and is accessible by foot, car, and cab from most area hotels. **Megabus** (www.megabus.com), the low-cost express bus service, now shuttles travelers between Cleveland and a number of cities like Columbus, Cincinnati, Chicago, Detroit, Buffalo, and Erie, Pennsylvania.

Getting Around

PUBLIC TRANSPORT

The **Greater Cleveland Regional Transit Authority** (216/566-5100, www.riderta.com), known locally as the RTA, operates buses, light-rail, community circulators, and downtown trolleys throughout Greater Cleveland. Fares are $2 for buses and trains, $1.25 for trolleys and circulators. Four rail lines make up the Rapid Transit System. With Tower City as the center, lines take riders as far west as Cleveland Hopkins International Airport, north to the lakefront and North Coast Harbor, and east to East Cleveland and Shaker Heights. Fares on trains are typically paid when entering or exiting at Tower City station.

All of RTA's buses are equipped with external bike racks. To use the service, riders should visually signal the bus driver before loading his or her bike onto the rack. Additionally, bikes are permitted on all RTA trains at all times. Just cautiously roll your bike onto the train and stand with it. In 2007, RTA was named by the American Public Transportation Association as North America's Best Public Transportation System.

Completed in the fall of 2008, RTA's HealthLine offers quick and efficient transit service between Public Square and University Circle, with stops in between, on electric-hybrid buses.

DRIVING

To take advantage of most of the attractions and activities in this book, a comfortable pair of shoes and access to the RTA are all that is required. The trains quickly and safely move people between the airport, downtown, and University Circle, and the city center isn't so large that walking between destinations is a marathon. Toss in some inclement weather, however, and those leisurely strolls can become rather unpleasant. When weather or distance prevents walking or riding, a car might come in handy. If renting one, make your life easy and spring for GPS; Cleveland's East Side contains more roundabouts than straight roads. Do your wallet a favor and obey posted speed limits and traffic signals; Cleveland has installed a slew of automated cameras that snap speeders and red-light runners. For those drivers with AAA memberships, emergency roadside assistance is available 24 hours a day, seven days a week by calling 800/AAA-HELP.

CAR RENTAL

Naturally, Cleveland Hopkins International Airport hosts a full lineup of national car rental agencies. While agents are located in the airport, the rental car agencies are off the airport grounds. Nonstop shuttle service transports rental car customers from the baggage claim level of the main terminal to the rental car facilities. As for downtown rental agencies, consider contacting **Budget** (1717 E. 9th St., 216/696-7133, www.budget.com), **Avis** (1717 E. 9th St., 216/696-1568, www.avis.com), **Hertz** (1701 E. 12th St., 216/685-1790, www.hertz.com), or **Enterprise** (1802 Superior Ave. E., 216/696-7500, www.enterprise.com).

PARKING

There is no shortage of parking lots and garages to take your money in return for a small patch of concrete. For a good interactive map of downtown lots, visit **Parking Carma** (www.parkingcarma.com).

TAXIS

To put it bluntly, hailing a cab in Cleveland can be like waiting for Godot: Hope quickly fades to frustration. If you want a cab and you are not at the airport or a hotel, call one on the phone. A few

RTA HealthLine

This massive infrastructure project took two years to complete and cost $200 million. But supporters say it has already spurred more than $4 billion in new investment along the seven-mile route.

What some deride as simply a fancy new bus system is being billed by others as the rebirth of Euclid Avenue. Once called "Millionaire's Row," Euclid was known the world over for its unparalleled beauty and unrivaled concentration of wealth. Prosperous industrialists like John D. Rockefeller, Charles Brush, and Marcus Hanna all had stately mansions along the tree-lined avenue. Famous department stores like Higbee's, May Co., Halle Bros., and Sterling-Linder-Davis attracted well-heeled shoppers from all over the region and beyond. But thanks in large part to suburban sprawl, once-great Euclid Avenue crumbled like a sand castle at high tide.

These days, Euclid is making a comeback. This major artery connects Cleveland's two most dynamic employment zones, Public Square and University Circle. It bisects Cleveland State University, PlayhouseSquare, the Cleveland Clinic, and the region's burgeoning Midtown tech sector. And the Euclid Corridor Project, now called the RTA HealthLine (www.rtahealthline. com), is making life a whole lot better for everybody along the way.

In addition to new roadways, bike lanes, sidewalks, transit stations, and streetscaping, the most noticeable newcomers are the buses themselves. Called rapid transit vehicles (RTVs), these extra-long hybrid-electric buses produce 90 percent less emissions than a traditional bus and zip passengers from downtown to University Circle in 20 minutes flat. To accomplish that feat, the RTVs travel in dedicated bus lanes down the middle of the street and GPS systems communicate with traffic signals. Also, riders pay fares before boarding, resulting in faster pickups.

Because of the unconventional traffic arrangement caused by the dedicated bus lanes, drivers need to be hyperaware when traveling along Euclid Avenue. To avoid traffic tickets and collisions with large moving objects, drive only in the marked car-only lanes. There are close to 60 new stations, also located in the middle of the street, and crosswalks are everywhere, so keep a vigilant eye out for pedestrians. To make a left turn, look for the marked left-turn lanes. When you see the green left arrow, it is safe to turn, even in front of a bus.

To ride the HealthLine, use the crosswalk to reach the station. Some dual-purpose stations service both east and west routes, while others are dedicated for only east or west travel; they are marked. Vending machines at all stations dispense single-trip, all-day, seven-day, and monthly passes. They are good for use throughout the RTA public transportation system. When boarding, there is no need to show your ticket to the driver—just enter through either door and sit down.

The HealthLine runs 24 hours a day, seven days a week. During peak times, buses come every five minutes. Between 11pm and 5am they slow to one every half-hour. Fares are $2.25 for a single trip.

Innerbelt Bridge

Since 1959, the Innerbelt Bridge was the main link into and out of downtown Cleveland, handling at last count more than 138,000 vehicles every day. In 2009, the Ohio Department of Transportation revealed plans for a new two-bridge highway that would replace the original aging Inner Belt Bridge over the Cuyahoga River. The first new bridge was completed in 2013, at which point all eastbound and westbound traffic from the original bridge was diverted to the new span. Upon completion of the first bridge, the old bridge was demolished and the second new bridge is now being built. When the second bridge is completed in 2016, one bridge will be dedicated to westbound traffic and the other to eastbound traffic. Throughout it all there will be road closures, detours, and other traffic hiccups typically associated with major construction projects. In addition to sturdy bridges with free-flowing traffic, the project has made some much-needed improvements to the street infrastructure near the "touch down" points. The intersection of Ontario Street and Carnegie Avenue, for one, features a new pedestrian plaza with granite block pavers and curbs, great news for those approaching Progressive Field on foot or bike.

popular companies are **Ace Taxi** (216/361-4700), **Americab** (216/881-1111), **Yellow Cab** (216/623-1550), and **Wolley** (216/671-5555).

BICYCLING

While far from two-wheeled nirvana, Cleveland is beginning to see the light when it comes to providing access for riders. New bike lanes, bike racks, and bike-awareness programs are converging to make the city much more conducive to pedal power. After much debate, bike lanes were added to the final design for the Euclid Corridor Project. A new city law requires all downtown parking lot operators to install bike racks. And the RTA installed bike racks on all of its buses, making bike-and-ride commuting a reality.

MOTORCYCLING

Like many states in the United States, Ohio requires only riders under the age of 18 years old or riders in their first year of motorcycle licensure to wear a protective helmet. Passengers riding with such young or novice drivers must also wear helmets.

DISABLED ACCESS

RTA is one of the first transit authorities in the country to operate a bus fleet that is 100 percent wheelchair accessible. Buses have a low-floor design that makes it easier for senior citizens, persons with disabilities, and everybody else to board and exit the vehicles. They also feature an easy-to-use ramp that works faster than traditional wheelchair lifts found on other buses. **Ace Taxi** (216/361-4700) operates wheelchair-accessible vans that can accommodate one wheelchair passenger and three other riders, or two wheelchair passengers and one additional rider. Call for reservations. **Hopkins Transportation Service** (800/543-9912) offers door-to-door service to the airport for everyone, including travelers with disabilities.

Tips for Travelers

WHAT TO TAKE

Common sense and a good **umbrella** go a long way in Cleveland: This city fully experiences all four seasons (sometimes in the course of a single day). If attending a Browns game, for instance, it might be wise to dress as if one were leading an Antarctic expedition—baseball games at Progressive Field, depending on the month, weather, and time of day, can be scorching hot, miserably wet, or, in early spring, even snowy. For much of the summer, the plan of attack is layers, a wide-brimmed hat, sunglasses, and sunscreen.

Appropriate footwear in C-Town can range from flip-flops to mukluks. **Lightweight rain gear** is always nice to have on hand, as is a sweatshirt. In the fall, temps can plummet from a balmy 75 degrees to a chilly 55 degrees just a minute after sundown.

Upscale-casual dress will work at almost any Cleveland restaurant. Most do get dolled up, however, when attending concerts at Severance Hall or the theater at PlayhouseSquare.

Golfers should really consider bringing their clubs when visiting between May and October. Northeast Ohio has some spectacular golf courses, with more than 120 public courses reachable in under an hour's drive.

VISITORS CENTER

Cleveland Visitors Center, which is operated by Positively Cleveland, is conveniently located downtown at the corner of Euclid Avenue and E. Fourth Street (334 Euclid Ave., 800/321-1001, www.positivelycleveland.com). Stop in every day but Sunday for maps and directions, customized itinerary planning, sightseeing tour information, event ticket sales, and restaurant, hotel, and car rental reservations.

SMOKING

Despite the state's relatively high number of smokers, Ohio voters approved a comprehensive smoking ban that went into effect in late 2006. The sweeping ban covers most public spaces and places of employment, including bars, restaurants, and bowling alleys. What does this mean for smokers? It means they spend a lot more time standing around on sidewalks, for starters. Bars and restaurants with patios have become popular with smokers as they are one of the few remaining public places to puff. Some restaurants, especially those that offer more upscale dining, do not allow their patios to become smoke havens. It's always wise to seek permission before lighting up.

TIPPING

Considering that restaurant servers earn $3.50 an hour, it is reasonable to assume that most rely on tips as their major source of income. It is customary to tip between 15 and 20 percent of the pretax total for competent service. And it is never fair to penalize a server for the faults of a kitchen. If the food is poor, send it back and get something else. Don't stiff the waiter because the cook is lousy. At bars, the going rate is about a buck per drink when ordering one or two, less when picking up a round. Cabbies expect a tip; no surprise there. A good rule of thumb is to round up to the nearest dollar and then add another dollar or two, depending on the distance. For long trips, 10 percent of the fare may be appropriate, assuming you ended up at the proper destination.

GAMBLING

In 2009, Ohio voters said yes to a ballot measure that allowed four full-scale, Vegas-style casinos to be built in the entire state. Cleveland's is the Horseshoe Casino downtown. Additionally, the state later allowed Ohio's seven horse-racing tracks to install slot machine-style video lottery terminals (or VLTs). Two, Northfield and Thistledown, are located close to Cleveland.

GAY AND LESBIAN

Thanks to a thriving arts and culture scene, Cleveland enjoys a robust gay and lesbian population. In fact, in 2014, the Gay Games will take place here. Lakewood likely contains the largest concentration of gay residents, and thus it boasts many gay-owned and gay-friendly businesses. Cleveland's annual Pride Parade and Festival, held in June, is well attended by both gay and straight revelers. Some bed-and-breakfasts, like Ohio City's Stone Gables, are both gay-owned and gay-friendly. For more information contact the **Lesbian, Gay, Bisexual and Transgender Community Center of Greater Cleveland** (216/651-5428, www.lgbtcleveland.org).

Health and Safety

While the rates of homicides and other violent crimes are down overall across the city compared with previous years, there is no shortage of danger lurking in and around Cleveland. But by and large, the bulk of the hazardous activity is confined to a handful of impoverished and gang-riddled neighborhoods well outside the scope of most visits. That doesn't mean that care should not be taken everywhere, especially at night. Whenever possible, travel in groups, stick to well-lighted and well-traveled lanes, and know your route. Need an escort? Call the **Downtown Cleveland Alliance** (216/621-6000), and they will send out one of their ambassadors to lend a hand.

Downtown is very safe, even at night. Most parts of Ohio City and Tremont are well-traveled and thus safe, but as one ventures toward the fringes, things get a bit dicier. Same goes for Detroit Shoreway. Neighborhoods to avoid include those east of East 55th Street and south of Shaker Heights, and east of MLK Jr. Drive and north of Superior Avenue.

EMERGENCIES, HOSPITALS, AND PHARMACIES

Dial 911 for all fire, police, or medical emergencies. The **Greater Cleveland Poison Control Center** can be reached at 800/222-1222. The **Cleveland Clinic** (800/223-2273, www.clevelandclinic.org) operates dozens of regional hospitals, family health centers, emergency rooms, and surgery centers throughout Cuyahoga County and beyond. When traveling in the University Circle area, visit the main campus at 9500 Euclid Avenue. If downtown or in Ohio City, visit **Lutheran Hospital** (1730 W. 25th St., 216/696-4300). When in Lakewood consider **Lakewood Hospital** (14519 Detroit Ave., 216/521-4200). Other hospitals of note include **St. Vincent Charity Hospital** (2351 E. 22nd St., 216/861-6200) and **University Hospitals Case Medical Center** (11100 Euclid Ave., 216/844-1000). Most hospitals offer emergency treatment.

Communications and Media

PHONES AND INTERNET ACCESS

For the most part, Cleveland telephone numbers fall within the 216 area code. As one travels west or east, 216 gives way to area code 440. Well south of town, 330 is the name of the game. When calling from one area code to another, it is necessary to dial a "1" before the 10-digit phone number. Time and weather reports can be accessed by calling 216/931-1212 or #622 on Verizon Wireless phones.

Cleveland is served by all major cellular carriers, including Verizon, Sprint, and ATT.

Free wireless Internet service is available at most Cleveland Public Library branches, including the main branch downtown and those in Tremont and Ohio City (and all branches have public computers with Internet access). Free wireless Internet also blankets much of the University Circle area. Countless coffee shops, restaurants, and hotels offer free access as well, guaranteeing that a hotspot is never far away.

POSTAL SERVICES

Those who need to send mail or set up a P.O. box can do so throughout town at numerous **United States Postal Service** locations. Call 800/275-8777 or visit www.usps.com to find the closest one. For additional mail and shipping services, contact The **UPS Store** (800/789-4623, www.theupsstore.com) or **FedEx** (800/463-3339, www.fedex.com), both of which maintain numerous Cuyahoga County outposts. To speedily move items from one location to another within the city, it might make sense to employ a courier service. Some popular companies include **Bonnie Speed Delivery** (216/696-6033) and **BOBCAT Same Day Delivery** (440/458-5374).

NEWSPAPERS AND MAGAZINES

Cleveland's one major newspaper, the *Plain Dealer* (www.cleveland.com), recently stopped seven-day delivery in favor of a daily online version coupled with a four-day printed and delivered version. The *Sun News* (www.cleveland.com/sun) publishes approximately 20 different community-specific weekly newspapers that come out on Thursday. For some of the best arts, entertainment, and political coverage, grab a copy of *Cleveland Scene* (www.clevescene.com), a free alternative weekly that is available all over town. For a more in-depth look into the goings on in and around Northeast Ohio, purchase the latest issue of *Cleveland* magazine (www.clevelandmagazine.com), a glossy. For all the latest business news, Crain's *Cleveland Business* (www.crainscleveland.com), a weekly news magazine, is tough to beat. Owned by the famous boxing promoter Don King, the *Call and Post* (www.call-post.com) is a 90-year-old newspaper that covers African American events and affairs. The *Gay People's Chronicle* (www.gaypeopleschronicle.com) is a biweekly publication covering Ohio's lesbian, gay, bisexual, and transgender community. For comprehensive coverage of the local arts scene, including a breakdown of every worthwhile gallery and exhibit, grab a copy of the latest *Collective Arts Network Journal* from any coffee shop. Better yet, visit it online (www.canjournal.org). Foodies should seek out *Edible Cleveland* each quarter for in-depth coverage of the local food scene, from farm-to-table and beyond.

RADIO AND TV

All major television affiliates are present and accounted for in Cleveland, while public television fans are serviced by **WVIZ/PBS** (www.wviz.org). The Cleveland radio dial has a little bit of everything when it comes to sports, news, talk, and music. For classic rock tune into WMMS 100.7 FM and WLFM 87.7 FM; for Top 40 try WQAL 104.1 or WMVX 106.5; for hip-hop and R&B hit WENZ 107.9 FM; for country music tune into WGAR 99.5 FM; for news, talk, and sports visit WTAM 1100 AM and WKNR 850 AM; for talk and oldies hit WMJI 105.7 FM; for Christian go to WFHM 95.5 FM; for classical and public radio WKSU 89.7 FM or WCPN 90.3 FM.

Resources

Suggested Reading

HISTORY AND GENERAL INFORMATION

Cayton, Andrew R. L. *Ohio: The History of a People.* Columbus, OH: Ohio State University Press, 2002. This contemporary text covers a lot of ground, from the attainment of statehood in 1803 all the way to the new millennium. Way more than a dusty history book, this entertaining read relies on letters, fiction, art, architecture, and sports to tell the story of this complicated state in the heartland.

Franklin, David. *Cleveland Museum of Art: Director's Choice.* New York: Scala Arts & Heritage Publishers, 2012. Part of the Director's Choice series, this book is penned by the museum's new director, David Franklin, who offers a personal tour of some of his favorite objects selected from holdings that span 6,000 years of artistic achievement. Each entry offers a reflection on the work of art, explaining why it is one of his highlights.

Glanville, Justin, and Julia Kuo. *New to Cleveland: A Guide to (Re)Discovering the City.* Cleveland: New to Cleveland, 2011. With more than 50 illustrations by local artist Julia Kuo and text by writer and urban planner Justin Glanville, this is no ordinary guidebook. Inside are sections on choosing the best neighborhoods for students, artists, and professionals; advice on where to send your kids to school; and insights on the Cleveland real estate market.

Grabowski, John J. *Cleveland, Then and Now.* Berkeley, CA: Thunder Bay Press, 2002. Serving as a sort of visual narrative, this unique book juxtaposes historical photographs with modern color images of the identical scene. In order to know who we are, we must know from whence we came, and this book offers a unique vehicle to get there.

Miller, Carol Poh. *Cleveland: A Concise History, 1796-1996.* Bloomington, IN: Indiana University Press, 1997. While indeed concise, this thorough book spans 200 years of Cleveland history, from the moment Moses Cleaveland stepped off his dinghy in the Flats to the city's bicentennial celebration. Augmented by wonderful illustrations and photographs, this methodical book brings people up to speed in record time.

Nickel, Steven. *Torso: The Story of Eliot Ness & the Search for a Psychopathic Killer.* Winston-Salem, NC: John F. Blair, 2001. Most know only about Eliot Ness through his dealings with Al Capone and his depiction in *The Untouchables* of TV and film. But as Cleveland's safety director, Ness was placed in charge of tracking down one of the most heinous serial killers of all time, the Mad Butcher of Kingsbury Run. This book tells the tale.

Van Tassel, David. *The Encyclopedia of Cleveland History.* Bloomington, IN: Indiana University Press, 1996. There may be no more comprehensive historical text of any city than this exhaustive tome. This 1,100-page hardback covers seemingly every aspect of Cleveland's first 200 years, with entries on industry, philanthropy, art, music, and flight. Add to that hundreds of photos, numerous maps, and the sharp writing of more than 200 journalists, and you get an encyclopedic digest that makes others in the genre look like tourist pamphlets.

Woods, Terry K. *Ohio's Grand Canal: A Brief History of the Ohio & Erie Canal.* Kent, OH: Kent State University Press, 2008. The Ohio & Erie Canal was so influential in the development of Cleveland and the entire state of Ohio, it is no wonder there are so many titles on the subject. Few, however, can match the level of detail captured in this thoroughly researched and well-penned account of the events surrounding Ohio's most ambitious infrastructure project.

RECREATION, ART, FOOD, MUSIC, AND SPORTS

Adams, Deanna R. *Rock 'N' Roll and the Cleveland Connection.* Kent, OH: Kent State University Press, 2002. Weighing in at more than 600 pages, this comprehensive tome leaves no doubt as to why Cleveland landed the Rock and Roll Hall of Fame. The book tracks the history of rock as it applies to Cleveland, touching on early musicians, local DJs, trendsetting radio stations, and the lead up to acquiring the Rock Hall.

Gorman, John. *The Buzzard: Inside the Glory Days of WMMS and Cleveland Rock Radio.* Cleveland: Gray & Co., 2008. Gorman, who served as WMMS's program director in the 1970s, offers readers a salacious glimpse into life at one of the most influential rock radio stations in the country. No surprise: This one includes tales of sex, drugs, and rock and roll.

...skins, Patience Cameron. *Cleveland on Foot: 50 Walks & Hikes in Greater Cleveland.* Cleveland: Gray & Co., 2004. Walkers, hikers, and outdoors enthusiasts will have a field day with this guide, which points folks in the direction of some of the most picturesque walks around town. Northeast Ohio is blessed with great parks, and this handy book will help you explore them.

Latimer, Patricia. *Ohio Wine Country Excursions.* Cincinnati: Emmis Books, 2005. Few people outside Ohio realize just how much quality wine production goes on in the state. For those who are eager to learn more, this great guide offers detailed info on more than 60 Ohio wineries. In addition to some historical context, the indispensible book contains maps, photos, and tasting guides.

Piiparinen, Richey, and Anne Trubek. *Rust Belt Chic: The Cleveland Anthology.* Cleveland: Rust Belt Chic Press, 2012. Answering a call for entries, dozens of established Cleveland writers such as David Giffels, Connie Schultz, and Michael Ruhlman offer "the longer view" of what it means to live in a recovering Rust Belt city. Within are narratives of failure, conflict, growth, and renewal—the same themes we find in Cleveland.

Pluto, Terry. *The Curse of Rocky Colavito: A Loving Look at a Thirty-Year Slump.* Cleveland: Gray & Co., 1995. Pluto, who covers sports for the Cleveland *Plain Dealer,* is one of the country's best sports reporters. He has penned a number of books on Cleveland sports, including those on the Browns and the Cavs. This one links the Cleveland Indians' lengthy championship drought to the fateful day in 1960 when the team traded away beloved slugger Rocky Colavito.

Raab, Scott. *The Whore of Akron: One Man's Search for the Soul of LeBron James.* New York: HarperCollins, 2011. Writer-at-large for *Esquire* and Cleveland-born expat, Scott Raab is a lifelong Cleveland sports fan who suffers right along with the rest of us. But when LeBron James announced his defection to South Beach on a nationally televised show, Raab snapped and penned this biting look at the man, myth, and meanie who broke the hearts of too many.

Suszko, Marilou, and Laura Taxel. *Cleveland's West Side Market: 100 Years and Still Cooking.* Akron, OH: University Of Akron Press, 2012. Penned by two well-known Cleveland food writers, this book takes readers on a nostalgic tour of the West Side Market and into the lives of many vendors and market families, who are the true foundation of this historic public space. The volume is rich with many rare, and previously unpublished, vintage and contemporary photographs, and images that provide a delightful armchair tour of this magnificent landmark, which is a must-see destination for food lovers.

Taxel, Laura. *Cleveland Ethnic Eats: The Guide to Authentic Ethnic Restaurants and Markets in Greater Cleveland.* Cleveland: Gray & Co., 2006. In this helpful guide, Cleveland-based food writer Laura Taxel documents hundreds of ethnic restaurants and markets in and around the Cleveland area. Adventurous foodies would do well to grab a copy.

FICTION, POETRY, AND CHILDREN

Holbrook, Sara. *What's So Big About Cleveland, Ohio?* Cleveland: Gray & Co., 1997. When a well-traveled 10-year-old is dragged by her parents to dull old Cleveland, she expects to be bored to tears. And she is—until she discovers a secret about the city that changes her outlook. What better way to get your kids excited about C-Town than with this illustrated children's book?

Lax, Scott. *The Year That Trembled.* Forest Dale, VT: Paul S. Eriksson, 1998. This coming-of-age novel by Cleveland writer Scott Lax is set in Northeast Ohio and tracks a close-knit group of friends in the days leading up to the Vietnam draft. In 2002, the book was adapted into an independent film.

Roberts, Les. *Pepper Pike.* Cleveland: Gray & Co. Roberts, the recipient of the prestigious Cleveland Arts Prize for Literature, is a mystery writer with dozens of novels under his belt. He is best known for his Milan Jacovich series, which revolve around a likable blue-collar private eye of the same name. In addition to the above title that kicks off the series, other books include *Full Cleveland, The Lake Effect,* and *Deep Shaker.* No surprise that the novels are set in and around Cleveland.

Swanberg, Ingrid (ed.). *D. A. Levy and the Mimeograph Revolution.* Huron, OH: Bottom Dog Press, 2007. Underground poet d. a. levy used his relationship with Cleveland as the fuel for his stirring poetry, prose, and art. Modern readers walk away with a unique and moving perspective of 1960s Cleveland. Levy used his own photocopier to self-publish his works, essentially kick-starting the local alternative press movement. This anthology of his work is supplemented with interviews, essays, and letters.

Winegardner, Mark. *Crooked River Burning.* Orlando: Harcourt, 2001. In this ambitious American novel, Winegardner weaves fictional and nonfictional events into a patchwork tale of a once-great city in decline. The stars of this drama hail from opposite sides of town—he from blue-collar Old Brooklyn, she from affluent Shaker Heights—but fate has a way of bridging divides. In spite of its negative circumstances, Cleveland somehow shines through it all.

Internet Resources

GENERAL INFORMATION

About.com
www.cleveland.about.com
Like other About.com sites, this one compiles a broad swath of information on a host of Cleveland-related topics. Good for the casual visitor and the potential relocater, the site melds info on tourist attractions, specific neighborhoods, dining and nightlife, and current events.

ArtHopper.org
www.arthopper.org
This Cleveland-based website keeps tabs on the Midwest's art scene with high-quality arts journalism that covers the Greater Lake Erie region, including Cleveland, Columbus, Akron, Cincinnati, Dayton, Detroit, Pittsburgh, Toledo, and Youngstown.

City of Cleveland
www.city.cleveland.oh.us
The official City of Cleveland website is intended as a portal to government services, residential information, and city jobs listings. This is also where folks pay their parking tickets online.

Cleveland.com
www.cleveland.com
This online version of the Cleveland *Plain Dealer* tracks local, regional, national, and international news, but also sports, weather, entertainment, and seasonal events. There are scores of bulletin boards where lively discussions on every conceivable topic take place 24 hours daily. This is also the online home for *Sun News,* a family of community newspapers that cover the Greater Cleveland area.

The Cleveland Memory Project
www.clevelandmemory.org
Get lost in the Special Collections archives of the Cleveland State University Library at this beautiful website. Compiled here are more than 500,000 newspaper photographs, covering decades of

Cleveland history, architecture, and events. There are 6,000 images documenting the construction of the Terminal Tower alone. Bridge fans will go nuts over the vast catalog of historic bridge pics. Also here is the full text of hundreds of rare books.

Cleveland Plus Living
www.clevelandplusliving.com
Hosted by area chambers of commerce, regional business-growth associations, and travel and tourism professionals, Cleveland Plus Living is designed to attract skilled residents to Northeast Ohio. More stuff than fluff, the site contains hard info on the region's top employers, housing and cost of living, and education from kindergarten through postgrad. There is also a comprehensive listing of visitors' sites for nearby counties, cities, and attractions.

Cuyahoga Valley National Park
www.nps.gov/cuva
This is the official U.S. National Park Service site for Cuyahoga Valley National Park, a 33,000-acre sanctuary 15 minutes south of Cleveland. The well-organized site includes information on the park's history, its diverse flora and fauna, and the numerous recreational activities that exist throughout the park. The downloadable PDF maps of the park, its trails and waterfalls, and the popular Ohio & Erie Canal Towpath Trail make this site an indispensable resource.

GreenCityBlueLake
www.gcbl.org
For followers of the green movement, the smartly written content from this nationally recognized nonprofit serves as a how-to guide for modern times. Promoting environmentally friendly redevelopment, stemming the tide of urban sprawl, and improving the quality of life for all residents are the breezes that propel this organization. Visit this site to read about living sans car in Cleveland, where to find green housing, and why moving to cornfields is bad for everybody.

The Encyclopedia of Cleveland History
http://ech.cwru.edu
This is the online version of the book listed in the previous section, which is the authoritative text on historical information about Cleveland. In addition to all the articles from the print version of *The Encyclopedia of Cleveland History,* this easy-to-search website also includes revised text, tons of new content, and high-res photos and documents.

Ohio Division of Travel and Tourism

www.discoverohio.com

This official travel and tourism site covers the great state of Ohio from border to border. In addition to information on where to go, what to do, and when to do it, the well-designed site also features interactive maps, glossy publications, and special deals and discounts. Here travelers will also find listings for every local tourism organization throughout the entire state.

Positively Cleveland

www.positivelycleveland.com

The official website for the Convention and Visitors Bureau of Greater Cleveland, Positively Cleveland is extremely useful for tourists, potential new residents, travel professionals, and meeting planners. It is chock-full of info regarding attractions, accommodations, shopping, transportation, and excursions from town. Suggested itineraries take all the guesswork out of planning a short stay.

University Circle Inc.

www.universitycircle.org

University Circle is the epicenter of arts, culture, education, and health care in Northeast Ohio, and this official website is a great place to begin your exploration. Geared both to visitors and job seekers, this thorough site has information on major cultural attractions, seasonal events and exhibits, dining and nightlife, accommodations, career listings, and real estate.

EVENT LISTINGS

Cleveland.com

www.cleveland.com/events

This helpful tool searches upcoming events by day, week, or month. Further sorting by event type, location, and entertainment genre makes it easy to pinpoint your way to fun.

Cleveland Scene

www.clevescene.com

Cleveland's premier alternative weekly publishes comprehensive entertainment listings covering art, music, dance, theater, film, dining, and nightlife.

Cool Cleveland

www.coolcleveland.com

Tens of thousands of Clevelanders get a weekly email newsletter from this organization detailing all the cool stuff going on around town. One of the most complete listings of arts and culture events, it is worth checking out before stepping out.

www.pluggedincleveland.com/events

Check out this site for a decent listing of upcoming events in a broad range of entertaining pursuits.

BLOGS

Brewed Fresh Daily

www.brewedfreshdaily.com

This group-effort blog compiles comments from leading Cleveland voices on news, politics, and current events.

I Heart Cleveland

www.heartcleveland.com

Designer Charity D'Amato does a good—and visually compelling—job of keeping tabs on the social scene, with specific attention placed on parties, events, and restaurants.

Unmiserable Cleveland

www.unmiserablecleveland.com

This well-tended website covers a broad spectrum of local topics, including food, music, neighborhood happenings, and the arts.

Writes Like She Talks

www.writeslikeshetalks.com

Cleveland blogger—and rising star politician—Jill Miller Zimon is a regular contributor to radio show panels, and she was pegged by *WE* magazine as one of its 101 Women Bloggers to Watch. She writes about politics, among other topics, at her award-winning site.

Index

A

activities: 151-179
Adventure Zone: 244
African Safari Wildlife Park: 258
air travel: 292
Akron Aeros: 235
Akron Art Museum: 235
Akron: 235
Alpine Valley Ski Resort: 174
American Toy Marble Museum: 236
Amish & Mennonite Heritage Center: 263
Amish Country: 263
Apollo's Fire: 149
Arcade, The: 32
Art Gallery at Cleveland State University: 130
arts: 125-150, 279
Ashtabula County: 244
Atma Center: 167

B

background: 269-290
baseball: 157
basketball: 158
beaches: 170
Beck Center for the Arts, The: 54, 147
bicycling: 154, 162, 170, 176, 296
bike rentals: 154, 162, 170
bike trails: 170, 176, 265
Blank Canvas Theatre: 140
Blossom Music Center: 148, 236
Bonfoey Gallery: 132
Boston Mills/Brandywine: 175
bowling: 154, 163, 168
Brite Winter Fest: 280
Burning River Fest: 284
Burning River Roller Girls: 179
bus transportation: 293

C

Caddy Shack Square: 256
Cain Park: 51
Cain Park Arts Festival: 284
Capitol Theatre: 139
car rental: 294
Carnegie West Library: 42
Cedar Lee Theatre: 145
Cedar Point Amusement Park: 259
Century Cycles: 170

Chenga World: 174
Children's Museum of Cleveland: 143
Christmas Story House, A: 42
cinema: 128, 139, 142, 145
City of Cleveland: 179
CityProwl: 176
Cleveland Agora: 129
Cleveland Asian Festival: 282
Cleveland Bike Rack: 154
Cleveland Botanical Garden: 48
Cleveland Browns: 160
Cleveland Cavaliers: 158
Cleveland Cycle Tours: 176
Cleveland Disc Association: 179
Cleveland Flea: 289
Cleveland Gladiators: 161
Cleveland Heights and Shaker Heights: 23; map 5 12-13
Cleveland Institute of Art Cinematheque: 142
Cleveland Institute of Music: 144
Cleveland International Film Fest: 281
Cleveland Metroparks: 178
Cleveland Metroparks All-Purpose Trails: 176
Cleveland Metroparks Zoo and RainForest: 55
Cleveland Museum of Art: 49
Cleveland Museum of Natural History: 143
Cleveland National Air Show: 287
Cleveland Orchestra: 145
Cleveland Play House: 135
Cleveland Police Historical Society and Museum: 133
Cleveland Pride Parade and Festival: 284
Cleveland Public Library (Main Branch): 32
Cleveland Public Library Eastman Reading Garden: 156
Cleveland Public Theatre: 140
Cleveland Rock Gym: 173
Cleveland State University Vikings: 158
Cleveland Tours: 154
Cleveland WinterFest: 281
Cleveland Yoga: 166
Clifton Arts & Musicfest: 285
climate: 270
comedy clubs: 128, 147
Commercial Districts of Cleveland

Heights, The: 52
communications: 300
concert venues: 129, 146, 148
Convergence-Continuum: 138
Convivium33 Gallery: 132
Corner Alley, The: 154
Critical Mass: 176
cross-country skiing: 171
culture: 125-150, 278
Cuyahoga County Courthouse: 33
Cuyahoga Valley National Park: 56
Cuyahoga Valley Scenic Railroad: 173

DE

DANCECleveland: 135
Detroit Shoreway and Edgewater: 23;
    map 3 8-9
Dickey's Lanes: 163
disabled access: 296
Dobama Theatre: 147
Don Drumm Studios and Gallery: 240
Downtown: 22; map 1 14-5
driving: 293, 294
Dyngus Day Cleveland: 282
economy: 276
Edgewater: see Detroit Shoreway and
    Edgewater
emergencies: 299
environmental issues: 271
essentials: 291-301
Euclid Corridor Project: 277
Evans Amphitheater: 146
events: 280
excursions: 229-268

F

Fairmount Boulevard District: 52
Fairview Park/Kentucky Gardens: 163
Feast of the Assumption: 285
Federal Reserve Bank: 33
festivals: 280
Football: 160
Fortune 500: 277
41° North Kayak Adventures: 169
Franklin Castle: 43
Free Stamp: 33
Front Room Gallery: 132

G

galleries: 130, 138, 139, 142, 146, 147
gambling: 298
gay and lesbian: 298
Geneva on the Lake: 245
Geneva State Park: 245
geography: 270

Glacial Grooves: 256
Golf: 172
Goodtime III: 155
Gordon Square Arts District: 46
government: 275
Great American Rib Cook-Off: 282
Great Lakes Science Center: 34
Great Lakes Theater Festival: 137
greater Cleveland: 23; map 7 16-17
Greater Cleveland Aquarium: 134
GroundWorks Dancetheater: 150
gyms: 156

H

Hale Farm & Village: 237
Halloran Ice Skating Rink: 168
Harry London Candies: 242
Hartville MarketPlace and Flea Market:
    242
Headlands Beach State Park: 170
health: 276, 299
Heights Arts Gallery: 146
Hessler Road and Hessler Court: 49
Hilarities 4th Street Theater: 128
history: 272
hockey: 161
Holden Arboretum: 56
Hope Memorial Bridge: 35
Horseshoe Lake Park: 167
hospitals: 299
hotels: 212-228; see also Hotels Index
House of Blues: 129
Huntington Beach: 170

IJ

ice-skating: 168, 171
Improv, The: 129
IngenuityFest: 288
internet access: 300
internet resources: 306
Inventor Now Museum & Store: 237
itineraries: 25-28
Jacobs Pavilion at Nautica: 130
Jay Avenue Homes: 43
John Heisman's Birthplace: 43
Joy Machines Bike Shop: 162

KL

Kalahari Waterpark: 259
Karamu House: 149
kayaking: 156, 169
Kelleys Island: 256
Kelleys Island State Park: 256
Kendall Lake Winter Sports Center: 171
Kidron Auction: 264

Kiraly's Orchard: 246
Lake Erie Islands: 251
Lake Erie Monsters: 161
Lake Metroparks Farmpark: 247
Lake View Cemetery: 53
Lakefront Reservation: 46, 165
Lakewood: 23; map 6 14-15
Lakewood Off-Leash Dog Park: 169
Lakewood Park: 54
lesbian and gay: 298
Lincoln Park: 44
Little Italy: see University Circle and
    Little Italy

M

magazines: 300
Mahall's Twenty Lanes: 168
Maltz Museum of Jewish Heritage: 57
Marblehead Lighthouse: 259
media: 300
Memphis Kiddie Park: 57
Mill Stream Run Reservation: 175
Money Museum at Federal Reserve
    Bank: 134
motorcycling: 296
Mountain Biking: 171
Murray Hill School House Galleries: 142
Museum of Contemporary Art: 144
museums: 133, 143, 148; see also sights

NO

Nature Center at Shaker Lakes: 53
Near West Theatre: 138
neighborhoods: 22-24
newspapers: 300
nightlife: 103-124; see also Nightlife
    Index
North Union Farmers Market: 285
Ohio & Erie Canal Reservation
    Mountain Bike Trail: 171
Ohio & Erie Canal Towpath Trail: 170
Ohio City and Tremont: 22; map 2 6-7
Ohio City Bicycle Co-Op: 162
Ohio Hot Air Balloons: 263
Oktoberfest: 288
Old Federal Building: 35
Old Stone Church: 37
Oldest Stone House: 55
OMNIMAX Theater: 128
1point618 Gallery: 139
OneWorldFest Cleveland: 286

P

Parade the Circle: 286
parking: 294

parks: 156, 163, 165, 166, 167, 169, 178
Paul Duda Gallery: 138
people: 278
performing arts: 135, 138, 140, 144, 147,
    147, 149, 149
Peter B. Lewis Building: 50
pharmacies: 299
phones: 300
planning tips: 22
PlayhouseSquare: 137
Polka Hall of Fame Museum: 148
Pop Up City: 289
postal services: 300
Pro Football Hall of Fame: 237
Progressive Field: 157
public transportation: 293
Puma Yoga: 169

QR

Quicken Loans Arena: 130
radio: 301
Rapid Transit System: map 18-19
Ray's MTB Indoor Park: 171
reading, suggested: 302
Reinberger Galleries: 142
resources: 302-309
restaurants: 58-102; see also
    Restaurants Index
Rite Aid Cleveland Marathon: 283
Rock and Roll Hall of Fame and
    Museum: 37
Rock and Roll Hall of Fame Library and
    Archives: 135
rock climbing: 173
Rockefeller Park: 166
roller derby: 179
rowing: 156, 169

S

safety: 99
scenic drives: 264
Screw Factory Artists: 147
Serpentini Arena: 168
Severance Hall: 50
Shaker Heights: see Cleveland Heights
    and Shaker Heights
Shaker Square: 54
Shaker Square Cinemas: 146
Shawnee Hills Golf Course: 172
shops: 180-211; see also Shops Index
skateboarding: 174
skiing: 174
Sleepy Hollow Golf Course: 172
smoking: 297
Smolen-Gulf Bridge: 244
snowboarding: 174

snowshoeing: 171
Soldiers and Sailors Monument: 39
Something Dada: 147
South Bass Island: 251
SPACEGallery: 133
Sparx City Hop: 289
spectator sports: 157, 179
sports: 151-179
Stan Hywet Hall: 238
St. Ignatius High School: 44
St. John's Episcopal Church: 44
St. Patrick's Church: 45
St. Patrick's Day Parade: 281
St. Stephen Catholic Church: 48
St. Theodosius Russian Orthodox
    Cathedral: 45
Studios at West 78th Street: 140
swimming pools: 179

T
Taste of Tremont: 287
taxis: 294
television: 301
Terminal Tower: 39
There's No Place Like OM: 165
tipping: 298
tips for travelers: 297
tobogganing: 175
tours, guided and walking: 154, 163,
    173, 176, 267
Tower City Cinemas: 128
trains: 293
Transformer Station: 138
transportation: 292, 293

Tree Frog Canopy Tours: 265
Tremont: *see* Ohio City and Tremont
Tri-C JazzFest: 283
trolleys, downtown: map 8 18-19
Trolley Tours of Cleveland: 40, 155
tubing: 174

UVWXYZ
Ultimate Frisbee: 179
University Circle and Little Italy: 23;
    map 4 10-11
U.S.S. COD Submarine: 41
Verb Ballets: 150
Veterans Memorial Bridge Tour: 163
Vision Yoga & Wellness: 164
visitors center: 297
Wade Oval Wednesdays: 287
Wade Park: 51
War Memorial Fountain: 41
Weapons of Mass Creation Fest: 287
Weekend in Ohio City: 283
Wendy Park at Whiskey Island: 164
West Side Market: 45
Western Reserve Historical Society: 144
Western Reserve Rowing Association:
    156
wineries: 247
Wolstein Center: 130
Wooltex Gallery: 133
YMCA of Greater Cleveland: 156
Yoder's Amish Home: 265
yoga: 164, 165, 166, 167, 169
Zygote Press: 133

Restaurants Index

Aladdin's Eatery: 90
Algebra Tea House: 86
Anatolia Café: 94
Arabica Café: 86
B Spot Burgers: 100
Bac: 68
Bar Cento: 78
Barrio: 78
Barroco Grill: 99
Big Al's Diner: 92
Black Pig: 73
Blackbird Baking Company: 98
Blue Point Grille: 67
Bogtrotters Doorstep: 75
Bonbon Pastry & Café: 69
Buckeye Beer Engine: 95
Civilization: 72

Cleveland Pickle: 66
Club Isabella : 88
Cookie and a Cupcake, A: 76
Coquette Patisserie: 87
Corbo's Bakery: 86
Corky & Lenny's: 102
Cowell & Hubbard: 63
Crop Bistro: 74
Dante: 78
Deagan's Kitchen & Bar: 95
Dervish Turkish Cuisine: 77
Dewey's Pizza: 94
Diner on Clifton: 82
District: 63
El Carnicero: 99
Erie Island Coffee: 62
Fahrenheit: 74

Fat Cats: 77
Felice Urban Café: 91
Fire Food & Drink: 91
Flour: 101
Flying Fig: 74
Ginko: 68
Greenhouse Tavern: 64
Grovewood Tavern and Wine Bar: 101
Gypsy Beans & Bakery: 82
Harp, The: 80
Inn on Coventry: 93
Johnny Mango: 72
Johnny's Little Bar: 67
Katz Club Diner: 92
Koko Bakery: 62
La Dolce Vita: 88
L'Albatros: 88
Le Petit Triangle Café: 69
Li Wah: 61
Lola: 65
Lolita: 77
Loop Café: 73
Lucky's Café: 70
Luna Bakery and Cafe: 90
Luxe Kitchen & Lounge: 83
Malley's Chocolates: 98
Market Café: 63
Melt Bar & Grilled: 96
Mi Pueblo: 89
Michaelangelo's: 88
Minh-Anh Vietnamese Restaurant: 85
Mitchell's Homemade Ice Cream: 87
Momocho Mod Mex: 80
Moxie: 101
Nate's Deli: 76
Nauti Mermaid: 68
Noodlecat: 61
Old Angle: 81
On the Rise: 90

Orale!: 80
Pacific East: 93
Parallax: 75
Parkview Nite Club: 83
Pier W: 99
Players on Madison: 100
Presti's Bakery & Café: 86
Provenance Restaurant and Café: 89
Pura Vida: 66
Red, the Steakhouse: 68
Rising Star Coffee Roasters: 73
Root Café: 97
Sasa Matsu: 93
Slyman's Deli: 66
SOHO Kitchen & Bar: 75
Sokolowski's University Inn: 78
Souper Market: 76
South Side: 81
Spice Kitchen & Bar: 82
Stone Oven: 91
Superior Pho: 61
Sweet Moses Soda Fountain: 83
Sweet Spot, The: 98
Sweetie Fry: 92
Szechuan Gourmet: 62
Table 45: 87
Tartine Bistro and Wine Bar: 98
Tommy's: 91
Tremont Scoops: 76
Tremont Taphouse: 81
Ty Fun Thai Bistro: 69
Umami Asian Kitchen: 100
Valentino's Pizza: 89
Vero Bistro: 94
Washington Place Bistro: 85
West End Tavern: 95
West Side Market Café: 71
Wonton Gourmet BBQ: 62
XYZ the Tavern: 85

Nightlife Index

ABC the Tavern: 110
Anatomy: 106
Around the Corner Saloon: 121
Barking Spider Tavern: 118
bars: 106, 110, 116, 117, 118, 121
Beachland Ballroom: 124
Beer Market, The: 117
Bottlehouse Brewery: 119
breweries: 111, 119, 123
Brothers Lounge: 117
casinos: 106, 124
dance clubs: 106, 113, 117

D'Vine Wine Bar: 108
Fat Head's Brewery & Saloon: 123
Five O'Clock Lounge: 121
Flying Monkey Pub: 110
Great Lakes Brewing Co.: 111
Grog Shop: 119
Happy Dog: 116
Hard Rock Rocksino Northfield: 124
Horseshoe Cleveland: 106
Humble Wine Bar: 122
Katz Club: 120
Kevin's Martini Bar: 108

La Cave du Vin: 120
Lava Lounge: 115
live music: 107, 117, 118, 119, 121, 124
lounges: 108, 115, 120
Market Avenue Wine Bar: 115
Market Garden Brewery: 112
McNulty's Bier Markt: 110
Nano Brew: 112
Nighttown: 119
Parnell's Pub: 118
Peabody's Concert Club: 107
Prosperity Social Club: 111
Shooter's: 106

Society Lounge: 108
Spotted Owl: 111
Stone Mad Irish Pub: 116
Thistledown Racino: 124
Twist: 117
Union Station/Bounce: 113
Velvet Dog: 107
Velvet Tango Room: 115
Wilbert's Food & Music: 107
Winchester Tavern and Concert Club:
    121
wine bars: 108, 115, 120, 122
Winking Lizard Tavern: 118

Shops Index

Anne van H. Boutique: 196
arts and crafts: 186, 197
b.a. Sweetie Candy Company: 210
Banyan Tree: 187
Barkley Pet Hotel and Day Spa: 208
Beachwood Place: 208
Bent Crayon Records: 191
Big Fun: 199
books: 186, 191, 198, 202, 205
Campbell's Sweets Factory: 189
Carol & John's Comic Book Shop: 202
Christophier Custom Clothier: 192
City Buddha: 200
CLE Clothing Co.: 183
Cleveland Brew Shop: 186
Cleveland MetroBark: 184
Cleveland Shop, The: 193
clothing: 187, 192, 196, 198, 205
Coventry Cats: 201
Crocker Park: 209
Deering Vintage: 190
duoHOME: 200
Elegansia: 190
Eton Chagrin Boulevard: 209
Evie Lou: 187
5th Street Arcades: 184
Fine Points: 197
Flower Child: 193
Gallucci's Italian Foods: 211
Geiger's Clothing & Sports: 204
Gentleman's Quarters/Frog's Legs: 198
gifts: 183, 187, 199
Glass Bubble Project: 186
Guide to Kulchur: 192
Hansa Import Haus: 189
Hausfrau Records: 192
health and beauty: 184, 188, 200, 202,
    207
Heck's Revival: 195

Heide Rivchun Conservation Studios:
    201
home furnishings: 183, 187, 199
Inn the Doghouse: 204
Johnnyville Slugger: 187
kid's stores: 201, 204, 208
Kilgore Trout: 205
Knuth Shoes: 206
Legacy Village: 209
Lilly Handmade Chocolates: 189
Loganberry Books: 198
Lorain Avenue Antiques District: 195
Mac's Backs Books: 198
malls: 184, 208
Marengo Luxury Spa: 184
Market at the Fig: 190
music: 186, 191, 198, 202, 205
Music Saves: 205
My Mind's Eye Records: 202
Nicky Nicole: 208
Only Cleveland Store, The: 183
Open Air in Market Square: 191
Paisley Monkey: 204
Passport to Peru: 197
pet stores: 184, 193, 201, 204, 208
Pet-Tique: 193
Pinky's Daily Planner: 187
Play it Again, Sam: 204
Playmatters Toys: 201
Quintana's Barber Shop: 200
Reagle Beagle: 202
Record Revolution: 198
Reincarnation Vintage Design: 195
Room Service: 188
Russian-Turkish Baths: 208
Sausage Shoppe, The: 211
Scott Metzger Systems: 207
shopping centers: 184, 208
Something Different: 188

specialty foods: 185, 189, 204, 210
Suite Lorain: 196
Surroundings Home Décor: 183
Tink Holl: 185
Tower City Center: 185
Unique Thrift: 191

Utrecht Art Supplies: 197
vintage and antiques: 190, 193, 201, 204
Visible Voice Books: 186
Yellowcake Shop: 192
Zen Metro Spa: 188

Hotels Index

Alcazar, The: 225
Aloft Cleveland Downtown: 215
Brownstone Inn: 216
Cleveland Airport Marriott: 226
Cleveland Clinic Guesthouse: 222
Cleveland Hostel: 220
Clifford House Bed and Breakfast: 220
Club at Hillbrook, The: 227
Comfort Inn Downtown: 216
Courtyard by Marriott: 222
Days Inn: 226
DoubleTree by Hilton: 222
Embassy Suites Cleveland Rockside: 227
Emerald Necklace Inn: 226
Glidden House: 223
Hampton Inn Beachwood: 227
Hilton Garden Inn: 216

Holiday Inn Express Hotel and Suites: 218
Hyatt Regency at The Arcade: 218
Inn at Brandywine Falls: 228
Inn of Chagrin Falls: 228
InterContinental Hotel and Conference Center: 223
InterContinental Suites Hotel: 224
J. Palen House: 221
Marriott Downtown at Key Center: 218
Renaissance Cleveland Hotel: 218
Ritz-Carlton, The: 219
Stone Gables Bed and Breakfast: 222
University Circle Bed and Breakfast: 224
Westin Cleveland Downtown: 219
Wyndham Cleveland at PlayhouseSquare: 220

Photo Credits